Paradigms of Research
for the 21st Century

Studies in the
Postmodern Theory of Education

Shirley R. Steinberg
General Editor

Vol. 436

The Counterpoints series is part of the Peter Lang Education list.
Every volume is peer reviewed and meets
the highest quality standards for content and production.

PETER LANG
New York • Washington, D.C./Baltimore • Bern
Frankfurt • Berlin • Brussels • Vienna • Oxford

Paradigms of Research for the 21st Century

PERSPECTIVES AND EXAMPLES FROM PRACTICE

EDITED BY Antonina Lukenchuk

PETER LANG
New York • Washington, D.C./Baltimore • Bern
Frankfurt • Berlin • Brussels • Vienna • Oxford

Library of Congress Cataloging-in-Publication Data
Paradigms of research for the 21st century:
perspectives and examples from practice / edited by Antonina Lukenchuk.
p. cm. — (Counterpoints: studies in the postmodern theory of education; v. 436)
Includes bibliographical references and index.
1. Education research. 2. Education—Research—Methodology.
3. Education—Research—Philosophy. I. Title.
LB1028.L84   370.72—dc23   2012025611
ISBN 978-1-4331-1803-6 (hardcover)
ISBN 978-1-4331-1802-9 (paperback)
ISBN 978-1-4539-0880-8 (e-book)
ISSN 1058-1634

Bibliographic information published by **Die Deutsche Nationalbibliothek**.
Die Deutsche Nationalbibliothek lists this publication in the "Deutsche
Nationalbibliografie"; detailed bibliographic data is available
on the Internet at http://dnb.d-nb.de/.

Cover image based on the artwork "Paradigm Shift:
The Coming of the Indigo-Crystal Children" © 2011 by Maria Celeste Garcia.
www.mariacelestegarcia.com. Reprinted by permission of the artist. All rights reserved.

The paper in this book meets the guidelines for permanence and durability
of the Committee on Production Guidelines for Book Longevity
of the Council of Library Resources.

To all lovers of wisdom

Contents

List of Figures   xi

List of Tables   xiii

Preface   xv

Acknowledgments   xix

Introduction   xxi
Antonina Lukenchuk

PART ONE: PARADIGMS OF RESEARCH: MULTIPLE WAYS OF KNOWING

1. Presaging Educational Inquiry: Historical Development of Philosophical
    Ideas, Traditions, and Perspectives   3
    Baudelaire K. Ulysse and Antonina Lukenchuk

2. Epistemology and Philosophy of Science: Traditions, Perspectives,
    and Controversies   31
    Antonina Lukenchuk and Baudelaire K. Ulysse

3. Paradigms and Educational Research: Weaving the Tapestry   61
    Antonina Lukenchuk and Eileen Kolich

PART TWO: PARADIGMS AS EDUCATIONAL RESEARCH EXEMPLARS

4. The Passage beyond Self: An Autoethnographic Journey into My
Cultural Roots, Personal and Educational Transformations   91
Vladimir Trostin

5. Sociocultural Perspectives of First-Generation Asian Indian Leaders in
U.S. Higher Education: An Ethnographic Study   103
Matthew A. Woolsey

6. Hermeneutics of Hispanic Parenthood: Reframing Conceptions
through Personal Voices   121
Maria E. Hernandez-Rodriguez

7. In Pursuit of Change: A Study of a Principal's Application of
Transformational Leadership Strategies   136
Christine L. Kramp Pfaff

8. Is There a Model for Success? Exploring Sustainable Professional
Employment among Clinical Exercise Physiology Program's Graduates   148
Regina Schurman

9. The Impact of Cognitive Information Processing on the Career
Decision Making of First-Year College Students   166
Anne Perry and Nancy W. Bentley

10. Greek Parents' Perceptions and Experiences Regarding Their
Children's Learning and Social-Emotional Difficulties   176
Eirini Adamopoulou

11. Successful Practices and Models of Enrollment Management in
Illinois Community Colleges: An Explanatory Mixed-Methods
Research Case Study   189
Andrea Lehmacher

12. Paradigmatic Consciousness Raising: What Moves Me   204
Krista Robinson-Lyles

13. Culling Methodological Tools, Honing Research Skills: A Paradigm of
Critical Discourse Analysis on Neoliberalism   219
Baudelaire K. Ulysse

14. Locked Gates and Chain-link Fences: A Generational
    Phenomenological Story of Disability   234
    Sharon Duncan

Postscript: Once upon a Time, the Message of Love Was Born   251
    Antonina Lukenchuk

    About the Contributors   257
    Index   263

Figures

Figure 1   Paradigm Pyramid   xxvi

Figure 1.1   Jastrow's Duck-Rabbit Image   17

Figure 3.1   Conceptual Relationships between the Paradigms of Research   69

Figure 3.2   Paradigms of Research: Mapping the Final Journey   85

Figure 8.1   Model of Sustainable Professional Employment for Clinical Exercise Physiologists   163

Figure 9.1   Data Collection Structure   169

Tables

Table 3.1   Typology of Paradigms as Major Systems of Inquiry, Models, and Ways of Knowing, and Their Corresponding Conceptual Repertoire, Epistemologies, Methodologies, and Selected Methods   67

Table 3.2   Positioning Part 2 Chapters within the Paradigms of Research   77

Preface

What is research and who is a researcher? Why engage in research and what is its value? How do we come to know what we know? What can we *really* know? *Paradigms of Research for the 21st Century* opens the door for wondering about these and many other important questions pertaining to the nature and process of educational research. Conceived as a journey into the familiar and the uncharted territories of knowledge, this book offers an insightful and detailed account of Western and non-Western worldviews and perspectives on reality, knowledge, and values, many of which have been instrumental to the development of different research traditions and methods in North America.

This book demonstrates how essential components of educational inquiry such as ideas, theories, philosophies, ideologies, epistemologies, value statements, methodologies, and methods can be applied to conducting and implementing robust research projects. The aforementioned essential components form a *paradigm*—a system of inquiry, a model, and a way of knowing. Empirical-analytic, pragmatic, interpretive, critical, poststructuralist, and transcendental paradigms are delineated as alternatives to a more orthodox division of conceptualizing research as quantitative or qualitative. The discussions on the nature of science and scientific method shed light on a number of misconceptions of these notions in educational research. Resulting from these discussions is an exposure of misconceived and misrepresented links between positivism and quantitative research.

Venturing on a paradigm journey are the dedicated contributors to this edition who share their tales of learning to theorize and practice educational research. Their hope is that graduate students, professional researchers, and scholars will benefit from this project and it might be of interest to all lovers of wisdom.

Welcome to a paradigm journey!

A Preneopragmatic, Postmodern ditty about Existential Phenomenon

Walking in the classroom
I was feelin' fine.
Asked about some questions
What's a Paradigm?
Naturally my fears grew
I felt so abused.
Looked around for confidence
You all seemed so confused.

"Hey folks have some handouts."
"Take 'em, have a ball"
Rorty, Kant, and Hegel
Dewey and Foucault.
Habermas, Adorno, take Nietzsche
For some sparks.
What's a Timbred Research?
Giroux, Freire, and Marx

We climbed out from an Existential mineshaft.
There is no deny'n,
the class became Gemeinschaft.
Feyerabend tells us
"You can bend the rules.
Research call for
using all the tools"
Look beyond the task when
Conceptualizing Framework
The threads of solid research exist
On many spools

Now we've all survived it
ESR610
A world of information
Shall we do it all again?
Adapting Methodology will help us in our showing.
Hermeneutics finds a way,
Cartesian ways of knowing.
To make our journey forward,
we must use the past
To Bacon, Locke, and all the rest
Thanks I've had a blast

—COURTESY OF KERRY MULDOWNEY,
COLLEAGUE AND FORMER STUDENT
OF PARADIGMS OF RESEARCH

Acknowledgments

I would like to express my warm gratitude to all contributors to this book—my colleagues and friends without whose assistance this manuscript would be an impossible undertaking. I am especially indebted to Baudelaire Ulysse and Eileen Kolich for sharing their talent and knowledge in our collaborative work.

To my former and current ESR610 students—thank you for sustaining my sense of curiosity and inspiring me to pursue this project. I am grateful to Kerry Muldowney for supporting my first steps in teaching paradigms and sharing his big heart, wit, humor, and the gift of poetry and music with me.

I wish to acknowledge the support from the staff at Peter Lang Publishing: managing director Christopher S. Myers, series editor Shirley Steinberg, editorial assistants, production managers, and all unnamed persons who have contributed to the production, marketing, and publication of this edition.

Introduction

ANTONINA LUKENCHUK

> Once upon a time, through wonder, the message of love was born in the midst of chaos, confusion, and the scatterings of the un-wisdom of the world. Wisdom was born in and through the markings left along the journeys which some persons ... have risked. These personal journeys have moved through the concrete feelings, experiencing, reflecting, and meditating along the pathways of our routine personal lifeworlds ....I, a lover of wisdom, that is a philosopher, speak of wisdom.
>
> —SHERMAN STANAGE

The Beginning—the Wondering

This book has been writing itself for a number of years, at least since the time I started teaching a graduate course in paradigms of research at a Midwestern private university. However, I can probably trace the deeper roots of this project to as far back as my childhood memories. Faded and almost forgotten, they nonetheless elicit recollections imbued with enchanting images. I enjoyed a highly imaginative childhood. My less-than-exciting external surroundings led me to search for wonder in the realm of the transcendent. This imaginary land of myths, folk songs, and stories became my safeguard and a lovely haven in the midst of the crude and dreary reality of the outside world. Entrance into adulthood brought with it the experiences that demystified a great deal of my childhood's imaginings, but the wonderings about the world and what lies beyond its horizon has persisted.

My first encounter with the word *philosophy* during my undergraduate studies has turned into an affectionate and lasting affair, and throughout the years of academic training, philosophical inquiry has been sustaining my sense of curiosity and the purpose of my educational pursuits. I feel intuitively drawn to the word *philosophy* because it speaks to me in a female voice in the language of my origin. The affectionate words *phileo* (Greek for love) and *sophia* (Greek for wisdom) that comprise philosophy are, in fact, of a female gender. I am a lover of wisdom, that is, a woman who loves and seeks wisdom. I become a philosopher by default the moment I wonder who I am by nature or what the meaning of this project is. There is hardly a person in this world who is not a philosopher *by nature* (the drive to know is evidently intrinsic to a human being). The questions that Paul Gauguin (1848–1903) assigns to his painting are endemic to humankind: *Where do we come from? What are we? Where are we going?* These questions impel people to fly to the moon, to delve into the depths of the oceans, to penetrate the nuclear layers of energy and the human body, and to create ambitious social projects. What would our lives be like if it were not for some courageous individuals who dared to pursue unimaginable projects?

Education makes an inquiry attainable and, until fairly recently in Western modern history, education has been inseparable from philosophical pursuits. Seekers of wisdom in ancient Western and non-Western world cultural traditions have been philosophers, scientists, *and* educators—catalysts of intellectual, moral, and political transformations in their respective societies. The modern age of scientific and technological advancements in the West provided an impetus for a sharp division of sciences into "natural" and "human" and the ensuing methodological debates surrounding these sciences. Educational inquiry was forced to find its place within the new division of sciences and to develop methods best suited for its needs and purposes.

Since the nineteenth century in the West, education has been defined as a human, social, or behavioral science, depending on the object of its inquiry and its juxtaposition to natural sciences. The twentieth-century revolutionary theories of relativity and quantum mechanics overturned the Newtonian explanation of the universe as the only true scientific paradigm, and the discovery of DNA radically changed the understanding of living things (Grof, 1985). These revolutionary events also represented the strongest challenge to the positivistic assumption of science. Twentieth-century philosophy had to engage with a scientific world and rethink its role in providing the all-encompassing metaphysical systems of explanation of the universe and the predicament of a human being within it. Subsequently, the new conception of science was to be developed to account for the paradigm shifts in twentieth-century physics, biology, chemistry, and other natural sciences.

Contemporary science is no longer expected to produce certain knowledge, and scientific method is employed by natural sciences to generate alternative paradigms of knowledge, some of which can be accepted as the best explanations available, and in the long run, they can be discarded and replaced by new paradigms. The present-day philosophy of human and social sciences is concerned with the study of both the human realm and the natural realm, which until very recently were regarded as distinct and different and, therefore, required different methods of investigation. Moreover, natural science is viewed by today's scientists as an effectively human practice in which a researcher is actively engaged (Polkinghorne, 2004). Contemporary scientific, philosophical, and educational inquiries focus on a variety of issues pertaining to individual areas of study that can only incrementally contribute to the whole of the understanding of various phenomena. To keep up with the aforementioned changes in the conception of science, educational researchers need to reconsider the obsolete methodological debates still raving on the pages of some academic publications (e.g., Howe, 2009).

This book was conceived out of love of wisdom and the desire to provoke imaginative thinking about educational inquiry. Gaston Bachelard (1884–1962) once said that when imagination works, everything works. We first imagine things before we know them. Bachelard's poetic turn led him to reconsider his epistemology as a project of a scientific mind, thus, giving primacy to imagination in the process of inquiry. Scientific knowledge "emerges only after we use some imagination, both in formulating questions and in framing hypotheses to answer them" (Audi, 2003, p. 260). Bachelard's name is important to consider in context of this book because he was an originator of the theory of epistemological breaks (1938/2002) in the philosophy of science that was developed many years prior to the similar theory of paradigm shifts put forth by Thomas Kuhn (1962/2000).

This book intends to bring to light obscure, forgotten, or unknown facts pertaining to educational research that can be instrumental to its conceptual rigor and accuracy. Like any pursuit, this work represents an open-ended inquiry that is subject to critics' scrutiny and questioning, which we would welcome. This book is an invitation to readers to join the *paradigm journey* undertaken by a few dedicated persons with the purpose of gathering their patches of wisdom that are scattered around the world and sharing their love messages with others.

Why This Book and What Is It About?

Paradigms of Research for the 21st Century contributes significantly to the field of educational research in the following ways: it is (1) filling in considerable gaps in the existing educational research publications, which lack philosophical foundations;

(2) expanding on the definition of *paradigm* and its alternatives for educational research grounded in various philosophical traditions since most current definitions of paradigm are insufficient; (3) amplifying the importance of vital links between epistemological and methodological assumptions; (4) exposing and clarifying misconceived links between positivism and quantitative methods of analysis; (5) elucidating a new conception of science and its impact on educational research, information that is rarely, if ever, mentioned in current research sources; and (6) advocating epistemological and methodological pluralism be on equal footing in all educational inquiries.

For the past eight years or so, I have been teaching a doctoral-level course, Paradigms of Research: Multiple Ways of Knowing (ESR 610), at National Louis University in Chicago, Illinois. ESR 610 is a required course within a sequence of research courses that acquaints students with a broad range of philosophical, ideological, and theoretical perspectives on educational research as the tools to conceptualize research and scholarly projects such as dissertations. ESR 610 is typically followed by introductory and advanced quantitative and qualitative methodology courses. The recurring discussions that I have with my colleagues who teach research courses and serve on dissertation committees reveal how ill prepared some of our doctoral candidates are to conduct dissertation research projects, even after taking a number of research courses. The lack of students' knowledge and skills is especially apparent when they are faced with making appropriate choices regarding research methodologies and conceptual tools that adequately fit their research purposes. Our doctoral candidates often face the proverbial chicken or the egg conundrum and which comes first. In other words, should they first consider a paradigm and then a toolbox of methods, or vice versa? Students must be equipped to answer other related questions. What are the relationships between theoretical frameworks and specific methods of investigation? To what extent can a research project be successful in terms of properly made epistemological and methodological choices?

Most educational researchers agree that "methods of analysis do not emerge out of thin air. They are informed by, and extend out of, particular theoretical sensibilities" (Holstein & Gubrium, 2012, p. 5). All research is anchored to basic beliefs about the nature of the world, knowledge, and values. How each researcher "conceptualizes the best way to apprehend the social world is clearly dependent upon what she or he believes about the nature of existence. What constitutes data? What constitutes a pattern in data? What does the pattern mean?" (Pascale, 2011, p. 5). Theoretical models, frameworks, philosophies, ideologies, beliefs, or perspectives, the terms that can be housed under the umbrella definition of *paradigm*, provide a roadmap for successful research or scholarly projects. The definition of *paradigm* generates interesting discussions and debates among contemporary educational researchers (Anfara & Mertz, 2006; Creswell, 2003; Lather, 2004; Polkinghorne, 1983). The notion of paradigm permeates this book and renders its content relevant to the educational research process.

While the consensus on the importance of the role of paradigms in educational research is widely acknowledged, most research methods texts provide fairly limited space to philosophical discussions pertaining to educational inquiry. There are only a handful of current editions that offer in-depth accounts of the theoretical foundations of research (Anfara & Mertz, 2006; Cohen, Manion, & Morrison, 2008; Jackson & Mazzei, 2012; Merriam & Simpson, 2000; Olsen, 2010; Pascale, 2011; St. Pierre & Pillow, 2000; Yu, 2006). Moreover, most of these sources focus exclusively on either theoretical frameworks of qualitative research (e.g., Anfara & Mertz) or particular areas of study such as, for instance, feminist poststructuralist theory (e.g., St. Pierre & Pillow). By comparison, *Paradigms of Research for the 21st Century* provides a more comprehensive and detailed historical and philosophical analysis of educational inquiries pertaining to all types of research: qualitative, quantitative, or mixed methods. This book abounds in philosophical terminology, which is rarely given proper attention in research methods textbooks (e.g., McMillan, 2008).

Despite an unequivocal repudiation of positivism in the mid-twentieth century, some contemporary researchers continue to misrepresent quantitative methods of analysis as positivistic (e.g., Hesse-Biber & Leavy, 2011; Pascale, 2011). The agreement has been reached by the philosophers of science that *all* of our knowledge is conditional and constructed within the contingent conceptual systems relative to time and place (Nelson, 2012). Given the contingency of truth/knowledge, what can educators count on as effective and critical methods of investigation? Paradigms of educational research represent a rich bricolage of methodological possibilities, and this book considers and discusses six of these.

The word *paradigm* is derived from the two Greek words *para* (beside) and *deigma* (example). The etymology of paradigm clearly presumes a relational construct, a pairing of sorts. Modern dictionary definitions elaborate on paradigm as follows: model, conjugation, giving all the inflections of a word, example, archetype, beau ideal, chart, criterion, ensample, exemplar, ideal, mirror, model, original, pattern, prototype, sample, standard (Kipfer, 2010). Kuhn's definition of paradigm is most frequently cited as "constellations of law, theory, application and instrumentation . . .; models from which spring particular coherent traditions of scientific research" (Runes, 1983, p. 240).

Our conception of paradigm integrates its major existing definitions and the etymology of the word, all of which lead us to designate the following threefold meaning to paradigm: (1) a system of educational inquiry, (2) a model, and (3) a way of knowing. Chapter 4 elaborates on the justifications for this definition of paradigm. Figure 1 portrays a paradigm pyramid built on its multiple definitions.

Figure 1: Paradigm Pyramid

PARADIGM
Par-a-digm
archetype
example
pattern
sample
model
chart
ideal
theory
system
original
standard
exemplar
framework
worldview
belief system
way of knowing

Educational researchers tend to differentiate primarily between quantitative and qualitative research. While such distinction is valid in terms of data and methods of their analysis, paradigms as theoretical frameworks of research require more expanded philosophical renditions and more diverse differentiations. The construct of paradigm encompasses a number of conceptual tools (referred to in this book as "conceptual repertoire"), epistemological assumptions, and corresponding methods of analysis. Creswell (2003), for instance, distinguishes between the four "alternative knowledge claim positions": postpositivism, constructivism, advocacy/participatory, and pragmatism (p. 6). Lather (2004) proposes four paradigms in a slightly different configuration: prediction (positivist), understanding (interpretive), emancipatory (critical), and deconstruction (poststructuralist) (p. 207). The analysis of various philosophical traditions of inquiry in Western and non-Western cultural traditions allows us to delineate six paradigms of educational research: empirical-analytic, pragmatic, interpretive, critical, poststructuralist, and transcendental. These six paradigmatic constellations do not exhaust all possibilities; however, they encompass major existing positions on knowledge, reality, and value statements in the philosophy of science. An important message intersecting the content of this book and being advocated by its contributors is that of an epistemological and methodological pluralism that recognizes and validates all existing paradigms on equal ground.

Organization of the Book

The book consists of two conceptually related parts foreshadowing the interconnectedness of theory *and* practice. The constructs of theory and practice are often conceived as separate entities. The word *theory*—via Late Latin from Greek, *theoria* (contemplation or speculation)—means a "system of ideas intended to explain something," a "set of principles on which the practice of an activity is based," or an "idea used to account for a situation or justify a course of action" (Stevenson & Lindberg, 2010, p. 1799). Polkinghorne (2004) renders practice as an "engaged action or activity," a "tradition, tacit knowledge, worldview, paradigm, ideology, framework, or presupposition" (pp. 6–7). More than two centuries ago, Immanuel Kant (1724–1804) emphasized that experience without a theory is blind, and theory without experience is mere intellectual play. Present-day philosophers of science consider the quest for knowledge as an activity in which a researcher is actively engaged, thus affirming the *reciprocity of theory-practice relationships*. Accordingly, part 1 chapters of this book represent a theory component of this synergetic duo, and chapters 5 through 15 of part 2 of this books exhibit its practice piece. Hence, paradigms and examples from practice should be understood as relational and mutually dependent constructs, whereby one informs the other and in turn is being informed and enriched by the other's experience. Examples from practice represent research and scholarly projects conducted within the traditions of alternative paradigms.

Part 1

Chapter 1 takes readers on a fascinating philosophical journey across continents and traditions. It weaves the tales of ancient, modern, and postmodern worlds into a tapestry of beliefs that have been instrumental to the development of educational inquiry in North America. Chapter 2 amplifies the discussions on epistemology and philosophy of science and their relevance to educational research. It foregrounds the importance of methodological debates in natural and human sciences that have provided an impetus for radical changes in the conception of science and paradigm shifts in educational inquiry. Finally, chapter 3 integrates the content of the preceding chapters in terms of relevant links among philosophical, epistemological, and methodological assumptions. Chapter 3 also provides a brief analysis of the part 2 research exemplars and portrays a pluralistic paradigmatic image by means of graphical and textual representations.

The contributors to the scholarly work presented in this book are women and men of diverse socioeconomic, racial, ethnic, and immigrant backgrounds, lifestyles, and political persuasions. What binds them together is a sheer love of and dedication to intellectual pursuits resulting in utilitarian and scholastic benefits to communities of inquirers.

Part 2

The configuration of part 2 of this book is an intentional act of positioning the chapters in a specific order that metaphorically represents a circle. Research begins in wonder and thus bears an imprint of thousands of years of the human history recorded in tales, dialogues, teachings, myths, legends, and stories. Storytelling is the most primordial form of research and it continues to cast its spell on storytellers and their followers. The ancient art of storytelling gave rise to narrative research, which, since the 1960s, has been gaining considerable popularity among educational researchers (Goodall, 2008; Holstein & Gubrium, 2012; Riessman, 2008).

Part 2 begins with the story of an educational leader (chapter 4) and ends with the story of disability (chapter 14), thus representing a circle of the tradition of storytelling enveloping more recently developed research methodologies. The opening autoethnographic study by Vladimir Trostin (chapter 4) is followed by a number of research projects conducted within the interpretive paradigm. Matthew Woolsey (chapter 5) presents an ethnographic investigation of first-generation Asian Indian immigrants who have attained senior-level leadership positions in U.S. higher education. Woolsey explores the evolution of the field of leadership since the Industrial Revolution onward and its global perspectives. His purpose is to offer a "lantern" that sheds light on the unchartered territory of insight into the sociocultural contexts that enable Asian Indians to gain extraordinary heights in higher education leadership. Maria Hernandez-Rodriguez (chapter 6) offers a hermeneutic analysis of Hispanic parents' perspectives on their children's kindergarten education. She challenges the misconceptions of many teachers about Hispanic parents and their involvement in their children's education. Hernandez-Rodriguez creates an intricate analysis of multilayered perspectives on the role of school professionals and parents as a shared responsibility for children's educational attainment and advancement.

Christine L. Kramp Pfaff (chapter 7) presents an ethnographic case study that portrays her personal journey into elementary school principalship and her attempts to implement transformational leadership strategies. As a new principal, she sought for the most effective ways to lead the school staff and to transform the school community into a culture of shared values, responsibilities, professional growth, caring, and academic success. A grounded theory study by Regina Schurman (chapter 8) demonstrates how the classical Glaserian approach can be applied to generate a model of sustainable professional employment for clinical exercise physiologists. Schurman's research is firmly positioned within the pragmatic paradigm that enables her to recast Peirce's (1839–1914) method of rigorous scientific inquiry and his proverbial flash of insight. The pragmatist view allows the features of grounded theory to become clearer and more understandable in terms of generating substantive theory.

The following two chapters after Schurman's study exemplify the potential of quantitative studies. Anne Perry and Nancy W. Bentley (chapter 9) propose a robust investigation of the impact of cognitive information processing on first-year college students' career decision making. Higher education institutions often require a career development course during the senior year as preparation for the job search process. In these courses, students are taught how to create a resume, research a company, prepare for an interview, and often mock interviews are conducted with faculty and staff. While this may be valuable and appropriate for seniors anticipating graduation, there is also a need to assist students much earlier with making an informed career choice. This experimental research study employs the Career Thoughts Inventory (CTI), a standardized career assessment tool that categorizes participants into a specific construct area, and an intervention based on Cognitive Information Processing (CIP) theory. Eirini Adamopoulou (chapter 10) presents an empirical-analytic study of Greek parents' perceptions and experiences regarding their children's learning and social-emotional difficulties in elementary schools. Adamopoulou employs the Test of Psychosocial Adaptation and the Parent Survey to identify Greek parents' perceptions of the causes and responsibility for solving their children's problems, the level and type of parental perceived burden due to their children's challenges, and their actions to support their children's learning and social-emotional difficulties, including their use of available community services.

Logically positioned in the middle of part 2, chapter 11, by Andrea Lehmacher, explicates an *in-between* paradigm of mixed-methods research. Lehmacher examines the practices of enrollment management in Illinois community colleges. The theoretical framework for this study includes three constructs: (1) community colleges as open systems adapting to the internal and external environment; (2) enrollment management as an integral process throughout the community college system; and (3) collaboration among internal departments as a critical component for successful enrollment management. Qualitative interviews and the Strategic Enrollment Management Health Assessment survey yield the two sets of data for analysis and the resulting integrated model of successful enrolment management practice.

Next in the constellation of research exemplars are the studies conducted within the interpretive and critical paradigms. Krista Robinson-Lyles (chapter 12) urges readers to think critically about preservice teacher practices in public schools. Preparing preservice teachers to teach for social justice is at once a necessary as well as a challenging journey. While the need to guide teachers on this journey has publically become more widely recognized, theorized, debated, and a more visible part of scholarship and professional educational discourse, the research and discourse around how teacher educators embark upon this same journey is less evident. This work amplifies the praxis of critical democratic education embodied through the experiences of four female teacher educators at Midwestern American universities. Chapter 13, written by Baudelaire K. Ulysse, presents a sophisticated discourse analysis of the politics and economics of neoliberalism in local and global perspectives. Ulysse poses the two following questions: In what way does neoliberalism embody imperialism and breed hegemony, exploitation, inequity, and inequality? Why does neoliberalism pervade education, and what effect does it have on the orientation of education? As an educator, Ulysse has a deep conviction that it is his vocation to be involved in the political process and, more important, to shun political neutrality on issues that concern society and the human condition.

Sharon Duncan's (chapter 14) generational phenomenological story of disability closes the circle of the storytelling tradition represented in this part of the book. Compelling, moving, and empowering, this study uncovers the meaning of the lived experiences of four individuals with intellectual disabilities and their families over three generations. Through the stories of resistance and resilience, the voices of the individuals with intellectual disabilities and their families reach out to the world beyond illusory or self-imposed fences, and gain prominence and power.

Finally, the postscript reflects on the experience of walking through the paradigm journey and offers a parting message to all lovers of wisdom.

Bibliography

Anfara, V. A., Jr., & Mertz, N. T. (Eds.). (2006). *Theoretical frameworks of qualitative research.* Thousand Oaks, CA: Sage.

Audi, R. (2003). *Epistemology: A contemporary introduction to the theory of knowledge* (2nd ed.). New York: Routledge.

Bachelard, G. (1938/2002). *The formation of the scientific mind: A contribution to a psychoanalysis of objective knowledge* (M. McAllester Jones, Trans.). Manchester, UK: Clinamen.

Bachelard, G. (2004). *The poetics of reverie: Childhood, language, and the cosmos* (D. Russell, Trans.). Boston: Beacon.

Cohen, L., Manion, L., & Morrison, K. (2008). *Research methods in education* (6th ed.). New York: Routledge.

Creswell, J. W. (2003). *Research designs: Qualitative, quantitative, and mixed methods approaches* (2nd ed.). Thousand Oaks, CA: Sage.

Goodall, H. L. (2008). *Writing qualitative inquiry: Self, stories, and academic life.* Walnut Creek, CA: Left Coast.

Grof, S. (1985). *Beyond the brain: Birth, death, and transcendence in psychotherapy.* New York: State University of New York Press.

Hesser-Biber, S. N., & Leavy, P. (2011). *The practice of qualitative research* (2nd ed.). Los Angeles: Sage.

Holstein, J. A., & Gubrium, J. F. (Eds.). (2012). *Varieties of narrative analysis*. Los Angeles: Sage.

Howe, K. R. (2009). Epistemology, methodology, and education sciences: Positivist dogmas, rhetoric, and the education science question. *Educational Researcher, 38*(6), 428–440.

Jackson, A. Y., & Mazzei, L. (2012). *Thinking with theory in qualitative research: Viewing data across multiple perspectives*. New York: Routledge.

Kenny, A. (Ed.). (1997). *The Oxford illustrated history of Western philosophy*. New York: Oxford University Press.

Kipfer, B. A. (Ed.). (2010). *Roget's international thesaurus* (11th ed.). New York: Collins Reference.

Kuhn, T. (1962/2000). The structure of scientific revolutions. In S. Rosen (Ed.), *The philosopher's handbook* (pp. 503–519). New York: Random House.

Lather, P. (2004). Critical inquiry in qualitative research: Feminist and poststructural perspectives: Science "after truth." In K. deMarrais & S. D. Lapan (Eds.), *Foundations for research: Methods of inquiry in education and the social sciences* (pp. 203–215). Mahwah, NJ: Lawrence Erlbaum.

McMillan, J. H. (2008). *Educational research: Fundamentals for the consumer* (5th ed.). Boston: Pearson.

Merriam, S. B., & Simpson, E. L. (2000). *A guide to research for educators and trainers of adults*. Malabar, FL: Krieger.

Nelson, G. (2012). Fighting for the humanities. *Academe, 98*(1), 16–21.

Olsen, W. (2010). *Realist methodology*. Los Angeles: Sage.

Pascale, C. M. (2011). *Cartographies of knowledge: Exploring qualitative epistemologies*. Los Angeles: Sage.

Polkinghorne, D. E. (1983). *Methodology for the human sciences: Systems of inquiry.* Albany: State University of New York Press.

Polkinghorne, D. E. (2004). *Practice and the human sciences: The case for a judgment-based practice of care*. New York: State University of New York Press.

Riessman, C. K. (2008). *Narrative methods for the human sciences*. Los Angeles: Sage.

Runes, D. D. (Ed.). (1983). *Dictionary of philosophy*. Savage, MD: Littlefield, Adams.

Stevenson, A., & Lindberg, C. A. (Eds.). (2010). *New Oxford American dictionary* (3rd ed.). New York: Oxford University Press.

St. Pierre, E. A., & Pillow, W. S. (Eds.). (2000). *Working the ruins: Feminist poststructural theory and methods in education*. New York: Routledge.

Yu, C. H. (2006). *Philosophical foundations of quantitative research methodology*. New York: University Press of America.

PART ONE

Paradigms of Research

Multiple Ways of Knowing

Presaging Educational Inquiry

Historical Development of Philosophical Ideas, Traditions, and Perspectives

BAUDELAIRE K. ULYSSE AND ANTONINA LUKENCHUK

Inquiry and the Pursuit of Wisdom

> Philosophy is a battle against the bewitchment of our intelligence through the means of language.
>
> —LUDWIG WITTGENSTEIN, THE OXFORD
> DICTIONARY OF QUOTATIONS, 2001, P. 824

Inquiry has been a vital and constant element in the pursuit of knowledge. Education makes the pursuit of knowledge or the attainment thereof, either directly or indirectly, one of its main objectives. Therefore, education must embrace inquiry as a perpetual ally in order for it to succeed in its pursuit of knowledge. Hence, the term *educational research* ought to represent inquiries that are focused, albeit not exclusively, on pursuing knowledge and that are aimed at understanding knowledge of all types. The pursuit as well as the attainment of knowledge that is presumed in inquiry does not involve the teleological conjecture, as such conjecture varies from researcher to researcher and from project to project; rather, such pursuit aims to grasp the essence of, the process leading to, as well as the reliability of knowledge.

These aspects of knowledge—essence, process, and reliability—underscore the questions that have driven intellectual activities since the beginning of time. Moser (2006) discusses these aspects of knowledge respectively in terms of "defining features," "sources," and "justification" (p. 273). The essence of knowledge—that which comprises knowledge of any type—evokes the 'what' question and is presumed to exist, unbeknownst to us or not, until that knowledge is accessed, uncovered, or discovered. Further, Moser breaks down the essence of knowledge into distinct kinds, which he labels "explicit" and "tacit":

> Explicit knowledge is self-conscious in that the knower is aware of the relevant state of knowledge, whereas tacit knowledge is implicit, hidden from self-consciousness. Much of our knowledge is tacit: it is genuine but we are unaware of the relevant states of knowledge, even if we can achieve awareness upon suitable reflection. (p. 273)

Moser's perceptive remarks seem to establish an equation that accounts for the link or the missing link between the known and the unknown, and evidently the nexus of the knower, the known, and the unknown. In addition, Moser (2006) asserts:

> Philosophers have identified various species of knowledge: for example, propositional knowledge (that something is so), non-propositional knowledge of something (i.e., knowledge by acquaintance, or by direct awareness), empirical (a posteriori) propositional knowledge, non-empirical (a priori) propositional knowledge, and knowledge on how to do something. (p. 273)

While the plethora of epistemic species might seem overwhelming, they, however, exude and underscore the cognitive diversity and relativity, which drives the vehicle of inquiry pertaining to the attainment of wisdom. This effectively led philosophers to surmise whether "extent of our a priori knowledge [was] relative to the extent of our a posteriori knowledge" (Moser, 2006, p. 273). Evidently, contemporary scholars and educators embrace inquiry as an effective method in the pursuit of knowledge. But the effective use of inquiry, particularly in educational research, requires a refined grasp of the history of inquiry as well as its historic contribution to the pursuit of knowledge. The Greek origin of the word *philosophy* means love of wisdom (Foley & Mohan, 2003; Ozmon & Craver, 2008). However abstract, this meaning is suggestive of a relentless and unrestrained pursuit of wisdom. This pursuit is neither characterized by aimless and desultory meandering in epistemological terrains, nor contained by ideological commitments; rather, it embodies a judicious and vigorous investigation of complex and open-ended questions regarding both the immaterial and the material realms.

Knowledge, in its variegated forms and sources, may exist independently of human existence, but the pursuit of knowledge by intelligent beings has largely been a human enterprise. There might be other intelligent beings that exist and inhabit places lying beyond earth's orbital threshold, but insofar as our general knowledge of the material world is concerned, one cannot assert with even the slightest degree of certainty that there are, in fact, intelligent beings inhabiting other planets or coexisting planet Earth with human beings. A concession must be made regarding the immaterial realm, which becomes largely a matter of speculation and belief as truth that can be deduced from reason (Plato), and/or experienced through faith and reason (Aquinas). While this concession is plausible, its subject lies outside the scope of the current project.

Granted knowledge writ at large is and has been a project of human enterprise, it follows then that the pursuit of knowledge as well as the grasp thereof remains inextricably linked to the human species. Further, knowledge writ at large, widely conceived as the objective of human intellectual enterprise or activity, is neither new nor old—it is evolving. Knowledge as such represents a diversely adorned and intricate tapestry with billions of pieces being potentially scattered across a wide array of intercontinental spaces that have been gathered by lovers of wisdom from distant and disparate lands. This creates a whole that is paradoxically unified and diversified. Each piece of this intricate and gigantic tapestry that is collected is valuable in time and space to the group of peoples living in those spaces, and it embodies answers to puzzling questions germane and relative to their material conditions and metaphysical assumptions. One might raise the question of whether the ultimate goal ought to be to find all these pieces and connect them so the big picture might become visible. Still, another might ask whether the ultimate goal ought to be for people in those respective places to use whatever piece or pieces they have culled from this intricate and beautifully adorned tapestry and direct them toward the creation of additional pieces based on what they already have in order to portray or convey their vision of that tapestry, however relative such vision might be in respect to their distinct perception.

Relevance of Philosophical Inquiries to Research

Let us suppose that this painting referred to hitherto represents a tapestry embedding various forms and sources of knowledge. Assuming this is the case, whether symbolically or actually, the forms and sources would have to be both universal and evolutionary. This is to say then that there are forms of objective knowledge, both material and metaphysical, accessible to intelligent human beings from different places across all continents. Once accessed, these forms of knowledge are extracted, analyzed, interpreted, elaborated on, and applied by intelligent human beings to material conditions relative to these beings while at the same time metamorphosing into new forms and laying foundations for further investigations. Could this then be the way human beings have been interacting with their world? Are human beings always eager to grasp what is immediately available and known while at the same committing themselves to know more about that which has been grasped in order to develop a multidimensional view of it for further inquiry, elaboration, explication, and articulation?

The known always triggers the search for the unknown, creating an unending cycle of epistemological quest, at the core of which lies the assumption that knowledge is not final but evolutionary. Philosophers and scholars alike have conceptualized this epistemological cycle as the pursuit of wisdom, a pursuit that has continued to fascinate philosophers and scholars from all parts of the world. Hence, the pursuit of wisdom epitomizes research. By research is meant the inquisitive process that seeks to uncover and discover new phenomena as well as explain and expand existing ones. Research, being proper, may be qualified in accordance with the objectives or the disciplines, in which case such research could be educational, psychological, neurological, or economic. The process and the impetus of research do not change but are only varied by the methods used (e.g., empirical-analytic, interpretive, or mixed).

The cumulative work gathered within this book is geared toward research in the discipline of education; hence the focus is educational research. As the introductory chapter has stipulated, the objective of this project is to show how research in education is grounded in various enduring philosophical traditions of inquiry. Because educational research is grounded in the philosophical traditions of inquiry, it necessarily follows that properly conducted educational research must factor in the philosophical schools or paradigms that embody this inquiry and its pursuit of wisdom.

Properly situating academic works in these larger philosophical frameworks is the act of a skilled researcher. This postulate is consistent with the premise of this book and with the notion that knowledge of any type is somehow predicated upon previously known facts or proposed theories. Therefore, if an academic work should be considered credible, that work must reflect familiarity with or be interconnected to previous works. For instance, if one conducts research in political science using rationalism as a tool of analysis, that person will demonstrate a more refined knowledge of rationalism by tracing its origin to idealism and realism. By the same token, if another person conducts research in political science using liberalism as a tool of analysis, that person will provide a more rounded treatment of liberalism by tracing liberalism back to John Locke and rationalism. Countless other examples could be provided to illustrate the imperativeness for researchers to show the connection they claim to philosophical traditions that preceded, informed, and shaped contemporary tools, or the theoretical perspectives underpinning the respective researches of these researchers. It is for that reason that the focus of this book is on delineating the most influential philosophical schools in the history of ideas while showing their interlinks to tools and theories researchers currently employ. The understanding of these philosophical schools is vital for the effective use of tools and theories in research projects, but such understanding is best served with an intro-duction of philosophy writ at large, particularly considering its major components such as metaphysics, epistemology, and axiology.

Branches of Philosophy: Metaphysics, Epistemology, and Axiology

Metaphysics is one of the branches of philosophy. The etymological makeup of the term *metaphysics* is telling and relevant to its meaning and focus. Two Greek words, *meta* and *phusia*, are joined to form the word metaphysics. *Meta* is a prepo-sition, which could mean with, after, or behind. If it is accompanied with the gen-itive case, it could mean with, among, or against (Trenchard, 1998); if it is accompanied with the accusative case (direct object), then its meaning could be after or behind (Wallace, 2000). The term *metaphysics* does not provide sufficient syntactical context to determine whether the construction is genitive or accusative, but drawing from its emphases and orientations, we may infer that *meta* in meta-physics stands for after or behind.

Whereas the modern science of physics concerns itself primarily with the phe-nomena of "the natural world, that is, in the realm of things existing in space and time" (Lowe, 2002, p. 2), metaphysics, on the other hand, focuses on as well as in-vestigates "the nature of things existing in space and time, with the nature of space and time themselves, and with the nature of causation" (p. 2). In addition, other ab-stract subjects such as being (ontology), mathematics, logic, time, space, and re-lated aspects of the universe (cosmology) belong to the domain of metaphysics. Here lies the fine line between physics and metaphysics—the scope of physics is confined to the realm of natural phenomena, while metaphysics subsumes the realm of natural phenomena and assumes the existence of another realm beyond the natural one. In addition, metaphysics goes even deeper by investigating the na-ture/essence of those entities existing within both realms.

The philosophical concept, epistemology, is formed by two Greek words—*epis-teme* (knowledge/justified or proven knowledge) and *logos* (explanation/study). Epistemology has been conceptually posited as a branch of philosophy whose pri-mary objective lies in "the study of the nature of knowledge and justification [thereof]" (Moser, 2006, p. 273). This study is both reflective and analytic, revolving around the questions of whether humans truly know, the nature of what humans really know, and the certainty of what humans claim to know. The emphases and orientations of epistemology make it a "theory of knowledge" (Moser, Mulder, & Trout, 1998). Philosophical reflection on the conditions of knowledge and sources of knowledge goes back at least to the ancient Greek philosophers Plato (c. 427–347

BC) and Aristotle (384–322 BC). Plato's *Theaetetus* and Aristotle's *Analytics*, more than any other writings, set the stage for epistemology "by delimiting the concept and the structure of human knowledge" (Moser et al., 1998, p. 4). Congruently, justification of knowledge, aimed at a high degree of certitude, has dominated the discourse on epistemology.

This need for the justification of knowledge has yielded two different schools of thought—foundationalism and non-foundationalism (Grayling, 1996). The former school maintains that knowledge can be justified in terms of finite claims or grounds. In other words, knowledge can be objective. Philosophers such as René Descartes (1596–1650), John Locke (1632–1704), and David Hume (1711–1776) shared that view. Those philosophers did not necessarily agree on the ground on which knowledge may be justified. For instance, Descartes posited that reason was the main purveyor of knowledge, while Locke and Hume posited experience as the source from which knowledge emanates. Locke, in particular, believed the human brain/mind is a blank slate until knowledge is wrought on it by experience, experience through the senses that forms the basis for the thesis of empirical knowledge. Similarly, Hume stressed the senses, particularly feeling or human emotion, as the purveyor of knowledge. Like Descartes, Kant (1711–1804) maintained knowledge can be sufficiently justified and stressed reason as an adequate tool by which objective knowledge may be accessed and interpreted. Both Descartes and Kant rejected the thesis of skepticism that challenges the claims of knowledge and suggested "proposed justification [for knowledge] might be insufficient" (Grayling, 1996, p. 47). The latter school, non-foundationalism, stems from skepticism and remains largely skeptical about the justification, the certainty, and the objectivity of knowledge. Foundationalism and non-foundationalism ultimately revolve around the question of whether knowledge can be objective or subjective.

The concept of axiology and its investigative orientations derive from the Greek etymology of the cognate. The Greek *axios* means value and its combination with logos (study/explanation/reason) forms this branch of philosophy, which investigates "the nature of value and what kinds of things have value" (Lemos, 2006, p. 949). Other scholars, like Scruton (1996), refer to this branch of philosophy as ethics and aesthetics. But there are many others who, like Lemos, view axiology as encompassing ethics, aesthetics, and other practical aspects that fit perfectly under this branch of philosophy.

Ancient and Classical Philosophical Traditions

Thus far, this chapter has focused largely on delineating philosophical concepts, ideas, and thoughts that are particularly common in Western philosophy. It is often assumed that ancient Greeks were the first to develop speculative thought, yet a second-century Christian, Clement of Alexandria, claimed that the Greeks borrowed their ideas from the barbarians (in ancient times barbarians represented communities or tribes not belonging to the great civilizations of Greece and Rome). Whichever the truth might be, it is historically important to recognize the contributions of ancient Greeks to the subsequent development of Western philosophy, architecture, science, literature, and arts. No history of ancient thought "can avoid the mountain mass of Plato" (Kenny, 1997, p. 22). English mathematician and philosopher A. N. Whitehead (1861–1947) once said that the European philosophical tradition, generally speaking, consists of a series of footnotes to Plato. Plato was responsible for immortalizing his teacher Socrates (469–399 BC) in the dialogues that gave rise to Idealism. Aristotle of Stageira, a student of Plato and tutor of Alexander the Great, ushered in Realism and the development of natural sciences.

While Western civilizations have significantly contributed to the conceptualization as well as the systemization of the project of contemporary philosophy, philosophizing activities are not exclusive to the West. The philosophic temperament is "found throughout the world and may be assumed to have been present throughout the hundred thousand years of human being" (Kenny, 1997, p. 4). Furthermore, the questions that drive Western philosophy are not unique to Western societies either. By philosophizing activities, we mean the unflinching intellectual drive and quest by human beings that seeks to comprehend as well as explicate existence, and pertains to time and space, and includes the material and the immaterial world. The following sections feature Hinduism and Buddhism as ancient philosophical traditions in order to illustrate the claim that philosophy is not a project unique to Western societies. As such, the ensuing discussions should be construed as a continuity of the project of philosophy that engages metaphysical and physical questions, and more important, reflect the same intense human fascination with the pursuit of wisdom, as is evident in Western philosophical traditions.

Hindu Philosophical Inquiry, *Jñāna*, and *Moksha*

The Hindu worldview assumes that all beings are caught in a cycle of painful existence where they are bound to experience multiple lifetimes. But this worldview also maintains that the duration of a person's experience in the cycle of existence is contingent upon his or her karma; to the degree that this person's karma has a quality lesser than the requisite to be liberated from the cycle, he or she may consider three different paths toward existing—knowledge, devotion, and karma. Karma resurfaces, but it presupposes deeds of better quality.

The path of knowledge is of particular interest to the thesis of the pursuit of wisdom for the following reasons. The path of knowledge posits knowledge as a way out of the painful cycle of existence. Johnson (2009) suggests *jñāna* exudes the sense of gnosis as in "realization of ultimate reality" (p. 157). Further, he accurately identifies this path in Hinduism as "the quest for liberating knowledge, identified as the realization of the relationship between [B]rahman [*ultimate reality*] and atman [*human soul*], which informs much of the teaching of the Upanishads, and which subsequently becomes the characteristic means to liberation" (p. 157). While Johnson's view is accurate, the interpretive meaning he suggested is too narrow, limiting *jñāna* to spiritual enlightenment and excluding knowledge (episteme), the object of inquiry. In fact, Chethimattam (1971) offers a compelling case in favor of a more comprehensive view of *jñāna*, which encompasses but is not limited to knowledge (Greek equivalent gnosis) as a spiritual enlightenment. Chethimattam's interpretive meaning is, in our opinion, more accurate, considering *jñāna* is linked to the Vedas.

In fact, this postulation of knowledge as a way out of the cycle of existence presumes that something is lacking epistemologically, hence ignorance entrenches the human soul deeper into the cycle of ignorance (Chethimattam, 1971). Thus, knowledge becomes a requisite toward liberation. Particularly, it states that the acquisition of knowledge is potent enough to erase one's past that may include burdensome bad karma, at which point that person will be liberated from the cycle more quickly. Worth noting is that the knowledge a person is required to acquire is not a random or arbitrary kind of knowledge. Its object [*from the syntactical formulation: I know the Vedas*] is the Vedas; in other words, the Vedas are the content of this knowledge.

In Hinduism, the pursuit of wisdom is stressed, albeit confined, to the Vedas. Even then, the elevation of the Vedas in the Hindu pursuit of wisdom amplifies the thesis of inquiry that is espoused in the present work. The thesis maintains that the known and the unknown exist in an unending cycle of philosophical or scientific inquiry that continuously captures as well as captivates the interest of the human mind, even galvanizing the mind toward greater dimensions of epistemological depth and breadth. The Vedas are the most sacred and ancient texts in the Hindu worldview and were the primary texts in the earliest forms of Hinduism (Van Voorst, 2011). Fittingly, Veda in Sanskrit means "wisdom" or "vision," which underscores the notion of the pursuit of wisdom. The Hindu Vedas themselves are ritualistic and vastly metaphysical, embodying cosmological and ontological speculations, and as such are deeply philosophical, reflecting a profound interest in wisdom of all sorts.

While the Vedas remain vital to the current forms of Hinduism, the notion of knowledge as a pathway toward liberation represents a paradigm shift that was wrought by a series of new philosophical writings referred to as the *Upanishads*. The Upanishads infused the then-oldest forms of Hinduism, Vedism—whose relevance was threatened by the emergence of the vibrant and philosophically elaborate system of Buddhism—with new ideas as well as new deities. But, the *Upanishads* did not necessarily overhaul the Vedas. Instead, they deconstructed the Vedas, particularly the highly ritualistic and elitist elements thereof, while presenting more systematized and philosophical interpretations and elaborations of the Vedas (Chethimattam, 1971; Hiriyanna, 1975). Even with the turn of the philosophical tide, which is evident in the *Upanishads*, the search for enlightenment by the human mind through the grasp of wisdom has remained constant.

No other Hindu book best illustrates this claim than the *Bhagavad Gita*. Composed of eighteen chapters and nestled in the epic war between the Pandavas and Kouravas, the *Bhagavad Gita* is replete with references to the infiniteness of wisdom and is infused with repeated calls for the human soul to yearn and search that infinite wisdom. Paradoxically, the call to seek such wisdom should by no means be construed as an indication that such wisdom might be grasped or attained. That wisdom is there but is not there, making it quite elusive. However elusive, it dwells in the Ultimate Reality. In other words, the Ultimate Reality is wisdom, but wisdom is embedded in the Vedas. So, grasping wisdom as such necessitates the seeker or the philosopher to search and to intellectually grapple with the Vedas. Once the seeker or the philosopher has attained a relatively perfect understanding or knowledge of the Vedas, he or she becomes liberated from *samsara* (cycle of reincarnation). That attainment in and of itself is, according to Hinduism, the consummate enlightenment, or realized relationship between the Brahman and that seeker. Worth noting is that this attained knowledge, albeit metaphysical, did not bypass inquiry.

Buddhist Philosophical Inquiry, *Prajna*, and *Nirvana*

Emerging from the Hindu background, Siddhartha Gautama (586–466 BC) also stressed the pursuit of wisdom. As an Indian prince, Gautama grew up steeped in the Hindu system; like his contemporary Indian compatriots, he thought of himself as being caught in this cycle of painful existence. The difference between Gautama and many Indians of his generation was that Gautama had grown disenchanted as well as disillusioned about the viability of then existing Hindu ways for a person to escape the cycle of existence. Such disenchantment and disillusion later infused Gautama with indifference so intense that Gautama decided to abandon his domestic life, as he knew it then, so he could proceed to the third and fourth stages of life (respectively, forest dwelling and asceticism). His abandonment represented an act of nonattachment to what was as well as a striving toward reaching what had not yet been grasped.

That which Gautama pursued both sacrificially and passionately was wisdom, or *jñāna*. His quest, which was successful by his later claim, came to embody paradoxically the essence of what he had tried to vanquish—suffering. This is epitomized in his acknowledgment that suffering exists because of things we desire to grasp. Suffering he did experience, even as he strove to overcome suffering, for he nearly died from his extreme ascetic regimen of dieting and meditating, which illustrated his postulation that suffering, in fact, originates in the human heart. When he finally reached his goal, the attainment of a deep level of consciousness—nirvana or enlightenment—which supposedly brought him closest to ultimate reality or transported him deepest into realms of reality, he gasped in gratification and exulted subliminally as he shared his newly obtained wisdom with his followers:

> As long, O monks, as my knowledge and insight were not quite clear regarding each of Four Noble Truths, I was uncertain whether I had attained to the full insight of what wisdom that [is] unsurpassed in the heavens or on earth. But as soon as my knowledge and insight were quite clear regarding each of these Four Noble Truths, then I became certain that attained to the full insight of that wisdom that is unsurpassed in the heavens or on earth. Now this knowledge and this insight have arisen within me. The emancipation of my heart is immovable. This is my last existence. Now there will be no rebirth for me! (as cited in Van Voorst, 2011, p. 82)

Gautama's achievement has been conceived as *enlightenment* in and of itself—knowledge surpassing the bounds of earth and heavens. For his achievement to be properly understood, Gautama's inquiry must be placed within the Hindu cultural and religious background as discussed earlier. The discourse excerpted above introduces the Four Noble Truths that represent one of the major teachings of the Dharma. It was part of the Buddha's first sermon wherein he outlined this Buddhist Dharma that contains two major teachings—the three characteristics of existence (suffering, non-existent self, and impermanence) and the Four Noble Truths (knowledge of suffering, origin of suffering, cessation of suffering, and knowledge of the path) (Prebish & Keown, 2010; Van Voorst, 2011).

The knowledge of the path contains eight teachings or principles referred to as the *noble eightfold path*, of which the first two are *right view* and *right resolve/thought*. Right view and resolve/thought are particularly noted because they embody *prajna* (Prebish & Keown, 2010). Literally, *prajna* means wisdom. Thus, *prajna* can be said to embody intellectual activities, or to be manifest in intellectual activities (Murti, 2010). In other words, knowledge and *prajna*, as conceptualized in the Buddhist Madhyamika system, are coupled, if not inextricably linked, to create a type of dialectic. That dialectic is knowledge and thus philosophy itself.

The examples of Hinduism and Buddhism, as ancient ways of knowing, illustrate the close link between knowledge and philosophical inquiry (research). Evidently, fascination with wisdom and the quest to grasp wisdom are imprinted on the human psyche regardless of their geographical or geopolitical status. Philosophizing activities within Hinduism and Buddhism embody such fascination and quest.

Modern Western Philosophy

Western classical systems of Plato's idealism and Aristotle's realism gave rise to the corresponding traditions of rationalism and empiricism. Stemming from metaphysics, idealism embodies a philosophical approach that separates the mind from the material world (Blackburn, 1996). In this philosophical tradition, "facts about mental life form the familiar class, and the ones about the physical world need some kind of certification from them" (Blackburn, p. 68). The idealist perspective has either informed or conceived various epistemological paradigms. In particular, the questions rationalism and empiricism have raised inevitably fall within the philosophical purview of idealism and realism.

Two philosophers tower over the emergence of rationalism and empiricism respectively—Descartes and Locke. Descartes and Locke were not necessary on the opposite side of the epistemological debate, but their respective ideas were different enough to yield polemical themes. For instance, Descartes postulated knowledge as "clear and distinct ideas," accessible through reason. To arrive at his conclusion, Descartes used the method of doubt. "He rejected as completely false any thought that could be doubted for any reason" (Bishop, 2011, p. 284). Descartes' principle, *cogito ergo sum*, became the basis of his ironic unwavering faith in reason (Bennett, 2001). Using the model inherent in his first principle, Descartes was able to infer "other perfectly clear and distinct ideas, including the existence of God, and the certainty of his own mathematical propositions" (Bishop, p. 285). Overall, Descartes' methodology for the certainty of scientific knowledge became the basis of modern *rationalism*, which maintains reason as the primary and "unique path to knowledge" (Garber, 2006, p. 771).

Like Descartes, Locke ushered in a new science of knowledge, and they both went on to etch lasting imprints on the Enlightenment Movement and, ultimately, on the history of intellectual ideas. Locke viewed knowledge as a product of experience. He argued that no ideas were innate to the mind and that all ideas came to the mind through sensuous experiences and "its own inner workings" (Bishop, 2011, p. 282). Finally, if we must have knowledge or acquire the certainty of knowledge, such knowledge must come "directly or indirectly through sensory experiences" (Moser & Nat, 1995, p. 22).

Philosophical schools of empiricism and rationalism have exerted a significant amount of influence on the history and development of ideas in the West and beyond its borders. These schools seldom agree with each other internally. Notwithstanding their lack of internal agreement, these schools share the profound preoccupation with understanding of both the material and the immaterial world. By the end of the nineteenth century, radical empiricism gave rise to logical positivism that embodies a philosophical approach that jettisons metaphysical claims. Otherwise known as the Vienna Circle, positivists were influenced by the empiricism of Hume and also by the *Tractatus Logico-Philosophicus* of Wittgenstein (1889–1951). The rejection of metaphysical claims by logical positivists was grounded almost entirely in their unequivocal commitment to empirical knowledge and to scientific method as the only tool that could access this knowledge. Any thought, knowledge, or tool outside the realm of empiricism and scientific method was deemed meaningless (Blackburn, 1996, p. 69).

Positivism

Positivism is often identified with several traditions that share common threads in the philosophical, linguistic, and sociological movements of the end of the nineteenth and the beginning of the twentieth centuries: logical atomism, logical empiricism, logical positivism, and logical (or linguistic) analysis. Auguste Comte (1798–1857) appropriated logical positivism as the ground for the development of the science of sociology. Comte was convinced that human phenomena could and should be studied with the methods employed by natural sciences. He attempted to create a positive science of human beings as opposed to theological and metaphysical speculations. Comte claimed to discover an "evolutionary law of three stages" (Runes, 1983, p. 259) that all societies pass through: theological, metaphysical, and positive, the latter being associated with the advent of sociology as the highest positive science in the hierarchy of sciences. Such positive science was meant to result in the discovery of the laws and regulations of human behavior calculated by mathematical formulas. A "perfect" society based on these laws of behavior would subsequently ensue. John Stuart Mill (1806–1873) adhered to a similar positivistic view, yet unlike Comte, he did not claim that the science of sociology could be based on absolutely certain knowledge.

R. Avenarius (1843–1896) and E. Mach (1838–1916) created a more rigid version of positivism. Avenarius' *empiriocriticism* asserts that pure experience should be the ground for certain knowledge, and Mach defends the view that knowledge should be limited to sensations. These ideas found their ultimate expression in the works of the scientists and philosophers who banded together in the 1920s to form the Vienna Circle group, which included Rudolf Carnap, Otto Neurath, Herbert Feigl, Felix

Kaufmann, and Kurt Gödel, under the leadership of Moritrz Schlick (1882–1936). Their purpose was to eliminate the so-called metaphysical and speculative errors. Fascinated by the progress of modern science, and especially by the theories of relativity and quantum mechanics, they elevated science to an insurmountable pedestal.

The Vienna Circle members were influenced by a number of prominent philosophers of the time: A. J. Ayer (1910–1989), G. E. Moore (1873–1958), B. Russell (1872–1970), G. Ryle (1900–1976), and especially L. Wittgenstein. Worth noting is the fact that Wittgenstein never associated himself directly with logical positivists and later made considerable revisions to his early philosophical works, particularly with regard to language, as will be discussed. One major preoccupation of logical positivists was with the language, the meaning of words, and how language statements reflect relations between words and the world. Logical positivists understood the link between language and the world as being directly related to sense data (Polkinghorne, 1983). *What you see is what you get!* This is a figurative expression that stands for the central principle of verification posited by logical positivism. The principle of verification, also known as *verificationism*, asserts that "no proposition can be accepted as meaningful unless it can be verified on formal grounds (through logic and mathematics) or verified on empirical or sense-data grounds" (Ozmon & Craver, 2008, p. 259). The only true and therefore meaningful propositions are either analytic (logical and mathematical) or synthetic (empirically verifiable), whereas claims such as "God is love," "This teacher is passionate about her job," or "The third-graders do not like taking tests" are considered nonsensical (Robinson & Groves, 2001).

Logical positivists encountered a series of problems associated with verificationism and other principles. Their disregard of the fact that there are unverifiable propositions in the language as well as some fundamental assumptions of science that cannot be verifiable led to a rapid decline and eventual refutation of positivism in the 1950s. Positivistic reliance on empirical sense data undermines the attempt to obtain an irrefutable knowledge precisely because these data depend on subjective perceptions. Despite its questionable reputation, positivism left an imprint on educational philosophy and research. In the 1950s, "Hardie and O'Connor criticized educational theories as vague and unscientific and hence as mere expressions of opinion" and recommended that educational research "become more scientific" (Kneller, 1984, p. 139). Positivism exerted considerable influence on behaviorism, cognitive science, and systems analysis.

Few professional philosophers can identify themselves with logical positivism today. Whereas positivism has been discarded as a scientific paradigm, it is often mistaken for "scientific" research in education. Yu (2006) points to the misconceived links between positivism and contemporary quantitative research, which might be due to the historical facts about the prominent founders of statistical methods such as Karl Pearson (1857–1936) and Ronald A. Fisher (1890–1962). The primetime of their careers coincided with the dominant position of positivism and fierce debates between evolutionary biologists and Mendel's (1822–1884) geneticists. While C. Darwin's (1809–1882) theory held that evolution is a result of accumulated small changes in traits over considerable periods of time, Mendel's theory of genetics contended that evolution is a discontinuous process and is driven by the mutation of genes. By the beginning of the twentieth century, both theories were blended into the so-called biometrics. Pearson initially adhered to Darwin's evolutionary biology, while Fisher came to support a blended view of a Mendelian-Darwinian-biometrician synthesis (Yu, 2006).

Arguably, statistics is not a subject-free methodology derived from timeless mathematical axioms: "biological themes and philosophical presumptions drove Karl Pearson and R. A. Fisher to develop their statistical schools" (Yu, 2006, p. 20). Different philosophies underlie the various schools of quantitative methods. It is certainly impossible to divorce the names of Fisher and Pearson from their association with positivism, yet it is equally inappropriate to regard the methods they developed and that were eventually accepted (with modifications) by quantitative researchers as positivistic. Yu presents compelling arguments in support of this thesis, which will be further elaborated in chapters 2 and 3.

By the second half of the twentieth century, positivism had been largely rejected by the Anglo-American and Continental philosophers of science. Frederick Suppe, Willard Quine, Stephen Toulmin, and Michael Polanyi are among the most outspoken critics of positivist view on science (Polkinghorne, 1983). Positivism has "failed in its attempts to reconstruct science into a logically unified system of theoretical statements grounded in the certainty of sense experience" (Polkinghorne, p. 93). A number of anti-positivist movements (e.g., Gestalt psychology, linguistic philosophy, structuralism, poststructuralism, and Wittgenstein's later work) signaled a paradigm shift in the conception of science. These movements shared a common belief, namely, that it is impossible to obtain absolutely certain knowledge in social and human sciences because human beings cannot stand outside their language systems and cultures. A skeptical response to logical positivism captures this assumption through the *Weltanschauungen* (world outlook) analysis, the thesis of which runs as follows: "One never has access to reality: one can only look through the opaque spectacles of the cognitive apparatus of one's historically given *Weltanschauungen*" (Polkinghorne, p. 103). It was Wittgenstein's later work on language games that played a "catalytic role in the origin of the *Weltanschauungen* analysis [for subsequent philosophers of science]" (Polkinghorne, p. 103).

Wittgenstein's departure from his earlier, positivistic position is expressed in *Philosophical Investigations* (1953/2009). In it, Wittgenstein proposes the language game theory, which questions the possibility that there is a direct relationship be-

Figure 1.1: Jastrow's Duck-Rabbit Figure

tween a word and an object (which is a positivistic position). The meanings of words, asserts Wittgenstein, are determined by various contexts, or rules of games (such as in a chess game), in which they are used. Wittgenstein maintains a position of radical pluralism on the possibility of different worldviews represented by many different languages, logics, and subsequently "truths"—all functioning within particular language games. It follows then that what we perceive and see as true depends on our world picture. In other words, human perception is fundamentally interpretive; it is always seeing something *as something*. Wittgenstein illustrates this principle of interpretive "seeing" by a duck-rabbit figure (see figure 1.1) adopted from American psychologist Joseph Jastrow (1863–1944).

With the decline and repudiation of positivism, philosophers of science abandoned the idea of searching for the foundations (or grounds) of knowledge and appropriated instead probabilistic and provisional "truth" statements conditioned by sociocultural and linguistic contexts. The metaphor of knowledge as an unbreakable foundation is often attributed to Descartes. As a counterpoint to this position, the twentieth-century philosophers of science W. Quine (1908–2000) and R. Rorty (1931–1650) proposed instead a net or spider web as a metaphor of knowledge, entertaining the idea that within the web of knowledge, some of its elements can be "weak" or "worn out" and we can subsequently "repair them while hanging on to the relatively stable parts, which still offer support" (Palmer, 2002, p. 108).

Subsequently, many philosophers of science turned to ideas developed prior to the reign of positivism in the 1920s. One of the richest sources of these ideas was American pragmatism and especially the philosophy of Charles S. Peirce, who claimed that science does not represent a "systematized knowledge but the pursuit itself in which scientists are engaged" (Polkinghorne, 1983, p. 119).

American Pragmatism

The story of pragmatism begins in Cambridge, Massachusetts, in the 1870s, when several young and talented minds (C. S. Peirce, W. James, C. Wright, J. Fiske, and F. E. Abbot) who referred to themselves as members of "Metaphysical Club" would gather to discuss and debate philosophical problems. The most prominent of these thinkers, Charles S. Peirce (1830–1914) and William James (1842–1910), were considered the official founders of pragmatism. John Dewey (1859–1952) developed pragmatism further and made it central to his educational philosophy, which "encourages the process-oriented, problem-solving instruction that is so popular with American teachers" (Gutek, 2004, pp. 71–72).

James popularized pragmatism and applied it a great deal to his work in psychology, known as *functionalism*. James added a value component to the practicality thesis of ideas. From a pragmatic standpoint, one should not be concerned with whether ideas are true or false, but rather with the difference that they can make in our lives. The ideas should have "cash value" (James's famous expression).

Despite his major contributions to pragmatism, Peirce's name remained in obscurity until about the second half of the twentieth century when his collected works were published for the first time. Subsequently, Peirce's genius gained worldwide recognition. In his later career, Peirce became highly dissatisfied with the way James, Dewey, and others used the term *pragmatism*, which made him rename his original philosophy into *pragmaticism* (the word that he himself considered ugly). Peirce insisted that pragmatism is not a philosophy or a theory of truth, but rather a method to assist us in finding solutions to problems. His celebrated definition of pragmatism is expressed in the following passage:

> Our idea of anything *is* our idea of its sensible effects. It appears, then, that the rule for attaining the third grade of cleanness of apprehension is as follows: Consider what effects, that might conceivably have practical bearings, we conceive the object of our conception to have. Then, our conception of these effects is the whole of our conception of the object. (1998, p. 146)

Derived from the Greek word *pragma* (action or deed), pragmatism emphasizes the synergy of relations between theory and practice, knowledge and action. Pragmatism is said to be a distinctly American philosophy and a natural outgrowth of the American spirit and way of life (Sellars, 2010) that reflects the American experience of the early settlers in a new land and their demands for the ideas to solve everyday problems. American pragmatism emerged as a response to long-standing European philosophical influences that seemed too "abstruse and too remote from the immediate concerns of a young, vigorous nation" (Popkin & Stroll, 1993, p. 274) recovering from the devastation of the Civil War. There was a sense among many American philosophers that the European eschatological traditions exhausted themselves and were in need of a revival that would bring the new scientific discoveries to the forefront of philosophical inquiry.

Pragmatists embrace scientific inquiry as a radical departure from positivism. Peirce (1966) contends that although positivism has a "favorable influence upon scientific investigation, its fundamental position is false" (p. 137). Peirce's essential position on knowledge, in contrast to positivism, was that our knowledge about the world of objects is fallible and that scientific knowledge has limits. Peirce revered science and thought of it as a living and breathing process. Peirce's (1998) consensus theory of truth elaborates on the process of validating true ideas by the community of scientists. It is the "COMMUNITY" [Peirce's emphasis] that has "definite limits, and [is] capable of a definite increase of knowledge" (1998, p. 115). Peirce firmly believed that scientists and philosophers are motivated by pure love of the pursuit of truth. An inquiry begins because of a genuine doubt: "The irritation of doubt causes a struggle to attain a state of belief. I shall term this struggle inquiry....It is certainly best for us that our beliefs should be such as may truly guide our actions so as to satisfy our desires" (1998, p. 126).

Peirce's method of scientific inquiry translates perfectly into Dewey's problem-solving method. Known as instrumentalism, or experimentalism, Dewey's pragmatic philosophy combines a theory of logic and a principle of ethical analysis and criticism. His expression *warranted assertions* entered the philosophical and educational vocabulary to designate pragmatic truth. In his "Logic: The Theory of Inquiry" (1938), Dewey proposed the notion of intelligence as an essentially evaluative experience. We cannot separate experience as moral, scientific, practical, or theoretical, hence his notion of the reconstruction of human experience. The purpose of inquiry is thus to resolve a doubt or to solve a problem and, while doing so, to exhibit moral practical value of that experience. Dewey's philosophy connects the continuity of experience with the idea of education as growth: "The educative process can be identified with growth when that is understood in terms of active principle, *growing*" (as cited in Johnson & Reed, 2012, p. 111).

Dewey's instrumentalism and experimentalism are linked through the notion of evolutionary philosophy, which influenced a great number of thinkers of that time. (Interestingly, Dewey was born in 1859, the year when Darwin's *The Origin of Species* was published.) Dewey tested his ideas as the experimental method of education in the University of Chicago Laboratory School, which he directed from 1896 to 1904. It was against the metaphysical theories of reality and knowledge that Dewey defended his "unity of knowledge" system, designating the relation between knowing and doing and the active social conception of human intelligence (Gutek, 2004).

The recent revival of pragmatism finds its expression in the neo-pragmatist critique of normativity in Western analytic philosophy. Particularly, Richard Rorty is critical of the American philosophy as being greatly influenced by the search for objective knowledge and thus attempting to establish a "normal" discourse. As a counterpoint, Rorty proposes an "abnormal" discourse as a criticism of this position (Ozmon & Craver, 2008). Cornel West (b. 1953) advocates *prophetic pragmatism*, which merges the ideas of Emerson, liberation theology, and classical pragmatism (Ozmon & Craver). In Rorty's view, the current neo-pragmatists' agenda has to do with "reconciling the antimetaphysical antiabsolutist trends in twentieth-century English, American, and Continental philosophy" and with envisaging the role of philosophy as helping people and society to "break free from outworn vocabularies and attitudes, rather than to provide 'grounding' for the institutions and customs of the present" (as cited in Popkin & Stroll, 1993, p. 316).

The reconciliatory spirit of pragmatism makes itself manifest in educational inquiry through its attempts to do away with the so-called paradigm wars between quantitative and qualitative purists (see, e.g., Johnson & Onwuegbuzie, 2004). Wedded to this spirit are pragmatism's remarkable contributions to the theory of truth and the method of rigorous scientific inquiry that in turn have become instrumental to an overall nineteenth-century anti-positivist movement launched by European existential-phenomenological and hermeneutic philosophers.

Existential-Phenomenological and Hermeneutic Inquiries
Where do we come from? What are we? Where are we going?

Several philosophical traditions developed in nineteenth-century Europe would make the existential questions central to their inquiry as well as part of a concerted effort to articulate the anti-positivist response to the excesses of rationalism and the disputes over the methods by which to approach the study of human phenomena. In 1858, the German historian Droysen distinguished between the terms *erklären* (explanation) and *verstehen* (understanding), which further marked an important distinction between the methods used in natural sciences based on the explanation of natural phenomena, and the methods employed in human sciences that relied on the understanding of human phenomena (Polkinghorne, 1983). Henceforth, *verstehen* becomes not only a legitimate source of knowledge, but more important, an alternative to a foundationalist epistemology way of knowing that is firmly embedded in historically particular and contingent vocabularies (Westphal, 2006).

Giambattista Vico (1668–1744) is said to be the forerunner of the anti-positivist response. Yet it was the German Romantic movement of the nineteenth century that contributed to the response most significantly. The Romantics were philosophers, poets, writers, and artists who questioned the ultimate authority of human reason and its privileged status as espoused by Enlightenment thinkers. Romantics turned their attention to human emotions and desires, the "perennial features of human existence that haunt those who celebrate the rational" (Oliver, 1997, p. 116). Finding a creative outlet in art and aestheticism, the Romantics launched an era of sensibility as a counter-current to a systematic rationalized approach to life. Their purpose was to achieve harmony between the intellect and passion.

Schelling (1775–1854), Novalis (1772–1801), and Hölderlin (1770–1843) are perhaps the most prominent names associated with German Romanticism. Schelling's identity philosophy represents a complex, dialectic ontological system that integrates subject and object, real and ideal, the *uni*verse and the *multi*plicity of being or self. Schelling resolves the internal struggle between artistic eros and systematic reason in favor of art as a unifying principle and the ground for the ultimate expression and realization of self. F. von Hardenberg (Novalis) reifies the unifying principle through poetry and attempts poetic philosophy—an understanding of the self and its world not in abstractions but by romanticizing them. Romanticizing is understood as a portrayal of the unexpected that interrupts our ordinary life and shows what we are *not*, what we are potentially: *Die Welt muß romantisirt werden* (The world must be romanticized), proclaims Novalis. In his major work, *Hyperion*, Hölderlin advances the All-Unity principle as the ultimate self-knowledge and self-expression through aesthetics. The Romantics inspired other philosophers of the anti-positivist response (e.g., Dilthey, Husserl, Heidegger, Merleau-Ponty, Gadamer, Ricoeur, and Habermas) whose philosophies of life laid foundations for the existential-phenomenological and hermeneutic inquiries.

As a systematic philosophy, existentialism was founded by Søren Kierkegaard (1813–1855) and Friedrich Wilhelm Nietzsche (1844–1900) and further developed by a number of European and American thinkers, psychologists, literary figures, and educators: Sartre, de Beauvoir, Buber, Jaspers, Marcel, Tillich, Rogers, Maslow, Camus, and Greene, to name a few most widely acclaimed. Existential themes of freedom, passionate choice, and an acute sense of responsibility for creating one's own destiny and meaning of life in a seemingly absurd and lonely world; living the values that one espouses; and overcoming the fear of death in the situations that require an ultimate choice and subsequently displaying courage and integrity of one's character run across the spectrum of existentialism in a variety of its representations.

Kierkegaard, the leading figure in Christian existentialism, contends that a true Christian lives a life of constant internal conflict in his or her search for God, and it is not through doctrine, theological studies, or regular church attendance, but instead through the leap of faith that he or she can find God, the God from within. Assuming that God exists and one can find Him, the human being is still in a precarious situation—still absolutely alone and abandoned in a seemingly indifferent and hostile world. Out of this complete isolation and despair comes the cry of one in the wilderness. But instead of God's answer, there is only silence: "the human being's experience of nothingness before God, which is at the same moment the complete fulfillment of human existence" (Gutek, 1997, p. 109).

Along comes Nietzsche who proclaims, "God is dead!"—the expression that does not have much to do with a theological argument but rather with Nietzsche's critique of modernity with its reliance on speculative philosophy and slave Christian morality. Nietzsche's concerns with the expression of truth and falsehood leads him to explore the Greek culture in the light of rational (embodied by Apollo) and irrational (embodied by Dionysus) principles. From the synthesis of these two principles arises "the beauty of an art in which life is contained but not destroyed, and in which the terrible and the irrational exist side by side with the serene" (Kenny, 1997, p. 217). Art and aesthetic, not knowledge, are given ontological priority in Nietzsche's existentialist project. Unless one creates something, it would be better that one had never been born. Existence, therefore, can be justified only artistically: only as an "aesthetic product can the world be justified to all eternity," and only as the "genius in the act of creation merges with the primal architect of the cosmos can he truly know something of the eternal essence of art" (Nietzsche, 2000, pp. 261–62).

Art owes its continuous evolution in the Apollonian-Dionysian duality. Being a moral deity, Apollo persistently attempts to retain his self-control in the midst of the warring spheres of influence [non-Apollonian Titans and extra-Apollonian barbarians], until the "effects of the Dionysiac spirit struck the Apollonian Greeks as Titan and barbaric.... Their whole existence, with its temperate beauty, rested upon a base of suffering and *knowledge* which had been hidden from them until the reinstatement of Dionysos uncovered it once more. And lo and behold! Apollo found it impossible to live without Dionysos" (Nietzsche, 2000, p. 256). Nietzsche ultimately favors the Dionysian principle as an expression of will—the will to power, to be more precise. To put it differently, each and every one of us has the potential to become reborn into *Übermensch* (Superman), which is an unrealized potential within us, as long as we are *willing* to overcome the external limitations of our existence: "The individual, with his limits and moderations, forgot himself in the Dionysiac vortex and became oblivious to the laws of Apollo. Indiscreet extravagance revealed itself as truth, and contradiction, a delight born of pain, spoke out of the bosom of nature" (Nietzsche, p. 257).

Nietzsche's philosophy had a profound influence on twentieth-century thinkers, especially on Sartre and Heidegger. Existentialism as a European phenomenon became especially pronounced during and after WWII when philosophers, writers, and ordinary citizens questioned the rationality of the war machine and the sanity of decisions behind it that resulted in the death of millions of people, many of whom sacrificed their lives in the name of false and destructive ideologies. Jean-Paul Sartre's (1905–1980) existentialism was shaped by the anguish, atrocities, and devastation of war. Sartre was part of the French Resistance during WWII and experienced the confrontation with death directly when he was captured by the Nazis. Sartre explicitly positions himself as an atheistic existentialist. In "Existentialism and Humanism," he defines existentialism through his famous dictum, "existence precedes essence." What does he mean by that?

> Man first of all exists, encounters himself, surges up in the world—and defines himself afterwards ....There is no human nature, because there is no God to have conception of it. Man simply is. Man is nothing else but that which he makes of himself. (as cited in Ozmon & Craver, 2008, p. 249)

Regardless of God's presence or absence in our lives, we are doomed to freedom in our earthly existence with its little pleasures and sorrows, and with the burden of making our own choices and assuming full responsibility for them and for the world that we create. Sartre's lifelong partner and philosopher in her own right, Simone de Beauvoir (1908–1986), created an original version of existential philosophy and became widely known for her feminist classic, *The Second Sex* (1949/1989). The book details the analysis of patriarchal societies and the predicament of woman as the Other within them:

> Humanity is male and man defines woman not in herself but as relative to him; she is not regarded as an autonomous being. For him she is sex, absolute sex, no less. She is defined and differentiated with reference to man and not he with reference to her. He is the Subject, he is the Absolute—she is the Other. (1989, p. xxii)

Beauvoir's celebrated credo, "one is not born but becomes a woman," reifies the existential condition that renders the choice for emancipation both possible and justified.

The beginnings and development of phenomenology are most commonly attributed to Husserl, Schutz, Heidegger, Sartre, Merleau-Ponty, and Freire. Edmund Husserl (1859–1938), notably the father of phenomenology, studied the structures of human consciousness and developed phenomenology along rationalist lines (transcendental phenomenology). Phenomenology literally means the study of appearances (Gr. < phenomena) that are being structured by our consciousness in specific patterns and come in different shapes as objects, ideas, memories, or images. The phenomenological process of uncovering the structures of consciousness can be compared with an archeologist excavating a prehistoric site. One has to carefully describe the various strata in order to reveal the meaningful structures that are taken for granted in everyday experience, which Husserl calls "lifeworld" (*Lebenswelt*). Lifeworld designates the everyday world of our affairs (family, work, pleasure, etc.). We may think of this world as "objective and independent, yet it is we who sustain it and give it meaning" (Kneller, 1984, p. 30). The task of phenomenological inquiry is, therefore, to describe the phenomena as they appear to our consciousness and to endow them with meaning.

Alfred Schutz (1899–1959) brought Husserl's phenomenology to the social world and made human action central to its inquiry. Maurice Merleau-Ponty (1908–1961) developed phenomenology along the lines of embodied consciousness. As embodied beings we relate to the world primarily through senses. Sense perceptions that originate in our thoughts are rooted in childhood, when we learn how to move and experience things in a "prereflective" manner. We think, act, and feel as we do "because of the omnipresent, prerefletive stratum of [our] experience" (Kneller, 1984, p. 43). Our bodily perception of the world is "dehiscence, a splitting open of the body as touching and touched, as seer and seen that allows the body to experience things" (Low, 2000, p. 17).

Martin Buber (1878–1965) contributed immensely to the existential-phenomenological educational theory by advancing the argument of the *I-Thou* dialogue as an authentic and mutually appreciative form of relationships between individuals. *I-Thou* is counter-positioned with an *I-It* mode of objectified and self-interested relationships. Buber advocates the *I-Thou* relation among teachers and students and conceives of it as a communion of divine and human character, whereas "one's faith in God and in one's fellow human beings is witness to one's devotion to a higher end" (Ozmon & Craver, 2008, p. 227).

The tradition of hermeneutics has a long and fascinating history. The term comes from the Greek *hermeneuein*, "to interpret," and is linked to the name of Hermes, the Greek god messenger. Hermes was the son of Zeus and Maia, the daughter of Atlas, and was born out of wedlock. His regular duties included carrying messages to and from Zeus, between the other gods and mortals. Known for his devious character, Hermes was a protector of mischief makers (Couch, 1997). He is often portrayed as wearing winged-shoes or sandals, a round helmet-shaped hat, and carrying a staff entwined with serpents. Worth noting is the fact that Hermes has siblings in other cultural traditions, for instance, Mercury in Roman mythology, Garuda the mythical bird in Hinduism and Buddhism, and Slava the messenger bird of Perun (equivalent of Zeus) in Slavic mythology.

Hermeneutics acquired its revolutionary spirit from the Protestant Reformation of the sixteenth century when, in opposition to the Catholic Church's authority over biblical texts, the Protestants "called for a return to the text itself" (Polkinghorne, 1983, p. 219). With the spread of literacy and the printing press, it became possible for common people to have access to biblical texts. M. Luther's (1483–1546) translation of the Bible into modern German revolutionized and shifted the consciousness of the religious laity in Germany, and eventually throughout Europe, from the confines of church dogmas to the vast and open prairie of hermeneutics wherein they were able to read freely and interpret independently the word of God.

Wilhelm Dilthey (1833–1911) is recognized as the leading figure in hermeneutics, although he credited Friedrich Schleiermacher (1768–1834) with the development of the art. Dilthey attempted to shape hermeneutics as a human science capable of generating knowledge for social and political decisions. Dilthey realized that it would be impossible to gain certain and objective knowledge of the human realm, yet one could strive for approximation of such knowledge in which "there are degrees of truth which move closer to a sure understanding" (Polkinghorne, 1983, p. 223). Significant to the study of hermeneutics are also the philosophies of Martin Heidegger (1889–1976) and Hans-George Gadamer (1900–2002).

Heidegger's *Being and Time* (1927) marks a radical departure from conventional assumptions of knowledge and the ego-subject in Western philosophy. It is not about the way we know the world, but the way we *are*. The question of being, thus, acquires ontological priority over all other questions. Heidegger posits the question of being within the context of *Dasein*—the realm of our existence. Human existence constitutes the openness where being can be revealed. For something to be means for it to be revealed, uncovered, made manifest. We exist in the world because we understand what it means to be. Our authentic existence—being-in-the-world—is possible only when self as ego is eclipsed by the manifestation of our finitude. The modes of being in the world also include being-with-others and being-toward-death. "The being of *Dasein* means ahead-of-itself-being-already-in-(the world) as being-amidst (entities encountered in-the-world). This Being fills in the signification of the term '*care*' [Sorge]" (Heidegger, 1962, p. 237). I *am* care (Sorge), the unity of lived experiences, temporal transcendence, openness to and involvement with worldly affairs, my being "here" (the *Da* of *Dasein*). The more open and authentic I am, the more able I am to care for myself and others.

In his seminal work *Truth and Method* (1960/2004), Gadamer extended and applied the main concepts developed by Heidegger regarding the historical and interactive conditions of human understanding. As a model for his method, Gadamer suggests translation from one language to another. Interpretation is not just reconstruction of meaning, it also involves a fusion of horizons, an interaction between the interpreter and the meaning in the text. Interpretation is a mediated process that has a circular character. The parts of the text constitute a complex whole that is the meaning of the text. The horizon is "something into which we move and that moves with us. Horizons change for a person who is moving. Thus the horizon of the past, out of which all human life lives and which exists in the form of tradition, is always in motion" (Gadamer, 1992, p. 271). The process of movement from the first pre-judgmental notion of the meaning of the whole (in which the parts are understood) to a change in the sense of the meaning of the whole is called the *hermeneutic circle*. Hence, interpretation is never final, and the process of understanding does not result in finite and objective truth. Hermeneutic understanding is conditioned and mediated by language, culture, and context. Hermeneutic method aims at "maintaining the intersubjectivity of mutual understanding in ordinary-language communication and in action according to common norms" (Habermas, 1972, p. 176). More important, the philosophical hermeneutics of Heidegger and Gadamer call into serious question the very possibility of objective historical knowledge.

Existential-phenomenological and hermeneutic (life) philosophies have opened extraordinary venues for researchers to pursue the study of human phenomena as a multi-paradigmatic endeavor. Their emergence and development signaled a radical shift from a positivistic view of scientific knowledge to epistemological and methodological pluralism. The legacy of early hermeneutics and its rebellious spirit was inherited by the twentieth-century thinkers for whom it was not enough to understand the world—they ventured to change it. This iconoclastic spirit of the twentieth century emanating from a desire for change and a new voice might be framed as postmodernism.

Critical and Postmodern Inquiries

The paradigm of postmodernism, which gave rise to various critical projects, particularly critical theory, is set against the postmodern backdrop. These critical projects originated in Western thought, focused on the notion of truth and the certainty thereof, and objected to the view of knowledge as neutral and rational. In addition, reflecting a shift away from modernism, as well as being heavily informed by the works of Karl Marx (1818–1883), Friedrich Nietzsche (1844–1900), and Sigmund Freud (1856–1939), these critical projects conceived two important schools of thought—Frankfurt School and poststructuralism (Carrette, 2005).

While Michel Foucault and Jacques Derrida were the more prominent figures within poststructuralism, Frankfurt School featured Max Horkheimer, Marcus Adorno, and Habermas as its key thinkers. While these two critical schools had their differences, they nonetheless shared some basic assumptions about knowledge, society, and political institutions:

> Following Marx critical theory is aware that all knowledge is linked to economic and political ideology; following Nietzsche it understands that all knowledge is linked to the "will to power"; and following Freud it under-

stands that all knowledge is linked to things outside our awareness (the unconscious). (Carrette, 2005, p. 28)

Traces of these critical pioneers are evident in almost every critical work that has been undertaken since then, and the fact that the three thinkers highlighted above viewed critical work from various prisms are also signs that critical project is neither monolithic nor homogeneous.

Grounded in the historical materialist tradition, critical theory embodies an unflinching interest in the social, political, spatial, and economic conditions of humans (Rush, 2004). From a Marxist standpoint, historical materialism is a philosophical perspective that is strongly grounded in all things physical and material, and even empirical in many ways (Smart, 1999), while the dialectic method represents a tool of analysis that views "every social system as having within it immanent forces that give rise to contradictions that can only be resolved by a new system" (Rush, 2004, p. 12). Thus, dialectic materialism is critical at its core and vies that agency is imperative for humans to determine and transform their respective material conditions, or the realities of their physical existence, or "sensuous existence" (Rush, p. 20).

Emanating from that background, critical theory "represents a sophisticated effort to continue Marx's transformation of moral philosophy into social and political critique, while rejecting orthodox Marxism as a dogma" (Bohman, 2006, p. 324). Critical theorists may have had varying degrees of perspectives on the unfolding of critical endeavor, but they were unequivocally united on the questions and issues that led to the conception of their critical enterprise:

> The motivation for this enterprise appears similar for each of the theorists—the aim being to lay the foundation for an exploration, in an interdisciplinary research context, of questions concerning the conditions which make possible the production and transformation of society, the meaning of culture, and the relation between the individual, society and nature. (Held, 1980, p. 16)

Held (1980) underscores this unity on the questions and concerns of critical theory as the central and melding theme that underlie collaboration and co-existence among the Frankfurt School scholars. Indeed, this unity has contributed to the success of critical theory, legitimizing it as a theoretical analysis that concerns itself with the actuality of life as it unfolds.

Geuss (1981) breaks down the fundamentals of critical theory and posits them as its central theses. The first thesis, according to Geuss, claims that critical theory is "aimed at producing enlightenment in the agents" who subscribe to the framework, in terms of "enabling those agents to determine what their true interests are" (p. 2). A second prong to the first thesis is that critical theory is "inherently emancipatory"; that is to say, it liberates "agents from a kind of coercion which is at least partly self-imposed, from self-frustration of conscious human action" (p. 2). The second thesis maintains that critical theory has a "cognitive content" that makes this theory intrinsically a "form of knowledge" (p. 2).

Flowing logically from the second thesis, the third one maintains that critical theory is dissimilar "epistemologically in essential ways from theories in the natural sciences": while "natural science is objectifying," critical theory is "reflective" (Geuss, 1981, p. 2). Objectifying refers to natural science making human beings the objects of its studies and embracing empirical standards that supposedly make findings about humans objective; but the "reflective" qualification of critical theory underscores its interest in understanding and interpreting the human condition and inspiring actions to improve it (Geuss, 1981). Critical theory seeks to transform human conditions materially while aiming to shift and balance power dynamics between the oppressed and their oppressors, between those in power and their subordinates. As such, critical theory has been established as an effective tool to critique dominant establishments or discourse, and to foster human emancipation (Bohman, 2006; Freire, 1971/1998; McLaren & Farahmandpur, 2005).

In this chapter, we endeavored to trace the historical development of philosophical ideas, traditions, and perspectives while highlighting their prevailing theme of pursuit of wisdom, including their significance to various paradigms of knowledge and to educational research. Thus, the preceding discussions fittingly preface the discussion of epistemology in the next chapter.

Bibliography

Barhart, R. K. (Ed.). (2008). *Chambers dictionary of etymology*. Edinburg, UK: Chambers Harrap.

Bennett, J. (2001). *Learning from six philosophers: Descartes, Spinoza, Leibniz, Locke, Berkeley, Hume* (Vols. 1–2). New York: Oxford University Press.

Bishop, P. (2011). *Adventures in the human spirit* (6th ed.). Upper Saddle River, NJ: Prentice Hall.

Blackburn, S. (1996). Metaphysics. In N. Bunnin & E. P. Tsui-James (Eds.), *Blackwell companion to philosophy* (pp. 64–89). Cambridge, MA: Blackwell.

Bohman, J. (2006). Frankfurt School. In R. Audi (Ed.), *The Cambridge dictionary of philosophy* (2nd ed., pp. 324–325). New York: Cambridge University Press.

Butchvarov, P. (2006). Metaphysics. In R. Audi (Ed.), *The Cambridge dictionary of philosophy* (2nd ed., pp. 563–566). New York: Cambridge University Press.

Carrette, J. (2005). Critical theory and religion. In C. Partridge (Ed.), *Introduction to world religions* (pp. 28–31). Minneapolis, MN: Fortress.

Chethimattam, J. B. (1971). *Patterns of Indian thought*. London: Geoffrey Chapman.

Couch, M. (Ed.). (1997). *Greek and Roman mythology*. New York: Todtri.

de Beauvoir, S. (1989). *The second sex*. New York: Vintage.

Encyclopedia of ancient myths and culture. (2004). London: Quantum.

Foley, M., & Mohan, W. J. (2003). *Philosophic inquiry: An introduction*. Philadelphia: Xlibris.

Freire, P. (1971/1998). *Pedagogy of freedom: Ethics, democracy, and civic courage*. (P. Clarke, Trans.). Lanham, MD: Rowman & Littlefield.

Gadamer, H. G. (1960/2004). *Truth and method*. (J. Weinsheimer & D. G. Marshall, Trans.). New York: Continuum.

Gadamer, H. G. (1992). The historicity of understanding. In K. Mueller-Vollmer (Ed.), *The hermeneutics reader: Texts of the German tradition from the Enlightenment to the present* (pp. 256–292). New York: Continuum.

Garber, D. (2006). Rationalism. In R. Audi (Ed.), *The Cambridge dictionary of philosophy* (2nd ed., pp. 771–772). New York: Cambridge University Press.

Geuss, R. (1981). *The idea of a critical theory: Habermas and the Frankfurt School*. Cambridge, UK: Cambridge University Press.

Grayling, A. C. (1996). Epistemology. In N. Bunnin & E. P. Tsui-James (Eds.), *The Blackwell companion to philosophy* (pp. 38–63). Oxford: Blackwell.

Gutek, G. L. (2004). *Philosophical and ideological voices in education*. Boston: Pearson.

Habermas, J. (1972). Knowledge and human interests. (J. J. Shapiro, Trans.). Boston: Beacon.

Heidegger, M. (1962). *Being and time*. New York: Harper & Row.

Held, D. (1980). *Introduction to critical theory: Horkheimer to Habermas*. Cambridge, MA: Athenaeum.

Hesse-Biber, S. N., & Leavy, P. (2011). *The practice of qualitative research* (2nd ed.). Los Angeles: Sage.

Hiriyanna, M. (1975). *Outlines of Indian philosophy* (10th ed.). London: Lewis.

Johnson, R. B., & Onwuegbuzie, A. J. (2004). Mixed methods research: A research paradigm whose time has come. *Educational Researcher, 33*(7), 14–26.

Johnson, T. W., & Reed, R. F. (2012). *Philosophical documents in education* (4th ed.). Boston: Pearson.

Johnson, W. J. (2009). *Oxford dictionary of Hinduism*. New York: Oxford University Press.

Kaplan, A. (1977). *The pursuit of wisdom: The scope of philosophy*. Beverly Hills, CA: Glencoe.

Kenny, A. (Ed.). (1997). *The Oxford illustrated history of Western philosophy*. New York: Oxford University Press.

Kneller, G. F. (1984). *Movements of thought in modern education*. New York: Macmillan.

Knowles, E. (Ed.). (2001). *The Oxford dictionary of quotations* (5th ed.). New York: Oxford University Press.

Lemos, N. L. (2006). Value theory. In R. Audi (Ed.), *The Cambridge dictionary of philosophy* (2nd ed., pp. 949–950). New York: Cambridge University Press.

Low, D. (2000). *Merleau-Ponty's last vision: A proposal for the completion of "The visible and the invisible."* Evanston, IL: Northwestern University Press.

Lowe, E. J. (2002). *A survey of metaphysics*. New York: Oxford University Press.

McLaren, P., & Farahmandpur, R. (2005). *Teaching against global capitalism and the new imperialism: A critical pedagogy*. Lanham, MD: Rowman & Littlefield.

Moser, P. K. (2006). Epistemology. In R. Audi (Ed.), *The Cambridge dictionary of philosophy* (2nd ed., pp. 273–278). New York: Cambridge University Press.

Moser, P. K., Mulder, D. H., & Trout, J. D. (1998). *The theory of knowledge: A thematic introduction.* New York: Oxford University Press.

Moser, P. K., & Nat, A. V. (1995). *Human knowledge: Classical and contemporary approaches* (2nd ed.). New York: Oxford University Press.

Murti, T. R. V. (2010). *The central philosophy of Buddhism: A study of Madhyamika system.* New Delhi: Munshiram Manoharlal.

Nietzsche, F. (2000). The birth of tragedy and the genealogy of man. In S. Rosen (Ed.), *The philosopher's handbook: Essential readings from Plato to Kant* (pp. 243–266). New York: Random House.

Oliver, M. (1997). *History of philosophy.* New York: Metro.

Ozmon, H. A., & Craver, S. M. (2008). *Philosophical foundations of education* (8th ed.). Upper Saddle River, NJ: Merrill Prentice Hall.

Palmer, D. (2002). *Does the center hold? An introduction to Western philosophy* (3rd ed.). Boston: McGraw-Hill.

Peirce, C. S. (1966). *Selected writings (Values in a universe of chance).* New York: Dover.

Peirce, C. S. (1998). *The essential writings.* Amherst, NY: Prometheus.

Polkinghorne, D. E. (1983). *Methodology for the human sciences: Systems of inquiry.* Albany: State University of New York Press.

Popkin, R. H., & Stroll, A. (1993). *Philosophy made simple* (2nd ed.). New York: Broadway.

Prebish, C. S., & Keown, D. (2010). *Introducing Buddhism* (2nd ed.). New York: Routledge.

Robinson, D., & Groves, J. (2001). *Introducing philosophy.* Lanham, MD: Totem.

Rush, F. (2004). Conceptual foundations of early critical theory. In F. Rush (Ed.), *The Cambridge companion to critical theory* (pp. 6–39). New York: Cambridge University Press.

Runes, D. D. (Ed.). (1983). *Dictionary of philosophy.* Savage, MD: Littlefield, Adams.

Scruton, R. (1996). *Modern philosophy: An introduction and survey.* New York: Penguin.

Sellars, R. W. (2010). *The essentials of logic.* Boston: Houghton Mifflin.

Smart, N. (1999). *World philosophies.* New York: Routledge.

Trenchard, W. C. (1998). *Complete vocabulary guide to the Greek New Testament.* Grand Rapids, MI: Zondervan.

Van Voorst, R. E. (2011). *Anthology of world scriptures* (7th ed.). Boston: Wadsworth.

Wallace, D. B. (2000). *The basics of New Testament syntax: An intermediate Greek grammar.* Grand Rapids, MI: Zondervan.

Westphal, M. (2006). Hermeneutics as epistemology. In J. Greco & E. Sosa (Eds.), *The Blackwell guide to epistemology* (pp. 415–435). Malden, MA: Blackwell.

Wittgenstein, L. (1953/2009). *Philosophical investigations* (4th ed.). (G. E. M. Anscomber, P. M. S. Hacker, & J. Schulte, Trans.). Malden, MA: Blackwell.

Yu, C. H. (2006). *Philosophical foundations of quantitative research methodology.* Lanham, MD: University Press of America.

CHAPTER TWO

Epistemology and Philosophy of Science

Traditions, Perspectives, and Controversies

ANTONINA LUKENCHUK AND BAUDELAIRE K. ULYSSE

Epistemology and Philosophy of Science: Overview

Epistemological Legacies and Controversies

In chapter 1, we defined epistemology as a branch of philosophy whose primary objective lies in "the study of the nature of knowledge and justification [thereof]" (Moser, 2006, p. 273). Kenny (2010) suggests that the Greek word for the term *epistemology* has special significance: episteme "is often used to indicate a knowledge of a rather grand kind, so that one of its English equivalents is science" (p. 121). That is a valid point, considering the important role science has played explaining and justifying knowledge, hence epistemology has been conceptually defined as "the science of knowing" (Pojman, 1999, p. 1). Throughout chapter 1, we perused the philosophical concept of epistemology and showed how various schools of thought in the history of philosophy have captivated the human mind and have contributed to our understanding of knowledge and the pursuit thereof.

Here we purpose to focus primarily on knowledge—scientific knowledge of all sources. This primary focus will immediately thrust us into terrains that are already charted. This means that our intention is not to reinvent the wheel but to account for the spokes that hold the wheel together. In other words, we will attempt to identify, review, analyze, and synthesize various theories of knowledge while guiding the reader/researcher to the shore where he or she may coast, however comfortably or uncomfortably. We hope, however, that readers do not settle and feel comfortable and that they will continue to navigate critically the various currents ushered in their direction.

Moser, Mulder, and Trout (1998) suggest that a theory of knowledge should first and foremost differentiate between "genuine knowledge and merely apparent knowledge, between the real thing and likely counterfeits" (p. 23). This suggestion raises a fundamental question that is rather recurring. But is the supposed line between genuine knowledge and apparent knowledge real, or is it imaginary? Or, more important, could such supposed line represent an unnecessary dichotomy? Philosophers, both past and present, who spent countless hours investigating knowledge were indeed interested in distinguishing among various types or kinds of knowledge. In the process, they seem to have focused on the following questions, among others. How do we know what we know? What counts as knowledge? Whose knowledge is of most worth? What is the scope of knowledge? What are its limits?

Pojman (1999) highlights three different types of knowledge: *knowledge by acquaintance*, *competence knowledge*, and *propositional knowledge*. Pojman's types of knowledge are general categories that may be labeled differently in other literature, and we do not necessarily view them as exhaustive. However, Pojman makes a compelling point about the connection between epistemology and propositional knowledge:

> Person S knows that *p* (where *p* is some statement or proposition). Propositions have truth value; that is, they are true or false. They are the objects of propositional knowledge. When we claim to know that *p* is the case, we are claiming that *p* is true. Here are three examples of propositional knowledge: "I know that the sun will rise tomorrow," "I know that I have a mind," and "I know that Columbus discovered America in 1492." (p. 2)

All three examples of propositional statements provided above can be either verified or falsified. Logically, none of those statements can be both true and false simultaneously. Whereas one of such statements is false, then its opposite must be true; conversely, whereas one of such statements is true, then its opposite must be false. The verification process may use various methods that test both the true value of knowledge claim and the source of that knowledge.

It should be noted that philosophers' attempts to distinguish among various kinds of knowledge is not new. The Greek language, which has immensely informed philosophical discourses of knowledge, features various Greek equivalents for the verb "to know." In addition to *episteme*, *oida* is also a Greek word for "to know" and it is suggestive of experiential knowledge. *Ginosko* is another Greek equivalent for "to know." Perhaps more important than the Greek words affecting our understanding of knowledge are the notions of knowledge, which have been extensively and judiciously treated in the works of Greek thinkers. The list of Greek thinkers is without a doubt extremely long, featuring Protagoras, Pythagoras, Socrates, Plato, and Aristotle, along with other distinct groups of Greek thinkers such as the Sophists, the Epicureans, and the Stoics. All of the aforementioned thinkers have contributed to modern concepts of knowledge or to projects seeking to answer questions related to the sources, the essence, and the certainty of knowledge (Kenny, 2010).

The importance of Socrates, Plato, and Aristotle in understanding the concept of knowledge cannot be overstated. For instance, Plato's *Theaetetus* proposes knowledge be viewed as geometry, astronomy, shoemaking, and carpentry, and then goes on to propose that "to know something is to perceive it with the senses" (Kenny, 2010, p. 123). The notion of knowledge as perception was a position apparently held by Protagoras, and Plato set the stage for Socrates to take up that position in order to consider its soundness (Kenny). In his evaluation of perception as knowledge, Socrates readily granted that there are "ordinary cases" when this notion of knowledge as perception is not "erroneous," but he denied these might be cases of real knowledge:

> There are cases of perception without knowledge: we can hear a foreign language spoken, and yet do not the language (163b). There are cases of knowledge without perception: when we shut our eyes and recall something we have seen, we know what it looks like and yes are no longer seeing it (164a). But if knowing = perception, then both these must be cases of simultaneously knowing and not knowing, and surely that is an absurdity? (as cited in Kenny, 2010, p. 124)

Being determined to gain Socrates' assent on a definite understanding of knowledge, Theaetetus this time proposed that knowledge should be "thought (*doxa*), and thought is an activity of the soul by itself" (Kenny, p. 125). The assumption of this proposition is that when the mind thinks, it is engaging in an activity of questioning and answering on different topics while "forming opinions" in the process that are considered the equivalent of knowledge. Socrates rejected that proposition on the basis that "there are false thoughts" (Kenny, p. 125).

Expanding on the notion of knowledge as thought, Theaetetus then added *logos* as a buffer, claiming that knowledge is "true thought, plus *logos*" (Kenny, 2010, p. 125). Theaetetus hoped to further qualify true thought with logos. This seems an apparent effort to capitalize on Socrates' slight willingness to grant "knowledge as true thought." Hence, *logos* is expected to manifest in three different forms—expression, analysis, and description—which, in Socrates' assessment, turned out to be insufficient to support the proposition of knowledge as thought, plus logos (Kenny).

Like Socrates and Plato, Aristotle spent considerable energy unraveling questions pertinent to the sources and the essence as well as the validity of knowledge claims. Aristotle's elaboration on these questions takes place primarily in the *Nichomachean Ethics*. *Arete*, *techne*, *episteme*, *phronesis*, *ergon*, *poiesis*, and *praxis* are recurring terms in the *Nichomachean Ethics* (Kenny, 2010). The ultimate question for Aristotle is how these seemingly varying terms could work to produce knowledge:

> The nature of the *arete* of anything depends on its *ergon*, that is to say its job or characteristic output. The *ergon* of the mind and all its faculties is the production of true or false judgments (*NE* 6.2. 1139a29). That, at least is its *ergon* in the sense of its characteristic activity, its output whether it is working well or ill; its activity, when it is working well and doing its job, and therefore its *ergon* in the strict sense, is truth alone (2. 1139b12). The intellectual *aretai*, then, are excellences that make an intellectual part of the soul come out with truth. There are five states of the mind that have this effect—*techne*, *episteme*, *phronesis*, *sophia*, *nous*—which we may translate as skill, science, wisdom, understanding, and insight (3. 1139b16-17). (as cited in Kenny, 2010, p. 132)

For Aristotle, as far as knowledge pertaining to humans as subjects and the world (both material and immaterial) as the object of this knowledge, the human mind seems always at work. Hence, the human mind plays a central role in understanding as well as obtaining knowledge whose object is related to the material and the immaterial world.

Logocentric principle of knowledge in both Plato's and Aristotle's philosophies necessarily includes a value component. Both philosophers sought proper ways to apply reason for the ultimate benefit of a human being in order for him or her to live a fully satisfied life. Plato was convinced that his philosophy "could provide a science of the soul that would cure diseases of thought, judgment, and desire and deliver people from the sufferings of their ordinary lives" (Polkinghorne, 2004, p. 101). Conversely, Aristotle, although primarily agreeing with his mentor on the centrality of the reason-*logos* principle to make good judgments, claimed that living a fulfilling, happy and, therefore, a good life cannot be reduced to the skills of science-*techne* coupled with an ultimate (true) knowledge-*episteme*. Aristotle believed that people know from experience what happiness and fulfillment are about and he conceived of a human being as a "fully embodied entity" with both reason and emotions involved in "decisions about how to live the good life" (Polkinghorne, 2004, p. 109). Therefore, Aristotle's treatment of *phronesis* as "practical wisdom" acquires a more interesting and complex rendition than it does in Plato's philosophy.

Aristotle distinguished between the three major tasks in human life and their corresponding activities. First, we need to develop a theory (*theoria*), which requires an application of mathematical and logical reasoning (*episteme*); then follows the task of *techne*, or the scientific skills of making artifacts, which requires *poiesis*—the knowledge to produce objects; and finally, there is a need for *praxis*, or "acting for the good life of the other or the state," which requires the use of *phronesis* or practical reasoning (Polkinghorne, 2004, p. 112). *Praxis* acquires an important place in Aristotle's philosophy that intentionally connects the benefits we can reap from proper application of reason to make good decisions that consequently lead to a fulfilled and happy life. Aristotle's principles of *phronesis* and *praxis* influenced the works of such twentieth-century thinkers as Arendt, Collingwood, Habermas, Heidegger, and Lyotard.

In *The Human Condition* (1998), Arendt expresses deep concerns about the decline of genuine political life in contemporary Western democracies and urges us "to think what we are doing," to invigorate a sense of the good and purposeful life through the synergy of *vita activa* (active life) and *vita contemplativa* (contemplative life). Arendt revitalizes the Aristotelian notion of *bios politikos*—the life "devoted to the matters of the *polis*," the "realm of human affairs," stressing action, or *praxis*, as the activity that will "establish and sustain it" (p. 7). Through acting and speaking, or "good deeds" and "good words," which Arendt associates with full engagement in social and political life, we can reclaim the lost meaning of *bios politikos* and can thus restore the notion of the good life. In the evolutionary process of reawakening *bios politicos*, Arendt distinguishes between several fundamental human activities—labor, work, and action, of which only action epitomizes genuine *praxis* and a fulfilled life. Although labor and work are worthwhile practices, they cannot satisfy our political aspirations, for it is only action due to its condition of plurality that is "specifically *the* condition of all political life" (Arendt, p. 7).

The caveat of a logocentric principle in Western philosophy is that the mind must do its work well in order to arrive at any of the objectives such as skill, science, wisdom, understanding, and insight. Fast-forwarding to the eighteenth century, these terms—skill, science, wisdom, understanding, and insight—which were wrought on the history of ideas by Greek philosophers, had continued to dominate the discourse on knowledge. Medieval philosophy is similarly important, but we consider it beyond the scope and objectives of this project; hence we have advanced to the eighteenth-century era, which might arguably be the stepping-stone or precursor to contemporary philosophy.

As stated earlier, Greek philosophical ideas, as enshrined particularly in the works of Socrates, Plato, and Aristotle, have had an immense influence on modern and contemporary Western ideas; however, the relationship between Greek philosophers and European philosophers during the eighteenth century is seldom consonant. Kenny (2010) illustrates this with his observation on the anticlimactic end of the discourses between Theaetetus and Socrates:

> Perhaps Theaetetus gave up too soon. If he had offered a fourth account [the three accounts he gave were words of expression, analysis, and description] of *logos* as meaning something like "justification," "reason," or "evidence," then his definition of knowledge as true belief plus logos would have been found satisfactory by many a philosopher during the subsequent millennia of philosophy. (p. 126)

Indeed, Theaetetus would have found an eager audience among philosophers in the eighteenth century and today, not simply because logos is widely viewed as rational method to justify belief or ideas, but also because perception, which was rejected by Socrates, is widely accepted as a source of knowledge by contemporary philosophers. In this regard, Winkler (2006) wrote:

> For the most part, eighteenth century philosophers viewed the understanding as one of several "faculties" or powers of the human mind; perception (or one of its cognates) was their preferred label for its characteristic or most basic act or operation. In this they followed the example set by Descartes, Malebranche, and Locke. The word perception was also used, however, as a synonym for idea—that is, as a label for the object of an act of understanding. (p. 236)

If Winkler is right about how eighteenth-century philosophers viewed perception, which he is, then the result of whatsoever the human mind attempted to understand would be understood. According to those philosophers, the mind would yield an epistemological product, which would have been labeled perception. This is not the only instance where modern or contemporary philosophers have departed from their Greek patriarchal philosophers, Socrates, Plato, and Aristotle. The Sophists espoused a view of knowledge that Socrates and Plato loathed. Sophists shared a deep skepticism about absolute knowledge and truth. Essentially, they rejected the existence of absolute knowledge and truth that they rendered relative (cognitive relativism). Sophists embraced and taught rhetoric as a special skill, and they emphasized "process, skill, and technique" (Johnson, 1998, p. 202). Sophists believed that special skill, rhetoric, could be applied to personal and social matters. Hence, rhetoric, for sophists, was the only skill that mattered and was worth teaching.

The philosophical commitment of the Sophists was devoid of absolute truths and ethical standards, which undermined what Socrates, Plato, and Aristotle taught and propagated. Socrates in particular contended that having expert knowledge is important and is in fact requisite for anyone to be able to genuinely teach (Johnson, 1998, p. 208). Various modern and contemporary philosophers who have also raised reasonable doubt regarding the nature of knowledge have espoused this philosophical commitment of the Sophists.

In addition to reason and perception, many philosophers have proposed memory as a source of knowledge as well. For instance, Audi (2003) claims: "Our beliefs are countless and varied. A vast proportion of them are stored in memory, though beliefs do not originate there" (p. 330). The caveat with memory is that it supposedly preserves beliefs but does not produce them:

> Perception looks outward, and through it we see the physical world. Memory looks backward, and through it we see the past, or at least some of the past. Introspection looks inward, and through it we see the stream of our own consciousness. Reason looks beyond experience of the world of space and time, and through it we see concepts and their relations. Testimony, our chief social source of knowledge, looks to others and thereby draws on all of these individual sources in those who convey their knowledge to us. (Audi, p. 332)

For many philosophers, knowledge is belief justified by reason or other evidence. For instance, Lehrer and Paxson (1999) advance the thesis of knowledge as belief in asserting that undefeated justified true belief represents something someone believes to be true and that has been justified by something or someone other than that thing believed to be true or justified by someone other than the claimer. The importance of justifying claims of knowledge and the persistence of the view of knowledge as belief have conceived two different philosophical frameworks—foundationalism and non-foundationalism—within which issues of subjectivity, relativeness, objectivity, validity, and truthfulness of knowledge are raised.

Kuehn (2006) claims the seventeenth-century philosophical issues related to knowledge and the certainty thereof are antecedents of the philosophical concerns of the eighteenth century. Indeed, the mid-seventeenth century in Europe was marked by major paradigm shifts in the developments of philosophical ideas. Descartes and Locke indubitably represent two foremost and perhaps most influential thinkers of that era, and their ideas have laid the foundation for epistemological foundationalism. Conceptually, foundationalism embodies

> the view that knowledge and epistemic (knowledge-relevant) justification have a two-tier structure: some instances of knowledge and justification are non-inferential, or foundational; and all other instances thereof are inferential, or non-foundational, in that they derive ultimately from foundational knowledge or justification. (Moser, 2006, p. 321)

Thus, foundationalism represents a larger philosophical framework, which is underpinned by the presupposition that human beings can be certain of knowledge and that their knowledge claims can be objective. Both Descartes and Locke embraced scientific knowledge, but they disagreed sharply on the process to obtain such knowledge (method). For Descartes, "knowledge was essentially independent of sense perception" (Kuehn, 2006, p. 391). The process leading to the grasp as well as the certainty of knowledge involves belief and subjectivity but does not end at either one (Kuehn). However, Locke's view of knowledge was grounded in an unwavering commitment to sense perception, which one could say is empiricism at its purest. Essentially, Locke posited that the mind was an empty slate (tabula rasa) that has knowledge of its own, but has to rely on the experiences wrought on it by sensuous experiences.

While Descartes and Locke obviously disagreed on the process and method to obtain knowledge, they shared the belief that human beings are able to acquire knowledge and be certain of that knowledge once acquired. For Descartes, the certainty of cognitive objectivity can be acquired by deduction (mathematical), and for Locke such certainty can be reached through sense perception. The legacies of Descartes and Locke, particularly related to the justification of knowledge, are lived on the philosophy of science as well.

Philosophy of Science: Science Challenged and Redefined

Philosophy of science deals with the application of epistemological concerns to a variety of areas of study and with proposing the methods that can lead those areas of study to satisfactory results. Due to major scientific and technological advancements in nuclear physics, mathematics, neuroscience, chemistry, and biology, twentieth-century philosophy had to engage more vigorously with a scientific world in order to rethink its dominant role in liberal arts and sciences. Until about the seventeenth century, in the West philosophy's domain included both physical and metaphysical concerns and its reign as *philosophia vero omnium mater* (from Latin, "the mother of all arts and sciences") was unquestionable. This started to change rapidly from the industrial revolution onward, and by the end of the twentieth century, philosophy lost its ultimate authority in providing an all-encompassing picture of the world. This task was left to individual disciplines, whereas philosophy acquired a more supportive role in examining language statements and their meaning within these disciplines. Philosophers of science became preoccupied with the methods (and their critique) used by natural sciences and the analysis of a variety of concepts pertaining to scientific theories. It became apparent that a critical reexamination of scientific method was overdue. The very question of what counts as knowledge was subject to an unprecedented scrutiny by the twentieth-century advancements in theoretical physics.

Two sets of concerns dominate the current philosophy of science, creating "two broad areas" (Papineau, 1996, p. 290). The first broad area investigates the question "whether science ever uncovers permanent truths, whether objective decisions between competing theories are possible and whether the results of experiment are clouded by prior theoretical expectations" (p. 290). The last broad category, according to Papineau, focuses on the metaphysics of science, examining scientific claims about the natural and related phenomena.

Contemporary philosophy of science features various philosophers, but we want to highlight the contributions of Gaston Bachelard (1884–1962) and Thomas Kuhn (1922–1996). Because of the fact that the translations of the works of Continental philosophers from a variety of their respective languages into English can be a matter of time, many of their works often become available to English-speaking audiences later than their original publications. This was the case with French philosopher Gaston Bachelard who in the 1930s developed a theory of epistemological breaks, which was further elaborated in Thomas Kuhn's theory of paradigm shifts.

The corpus of Gaston Bachelard features work encompassing science, poetry, epistemology, and imagination. To Bachelard, imagination, more than reason, is a unifying force in the human soul. Bachelard's poetics is linked essentially to his epistemology and more general views on the history of arts and sciences. His widely acclaimed notion of *epistemological obstacle* (also known as *epistemological break* or, interchangeably, *epistemological rupture*) provides, on the one hand, a sharp criticism of positivism, and on the other, a solid justification for an integrated approach to knowledge and intuition, rational and irrational, and scientific and poetic. Yet, another fascinating feature of Bachelard's work is the integration epistemology and psychoanalysis. This integration of epistemology and psychoanalysis ends up functioning as a sort of therapeutic effect on objective knowledge, whereby utilitarian and mundane irrationalities that impede the progress of objective knowledge are removed. In addition, psychoanalysis helped him understand how blockages are formed in some people that prevent them from the formation of the scientific mind. He called these blockages epistemological obstacles. Even a healthy mind, he thought, still has some "dark areas, traces of the old in our new ways of thinking" (2002, p. 20). Eventually, his study of pre-scientific texts led him to conclude that the age of reason was also marked by unreason as he determined how even some among the so-called educated people of his era displayed disturbed minds about some scientific discoveries, such as electricity.

Bachelard posited that the formation of the scientific mind requires three stages of development: the concrete, the concrete-abstract, and the abstract. Having examined the epistemological obstacles to objective thought (2002), he changed his position on the primacy of the scientific mind. The impetus that caused the change in his position is that he came to understand that imagination is not an obstacle but an essential element of psychic dynamism. Epistemology thus represents two dialectical activities, intellectual and imaginative, which should form the rhythm of life (Bachelard, 2000). Hence, Bachelard (2004) claims, "Without the help of poets, what can a philosopher, weighted down with years, do if he persists talking about imagination? He has no one to test. He would immediately get lost in the labyrinth of tests and counter-tests" (p. 25).

Inspired by Bachelard's ideas, Kuhn developed a theory of paradigm shifts that shed additional light on a new conception of science and scientific knowledge. Kuhn spent about 15 years studying the history of science that resulted in his famous *The Structure of Scientific Revolutions* (1962). He came to the conclusion that the development of science is not a linear and cumulative process. Some theories can be contradictory. His central concept is that of a paradigm whose definition entered most etymological and philosophical dictionaries as a "constellation of beliefs, values, and techniques shared by the members of a given scientific community" (Runes, 1983, p. 240). In *The Structure of Scientific Revolutions*, Kuhn maintains that some paradigms are general and encompassing, while others guide scientific thinking within specific areas of study. A paradigm is essential in the process of observation and experiment:

> Paradigms provide scientists not only with a map but also with some of the directions essential for map-making. In learning a paradigm the scientist acquires theory, methods, and standards together, usually in an inextricable mixture. Therefore, when paradigms change, there are usually significant shifts in the criteria determining the legitimacy both of problems and of proposed solutions. (Kuhn, 2000, p. 519)

A scientist cannot avoid bringing a definite belief system into the area of study. Kuhn observed that early stages of most sciences went through pre-paradigm periods characterized by conceptual chaos and competing views of nature. Paradigm debates always involve the question: "Which problems is it more significant to have solved? Like the issue of competing standards, that question of values can be answered only in terms of criteria that lie outside of normal science altogether, and it is that recourse to external criteria that most obviously makes paradigm debates revolutionary" (Kuhn, p. 519). When the majority of the scientific community accepts a paradigm, this newly accepted paradigm becomes a warrant—a mandatory way of approaching problems (normal science). A new and radical theory is not an addition to the existing knowledge but its interruption.

Kuhn's theory of paradigm shifts reinforces the general assumptions held by twentieth-century philosophers of science—that our knowledge of the world is essentially fallible and, if acquired, it can only represent the best explanation available.

Any new discovery can potentially lead to a dramatic shift in our view of the world's picture. This new understanding of science proposes an expanded notion of reason supported by a hermeneutic and a pragmatic logic. Charles S. Peirce (see chapter 1), for instance, regarded the knowledge of science not as the Truth but only as its approximation. Truth thus represents the effectiveness of our knowledge as demonstrated by the effectiveness of our action. Peirce also believed that knowledge was a communal achievement and that the community (scientific community, as he would have it) had to make a decision to accept or reject a given paradigm of knowledge.

Considering the multifaceted constellation of existing beliefs, epistemological pluralism is the position from which one ought to approach the question of methods in both natural and human sciences. Contemporary inquiry often represents *syncretic* research that "proposes something more than the use of multiple systems of inquiry: it proposes the additional step of syncretizing the results of the multiple inquiries into a unified and integral result" (Polkinghorne, 1983, p. 254). For instance, German philosopher Otto Apel (b. 1922) proposed syncretic research in psychoanalysis in a form of "tacking," or "zigzagging," whereby the researcher "first is engaged in the research process, then distances himself from it, analyzes and reevaluates his position, and then returns to be a participant of the research again" (Polkinghorne, 1983, p. 255). Jürgen Habermas (b. 1929) developed the project that syncretized hermeneutic and empirical sciences to create guidelines for the logic of a critical science, and this will be the focus of our further discussion.

The Fallen Skies of Epistemological Certainty
"Positive" Knowledge Dethroned

The foundationalist assumptions of scientific knowledge, as enshrined in the philosophical works of Descartes and Locke, dominated epistemological discourses in the West for a long time. These assumptions have culminated in the positivist conception of science that held that only those things of which we are absolutely certain can be counted as knowledge. However, at the turn of the twentieth century, the fallen angels of logical positivism were overpowered by the new forces coming from several movements in the philosophy of science (see chapter 1). Logical positivism was dethroned as supposedly the only valid scientific paradigm by the new developments in nuclear physics and microbiology. The nature of science and its scope have changed dramatically through the expansion of the boundaries of scientific inquiry that shifted radically from positivistic and reductionist models to post-positivist. The pioneering philosophers of science who championed the cause of questioning the absolute certainty of positivistic science were Bachelard, Kuhn,

Frank, Popper, and Feyerabend, among a few others. Karl Popper (1902–1994) was one of the first to contest the claims of positivistic science by raising questions of scientific method that posit observation as its stepping-stone leading to theoretical formulations.

Paul Feyerabend (1924–1994) provided radical criticism of positivistic scientific methodology in his seminal work, *Against Method: Outline of an Anarchistic Theory* (1978). *Against Method* begins with Feyerabend's celebrated quote: "Science is an essentially anarchic enterprise: theoretical anarchism is more humanitarian and more likely to encourage progress than its law-and-order alternatives" (Feyerabend, 2000, p. 493). Feyerabend insists on the fact that science is not and cannot be governed by a system of firm, unchanging, and absolute principles and that all methodologies have their limits. The history of science "does not just consist of facts and conclusions drawn from facts. It also contains ideas, interpretations of facts, problems created by conflicting interpretations, mistakes, and so on" (p. 495). To put it differently, there is no single theory that agrees with all the facts in its domain. In agreement with Bachelard and Kuhn, Feyerabend asserts that history clearly shows us that epistemological breaks have been necessary to propel scientific progress. Accordingly, pluralistic methodology becomes a necessity when comparing rival theories and ideas. Feyerabend's principle of methodological anarchism finds its utmost expression in the following statement: "The idea of a fixed method, or of a fixed theory of rationality, rests on too naïve a view of man and his social surroundings. [It is clear that] the only one principle that can be defended under *all* circumstances and in all stages of human development is the principle: *anything goes*" (p. 502).

"Anything goes" is the principle that can be leveraged against the backdrop of the debate formulated by the skeptics who believed that there could be only two propositions of knowledge—apodictic and problematic (see the discussion above). It follows then that a proposition can be either "infallible and beyond doubt or dubious and, therefore, not *episteme*" (Polkinghorne, 1983, p. 12). However, and as Feyerabend claims, there can be indeed "assertoric" propositions that stand between apodictic (infallible) and problematic (dubious). Assertoric propositions "remain open to future confirmation and correction as more experience is gained" (Polkinghorne, 1983, p. 12). Hence, between the extremes of absolute certainly and absolute uncertainty, "statements of knowledge can be judged against each other, and some of them can be accepted and used as the base for action while others can be rejected" (Polkinghorne, 1983, p. 13). The acceptance of assertoric knowledge as a legitimate goal of science "has reopened a possibility for alternative epistemological frameworks" (Polkinghorne, 1983, p. 12).

The contributions of Hermeneutics to the development of alternative epistemologies and subsequently to the anti-positivist movement were discussed in chapter 1. Hermeneutics challenged the notion of knowledge as restricted only to *episteme* and instead proposed Understanding (*verstehen* in German) as a legitimate type of knowledge. The upper-case letter *U* underscores the importance of the notion. Without a capital letter *U*, understanding refers to any kind of comprehension. Yet when capitalized, it denotes a "specific type of understanding, the comprehension of meaning" (Polkinghorne, 1983, p. 217). *Understanding* thus becomes a way of knowing and a method whereby researchers apprehend the meaning and translate it into a variety of forms of data to serve the purposes of their research.

Hermeneutics emphasizes the "embededness of knowledge in historically particular and contingent vocabularies" (Westphal, 2006, p. 416). Philosophical hermeneutics of Heidegger and Gadamer represents, by far, one of the most influential anti-positivist responses. Heidegger, for instance, repudiates foundationalism in his account of the hermeneutic circle. He draws distinctions between linguistic and prelinguistic interpretation of the text. To him, interpretation is always *seeing-as*. There is, in other words, an a priori understanding before we enter the circle, and it is, in fact, our understanding of ourselves. Every act of interpretation thus presupposes our understanding of ourselves as a thrown projection in our dealings with things. Heidegger admits that knowledge does have foundations, but at "the basis of the linguistic expressions that are the bearers of truth or falsity are not those representations that are epistemically privileged, [but rather] practices that are not truth bearing" (Westphal, p. 424). Heidegger makes practice foundational to his epistemology and looks for a more primordial conception of truth that he often labels as unconcealment (along with some other terms).

Jürgen Habermas extended the hermeneutic tradition to the study of social theory, thus providing a sharp criticism of positivistic science. Habermas's ideas, along with those of other twentieth-century critical and postmodern philosophers, represent a concerted effort to deconstruct the very notion of episteme as a hegemonic construct advanced by Western philosophers.

Episteme Deconstructed

Critical hermeneutics positions Habermas within the milieu of the Continental postmodern/poststructuralist contemporary thinkers such as Jean-François Lyotard (1924–1998), Gilles Deleuze (1925–1995), Michel Foucault (1926–1984), Jean Baudrillard (1929–2007), Jacques Derrida (1930–2004), and Julia Kristeva (b. 1941), among a few others, who have been performing deconstructive works and situated themselves within the postmodern outlook, which views itself as essentially different from modernism. Loytard's description of postmodernism as "incredulity toward metanarratives" (as cited in Rose, 1991, p. 55) puts deconstruction in perspective. Hence, the project of deconstruction has been primarily about deconstructing metanarratives of any sort, including epistemological frameworks. Particularly, deconstructive works focus on delineating the political, social, and economic influences on what knowledge is accepted as valid and objective.

The history of postmodern outlook can be traced to the nineteenth-century British artists. In the beginning of the twentieth century, the label of postmodernism was attached to a broad movement in art also known as post-impressionist or post-industrial. Nietzsche is considered by many a presage of postmodern thought, which he expressed as the crisis of modernity [of his time] and the advent of a new age of *Übermensch* (see chapter 1). The modern era is typically associated with the rise of natural sciences and the decline of the centralized power of Christendom (predominantly Catholicism). Secular movements within the Age of Enlightenment are also referred to as the modern era. A modernist was regarded as a person committed to the modern age who believed that "traditions must be overthrown or redefined in order to do justice to the new forms of experience" (Scruton, 1996, p. 2). English-speaking philosophy is "modern, but not modernist. French philosophy … (e.g., Derrida, Foucualt) is modernist, without being particularly modern, i.e., without basing itself in the assessment of arguments, or in the desire to build on established truths" (Scruton, p. 2). At the turn of the twentieth century, the label postmodern was adopted by several French thinkers who had been sparking the debates of the "arching questions of the human spirit" (Scruton, p. 3).

The concern with these debates was unavoidable for Jürgen Habermas. In his opus magnum *Knowledge and Human Interests* (1972), Habermas brings forth the following three major theses: that (1) *"achievements of the transcendental subject have their basis in the natural history of the human species"*; (2) that *"knowledge equally serves as an instrument and transcends mere self-preservations"*; and (3) that *"knowledge-constitutive interests take form in the medium of work, language, and power"* (pp. 312–13). Especially important for educational inquiry, Habermas provides distinctions regarding the three different modes of research associated with human interests. First, in the empirical-analytic sciences, "knowledge is … predictive knowledge. However, the *meaning* of such predictions, that is their technical exploitability, is established only by the rules according to which we apply theories to reality" (Habermas, p. 308). Further, the historical-hermeneutic sciences

> gain knowledge in a different methodological framework. Here the meaning of the validity of propositions is not constituted in the frame of reference of technical control …. Theories are not constructed deductively and experience is not organized with regard to the success of operations. Access to the facts is provided by the understanding of meaning, not observation. (Habermas, p. 309)

And finally, the "systematic *sciences of social action*, that is economics, sociology, and political science, have the goal…of producing nomological knowledge" (Habermas, p. 310) [Nomological refers to rule-abiding knowledge]. Habermas vehemently emphasizes that a critical social science will never be satisfied with such an outcome. It should be "concerned with going beyond this goal to determine when theoretical statements grasp invariant regularities of social action as such and when they express ideologically frozen relations of dependence that can in principle be transformed" (Habermas, p. 310). The methodological framework that Habermas proposes for determining the meaning of the validity of critical propositions of this type of inquiry is established by self-reflection (reflexivity). Self-reflection designates an emancipatory cognitive interest.

Habermas' emancipatory and self-reflective practices incite social imaginations of postmodern and poststructuralist thinkers. Foucault (1967), for instance, proposes a metaphor of *heterotopia*, denoting a concept of human geography (place, space, dwelling, etc.). Heterotopia represents a *real* space (as opposed to utopia) that allows for generating non-hegemonic conditions of otherness. Foucault maintains that there are real places in every culture and in every civilization that are formed in the very founding of society, which are "something like counter-sites, a kind of effectively enacted utopia in which the real sites, all the other real sites that can be found within the culture, are simultaneously represented, contested, and inverted" (p. 3). Foucault's concern is with the spirit of individual and social imagination that should spur the societal and political change in an oppressive society.

Jacques Derrida, another prominent figure in postmodern and poststructuralist movement, is known for his radical hermeneutics. Derrida's main thesis is "nothing is outside the text." This means, epistemologically, that "being must always already be conceptualized," and, ontologically, that "the thing itself is a sign" (Westphal, 2006, p. 430). In maintaining that there will always be at least two interpretations of interpretation [of the text], Derrida not just overcomes metaphysics, he essentially abolishes it. The critique of logocentric principle in the history of Western philosophy finds its ultimate expression in the philosophy of Derrida that can be briefly captured in the notions of identity and difference, or in other words, of continuity and being *deferred*. Derrida coins the word *différance* to convey both the difference and deferral. There is no knowledge as such, concludes Derrida, and its use-value becomes a mere production for sale.

Jean Baudrillard's (1929–2007) postmodern critique of social realities in advanced Western powers is expressed through his extravagant images of simulacra and hyperreality. Assuming that we are the inhabitants of a postmodern world where the demarcation lines between what is real and what is not are simply impossible to draw, then, as Baudrillard suggests, most of us are confined to a hyperreality of Disneyland, a 'perfect model of all the entangled orders of simulation':

This imaginary world is supposed to be what makes the operation success-ful. But, what draws the crowds is undoubtedly much more the social mi-crocosm, the miniaturized and *religious* reveling in real America, in its delights and drawbacks. The objective profile of the United States…may be traced throughout Disneyland. All its values are exalted here, in miniature and comic-strip form. Embalmed and pacified. Whence the possibility of an ideological analysis of Disneyland…digest of the contradictory reality. But this conceals something else, and that "ideological" blanket exactly serves to cover a *third-order simulation*: Disneyland is there to conceal the fact that it is the "real" country, all of "real" America, which *is* Disneyland. (1999, p. 485)

Baudrillard urges individuals to reawaken their self-consciousness and break away from illusions, deceptions, and oppressive influences of omnipotent and transcen-dent powers of politics, ideology, religion, and consumerism.

The domino effect of critical poststructuralist Continental philosophers produced a vibrant constellation of Anglo-American thinkers. Critical feminists who followed in the footsteps of their foremothers such as Simone de Beauvoir (1908–1986) ush-ered in several movements critical to the development of gender and identity issues in contemporary educational inquiry. Sociologist Dorothy Smith (b. 1926), for in-stance, argued that women experience the world differently from men, since men encounter the world already processed (e.g., meals prepared, laundry done), while the work of women is the processing of the raw material into a form suitable for consumption (Longino, 2006). Psychologist Carol Gilligan "criticized her colleague Lawrence Kohlberg's account of moral development as resting too much on a pat-tern ascertained from male samples" (Longino, p. 330). Educational psychologist Mary Belenky and her colleagues suggest that "women learn through connection rather than separation"; and they claim this as a "way of knowing" (Longino, p. 330). One of the consistent themes running through the feminist rethinking of the sub-ject of knowledge is the "insistence on its embodiment" (Longino, p. 331), which concerns the mind-body problem in Western philosophy. The disembodied self is a Cartesian masculine subject. It is in fact displaced onto the bodies of "feminized and primitivized Others—European women and nonwhite women and men—who are thereby epistemologically disfranchised" (Longino, p. 332).

Haraway (1999) contributed to the feminist and postmodern critique of the phi-losophy of science as an essentially masculine project. Along with this critique, Haraway deconstructs the mythology of a unified women's movement on the basis of her argument of our fractured identities:

There is nothing about being "female" that naturally binds women. There is not even such a state as "being" female, itself a highly complex category constructed in contested sexual scientific discourses and other social practices. Gender, race, or class consciousness is an achievement forced on us by the terrible historical experience of the contradictory social realities of patriarchy, colonialism, and capitalism. (p. 540)

Haraway's concern is with feminists' "lapsing into boundless difference" and "giving up on the confusing task of making partial, real connections"; some differences are "playful; some are poles of world historical systems of domination. 'Epistemology' is about knowing the difference" (p. 543).

Embodiment is an important construct to delineate standpoint epistemologies championed by Donna Haraway in her essay, *Situated Knowledges* (1988). Standpoint epistemology represents an analysis of some Marxist ideas regarding the position of workers as opposed to capitalists. Workers' understanding of their condition gave them privilege over capitalists, and this superiority could be regarded as both epistemological and political. Additionally, sexual division of labor in childbearing provided the basis for the opposed structuring of material life of women and men. Although the standpoint epistemological assumptions shared the above Marxist-based ideology, they failed to account for women's diversity and particular locations of female oppression (Longino, 2006).

Another dimension of the embodiment of the knower is the denial of any essential difference between subjects and objects of knowledge. With this regard, reflexivity takes on an especially important dimension, that is, "the knower's awareness of her assumptions and values and of the ways in which these affect her beliefs and theorizing" (Longino, 2006, p. 334). Feminist epistemologists are convinced that current social arrangements "assign epistemic privilege to occupants of one social position," and that feminist standpoint theory "seeks to reverse the assignment and grants epistemic privilege to those in subordinated, socially unprivileged positions" (Longino, p. 338). Whichever the case, the poststructuralist feminists are working vehemently toward to the demise of the positivistic rhetoric of science (Lather, 2004).

Worth noting is the fact that poststructuralist position steers away from feminism's tendency to make generalizations based on the experiences and accounts of Western, white, middle-class women. Instead, it looks at "the intersection of the identity categories: race, class, gender, sexual orientation, ethnicity, nationality, age, wellness, etc" (St. Pierre & Pillow, 2000, p. 7). The issue of woman's subjectivity continues to be challenged by poststructuralist feminists who place a greater emphasis on language and discourse that shape the ways women experience oppression (St. Pierre & Willow). Poststructuralist feminists question the very possibility of finite definitions:

If "woman" is defined once and for all, then there is no hope of a reconfiguration that might offer different, strategic possibilities for ethical, political, and relational work. What kind of women and what kinds of feminism might we fail to produce if we define "woman" and "feminism" once and for all? (St. Pierre & Pillow, p. 8)

One of the strengths of poststructuralism lies in its ability to continue to "reinvent itself strategically, shifting and mutating given existing political agendas, power relations, and identity strategies" (St. Pierre & Willow, p. 8).

The issues of epistemic privileges and deconstructive practices are central to the critical race theory (CRT) framework. Critical race theories emerged in the 1980s as a reaction to critical legal studies and launched a critical examination of American society and culture in the intersections of race, law, and power. Later these theories included in the context of their investigations the constructs of gender, ethnicity, national identity, and sexual orientation CRT studies, which grounded themselves in the human and civil rights struggles for justice and equal opportunity for historically oppressed and disadvantaged groups in the United States (Ballard & Cintron, 2010; Bell, 2008; Delgado & Stefanic, 2001; Essed & Goldberg, 2001). Ballard and Cintron identify three elements of critical race theory: microaggressions, creation of counter-stories, and development of counter-spaces. *Microaggressions* is defined as "a type of subtle abuse aimed at minorities that can be visual, verbal, nonverbal, conscious, or unconscious" (p. 15). The creation of counter-stories is presented as "archives, testimonies, or discussions that marginalized groups use to respond to stories previously espoused by the dominant group" (p. 16). Finally, the development of counter-spaces is seen as a "means of conveying stories of experiences that have not been told, as well as a way to assess and counter dominant stories" (p. 16).

Critical race theory's concern is centered on W. E. B. Du Bois' (1868–1963) account of "double consciousness" as a "complex and constant play between the exclusionary conditions of social structure marked by race and the psychological and cultural strategies employed by the racially excluded and marginalized to accommodate themselves to everyday indignities as well as to resist them" (Essed & Goldberg, 2001, p. 5). Critical racial theories exert a significant influence on humanities and social science scholarship, especially critical ethnicity studies (Gaspar de Alba, 2003; Noriega, 2000; Saldívar, 1990).

Wedded to the cause of critical theories are the issues of queer studies whose task is to challenge "those U.S. legal and social structures that privilege heterosexuality, patriarchy, white supremacy, and class advantage, with the legal and social liberation of sexual minorities—queers—as its principal focus" (Lugg, 2006, p. 178). The queer legal theory (QLT) emerged in the 1990s in response to some political and legal events, and it "does not expect the researcher to remain 'neutral' on issues of social justice and queer Americans" (Lugg, p. 177).

Disability studies provide a sharp critique of the social model of disability (Gabel & Peters, 2004). Recent developments in disability studies moved away from the objective-subjective dichotomy while adopting a postmodern position that provides new space to deconstruct the notion of disability itself. Particularly, Gabel and Peters employ the postmodern perspective to critique medical and functionalist models of disability that marginalize and pathologize disability. Resistance theory is yet another powerful tool that adds to the deconstructive theory and practice of disability studies "to transgress, disrupt, and confront while also constructing a disability-centered notion of beauty and desire" (Gabel & Peters, p. 593). Resistance is inherently political, and the above discussion on its theorizing and practical application provides an indispensable forum for educators to consider their inquiry along the lines of critical theories intersecting socioeconomic class, race, ethnicity, gender, ability, or lifestyle issues pertaining to social justice.

Epistemological Pluralism on Equal Footing: Non-Western Ways of Knowing

Our quest to know often leads us to explore uncharted territories populated with different inhabitants having multitudes of different beliefs. These beliefs form a "structure of great complexity, with innumerable changing elements that reflect our continuing experience and thought, our actions and emotions, our learning and forgetting, our inferring and accepting, our revising and rejecting, our speaking and listening" (Audi, 2003, p. 336). An apparent diversity of worldviews is indicative of the fact that we live in the world of "pluralistic epistemologies" (Polkinghorne, 1983). According to Ogilvy (1977), there is "not *one truth* which corresponds to *reality*. Instead, there are *some truths* which hold within communities" (as cited in Polkinghorne, 1983, p. 250). Epistemological pluralism hinges on the notion of context—or community—that allows for an "understanding that is greater than the understanding of any one point of view" (Polkinghorne, 1983, p. 251). Epistemological pluralism incites the inquiry that can "reap significant methodological benefits from using multiple procedures for its research designs" (p. 252).

Whereas (for the most part) several preceding centuries were marked by the dominance of some epistemologies and the silencing—if not subjugation and ridicule—of others, this century (let us hope for the most part) brings to the forefront the power of knowledge unleashed from all four corners of the world on equal footing. The history of an epistemological journey of what can be labeled as non-Western traditions carries a record of extraordinary achievements and glory on the one hand, and colonialism and suppression on the other.

It should be noted that the terms *non-Western* and *Western* denote a great deal of ambiguity and confusion. If considered geographically, non-Western (as opposed to Western or Western European) applies to most of the world's locales and their inhabitants. It is estimated, for instance, that there are 196 countries in today's world (Glennon, 1995) (the number varies between 193 and 195 in other sources), out of which only 44 are officially recognized as Western European. If taken in political and economic terms, both Western and non-Western elicit the same amount of ambiguity. Western often refers to either Western European, or North American *and* Western European, or to both, designating several countries in Europe and North America with advanced economic and technological powers ascribed as dominant (until very recently) within the scope of global economy. The same countries are often regarded in opposition to non-Western because of the history of colonialism. However, the term *Western European* is especially ambiguous due to the history of its emergence after WWII, during the Cold War era launched by the United States and its allies against the former Soviet-bloc European countries. With the dissolution of the USSR, the political implication of the term lost its meaning, yet it still remains in popular use.

Today's Europe is essentially different from what it was even some 50 or 60 years ago. There are 44 northern, southern, western, and eastern European countries on the world map; out of these 44, only 9 are recognized by the UN as Western. The history of many Western European countries is one of foreign invasion, slavery, and colonialism. Many European countries, on the other hand, in their remote and recent historical past, have been fighting for liberty and independence from their next-door neighbors. The history of European revolutionary ideas and events continues to inspire social and political activism throughout the world. This brief and certainly superficial tour of European history reminds us of some facts that are important to consider when addressing non-Western traditions. It is from the position of the general context of vast diversity and complexity among and within the world's cultures that we approach non-Western ways of knowing. Both the scope of this book and the space limit of its printed edition allow for the inclusion of some but not other materials. Being selective by no means implies privileging some perspectives over others. On the contrary, the thesis that we advocate throughout this book is that of epistemological pluralism on equal footing, thereby recognizing and honoring all cultures and their respective ways of knowing.

The Eastern world abounds in rich and diverse philosophical thought. Chapter 1 deals in great detail with Hinduism and Buddhism—the ancient philosophical traditions that originated in India. China is the birthplace of Taoism and Confucianism. Taoism begins with the anthology known as the *Daode Jing* (*Tao-te Ching*) ascribed to the legendary Laozi (Lao-tzu) who lived in China in ~ 5 BC. At the heart of his message is Tao, translated as the Way. The Tao of Lao-tzu represents simultaneously the nature of reality, knowledge, and value perceived as a whole. It appears that to become knowledgeable means to act in harmony with the Tao, or natural rhythm of the universe, and hence embrace the ultimate value of experience. Actions that abuse consciousness may rebound and obtain their ecological retribution from persons and societies that have disrupted the equilibrium. The Tao illuminates the principle of reciprocity wherein the outer world reflects the inner conditions and vice versa. Chinese teachers brought Buddhism to Japan. Particularly, Eisai (1141–1215) is considered to be the father of Zen Buddhism in Japan. The monk Dogen (1200–1253) is responsible for spreading Ts'ao-tung or Soto methods and teachings from China to Japan.

In the twelfth and thirteenth centuries, the movement known as the Qabbalah (Kabbalah) or Tradition (originated in Provence and Spain) revived the mystical strand in the Jewish tradition. The Qabbalists explore the techniques of meditation and ecstasy, especially Avraham Abulafia (1240–circa 1291), who may have been influenced by Sufism or Islamic mysticism. Illuminationist, or Ishraqi, school of Persian philosophy, founded by the Sufi sheikh al-Suhrawardi (1154–1191) used a linguistic connection between the concept of "Eastern-ness" (*mashriq*) and that of "wisdom" or "light" or "illumination" (*ishraq*). Both words are derived from *sharq*, meaning "the sunrise." Suhrawardi and his followers claimed that Light was the foundation of all existence. Knowledge of the truth is thus achieved through an intuition of Light—an illumination. Rumi (1207–1273), a Persian Sufi mystic and the key exponent of Sufism, believed that the ultimate center of human consciousness, our inmost reality, is the heart (*dil, qalb*). People's hearts are often veiled by innumerable levels of dross and darkness. Transformation occurs when one's heart is completely purified. Love is, therefore, understood as a metaphysical and epistemological principle.

Mysticism and esoteric philosophy cross the geographical boundaries between the East and the West and represent an unbroken tradition from the Egyptians, Hebrews, and Greeks, through the Christian West, and continuing to the present. Central to esoteric world traditions is the system of "the One" that cannot be properly expressed in words and that has different interpretations specific to different cultures. The One is the supreme God that emanates in the form of the Intellect or Nous that further emanates in the Soul. It exemplifies the union of human beings with the Infinite. Gnosticism, the teaching of Gnostics, evokes the Sufi knowledge of the heart. Gnostics are said to have lived in 300 or 400 AD. Gnosis is also known as the knowledge of the heart and its basic precepts are esoteric.

> The terms *Gnostic* and *Gnosticism* are derived from the Greek word *gnosis*, which is usually (albeit somewhat misleadingly) translated as "knowledge." The knowledge the Gnostic seeks…is not rational knowledge. The Greek

> language distinguishes between theoretical knowledge and knowledge gained from direct experience. The latter is gnosis, and a person possessing or aspiring to this knowledge is a Gnostic. (Hoeller, 2002, p. 2)

Hoeller proposes the term *insight* as opposed to knowledge to denote Gnosis because it "involves an intuitive process that embraces both self-knowledge and knowledge of ultimate, divine realities" (p. 2). Gnosticism in the first century BC was represented by both Christian and non-Christian schools. Contemporary educational researchers may find it interesting that the hermeneutic tradition in interpretive research has strong conceptual links with a non-Christian school of Gnosis known as Hermeticism—supposedly the original birthplace of Hermes.

Gnostics should be rightfully credited for their treatment of the feminine principle in the eschatological scheme of world events. *Sophia* is the name that personifies the Divine Feminine in Gnosticism and other esoteric traditions. Literally, "wisdom" in Greek, *sophia* is a female constitutive element of *philosophy* (see previous discussion this chapter). Greek is a gendered language, and perhaps it is not coincidental that the word *philosophy* conveys the presence of a female principle in a nonetheless almost exclusively male domain. The image of Sophia appears in the Wisdom Books of the Old Testament as Chokmah. Gnostic Philo of Alexandria (circa 20 BC–circa 50 AD) repeatedly used the concept of Sophia (on a par with Logos, Nous) drawing from the Old Testament. He claimed that God created Sophia in the beginning of creation and then together with Her created the entire universe.

Greek philosophers wrestled with the questions of the origins of the world, the role of the divine wisdom-Sophia in the eschatological schemata, and the relationship between Sophia and Logos. Pythagoras, who is traditionally considered the first self-proclaimed lover of wisdom, recognized Sophia in Western philosophical tradition. In Plato's *Symposium*, Diotima (who might be Sophia personified) appears as the "great priestess of Mantineia" who "dictates to [her teacher, Plato] the ideal, idealized, and [the Platonic] concept of love" (Kristeva, 1987, p. 71). In contrast to the male-dominated structure of the possession-love, Diotima epitomizes the "uniting-love" principle, an "agent of synthesis," and the power of Phallus: "Diotima *is* it; she is that Phallus, even if she doesn't *have* it. She hands it over to the philosopher whose task is to possess it, to conquer it, and to use it to enslave or educate" (Kristeva, p. 74). Contemporary feminist scholars may find the Gnostic Sophia, if translated into secular imagery, refreshingly empowering.

Metaphysical beliefs permeate indigenous and aboriginal cultures. *Indigenous* and *aboriginal* are often used interchangeably to refer to the people and cultures native to North and South America, Africa, Australia, and Oceania. *Native, aboriginal*, and *indigenous* typically identify people inhabiting particular geographical territories from the earliest times or from before the arrival of colonists. In the Americas, for instance, the Toltec culture (~ eighth century) was native to Mexico and preceded the Aztecs in the tenth century. The Incas in Peru have been known since the ~thirteenth century. The Mayan civilization dates back to ~2000 BC. Each of these cultures has left a heritage of sophisticated cosmological systems, myths, rituals, and traces of scientific, technological, and artistic advances. The Toltec were known as women and men of knowledge (Ruiz, 2004). They were masters (*naguals*) and students. *Naguals* were forced to conceal the ancestral knowledge-wisdom because of European conquest and misuses of personal power by a few students (Ruiz). Yet the knowledge was passed through generations of *naguals*. The result of believing in the truth is "goodness, love, happiness" (Ruiz, p. 19). The Toltec truth, the "story," needs to be "experienced to become legitimate" (Ruiz, p. 23).

The beliefs of the people residing in the vast areas of the Pacific Ocean represent an array of diversity as well as common patterns. The words *mana* (sacred power associated with gods; holy forces of nature) and *tabu* (or taboo) (that which is forbidden), for instance, are common to most of the Pacific region's inhabitants (Smart, 1998). The Polynesian religion distinguishes between the spiritual (invisible) world and the world of experience (seen), with the two worlds being interconnected. The use of practices such as rituals, magic, witchcraft, wearing masks, and body painting are common to many cultures in Oceania. Essential to most aboriginals of Australia is the concept of the Dreaming, or Dreaming Time, which can be rendered as yet another way of knowing. Shamanism originated among the Tunguso-Manchurian people to whom the word *saman* meant "he or she who knows" (Grof, 2006, p. 29). Shamanism is at least 30,000 to 40,000 years old. The term also refers to Siberian native healers and it has been widely used for a variety of native healers in different parts of the world who have been popularly known as "medicine men, witch doctors, sorcerers, or wizards" (Grof, 2006, p. 29).

Plurality, depth, and scope of knowledge developed over thousands of years by indigenous peoples throughout the world and are evident in their ways of living. Indigenous knowledges are also diverse in themselves and unique to given cultures, geographies, and societies (Barnhardt & Kawagley, 2005). They have been passed through generations primarily through "storytelling, ceremonies, songs and dances from generation to generation" (Price, 2010, p. 2).

For the most part of their history, the cultures of Africa were viewed by Western colonizers and missionaries as "primitive, backward, and in need of radical reconstruction" (Brown, 2004, p. 4). And most of what has been known through literature about traditional African philosophical thought emerged through Eurocentric characterizations of African cultures (Brown, 2004). African conceptual languages have been replaced with "theoretical idioms from the West" (Appiah, 2004, p. 23). Yet throughout the same history of colonialism, the people of African descent have long engaged in philosophical thought of their own. Traditional

African thought was indigenous to sub-Saharan cultures prior to the infusion of Islamic, Judaic, and Christian ideologues (Brown, 2004).

Within the realm of traditional African worldview, a person consists of a body made from the "blood of the mother, an individual spirit [*sunsun*] which is the main bearer of one's personality, and the *okra* [from which *sunsun* derives from the father at conception, the kind of a life force sent to a person from Nyame, the high god, and departs the body at death]" (Appiah, 2004, p. 28). In contrast, Western rationalism interprets a person as consisting of a body and a mind (or brain). However, many Europeans and Americans—and Africans—believe that the "departure of the mind from the body is death, and that the mind, released from the body, renamed the 'soul,' survives somehow, perhaps even somewhere" (Appiah, pp. 28–29). This seems like a "different theory—*sunsun* and *okra* are dual non-bodily entities, [of] which the mind is one" (Appiah, p. 29).

The belief in the existence of a spiritual world is not unique to African cultures. Native Americans, for instance, embrace the notion that there are non-observable life forms (spirits) that can reside in birds, bears, or streams. The beliefs of many cultures that have been regarded as inferior to those of modern Western European views show more commonalties than differences regarding the nature of the universe and human being. The knowledge of indigenous societies derives from multiple sources, including traditional teachings, empirical observations, and revelations (Castellano, 2008). While traditional indigenous knowledge (a set of absolutes about the nature of reality and being) has been transmitted through generations without questioning, the empirical knowledge is gained through careful observation (e.g., knowledge of ecosystems).

To understand what the beliefs of African or Native American people are, one needs an investigation that "challenges the ways in which research is conducted *on* Indigenous communities, rather than *with*, or *by* Indigenous communities and researchers" (Langdon, 2009, p. 9). Most aboriginal people who write about aboriginal knowledge have spent a "good deal of their lives interacting with mainstream society and see a need to make explicit those elements of their culture which are at risk of being lost" (Castellano, 2008, p. 31). The knowledge that these cultures can share with us will be a "living fire, rekindled from surviving embers and fuelled with the materials of the twenty-first century" (Castellano, p. 34).

Most indigenous peoples are currently undergoing "major social upheavals as a result of transformative forces beyond their control"; many of their values, beliefs, and practices are "recognized as being just as valid for today's generations as they were for generations past" (Barnhardt & Kawagley, 2005, p. 9). The process is reciprocal:

> Native people may need to understand Western society, but not at the expense of what they already know and the way they have come to know it.

Non-native people, too, need to recognize the coexistence of multiple worldviews and knowledge systems, and find ways to understand and relate to the world in its multiple dimensions and varied perspectives. (p. 9)

Indigenous epistemologies continue to transform contemporary realities of Western advanced societies in the fields of medicine, health, law, politics, and education (Dei, Hall, & Rosenberg, 2008). The legacy of ancient worldviews, no matter how glorious or painful it might have been, represents a multifarious and, at times, surprisingly unified picture that finds its mythological expression in a poetic image of the necklace of the Vedic goddess Indra ("Indra's net"). The necklace is made of shining jewels, all interconnected. "It is told that if we take one jewel and look at it, we'll see the refection of all others, infinite in number. Each of the jewels reflected in one and it reflects all others simultaneously; thus there is an infinite reflecting process occurring" (Robertson, 2009, p. 145).

These ancient Indian and Chinese legends illustrate a holonomic principle of the universe signifying the unity of the whole and its parts. Interestingly, a similar principle was described by German philosopher and mathematician G. W. von Leibniz (1646–1716) in one of his major works, *Monadology* (1714). Likewise, contemporary scientists contemplate the unity principle of the universe. David Bohm (1917–1992), a co-worker of Einstein, who made important contributions to theoretical physics, philosophy, and neuropsychology, believed that "matter and consciousness cannot be explained from, or reduced to each other. They are both abstractions from the implicate order, which is their common ground, and thus represent an inseparable unity" (Grof, 1985, p. 76). Edgar D. Mitchell, the lunar pilot for NASA's Apollo 14 space mission, recalls his experience in space: "I could see the stars, see the separateness of things, but felt an inner connectedness of everything. It was personal. It was wild. It was ecstatic. And it made me ask myself, well, what kind of a brain-mind-body is this that reacts to this vision, this sighting? And it made me realize that our story of ourselves as told by science was probably incomplete, and maybe flawed" (Brown, 2005, p. 56).

What Can We Really Know? New Horizons and Possibilities

What can we *really* know about the world around us? The *truths* about it both tempt and elude. The twentieth-century paradigm shifts in hard sciences can be looked at through the prism of an ancient Chinese saying: To be uncertain is uncomfortable, but to be certain is ridiculous (Boyd, 2012). Albert Einstein's theories of relativity (1905, 1916), quantum mechanics, the discovery of DNA, and the ensuing advancements in biology, chemistry, physics, and mathematics have irrecoverably transformed our thinking about the universe and ourselves in terms of certainty of knowledge. Quantum mechanics, more so than other discoveries of the twentieth century, was the "first crack in the wall of the naïve determinism" and produced a domino effect rendering all methods of encryption obsolete in quantum computation, which in turn made us wonder how "our grandchildren will manage to keep their secrets" (Rota & Crants, 2000, p. 479). Quantum mechanics raised the questions regarding the prediction of the events at the subatomic level. Matter was no longer conceived as to be comprised of solid atoms; the atom itself was divided into constitutive particles held by different forces. At the subatomic level, particles did not obey to fixed mechanical laws. Quantum mechanics made us give up not only the conventional reality of the particle picture of electrons but also the nature of reality itself—no longer completely predictable, causal, and ordered.

What will the twenty-first century hold? Perhaps it will be as "much an age of philosophy as an age of science," wherein they become equal partners in "our project of understanding the world" (Rota & Crants, 2000, p. 491). In the history of Western and non-Western worlds alike, chaos, creativity, and transformation were understood as forming the fabric of a spontaneous cosmos. The principles of multiplicity, diversity, and seemingly random occurrences as the inheritance of many ancient traditions echo similar principles of contemporary fractal geometry, holographic images, and chaos and complexity theories. The new sciences of chaos and complexity and the study of nonlinear dynamic systems have opened venues for Western scientists to consider the pathways toward the interconnected system of a *conscious* universe.

Much like their alchemist counterparts of the Dark Ages, contemporary scientists are on the quest to solve the mysteries of the universe. Today we are witnessing the "beginning of a restructuring of our idea of what a scientific theory should be. The old prejudice that all science should be eventually 'reduced' to physics was prodded by the simplistic positivism that truculently dominated the philosophy of science in the latter half [of the twentieth] century, and that we can now safely relegate to the dustbin of history" (Rota & Crants, 2000, p. 480). With almost 2,500 years of history on its record, contemporary science consists of "extending only incrementally what we can do, or what we can know. But now and then, unpredictably yet inevitably, an event occurs that crystallizes a new insight and reshapes how we perceive things" (Crease, 2003, p. xvi):

> We choose to examine a phenomenon which is impossible, *absolutely* impossible, to explain in any classical way, and which has in it the heart of quantum mechanics. In reality, it contains the only mystery.
>
> —RICHARD FEYMAN (AS CITED IN CREASE, 2003, P. 191)

For thousands of years, science and philosophy have shared the thrill of discovery and perceived an "intimate connection between the true, the beautiful, and the good, seeing these as 'entangled,'...inseparably bound up together in a common and deeply lying origin" (Crease, 2003, p. 216). Yet, the world is never fully transparent to us; the world that we want to explore is a "largely unknown entity," and we certainly must "keep our options open" (Feyerabend, 2000, p. 496). As long as we continue the pursuit of knowledge, moving from one location to another and allowing ourselves to be led upward, we can "achieve a more intimate connection with ourselves and the world, and thereby become more human" (Crease, pp. 216–17).

> The scientist does not study nature because it is useful; he studies it because he delights in it, and he delights in it because it is beautiful. If nature were not beautiful, it would not be worth knowing, and if nature were not worth knowing, life would not be worth living.
> —HENRI POINCARÉ (AS CITED IN CREASE, P. 217)

Science, philosophy, and spirituality have been important forces in the history of humanity. Each operating within its own language games, they continue to tread the path toward new insights today as they have been for thousands of years. Whether there is a possibility for convergence of different pathways in pursuit of knowledge remains to be seen as the twenty-first century unfolds. Living in today's world means inhabiting the dwelling places within a *global* world and, by virtue of an available and fast means of communication and travel, also acknowledging its obvious pluralistic milieu. Coincidently, this also means recognizing, on equal footing, all the diversity of worldviews from "quantum-relativistic physics, consciousness research, and neurophysiology" to the "ancient and Oriental spiritual philosophies, shamanism, aboriginal rituals, and healing practices" (Grof, 1985, p. 91). Even if it is against our wishes, a worldview is clearly emerging that may as well be envisaged as global epistemological pluralism.

References

Appiah, A. K. (2004). Akan and Euro-American concepts of the person. In L. M. Brown (Ed.), *African philosophy: New and traditional perspectives* (pp. 21–34). New York: Oxford University Press.

Arendt, H. (1998). *The human condition.* Chicago: University of Chicago Press.

Audi, R. (2003). *Epistemology: A contemporary introduction to the theory of knowledge* (2nd ed.). New York: Routledge.

Bachelard, G. (2000). *The dialectic of duration* (M. McAllester Jones, Trans.). Manchester, UK: Clinamen.

Bachelard, G. (2002). *The formation of the scientific mind: A contribution to a psychoanalysis of objective knowledge* (M. McAllester Jones, Trans.). Manchester, UK: Clinamen.

Bachelard, G. (2004). *The poetics of reverie: Childhood, language, and the cosmos* (D. Russell, Trans.). Boston: Beacon.

Ballard, H., & Cintron, R. (2010). Critical Race Theory as an analytical tool: African American male success in doctoral education. *Journal of College Teaching and Learning, 7*(10), 11–23.

Barnhardt, R., & Kawagley, A. O. (2005). Indigenous knowledge systems and Alaska native ways of knowing. *Anthropology and Education Quarterly, 36*(1), 8–23.

Baudrillard, J. (1999). Simulacra and simulations: Disneyland. In C. Lemert (Ed.), *Social theory: The multicultural and classical readings* (pp. 481–486). Boulder, CO: Westview Press.

Bell, D. A. (2008). *Race, racism and American law*. New York: Aspen.

Boyd, T. (2012). The clarity of coincidence. *Quest, 100*(2), 44–45.

Brown, D. J. (2005). *Conversations on the edge of the apocalypse: Contemplating the future with Noam Chomsky, George Carlin, Deepak Chopra, Rupert Sheldrake, and others*. New York: Palgrave.

Brown, L. M. (2004). Understanding and ontology in traditional African thought. In L. M. Brown (Ed.), *African philosophy: New and traditional perspectives* (pp. 158–178). New York: Oxford University Press.

Castellano, M. B. (2008). Updating aboriginal traditions of knowledge. In G. J. S. Dei, B. L. Hall, & D. G. Rosenberg (Eds.), *Indigenous knowledges in global contexts: Multiple readings of our world* (pp. 21–36). Toronto: University of Toronto Press.

Crease, R. P. (2003). *The prism and the pendulum: The ten most beautiful experiments in science*. New York: Random House.

Dei, G. J. S., Hall, B. L., & Rosenberg, D. G. (Eds.). (2008). *Indigenous knowledges in global contexts: Multiple readings of our world*. Toronto: University of Toronto Press.

Delgado, R., & Stefanic, J. (2001). *Critical race theory: An introduction*. New York: New York University Press.

Essed, P., & Goldberg, D. T. (Eds.). (2001). *Race critical theories: Text and context*. Malden, MA: Wiley-Blackwell.

Feyerabend, P. (2000). Against method. In S. Rosen (Ed.), *The philosopher's handbook* (pp. 493–502). New York: Random House.

Foucault, M. (1967). *Of other spaces*. Retrieved from http://foucault.info/documents/hetero-Topia/foucault.heteroTopia.en.html

Gabel, S., & Peters, S. (2004). Presage of a paradigm shift? Beyond the social model of disability toward resistance theories of disability. *Disability and Society, 19*(6), 585–600.

Gaspar de Alba, A. (2003). *Velvet barrios: Popular culture and Chicana/o sexualities*. New York: Palgrave.

Glennon, L. (Ed.). (1995). *Our times: An illustrated history of the 20th century*. New York: Pub Overstock.

Grof, S. (1985). *Beyond the brain: Birth, death, and transcendence in psychotherapy*. New York: State University of New York Press.

Grof, S. (2006). *The ultimate journey: Consciousness and the mystery of death*. Ben Lomond, CA: MAPS.

Habermas, J. (1972). *Knowledge and human interests* (J. J. Shapiro, Trans.). Boston: Beacon.

Haraway, D. (1999). The cyborg manifesto and fractured identities. In C. Lemert (Ed.), *Social theory: The multicultural & classic readings* (pp. 539–543). Boulder, CO: Westview.

Hoeller, S. A. (2002). *Gnosticism: New light on the ancient tradition of inner knowing.* Wheaton, IL: Quest.

Johnson, S. (1998). Skills, Socrates and Sophists: Learning from history. *British Journal of Educational Studies, 46*(2), 201–213.

Kenny, A. (2010). *A new history of Western philosophy.* New York: Oxford University Press.

Kristeva, J. (1987). *Tales of love* (L. S. Roudiez, Trans.). New York: Columbia University Press.

Kuehn, M. (2006). Knowledge and belief. In K. Haakonssen (Ed.), *The Cambridge history of eighteen-century philosophy* (Vol. 1, pp. 389–425). New York: Cambridge University Press.

Kuhn, T. (2000). The structure of scientific revolutions. In S. Rosen (Ed.), *The philosopher's handbook: Essential readings from Plato to Kant* (pp. 503–519). New York: Random House.

Langdon, J. (Ed.). (2009). *Indigenous knowledges, development and education.* Rotterdam, the Netherlands: Sense.

Lather, P. (2004). Critical inquiry in qualitative research: Feminist and poststructural perspectives: Science "after truth." In K. deMarrais & S. D. Lapan (Eds.), *Foundations for research: Methods of inquiry in education and social sciences* (pp. 203–215). Mahwah, NJ: Lawrence Erlbaum.

Lehrer, K., & Paxson, T. D. (1999). Knowledge: Undefeated justified true belief. In L. Pojman (Ed.), *The theory of knowledge: Classic and contemporary readings* (pp. 153–156). Belmont, CA: Wadsworth.

Longino, H. E. (2006). Feminist epistemology. In J. Greco & E. Sosa (Eds.), *The Blackwell guide to epistemology* (pp. 327–353). Malden, MA: Blackwell.

Lugg, C. A. (2006). On politics and theory: Using an explicitly activist theory to frame educational research. In V. A. Anfara Jr. & N. T. Mertz (Eds.), *Theoretical frameworks of qualitative research* (pp. 175–188). Thousand Oaks, CA: Sage.

Moser, P. K. (2006). Foundationalism. In R. Audi (Ed.), *The Cambridge dictionary of philosophy* (2nd ed., pp. 321–323). New York: Cambridge University Press.

Moser, P. K., Mulder, D. H., & Trout, J. D. (1998). *The theory of knowledge: A thematic introduction.* New York: Oxford University Press.

Noriega, C. (Ed.). (2000). *The Chicano studies reader: An anthology of Aztlan, 1970–2000.* Los Angeles: UCLA Chicano Studies Research Center.

Papineau, D. (1996). Philosophy of science. In N. Bunnin & E. P. Tsui-James (Eds.), *Blackwell companion to philosophy* (pp. 290–324). Cambridge, MA: Blackwell.

Pojman, L. P. (Ed.). (1999). *The theory of knowledge: Classic and contemporary readings* (pp. 153–156). Belmont, CA: Wadsworth.

Polkinghorne, D. E. (1983). *Methodology for the human sciences: Systems of inquiry.* Albany: State University of New York Press.

Polkinghorne, D. E. (2004). *Practice and the human sciences: The case for a judgment-based practice of care.* New York: State University of New York Press.

Price, M. W. (2010). Indigenous taxonomy, ethnobotany and sacred names. In P. Boyer (Ed.), *Ancient wisdom, modern science: The integration of native knowledge in math and science at tribally controlled colleges and universities* (pp. 1–13). Pablo, MT: Salish Kootenai College Press.

Robertson, R. (2009). *Indra's Net: Alchemy and chaos theory as models for transformation.* Wheaton, IL: Quest.

Rose, M. A. (1991). *The postmodern and the postindustrial: A critical analysis.* New York: Cambridge University Press.

Rota, G. C., & Crants, J. T. (2000). Introduction: Ten philosophical (and contradictory) predictions. In S. Rosen (Ed.), *The philosopher's handbook: Essential readings from Plato to Kant* (pp. 473–491). New York: Random House.

Ruiz, M. (2004). *A Toltec wisdom book: The voice of knowledge*. San Rafael, CA: Amber-Allen.

Runes, D. D. (Ed.). (1983). *Dictionary of philosophy*. Savage, MD: Rowman & Littlefield.

Saldívar, R. (1990). *Chicano narrative: The dialectics of difference*. Madison: University of Wisconsin Press.

Scruton, R. (1996). *Modern philosophy: An introduction and survey*. New York: Penguin.

Smart, N. (1998). *The world's religions* (2nd ed.). New York: Cambridge University Press.

St. Pierre, E. A., & Pillow, W. S. (Ed.). (2000). *Working the ruins: Feminist poststructural theory and methods in education*. New York: Routledge.

Westphal, M. (2006). Hermeneutics as epistemology. In J. Greco & E. Sosa (Eds.), *The Blackwell guide to epistemology* (pp. 415–435). Malden, MA: Blackwell.

Winkler, K. P. (2006). Perception and ideas, judgment. In K. Haakonssen (Ed.), *The Cambridge history of eighteen-century philosophy* (Vol. 1, pp. 234–285). New York: Cambridge University Press.

CHAPTER THREE

Paradigms and Educational Research

Weaving the Tapestry

ANTONINA LUKENCHUK AND EILEEN KOLICH

Paradigmatic Diversity and Educational Research

This chapter lends itself to the nexus of the issues concerning the notion of paradigm, the underpinning and, at times, misconceived assumptions of the nature and various types of educational research, and the value of philosophical inquiry into the underlying principles and constructs of research in human sciences. Our purpose is to establish a chain of interrelated links between epistemological and methodological questions that can lead to a more integrated and broader view of educational research.

One of the points of departure regarding educational research that we took in chapter 1 was to position it, first and foremost, within the tradition of *human science* research. This tradition has a long history in the West, which is significant to recall because of the great deal of ambiguity surrounding more recent use of the word *science* and its place within the classification of arts and sciences. The word *science* is derived from *scientia* (Latin for knowledge) and can be defined as (1) an "intellectual and practical activity encompassing the systematic study of the structure and behavior of the natural and physical world through observation and experiment," (2) a "particular area of this . . .," (3) a "systematically organized body of knowledge of a particular subject," and (4) a "knowledge of any kind" (Stevenson & Lindberg, 2010, p. 1564). This extended definition of science can be applied to education whose disciplinary boundaries include an intellectual and practical activity aimed at a systematic study of human phenomena. The science of education seeks knowledge and understanding of multitudes of complex issues pervading the realm of human affairs—cultural, social, political, moral, religious, and so forth.

In the West, until about the Industrial Revolution, the above concerns comprised the domain of philosophy, the task of which was to provide a systematic and all-encompassing account of the nature of the universe and human being in physical and metaphysical terms. Educational issues were integrated within the hierarchy of arts and sciences, all of which served overall philosophical goals. Most ancient and modern philosophers did not differentiate their activities as philosophical, scientific, or educational. Socrates, Plato, Aristotle, Confucius, Rumi, to name a few, were all great teachers in their own right. Milesian philosophers (6 BC Ionia, which is present-day Turkey), who became known as the first scientists, taught that life and nonlife, and matter and spirit were all one.

The scientific discoveries and technological advancements following the Industrial Revolution provided an impetus for a separation between and compartmentalization of arts and sciences as well as for a shifting role of philosophy from its royal to a supplementary status serving the purposes of individual disciplines. The eighteenth-century philosopher David Hume attempted the inception of a science of human nature based on observable and measurable moral behavior, which eventually gave rise to behavioral sciences (Polkinghorne, 1983, 2004). The nineteenth-century German historian Droysen marked the distinction between *erklären* (explanation) (as in natural sciences) and *verstehen* (understanding) (as in human sciences), a distinction that presaged methodological debates in educational research. Further, in nineteenth-century Germany, Dilthey coined the word *Geisten-wissenschaft*, which cannot be exactly translated into English. It is composed of *vershehen* (German for understanding) and *Wissenschaft* (German for science, learning, or knowledge). The science of understanding, also known as hermeneutics, has thus become a counterpoint to a natural science, the traditional purpose of which was explanation (see chapters 1 and 2).

At the turn of the nineteenth century, in the West, social sciences emerged as an attempt to study individuals and their behavior within societal groups at the micro- and macrolevels, for example, sociology, anthropology, economics, and political science. Durkheim, Weber, and Marx were the architects of grand social science projects that still continue to provoke the social and political imaginations of contemporary thinkers (Lemert, 1999). August Comte attempted an ambitious positive social science that did not withstand the test of time. By the second half of the twentieth century, all positivistic undertakings in natural and social sciences had failed. The time became ripe for a new vision of science and the methods of scientific inquiry.

Methodological debates surrounding natural and human sciences entailed the revisionist conceptions of knowledge and scientific method from positivistic to post-positivistic (see chapters 1 and 2). Einstein's relativity theory and quantum mechanics presented major challenges to the positivistic view of science. By the mid-twentieth century, the rejection of positivism by the philosophers of science, and their ensuing consensus that science could no longer produce certain knowledge, signaled radical changes in the understanding of methods applied to the study of human phenomena. Knowledge was conceived as fallible and subject to questioning, rejection, or acceptance as the best explanation available (temporary warrant) by a community of inquirers in a particular field of study.

Accordingly, the new conception of science assumed a critical stance toward scientific progress as an accumulation of and/or addition to the existing body of knowledge. Instead, the acquisition of knowledge represented the process of evolutionary change of paradigms competing for the best explanation of phenomena, accompanied by the process of occasional revolutionary epistemological breaks (paradigm shifts) that could invalidate the previously accepted warrants of knowledge. The tools of traditional scientific method were no longer sufficient to apply to an expanded notion of reason that included "systems logic, hermeneutic logic, pragmatic logic, the understanding and explanation of field theory, organic systems, linguistic statements, and consciousness" (Polkinghorne, 1983, p. 243). Since natural sciences were no longer restricted to the production of indubitable knowledge and, therefore, open to methodological alternatives, human sciences in turn became more receptive to the methods that could provide the most appropriate access to the study of human beings who present the most complex kinds of problems.

Feyerabend's proverbial anything goes (see chapter 2) propels the idea that it is no longer possible to rely on fixed methods of investigation in any type of research. Methods are "no longer considered correct or right in themselves"; instead, they should be "appropriate . . . in relationship to the kind of question being addressed" (Polkinghorne, 1983, p. 273). The above statements underscore our position on knowledge and methods in educational research that can be generally expressed as an epistemological and methodological pluralism. Epistemological pluralism necessarily entails the recognition of diverse beliefs and practices found in today's world cultures and societal groups, and these beliefs and practices should be recognized and legitimized on equal grounds with those that have been [historically] given exclusive privilege, authority, and power, namely with the Western epistemologies (see chapter 2).

In the previous chapters, we employed a number of metaphors to convey our messages with regard to educational inquiry, knowledge, and the research process. Chapter 1 opens with a spirited discussion of philosophy as a form of inquiry, a pursuit of wisdom or knowledge, which is intrinsic to a human being. Educational inquiry is a pursuit of knowledge writ at large driven by the primordial eros—an unsettling desire that accompanies the level-headed logos. Passionate search for wisdom can be translated into a tapestry of the world's cultural beliefs imbued within their original definitions: *jñāna* in Hinduism, the *Tao* in Chinese philosophy, *ishraq* in Persian tradition, *Sophia* in Gnosticism, and others (see chapters 1 and 2). Passion is the gateway to things imagined that have inspired the most daring projects in the history of humankind, and philosophers and scientists alike can testify to the passion's triumph over the levelheadedness of reason in their pursuit of knowledge. Nietzsche and Poincaré may have little in common except their shared conviction that life is not worth living if it is not for the pursuit of creating art or discovering nature's wonders.

Alas, there is so much we do not know. There are perhaps as many holes in the spider web of our knowledge of the universe as there are stars in it radiating luring light from above. Like philosophers and scientists, educational researchers venture on passionate journeys to discover what the twenty-first century holds.

So, what are the ways of knowing available for educational researchers to pursue their projects in this day and age? The analysis of numerous philosophical and educational sources pertaining to epistemology and philosophy of science (see chapters 1 and 2) allowed us to identify six paradigms of educational inquiry encompassing a great variety of beliefs, theories, assumptions, and practices. The number of identified paradigms is contingent on epistemological boundaries and is open to alternatives. The constitutive elements of each paradigm were delineated by taking into consideration existing scholarship on epistemology, philosophy of science, philosophical foundations of research, the accompanying vocabulary, and our own understanding of the conception of paradigm. The six paradigms identified for the purpose of this book are empirical-analytic, pragmatic, interpretive, critical, poststructuralist, and transcendental.

Table 3.1 depicts a typology of these six paradigms and their corresponding conceptual repertoire, epistemologies, methodologies, and selected methods. To fill in each cell of the table, we selected the terminology that is most frequently and widely used in philosophical and educational sources and captures the most important constitutive elements of each delineated paradigm. It is important to mention that that the six paradigms are not completely autonomous entities; instead, most of them exhibit conceptual relationships that can be either strong or weak. Figure 3.1 portrays these relationships wherein solid lines demonstrate strong links and broken lines, weak links. The description of the paradigms pertaining to table 3.1 will be accompanied by comments on the paradigmatic relationships in reference to figure 3.1.

There are numerous definitions of *paradigm* and contemporary educational researchers and scholars disagree on the use of the term. For instance, Yu (2006) prefers *tradition* to *paradigm* based on his association of the term with Kuhn's definition of *paradigm* (see introduction and chapters 1 and 2). Yu claims that Kuhn's definition inevitably leads to an incommensurability thesis. However, if we look closer at Kuhn's argument about competing paradigms of science in the history of Western philosophy of science, it becomes clear that the incommensurability thesis does not apply to competing paradigms across different sciences. It is only within a particular field of study such as physics, where the thesis of incommensurability can be applied—some theories become obsolete in time, others remain credible within limited parameters, yet other theories can become completely overturned.

Our understanding of *paradigm* includes but is not limited to Kuhn's definition. Many educational researchers (e.g., Anfara & Mertz, 2006; Merriam et al., 2002) use a variety of terms in reference to paradigm: theory, theoretical framework, conceptual framework, model, lenses, a set of ideas, guiding principles, or perspectives. We consider all of these definitions under the umbrella term *conceptual repertoire*. Conceptual repertoire is a figurative expression that means an "endless list of conceptual ingredients," comprising a particular paradigm of research and resembling a list of musical pieces whose endless and different configurations can generate multiple productions. Tapestry of beliefs (see chapter 1) is another metaphor to convey the same idea. The conceptual repertoire cell consists of ideas, concepts, theories, philosophies, ideologies, traditions, perspectives, and practices (see table 3.1).

Paradigm (from the Greek *para*, beside, and *deigma*, example) is an "example, a model, a worldview, a theory, or a methodology" (Stevenson & Lindberg, 2010, p. 1269). Other dictionary definitions of paradigm include "example, archetype, beau ideal, chart, criterion, ensample, exemplar, ideal, mirror, model, original, pattern, prototype, sample, standard" (Kipfer, 2010, p. 588). Introduction provides a definition of paradigm derived from several dictionaries, resulting in a paradigm pyramid construct (see figure 1, introduction). For the purpose of this book, we employ a threefold definition of paradigm: (1) a system of inquiry, (2) a model, and (3) a way of knowing.

Polkinghorne (1983) identifies three major paradigmatic possibilities for human science research: deductive-hypothetical, pragmatic, and existential-phenomenological and hermeneutic systems of inquiry. Our use of paradigm as a system of inquiry refers to such overarching historical and philosophical traditions (macro constructs). Based on this definition, five of the six paradigms were identified: empirical-analytic, pragmatic, interpretive, critical, and transcendental (see table 3.1). Inquiry is a broad term that can designate any research project as an "act of asking for information," posing a "question," and conducting an "official investigation" (Stevenson & Lindberg, 2010, p. 897). We consider this broad meaning of inquiry as integral to our understanding of paradigm as a system of inquiry, which can be subsequently extended to an act of posing research questions within a "set of [beliefs] connected [as] parts forming a complex whole" and following an "organized scheme or method" (Stevenson & Lindberg, 2010, p. 1763).

Our second use of paradigm as a model is based on the assumption of it as a micro construct, such as, for instance, a specific theory that can underpin an individual research project, or a theoretical model that can emerge as a result of conducting an individual research project (e.g., grounded theory). The chapters in part 2 of this book demonstrate various microlevel paradigms positioned within the macrolevel overarching systems of inquiry (see table 3.2). Finally, we conceive of paradigm as a discursive way of knowing that doesn't necessarily fit in within a well-delineated model or system of inquiry. Poststructuralist falls within this definition of paradigm.

The following detailed description of the six paradigms provides insights into the ways we conceptualize each of them individually and in relation to each other. The first row in table 3.1 shows the interconnections between a paradigm and its constitutive ingredients. The arrow that extends from the cell paradigms onward points to the conception of paradigm as encompassing conceptual repertoire, epistemologies, methodologies, and methods. The arrows that spread from the methodologies cell to the right and to the left point to epistemologies, conceptual repertoire, and methods as constitutive elements of methodology. Thus, the first row in table 3.1 provides an organizational framework for the description of each paradigm.

Empirical-analytic paradigm acquires its label from the longstanding traditions of Western rationalism and empiricism as well as the relevant educational research positions of materialism and behaviorism. Positivism exerted its influence on this paradigm for a relatively short time and was repudiated in the second half of the twentieth century. It is no longer acceptable to equate this paradigm with positivistic research (Yu, 2006); however, some educational researchers continue to do so (e.g., Hesse-Biber & Leavy, 2011; Lather, 2004; Pascale, 2011). Habermas (1972) distinguishes empirical-analytic sciences whose purposes are prediction and control. Polkinghorne (1983) refers to this paradigm as empirical, deductive, or deductive-hypothetical. Creswell (2003) singles out a similar paradigm he identifies as post-positivistic. *Scientific* also stands for empirical-analytic research paradigm (e.g., Cohen, Manion, & Morrison, 2008) and its use is appropriate as long as a post-positivistic conception of science is implied. The term that is most frequently used to designate this paradigm is *quantitative* (e.g., McMillan, 2008).

Empirical-analytic research in education yields probabilistic, formal, theoretical, explanatory, and warranted truths/knowledge claims obtained as a result of experiment, analysis of variables, or causal-comparative studies within the theoretical boundaries delineated by each individual project. Although the purpose of empirical studies is to produce foundational knowledge, it can be at best weak foundationalism (see chapters 1 and 2). Until about the 1970s, empirical-analytic research held an epistemological and methodological privilege over other systems of inquiry in human

Table 3.1: Typology of Paradigms as Major Systems of Inquiry, Models, and Ways of Knowing, and Their Corresponding Conceptual Repertoire, Epistemologies, Methodologies, and Selected Methods

PARADIGMS AS SYSTEMS OF INQUIRY MODELS WAYS OF KNOWING	Corresponding CONCEPTUAL REPERTOIRE ideas, concepts, theories, philosophies, ideologies, traditions, perspectives	Corresponding EPISTEMOLOGIES types of knowledge and knowledge claims	Corresponding METHODOLOGIES	Selected METHODS within corresponding methodologies
EMPIRICAL-ANALYTIC	rationalism, empiricism, materialism, behaviorism, *positivism (minimal and short-lived influence)	probabilistic, fallible, formal, theoretical, approximation to *truth* (small "t") warrant	quantitative can be critical	experimental, quasi-experimental, correlational, survey, causal-comparative, ex post facto
PRAGMATIC	pragmatism, empiricism, rationalism, experimentalism, instrumentalism, utilitarianism, materialism	provisional, fallible, best possible explanation, trial-and-error, warrant	quantitative, qualitative, or mixed can be critical	grounded theory, action and practitioner research, case study, various quantitative and qualitative methods
INTERPRETIVE	existentialism, phenomenology, hermeneutics, constructivism, ethnomethodology, symbolic interactionism	understanding (*verstehen*), description, interpretation, meaning-making, contextual	qualitative often coupled with critical	great variety of methods: e.g., case study, [auto]-ethnography, narrative, phenomenology, unobtrusive methods (content, text, discourse analysis), visual, arts-based research
CRITICAL	neo-Marxism, critical theory, feminism, critical race and ethnicity theories, queer theory, disability studies, social reconstructionism, social and political activism	emancipation, advocacy, consciousness-raising, social and political transformation, standpoint epistemologies, contextual	predominantly qualitative can be quantitative or mixed	various qualitative, quantitative, or mixed methods

| POST-STRUCTURALIST | antifoundationalism, postmodernism, simulacra, chaos and complexity theories, social and political activism | deconstruction of *episteme* as the only 'true' knowledge, epistemological anarchism, discursive, contextual, socially and politically transformative | predominantly qualitative and critical | experimentation with various methods and ways of representation (textual and visual), unobtrusive methods |
| TRANSCENDENTAL | foundationalism, Western and non-Western metaphysical systems, world esoteric and spiritual traditions, Gnosticism, most indigenous and aboriginal traditions | ultimate Truth (capital 'T'), finite, intuitive, emotive, spiritually, socially and politically transformative, body-mind-soul unity, revelation | predominantly qualitative can be critical | variety of qualitative methods |

and social sciences, and it remains highly influential among contemporary educational researchers. Part 2 features several quantitative research projects described further in this chapter. Empirical-analytic paradigm exhibits several links with other paradigms (see figure 3.1). In epistemological terms, it is closely linked to pragmatic paradigm, hence a solid line depicting a strong link. Although rare, empirical studies can also be critical in terms of their research purposes. A broken line shows a weak relation between empirical-analytic and critical paradigms (see figure 3.1).

Pragmatic paradigm is important to distinguish because of its unique position on knowledge claims Polkinghorne (1983) defines, via Peirce (see chapters 1 and 2), as trial-and-error truths that withstand the test of experiment, time, and utility. Pragmatic truth is a not a justified belief in a strict epistemological sense, but rather the effectiveness of knowledge demonstrated by the effectiveness of action (Polkinghorne, 1983). Pragmatic truths are warranted assertions that have to be agreed upon and accepted (or rejected) by a community of inquirers. Creswell (2003) singles out pragmatic paradigm as problem centered and action oriented and as such it is highly appealing to practitioner and action researchers. Conceptually, pragmatism has the strongest connection with empirical-analytic paradigm and tentative connections with interpretive and critical paradigms (see figure 3.1). Precisely because of these links, pragmatism is often positioned as an in-between and reconciliatory paradigm (between supposedly pure empirical-analytic and interpretive paradigms) (see Johnson & Onwuegbuzie, 2004). Pragmatism is an overarching paradigm undergirding a variety of qualitative, quantitative, and mixed methods research projects.

Interpretive paradigm has roots in several traditional arts and sciences: anthropology, psychology, sociology, political science, linguistics, and philosophy. Polkinghorne (1983) provides a sophisticated analysis of the origins of this paradigm in the existential-phenomenological and hermeneutic systems of inquiry (see chapters 1 and 2). Germinating from several nineteenth-century European movements, existential-phenomenology and hermeneutics represented the strongest anti-positivist response (Polkinghorne, 1983) that triggered radical changes in the conception of science, knowledge, scientific method, and appropriate methodologies for the study of human phenomena. *Phenomenological* (or descriptive) and *hermeneutic* (or interpretive) are the historical terms associated with this paradigm. Other terms for it found in research textbooks are *interpretivist*, *qualitative*, or *naturalistic*, which are often used interchangeably. Habermas (1972) distinguishes historical-hermeneutic sciences that aim at knowledge as understanding. *Understanding* (capital *U*) underscores the nature and type of knowledge uniquely attributed to this paradigm. Lather (2004) identifies this paradigm as understanding. Similarly, Creswell (2003) emphasizes understanding as part of constructivist paradigm, which is synonymous with interpretive. Symbolic interactionism and ethnomethodology sprang from the interpretive tradition (Cohen et al., 2008). Interpretive paradigm is most strongly linked to critical, and tentatively to pragmatic,

Figure 3.1: Conceptual Relationships between the Paradigms of Research

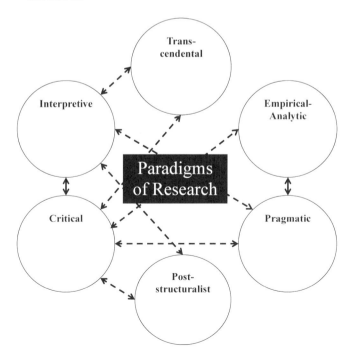

poststructuralist, and transcendental (see figure 3.1). Contemporary interpretive research represents a flourishing field of qualitative studies with many diverse and innovative designs (see table 3.1). Table 3.2 and its description features several interpretive research projects presented in part 2 of this book.

Critical paradigm is singled out based on its strong conceptual repertoire grounded in the political perspectives on knowledge and research and especially in neo-Marxist or critical theory perspectives. It is by the association with these perspectives that we denote this paradigm as critical. Critical epistemology takes hermeneutics to the next level—the level of emancipation with regard to knowledge now understood as power. One of the leading contemporary critical theorists, Habermas (1972), proposes critical social science grounded in knowledge as emancipation. Following his lead, Lather (2004) employs the term *emancipatory* and Creswell (2003) uses *advocacy/participatory* to identify this paradigm. Lather (2004) reminds educational researchers that the key issue is "how to bring scholarship and advocacy together in order to generate ways of knowing that interrupt power imbalances" (p. 208). Critical paradigm is linked conceptually with all others in terms of its research purposes, and its strongest connection is with the interpretive system of inquiry. Critical inquiry is exceedingly popular among educational researchers, and it inspires an array of research and scholarly projects in feminism, critical race and ethnicity, queer, and disability studies. Table 3.2 and its description in the next section feature several critical inquiry chapters.

The four paradigms that have been described thus far share several important features. First, they encompass major methodologies employed in current educational research (Creswell, 2003, 2012) with various terms ascribed to them. In epistemological terms, all four paradigms designate knowledge claims as provisional, contextual, and contingent. This means that the knowledge/truth that is produced as a result of the research projects conducted within these paradigms is "constructed within [particular] conceptual systems" and is "relative to time and place" (Polkinghorne, 1983, p. 3). Given the characteristics of the knowledge claims of these four paradigms, poststructuralist and transcendental paradigms represent their counterparts, each in their own terms. Between themselves, transcendental and poststructuralist paradigms are epistemological opposites and there is absolutely no connection between them (see figure 3.1).

Poststructuralist can be best described as a discursive way of knowing due to its complete rejection of foundational knowledge. Poststructuralism is an essentially anti-foundationalist project seeking to deconstruct episteme as the only true and privileged knowledge. There is no knowledge as such, according to poststructuralist thinkers; all that we have is text and its endless interpretations—the copy of the copy of the copy, *simulacra*, or *hyperreality* (see chapters 1 and 2). The poststructuralist way of knowing is conceptually at odds with many structured models of inquiry, yet its representatives ally with emancipatory research agendas proposed by critical researchers. Poststructuralist research does not stand on its own ground—which it resists and rejects—and is typically conducted within interpretive and critical inquiries. Poststructuralist feminist research is especially appealing to educators (e.g., Lather, 2004, 2008; St. Pierre & Pillow, 2000). Poststructuralist thinkers generate innovative ways of conducting research by experimenting with expressive means and genres such as art, literature, cinematography, or digital imaging. Although elusive in terms of its own definition and suspicious of structured approaches to research, poststructuralism is important to singling out creative ways of generating research projects that stir our social imaginations.

Finally, we distinguish *transcendental paradigm* as truly unique among the constellation of contemporary educational research paradigms. It represents a metaphysical alternative to all other paradigms (which are grounded in a materialistic conception of reality) in that it posits the existence of the ultimate reality and Truth (capital letter *T*) and asserts the importance of reason and intuition, or revelation, as the ultimate ways of knowing. What follows from this position is that reality and a human being have at least two dimensions: physical and metaphysical, or body and mind, as in most ancient and classical philosophical traditions. Some similar non-Western traditions identify a threefold conception of the universe and a human being: body, mind (soul), and spirit (see chapters 1 and 2). Transcendental paradigm deals with the issues of spirituality. *Transcendental* is a conditional term that we use to designate an array of traditions, ranging from Western mysticism to aboriginal and indigenous beliefs. *Transcendental* means "relating to a spiritual or nonphysical realm" (Stevenson & Lindberg, 2010, p. 1838). The word also evokes Transcendentalism, an idealistic philosophical movement begun in New England in the 1830s. Its major representatives, Ralph Waldo Emerson (1803–1882) and Henry David Thoreau (1817–1862), believed in the divine order of nature and humanity and held progressive views on abolitionism, feminism, and communal living. *Transcendental* can be interpreted in both religious and secular terms. In either case, it implies the existence of an internal moral compass according to which a human being establishes her or his relations with others and the surrounding world. Immanuel Kant (1724–1804) calls this compass a "categorical imperative," or a sense of moral obligation. Metaphysical arguments are not easy to discard. Contemporary professional philosophers continue to wrestle with a metaphysical conundrum and its sources: consciousness and freedom (Scruton, 1996). Self-consciousness presents us with a "peculiar idea of unity," which Kant described as a "transcendental unity of apperception" (Scruton, p. 226).

The issues of spirituality are rarely explored by educational researchers, and when they are, the studies focused on these issues are typically conducted in conjuncture with interpretive or critical (or both) types of research. For instance, Dantley (2005) contends that faith grounds contemporary educational leadership when it is inclusive and politically effective. He aligns faith with leadership, specifically with transformational leaders who wrestle with undemocratic practices such as tracking and ability grouping, inequitable funding, and high-stakes testing. According to Dantley, these leaders exercise faith as they "envision schools grounded in democracy and social justice but they labor to bring about what they have created by faith into existence" (p. 11). Tisdell's (2000) study seeks to determine "how spirituality influences the motivations and practices of a multicultural group of women adult educators who are teaching for social change" (p. 67). Tisdell positions her research within the critical and poststructuralist feminist framework, and she discovers that spirituality is elusive as well as all-encompassing and is a force that "gives meaning and coherence to life" (p. 86). And it is this compelling realization that adds an immense value to the participants' efforts to teach for social change.

The examples of research projects presented in part 2 do not intersect with either the transcendental or poststructuralist paradigms directly. However, tentative links with the transcendental paradigm, for instance, can be established in the content of chapters 4 and 5, and the content of chapter 14 has an implicit poststructuralist ring to it.

The description and graphical representation of the six paradigms identified for the purposes of this book are yet another conceptual version, among others, of educational research. These paradigms do not exhaust all possibilities, yet we believe that they are sufficiently encompassing in terms of existing educational research alternatives. A different number of paradigms can be potentially identified. Ours is not a matter of concern with the number but, more effectively, with the purpose of this paradigm journey to broaden the conception of educational inquiry and the spectrum of its methodological choices.

Toward Methodological Pluralism

Although the fierce battles between positivistic and post-positivistic camps of philosophers are the remnants of the past, today's researchers continue to debate the issues surrounding appropriate methods of educational inquiry whereby placing positivism in the center of debates. For instance, Howe (2009) posits the existence of a tacit form of positivistic research (new scientific orthodoxy) that presumably is still thriving in educational research. Yu (2006) would question this and similar statements on the grounds of persisting misconceptions and misrepresentations of positivism in educational research (see chapters 1, 2, and the discussion above).

Current research in hard and soft sciences is engaged in multischematic and multiparadigmatic inquiries choosing among available and often competing methodological alternatives (Polkinghorne, 1983; Yu, 2006). Epistemological and methodological pluralism, which is the reality of the day, calls into question any assumption of certainty regarding the knowledge of the world and any fixed method designed to unravel all its mysteries. The existing theoretical frameworks and methods in educational research do not represent impervious to criticism or annihilation models but rather alternative and multiple paradigms of research, each of which can represent the best available and most *appropriate* model for individual inquiry, and each of which can be eventually subject to questioning and rejection. Choosing appropriate paradigm(s) for a particular research project is the key to the project's successful planning, that is, selecting appropriate methodologies and that project's subsequent implementation.

Relevant to our discussion on research methodologies is the question of definitions. The terms *methodology* and *methods* are often used synonymously, even though they have very distinct meanings and purposes. Both words have their origins in Latin and their etymology partially was addressed in chapters 1 and 2. Consulting the etymology of many terms that we use in education is essential to their proper understanding. The roots, prefixes, or endings of these terms often bear important connotations that, if not accounted for, could create controversies and debates around their use (and these occur fairly often among educational researchers and scholars). *Method*, for instance, designates

> particular activities that are used to achieve research results. Methods include various experimental designs, sampling procedures, measuring instruments, and the statistical treatment of data. The word *method* retains the mean of its etymological roots. It is made up of the root words *meta* and *hodos*: *meta* means "from" or "after," and *hodos* "journey." The word *method* is thus a "going-after" or "a pursuit."…it is a pursuit of knowledge. (Polkinghorne, 1983, p. 5)

deMarrais and Lapan (2004) define method as specific research techniques used to gather evidence about a phenomenon, and it typically utilizes such research tools as surveys, observations, interviews, and the like. Bogdan and Biklen (2007) define *method* as "consistent with the logic embodied in the methodology" (p. 35).

Methodology, on the other hand, reflects an overarching process or plan for researching phenomena. Methodology includes the root word *logos*, which has a rich history beginning with Greek philosophy where it was used to refer to the principle of reason, the source of world order and intelligibility (see above). Methodology is "the examination of the possible plans to be carried out—the journeys to be undertaken—so that an understanding of phenomena can be obtained" (Polkinghorne, 1983, p. 5). Methodology is typically informed by major systems of inquiry, or paradigms, and includes under its umbrella definition specific ideas or theories as part of the conceptual repertoire and corresponding epistemological positions and methods. Epistemological and ontological assumptions ought to be especially carefully crafted since they have a significant impact on how we generate knowledge (Pascale, 2011).

deMarrais and Lapan (2004) reiterate a similar position claiming that our assumptions about what we believe knowledge is "are embedded in methodological discussions, and therefore have consequences for how we design and implement our research studies" (p. 5). For example, ethnographic research can be grounded in a range of epistemological and methodological positions such as symbolic interactionism or critical theory (deMarrais & Lapan), cultural and cognitive anthropology, or feminism (Creswell, 2012). Specific theoretical assumptions about how one defines culture are certainly paramount for ethnographic research (deMarrais & Lapan). Determining which methods to use (e.g., observations, interviews, document analysis, etc.) should first be based on a thorough review of methodologies, which addresses phenomena that can be studied as the method emerges in a related way. Thus, it is imperative that researchers qualify their inquiries by demonstrating how their research is connected to larger theoretical and philosophical dispositions on knowledge that often constitute a system or tradition of inquiry—paradigm (e.g., empirical-analytic, pragmatic, interpretive, critical)—that provides a substantive context for situating and crafting a credible research plan (methodology) that is aligned with appropriate activities and tools for collecting and analyzing data (methods).

Selecting a methodology and accompanying methods can be a daunting task for novice researchers, given the varied and sometimes unique ways in which the overarching research paradigms and methodologies are interpreted by the respective researcher, authors of research methods texts, and articles addressing methodological assumptions. It should be noted that the assumptions of what research is in the field of human and the social sciences has changed significantly over the last several decades. The repudiation of positivism and subsequent changes in the understanding of scientific method, along with the emergence and growing popularity and legitimacy of interpretive methodologies, have changed the nature and scope of educational research.

Although over the years interpretive (qualitative) research has gained proper recognition and place within the constellation of methodologies in social and human sciences, many contemporary educational researchers and scholars continue to debate the nature of the scientific method, which supposedly puts a demarcation line between more scientific quantitative research and its less scientific qualitative counterpart. Moreover, many partisan researchers on both sides of the debate continue to misrepresent positivism by associating it with quantitative research. It is imperative for educational researchers to develop a deeper and clearer perspective on the philosophical underpinnings of quantitative inquiry. We rely primarily on Yu (2006) to demystify positivism in general, especially its misconceived relation to quantitative research. Yu presents a detailed analysis of positivism, its history and its relevance or absence thereof to quantitative methods of analysis:

> While positivism has been universally rejected by philosophers of science over the past fifty years, the current textbooks still either associate quantitative methods with positivist ones or cover quantitative methods within a positivist frame of reference. Despite the fact that newer epistemologies and methodologies, such as post-positivism, critical realism, and critical multiplism, have been discussed in numerous books and articles, the debate regarding the paradigm of quantitative methods seems to be trapped in a time warp. (p. 23)

There are several reasons for the misunderstanding of the relationships between positivism and quantitative research:

> The misunderstanding is due to the association between the one-way reductionism endorsed by certain logical positivist and quantitative methods. In addition, quantitative research includes time-series analysis, repeated measures, and other trend-based inquiries, and thus it is inaccurate to describe quantitative research as merely orienting towards outcomes and lacking the process orientation. (Yu, 2006, p. 24)

Further, the perception that quantitative research assumes static reality is attributed to the myth that logical positivists are realists, which is conceptually erroneous. Whereas from a positivistic standpoint reality is equated with experience, quantitative researchers typically posit objective reality as the point of departure for pursuing research. Logical positivism represents conventionalism, relativism, and subjectivism—a position that is essentially antirealist (Yu, 2006). Yu contends that at the ontological, epistemological, and methodological levels, "the Fisherian School, the Neyman/Pearson School, the Bayesian school, the Resampling School, and the Exploratory Data Analysis (EDA) school are fundamentally different, and to some extent are incompatible" (pp. 24–25). This statement clearly supports the epistemological and methodological pluralism position relevant to quantitative *and* qualitative methods as well as the methods *within* each of these categories.

Positivists' major principle of verification represents another dilemma with regard to misconceived relations between positivism and quantitative research. The principle of verification concerns statements of meaning and posits that a statement is meaningless if verification is not possible. Therefore, if statistical methods that are applied cannot yield verifiable results, the effort is useless. In the tradition of quantitative research, there is no evidence that any major quantitative researchers subscribe to this radical epistemology. For example, Cronbach, the famous statistician who introduced Cronbach coefficient Alpha and construct validity, did not restrict his inquiry to only verifiable materials in the logical positivist sense. When Cronbach contemplated the problem of causal inferences in research, he did not employ LISREL or other quantitative causal modeling techniques. Instead, he looked to the more qualitative methods of the ethnographer, historian, and journalist (Yu, 2006). Statistical methods do not provide verification in the logical positivist sense:

> The logic of statistical hypothesis testing is not to verify whether the hypothesis is right; rather, the logic is to find the probability of obtaining the sampled data in the long run given that the null hypothesis is true. However, if we put any theory in the perspective of the "long run," *nothing can be conclusively verified* [our emphasis]. (Yu, p. 29)

In agreement with Yu (2006), we contend that many educational researchers incorrectly attribute causal inferences to logical positivism. Quantitative methods, which include randomized experiments, quasi-experiments, meta-analysis, and structural equation modeling, are not compatible with the anti-cause notion of logical positivism. Yu further argues that it is questionable to attribute positivist reductionism to quantitative research. The history of positivism shows how the originators of many statistical methods—which are still widely used in quantitative research— such as Pearson and Fischer, initially adopted positivistic assumptions predominant at that time. Yet shortly after the overall repudiation of positivism, most if not all scientists abandoned its positions (see chapters 1 and 2). The point that logical positivism is not—and cannot be—the modern scientific paradigm can hardly be overestimated. Positivistic assumptions of science have become obsolete by default due to the scientific and technological advancements of the recent century, and current methods of going after knowledge are not a matter of certainty but rather a choice that can yield the best explanation or understanding among the existing alternatives.

Various schools in quantitative research utilize different assumptions and could be treated as independent traditions; therefore, methodological pluralism is encouraged by quantitative researchers:

> What is needed is to encourage researchers to keep an open mind to different methodologies by allowing research methods being driven by research questions, while retaining skepticism to examine their philosophical assumptions of various research methodologies instead of unquestioningly accepting popular myths. (Yu, 2006, p. 43)

The perspectives provided by Yu (2006), Polkinghorne (1983), and Ozmon and Craver (2008) suggest the need for (1) carefully scrutinized philosophical frameworks, (2) utilizing a syncretic process that incorporates a multi-paradigmatic approach to educational research, and (3) exploring new philosophical directions in an effort to maximize the potential of the researcher's inquiry.

In this chapter, we illustrate how twelve burgeoning researchers coming from various fields of educational study have approached their respective projects using various epistemological and methodological perspectives informed by specific overarching systems of inquiry in an effort to gain a more in-depth understanding of their research and its ramifications (see chapters in part 2). The works of these authors originated from their dissertation research projects that effectively represent inquiries into significant human problems and the attempts to solve them. Table 3.2 exhibits the approach that we take to position the chapters in part 2 within the four major paradigms of research: empirical-analytic, pragmatic, interpretive, and critical. In what follows, we provide a brief analysis of these chapters

Table 3.2: Positioning Part 2 Chapters within the Paradigms of Research

CHAPTER NO.	TITLE	AUTHOR(S)	PARADIGMS	METHODOLOGIES/METHODS	
				DESIGNS INSTRUMENTS	THEORIES PERSPECTIVES MODELS
CH 4	"The Passage beyond Self: An Autoethnographic Journey into My Cultural Roots, Personal, and Educational Transformations"	Vladimir Trostin	Interpretive	*Qualitative* Autoethnography Personal Narrative Writing as a method	Culture-Self relations Cross-cultural perspectives Transformational leadership
CH 5	"Sociocultural Perspectives of First-Generation Asian Indian Leaders in U.S. Higher Education: An Ethnographic Study"	Matthew Woolsey	Interpretive	*Qualitative* Ethnography Biographical narrative Interviews Field notes Documents Artifacts	Sociocultural lens, Bicultural, intercultural, and global perspectives on leadership
CH 6	"Hermeneutics of Hispanic Parenthood: Reframing Conceptions through Personal Voices"	Maria E. Hernandez-Rodriguez	Interpretive	*Qualitative* Hermeneutics Interviews	Philosophical Hermeneutics Natural Growth Model

Table 3.2 cont.

Table 3.2 cont.

CHAPTER NO.	TITLE	AUTHOR(S)	PARADIGMS	METHODOLOGIES/METHODS	
				DESIGNS INSTRUMENTS	THEORIES PERSPECTIVES MODELS
CH 7	"In Pursuit of Change: An Ethnographic Case Study of a Principal's Application of Transformational Leadership Strategies"	Christine L. Kramp Pfaff	Interpretive Pragmatic	*Qualitative* Ethnographic Case Study Interviews Survey	School culture Implementation of transformational leadership strategies
CH 8	"Is There a Model for Success? Exploring Sustainable Professional Employment among Clinical Exercise Physiology Program's Graduates"	Regina Schurman	Interpretive Pragmatic	*Qualitative* Grounded Theory (Glaser) Interviews Documents	Model of Sustainable Professional Employment
CH 9	"The Impact of Cognitive Information Processing on the First-Year College Student's Career Decision Making"	Anne Perry and Nancy W. Bentley	Empirical-Analytic Pragmatic	*Qualitative* Experimental Career Thoughts Inventory	Cognitive Information Processing Theory
CH 10	"Greek Parents' Perceptions and Experiences Regarding Their Children's Learning and Social-Emotional Difficulties"	Eirini Adamopoulou	Empirical-Analytic Pragmatic	*Qualitative* Survey Design Test of Psychological Adaptation Parent Survey	Ecological Perspective Learning and social-emotional difficulties (elementary level) International perspective (Greece)
CH 11	"Successful Practices and Models of Enrollment Management in Illinois Community Colleges: An Explanatory Mixed-Methods Case Study"	Andrea Lehmacher	Pragmatic Empirical-Analytic Interpretive	*Mixed Methods* *Quantitative:* Strategic Enrollment Management Health Assessment Survey *Qualitative:* Interviews	Open systems theory Models of collaborative enrollment management and marketing strategies in community colleges
CH 12	"Paradigmatic Consciousness Raising: What Moves Me"	Krista Robinson-Lyles	Critical Interpretive	*Qualitative* Phenomenological analysis Hermeneutics Interviews	Critical Theory Critical Pedagogy Praxis of Critical Democratic Education

Table 3.2 cont.

CHAPTER NO.	TITLE	AUTHOR(S)	PARADIGMS	METHODOLOGIES/METHODS	
				DESIGNS INSTRUMENTS	THEORIES PERSPECTIVES MODELS
CH 13	"Culling Methodological Tools, Honing Research Skills: A Paradigm of Critical Discourse Analysis on Neoliberalism"	Baudelaire K. Ulysse	Critical Interpretive	*Qualitative* Critical Discourse Analysis	Neoliberalism Critical Theory Critical Pedagogy
CH 14	"Locked Gates and Chain-Link Fences: A Generational Phenomenological Story of Disability"	Sharon Duncan	Critical Interpretive	*Qualitative* Phenomenological analysis Interviews Documents	Critical Theory Disability Studies Hermeneutic Phenomenology

focusing on how specific types of knowledge, theories, and theoretical orientations are linked directly with the steps of the research process.

For instance, several authors developed their studies within the empirical-analytic system of inquiry. In chapter 9, Anne Perry and Nancy Bentley explore the impact of the cognitive information processing approach (CIP) for career problem solving and decision making on first-year college students enrolled in freshman level core-college courses at an open enrollment, career-oriented, regionally accredited Midwestern proprietary university. In agreement with an experimental quantitative design, they proposed a hypothesis that the Career Thoughts Inventory (CTI) scores for subjects who complete the workbook intervention will be lower than for those who do not. The hypothesis was tested through utilization of the intervention strategy. Accordingly, the researches randomly assigned students to a control or experimental group, grounded their study in the principles of cognitive therapy as it applies to problem solving and decision making, and conducted the experiment. The results supported their assumptions regarding student perceptions about career planning as measured through the CTI.

In chapter 10, Eirini Adamopoulou's study employed a nonexperimental, descriptive survey design. Her intent was to describe a specific phenomenon: Greek parents' perceptions and experiences about their children's learning and social-emotional challenges in elementary school. Her survey included a large sample of parents who reside in different areas of Greece. In addition to the survey, she used the Test of Psychosocial Adaptation where parents rated their children's social-emotional learning functioning. The study was guided by Bronfenbrenner's ecological systems theory. Using the ecological perspective, she explored the impact of Greek society's limiting factors, constraints and opportunities, and the general environment. The large data sets, the multiple perspectives, and the statistical measures provided a wealth of information that enabled Adamopoulou to gain a depth of knowledge that informs and yet remains fallible and subject to further improvement.

Andrea Lehmacher, in chapter 11, employed mixed-methods design to explore the enrollment practices at two Illinois community colleges and the factors that contributed to or impeded the overall enrollment management process. Open systems theory was used as a framework to guide her thinking about the appropriate methodological approach that she would employ. The research process began with collecting quantitative data via the SEM Health Assessment survey. The results of the quantitative analysis provided statistical evidence that supported and, in some cases, refuted her assumptions regarding the impact of certain core values on successful enrollment management processes. Subsequently, she utilized qualitative semi-structured interviews to triangulate data and add credibility to her research study.

All three of the aforementioned projects were pragmatic in their underlying purposes, although their implementation was carried on within different theoretical frameworks and methods (table 3.2). Figure 3.1 points to conceptual connections between the six paradigms identified in this book. It is fairly common for actual research projects to be conceptualized within closely connected paradigms in terms of research purposes or designs. The pragmatic paradigm holds a worldview "that focuses on the outcomes of research, that include the actions, situations, and consequences of inquiry" (Creswell, 2012, p. 22). Pragmatism is an exceedingly practical and applied research philosophy (Creswell, 2003). The pragmatic worldview incorporates multiple methods that would best answer the research questions, utilize quantitative, qualitative, or mixed methods for collecting data, address practical applications of ideas, and emphasize the importance of the research problem as the context for conducting the research (see tables 3.1 and 3.2). In recent years, mixed-methods research has gained relative popularity because its purpose is to reach convergent validity or a stronger warranted assertion. Johnson and Onwuegbuzie (2004), for instance, provide a compelling position regarding the role of mixed-methods research and the need to promote the importance of the pragmatic viewpoint as researchers strive to inform practice with a perspective that reflects inductive and deductive approaches.

The pragmatic paradigm is the overarching framework shaping Regina Schurman's research in chapter 8. Schurman selected a grounded theory design for her study because she saw the need for a broad theory or explanation for her particular inquiry. The study reflects qualitative grounded theory and is firmly positioned within the pragmatic tradition. Pragmatism, which reflects Peirce's process of inquiry (abduction, deduction, and reduction), parallels the process Schurman utilized as she wrestled with her research inquiry. The grounded theory design fits her research purposes and questions and is sensitive to the individuals in her setting.

Schurman used semi-structured and unstructured interviews with the participants who had graduated from the clinical exercise physiology program. She stayed close to the data in this design by continually analyzing one set of responses that led to an analysis of the next set. Schurman appropriated the Glaserian version of grounded theory that was best aligned with her research purposes to address the employment challenges faced by graduates of clinical exercise physiology programs. Her study resulted in a model of sustainable professional employment that captures the processes that guide graduates to management positions in healthcare systems.

Several chapters in part 2 present studies conducted within the traditions of interpretive and critical research: hermeneutics, ethnography, autoethnography, phenomenology, case study, and critical discourse analysis (see table 3.2). Vladimir Trostin's research in chapter 4, for instance, was guided by the principles of autoethnography, which he has applied throughout his work as he describes his life story and the factors that have influenced his personal identity. Researchers using this approach attempt to create a more authentic or introspective account of self. Autoethnographers believe that all knowledge is grounded in subjective experience (deMarais & Lapan, 2004); thus they attempt to provide as much information as possible about themselves in their role as reporter of the research, since they are the focus of the study. Because the focus is on the researcher, others in the field appear to have a secondary or distant connection to the researcher. The field serves as the milieu for the self-reporter. Often, subjective researchers, while in the process of studying themselves, share critical events in their lives, personal tragedies, and professional accomplishments. These researchers are passionate about generating new knowledge through their self-disclosures and honest accounts of their personal experiences. One of the challenges with ethnography is establishing the credibility of the approach and its ability to establish "standards of truth" (deMarrais & Lapan, 2004, p. 177), which can be achieved through rich descriptions and we see evidenced in Trostin's work.

In chapter 5, Matthew Woolsey selected an ethnographic approach as a framework to shape his exploration of first-generation Asian Indian leaders because it directly addresses his intent to discover how individuals in different cultures and subcultures respond to and make sense of their lived experiences (see table 3.2). Ethnography is an effective way to understand social reality by directly observing behaviors and interacting with others within the research setting. Woolsey specifically wanted to know which salient features in their backgrounds enabled and nurtured their viability both in India and in the United States especially. He was also interested in identifying the key motivators that influenced Asian Indian expatriate college and university leaders to pursue higher education leadership positions in the United States.

Woolsey actively pursued data to inform his inquiry. He spent hours observing participants, maintaining field notes and reflections, using thick descriptions to establish credibility and capture behavioral nuances, and studying signs in the language (semiotics) that reflect a "stratified hierarchy of meaning structures" (Bogdan & Biklen, 2007, p. 30). He made every effort to become part of the culture in order to gain the trust and the respect of his participants and, moreover, to be able to "understand" what is communicated verbally and silently because he possesses "the insider's view" (Bogdan & Biklen, p. 31) and now has acquired shared meaning.

Christine Kramp Pfaff, in chapter 7, developed an ethnographic case study that addressed an elementary school principal's plan to incorporate transformational leadership in her school in an effort to enhance her leadership capabilities, expand teachers' instructional skills, and establish a more professional school culture, all with a focus on student improvement. Her research was guided by her intent to identify transformational leadership qualities that could affect change in her own leadership style, improve teaching effectiveness, and build a positive and forward thinking school culture (see table 3.2). Her study was grounded in transformational leadership theory. Kramp Pfaff used a case study approach to plan her process for improving the school culture, which is an indication that her research had pragmatic ends to it. Similar to Woolsey, she used an ethnographic approach as a framework to guide her data collection process, which included field notes that reflected the participants' perceptions of the cultural change process introduced. She supplemented this information with semi-structured interviews of four participants and substantiated her findings by triangulating her data.

Maria E. Hernandez-Rodriguez's research in chapter 6 is situated in a hermeneutic tradition, which is about searching for a deep understanding by interpreting the meaning that actions and interactions have for individuals. We can only understand social reality from the individuals immersed in it (Hesse-Biber & Leavy, 2011). Hernandez-Rodriguez applies this hermeneutic approach in her study as she relates the journey of her Hispanic parents and the challenges they faced raising and educating their children. She crafts a detailed account of her parents' experiences by providing a micro reality of Hispanic parenthood and its meaning. Her research questions focus on parent's preparation of their children for education, their conceptions of their roles in and responsibilities for their child's education, and the role and responsibility of the school relative to preparing parents for the education process. Hernandez-Rodriguez used observation and interviews to collect data to support and inform her interpretation of these experiences. The dialogues are captured in a hermeneutic circle, which creates a dynamic dialogue for understanding and taking this understanding to the next level (see table 3.2).

The critical paradigm has gained special dominance, drawing from the politically transformative events of the Civil Rights and counterculture movements. The political and philosophical ideas and events reflective of this paradigm's epistemological and philosophical underpinnings have given rise to such forms of educational inquiry as feminism, critical race, ethnicity, and queer theories; disability studies; critical discourse and semiotic analyses; and postmodern and poststructuralist inquiries. Critical inquiries are strongly aligned with the interpretive tradition, and this is evidenced in the works of Krista Robinson-Lyles in chapter 12, Baudelaire K. Ulysse in chapter 13, and Sharon Duncan in chapter 14.

Robinson-Lyles, for instance, introduces her study with reflection on the state of educational practices based on her experiences as a mother and teacher-educator. This reflection sets the stage for her research inquiry. Her inquiry is grounded in social phenomenology and critical hermeneutics and it is this methodological perspective that shapes her assumptions about which factors create awareness and promote transformation (see table 3.2). She uses narrative as the tool for collecting data and incorporates a process of storying, restorying, and restorying again in an effort to uncover participants' assumptions and perceived practices relative to her research intent. Robinson-Lyles elected to add herself as a participant, which she justified on the grounds that her personal narrative would add value to her overall inquiry and research expectations. As a result of her data analysis, she identified three emergent and recurring themes with accompanying subthemes. She concluded that transforming current thinking toward conscientization requires ongoing reflection, questions, and moments of discord, where current assumptions can be challenged and reframed, thus allowing for established mental models to be reconsidered in light of new and convincing perspectives. A significant result for Robinson-Lyles is that she herself experienced a sense of transformation as she carefully prepared a process for teaching teachers how to inform and transform their students.

Baudelaire K. Ulysse employs critical discourse analysis (CDA) that reflects a number of theories, sampling procedures, and analytic frameworks (Pascale, 2011) to explore his overarching research question: How is the current engine of economic globalization, or the global economy, being propelled by neoliberalism as the dominant discourse? Ulysse is committed to fair-mindedness, freedom of academic practice, and a genuine interest in the human condition, and his passionate commitments drive his thinking and actions. His analysis of the discourse of neoliberalism is informed primarily by the critical theory perspective. Through the use of CDA, and the process inherent within the tool, he has been able to dissect and decipher these texts and resources, determine the underlying messages associated with neoliberalism, and discuss these findings within the context of his research intent. Ulysse's study is a compelling case of the potential of unobtrusive methods of analysis (Hesse-Biber & Leavy, 2011).

Duncan's research is done in the intersections of phenomenology and critical inquiry into disability studies (see table 3.2). Her overall intent is to raise awareness of the lived experiences of individuals with disabilities and the impact these experiences have on their families. As Duncan shares the lived experiences of her participants, she inserts specific connections between the story and the research intent. Her purpose is to identify key themes that ground the phenomenology of disability in specific critical intentionalities as portrayed through the participants' experiences. Duncan reaches her ultimate research purpose as she elevates the level of readers' awareness so that able and disabled can meet at the fence and open the gate.

The above projects, rendered through the context of major theoretical frameworks of educational inquiry, provide ample opportunities for novice researchers to enhance their skills of data analysis, inferring meaning from individual lived experiences, creating theoretical models to improve practice, and emancipating consciousness to fight for social justice, and along the way, to learn to position research projects within appropriate paradigms. Journeying through a variety of research exemplars and paradigms inevitably leads to broadening one's horizons in terms of epistemological and methodological pluralism.

Paradigms of Research: Mapping the Final Journey

British philosopher, mathematician, and educator Bertrand Russell (1872–1970) believed that the value of philosophy can be found in the effects upon those who study it. Many philosophers have attempted to provide definite answers to the fundamental questions concerning the nature of the universe and human being without much success. The value of philosophy, therefore, should be sought in its very uncertainty. Philosophy has its chief value "through the greatness of the objects which it contemplates, and the freedom from narrow and personal aims resulting from this contemplation" (Russell, 1993, p. 4). It has to be studied

> not for the sake of any definite answers to its questions, since no defined answers can, as a rule, be known to be true, but rather for the sake of the questions themselves; because these questions enlarge our conception of what is possible, enrich our intellectual imagination and diminish the dogmatic assurance which closes the mind against speculation; but above all because, through the greatness of the universe which philosophy contemplates, the mind also is rendered great, and becomes capable of that union with the universe which constitutes its highest good. (p. 5)

Collingwood (2005) is critical of the excesses of the modern utilitarian mentality that suppresses emotions and ridicules superstitious beliefs in the irrational. He appeals instead to the intuitive and imaginative powers of our primordial being. Bachelard (2005) echoes in turn by exclaiming that when imagination works, everything works!

Figure 3.2: Paradigms of Research: Mapping the Final Journey

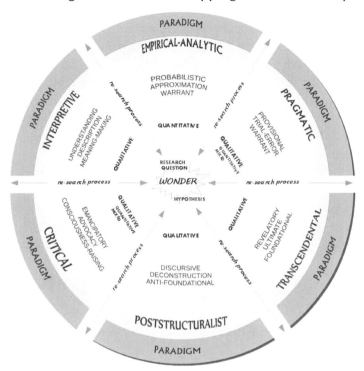

Educational researchers pride themselves on implementing the projects that serve practical purposes and solve daily human problems. Yet they also conceive of the value of educational inquiry in posing the questions that enlarge our conception of what is possible and what enriches our intellectual and social imaginations. Imagination is the gateway into the known and the unknown, the mysterious spark that instigates our thinking and desire to pursue daring projects. Imaginative thinking frees us from the constraints of prescriptive rules and standards that dictate how to conduct research projects. Like philosophy, research begins in wonder. Wondering and imagination take precedent over calculation and precision in launching successful and gratifying inquiries, and those of us who have ever experienced this, know *for sure* that it is true. Figure 3.2 has *wonder* as its heart center. Emanating from wonder are research questions, hypotheses, methods, epistemologies, theoretical frameworks—all the ingredients of the research process that are informed by the six paradigms. Figure 3.2 captures the image of the paradigm tapestry as a multiparadigmatic and holistic representation. Each of the six paradigms envelopes corresponding epistemological assumptions and major research designs. Intersecting the cells of the paradigms are the passages with the inscription "re-search process,"

which intends to convey the idea that the research process is informed from the beginning to end by specific paradigms and that it is circular in nature. Its circular nature is explicated in the word itself: re-search, meaning searching all over again. It implies that our knowledge of the world and human phenomena is never complete. The end of any research process, no matter how strongly it can be grounded in foundational knowledge, signifies a new question emerging from the results, and thus the process continues. Open spaces between the paradigms on the outer circle connote the holes in our knowledge and infinite possibilities of its pursuit through multidimensional and diverse paradigmatic research processes. The circle is never complete and the re-search process remains open.

Our paradigm journey ends on the pages of this chapter. It is final, but not complete or finite. We have endeavored this quest out of the desire to broaden our conception of what is possible in educational inquiry and to enlarge our intellectual imagination of it. We are grateful to the readers who joined in along the way. The search for truth begins with wonder at its heart center and continues as we speak.

References

Anfara, V. A., Jr., & Mertz, N. T. (Eds.). (2006). *Theoretical frameworks of qualitative research.* Thousand Oaks, CA: Sage.

Bachelard, G. (2005). *On poetic imagination and reverie* (C. Gaudin, Trans.). Putnam, CT: Spring.

Bogdan, R. C., & Biklen, S. K. (2007). *Qualitative research for education: An introduction to theory and methods* (5th ed.). Boston: Pearson.

Cohen, L., Manion, L., & Morrison, K. (2008). *Research methods in education* (6th ed.). New York: Routledge.

Collingwood, R. G. (2005). *The philosophy of enchantment: Studies in folklore, cultural criticism, and anthropology.* London: Oxford University Press.

Creswell, J. W. (2003). *Research designs: Qualitative, quantitative, and mixed methods approaches* (2nd ed.). Thousand Oaks, CA: Sage.

Creswell, J. W. (2012). *Educational research: Planning, conducting and evaluating quantitative and qualitative research* (4th ed.). Boston: Pearson.

Dantley, M. (2005). Faith-based leadership: ancient rhythms or new management. *International Journal of Qualitative Studies in Education, 18*(1), 3–19.

deMarrais, K., & Lapan, S. D. (Eds.). (2004). *Foundations for research: Methods of inquiry in education and social sciences.* Mahwah, NJ: Lawrence Erlbaum.

Habermas, J. (1972). *Knowledge and human interests* (J. J. Shapiro, Trans.). Boston: Beacon.

Hesser-Biber, S. N., & Leavy, P. (2011). *The practice of qualitative research* (2nd ed.). Los Angeles: Sage.

Howe, K. R. (2009). Epistemology, methodology, and education sciences: Positivist dogmas, rhetoric, and the education science question. *Educational Researcher, 38*(6), 428–440.

Johnson, R. B., & Onwuegbuzie, A. J. (2004). Mixed methods research: A research paradigm whose time has come. *Educational Researcher, 33*(7), 14–26.

Kipfer, B. A. (Ed.). (2010). *Roget's international thesaurus* (11th ed.). New York: Collins.

Lather, P. (2004). Critical inquiry in qualitative research: Feminist and poststructural perspectives: Science "after truth." In K. deMarrais & S. D. Lapan (Eds.), *Foundations for research: Methods of inquiry in education and social sciences* (pp. 203–215). Mahwah, NJ: Lawrence Erlbaum.

Lather, P. (2008). (Post)feminist methodology: Getting lost OR a scientificity we can bear to learn from. *International Review of Qualitative Research, 1*(1), 55–64.

Lemert, C. (1999). *Social theory: Multicultural & classic readings.* Boulder, CO: Westview.

McMillan, J. H. (2008). *Educational research: Fundamentals for the consumer* (5th ed.). Boston: Pearson.

Merriam, S. B., et al. (Ed.). (2002). *Qualitative research in practice: Examples for discussion and analysis.* San Francisco: Jossey-Bass.

Ozmon, H. A., & Craver, S. M. (2008). *Philosophical foundations of education* (8th ed.). Upper Saddle River, NJ: Merrill Prentice Hall.

Pascale, C.-M. (2011). *Cartographies of knowledge: Exploring qualitative epistemologies.* Los Angeles: Sage.

Polkinghorne, D. E. (1983). *Methodology for the human sciences: Systems of inquiry.* Albany: State University of New York Press.

Polkinghorne, D. E. (2004). *Practice and the human sciences: The case for a judgment-based practice of care.* New York: State University of New York Press.

Russell, B. (1993). The value of philosophy. In J. Perry & M. Bratman (Eds.), *Introduction to philosophy: Classical and contemporary readings* (pp. 2–5). New York: Oxford University Press.

Scruton, R. (1996). *Modern philosophy: An introduction and survey.* New York: Penguin.

St. Pierre, E. A., & Pillow, W. S. (Eds.). (2000). *Working the ruins: Feminist poststructural theory and methods in education.* New York: Routledge.

Stevenson, A., & Lindberg, C. A. (Eds.). (2010). *New Oxford American dictionary* (3rd ed.). New York: Oxford University Press.

Tisdell, E. J. (2000). Spirituality and emancipatory adult education in women adult educators for social change. *Adult Education Quarterly, 50*(4), 308–335.

Yu, C. H. (2006). *Philosophical foundations of quantitative research methodology.* Lanham, MD: University Press of America.

PART TWO

Paradigms as Educational Research Exemplars

The Passage beyond Self

An Autoethnographic Journey into My Cultural Roots, Personal and Educational Transformations

VLADIMIR TROSTIN

Contemplating the Inquiry

Inquiry into one's identity has been a preoccupation of people in many cultures and at different points in history. For William Shakespeare (1564–1616), life resembled a stage and the people were the actors decoding the moral motives of characters' behaviors and choices. I choose this metaphor to explain the variety of roles we are enacting during our lives. Feodor Dostoevsky (1821–1881), Anton Chekov (1860–1904), Leo Tolstoy (1828–1910), Carl Jung (1875–1961), and Erik Erikson (1902–1994), among other world-acclaimed writers, thinkers, and psychologists made efforts to penetrate the depths of human nature. They pondered the psyche of a human being and the dilemmas of society and the individual, mundane and metaphysical. The concept of self has been central to many psychoanalytic and social theories. To Erikson (1980), a person's identity formation is a lifelong developmental process. Identity is also shaped by the "nation, community, ethnicity, race, religion, gender, sexuality, and age" (Yon, 2000, p. 1). Yon conceives both self and culture as elusive phenomena. The two components—self and culture—exhibit the dynamic processes of tensions, contradictions, and mutual influences. Identity "takes shape as assumptions about sameness or difference between selves and communities" (Yon, p. 2).

Inspired by the thinkers of the past and present, I decided to embark on my own journey, anxious to access the hidden back roads of my psyche and to retrace the routes and byways I've taken thus far on my existential passage. This study situates my life story within the broader historical and sociocultural contexts of my life. The geographical locations—China, Russia, Kazakhstan, Latvia, and the United States—are not only the places of my childhood, adolescence, and adulthood, but more important, they are the diverse places where my identity has been shaped, challenged, tested, and tempered into the person that I am today. Mine is a multidimensional and multicultural story told on behalf of a "Chinese-of-Russian-origin-American." What does this mean, I wonder? What does it mean to be an educational professional who carries the baggage of such an identity? With these questions in mind, I contemplate the relevance of culture in the formation of my identity.

Identity, from my perspective, is an expression of self *and* others dyadic relations. An individual's identity is ultimately connected to a cultural group or groups within which one belongs. In the context of constantly changing historical and socioeconomic conditions, individuals participate in different social practices, and these practices in turn shape their identities (Pratt, 1994). Some scholars argue that preserving cultural identities and differences may become a divisive force in modern society, while others argue that multiculturalism and cosmopolitanism lead to shared citizenship (Gans, 2005).

Identity is an evolving process (Hall et al., 1992; Hall, 1996). Various contexts create various identities of possible selves and temporal commitments and interactions with others (Goossens, 2008). My life experiences, as they were, disclose the formation of my identity as evolving processes. Perhaps it was those diverse cultural processes that had the greatest impact on my identity formation through the years of my dwelling in different geographical locations of the world.

Culture appears to be a multidimensional growing crystal, symbolically representing our widening knowledge of the concept. It was my fascination with the study of culture and identity and their complex interrelations that eventually prompted me to pose the following research question within the tradition of autoethnography: *What are my paths of understanding, questioning, and moving beyond self toward a greater sense of personal and professional awareness and growth under changing and diverse sociocultural and political conditions?*

My Initiation into Autoethnography

My interest in autoethnography was sparked during the courses on qualitative research at National Louis University. The idea to make my life story central to the dissertation seemed both challenging and intriguing. At the time, I found myself strongly compelled to reflect on my life and to come to terms with who and what I was, as well as to rethink my personal and professional aspirations. I felt an urge to bring back the memories of the past, to analyze, to confess, to reconcile, to heal, to forgive, and to move ahead. While living in the former USSR, I was often restricted by the official ideology to express myself fully as an individual and as a professional. I followed the laws of the state and buried my unexpressed aspirations often for the sake of pure survival. Eventually, I left the USSR for the United States with the hope to fulfill my lifelong dreams.

Undertaking an autoethnographic study allowed me to explore the depths of the turning-point events in my life. I credit a lot of my knowledge of and passion for autoethnography to Carolyn Ellis. Carolyn deciphers the word ethnography into two parts: *ethno*, meaning people or culture, and *graphy*, meaning writing and describing. Ethnography is writing about people and culture. Ethnographers engage in a thorough research which, for the past few decades, signaled a shift from a more traditional scientific view on research to its interpretive counterpart. Interpretive research centers on individual lived experience and personal accounts as evidence for credibility and validity of studies in educational research. Carolyn affirms that stories are ways and means to make sense of the world.

Ellis (2004) argues that "stories should be both a subject and a method of science research" (p. 32). Autoethnography presumes that reality is socially constructed and that meaning is revealed through symbolic (language) interaction (Berger & Luckmann, 1966). Autoethnography is becoming the middle ground between social science and art where personal, cultural, societal, and political phenomena are intersecting with each other and being negotiated. In autoethnography, the author incorporates the "I" into research and writing, yet analyzes his- or herself as if studying an "other" (Ellis).

Autoethnography frees us to move beyond traditional methods of writing (Gergen & Gergen, 2002). The rigor of social science ethnography combined with the language arts is capable of evoking emotional response from the reader. "We all have our stories. We live by stories. We need stories to maintain our balance and our identity, and to express who we are" (Cleaver, 2002, p. 11).

The Making of Autoethnography
Positioning Autoethnography within the Interpretive Paradigm

In contrast to scientific research in natural sciences, interpretive or qualitative researchers "seek answers to questions of how social experience is created and given meaning" (Denzin & Lincoln, 2003, p. 5). Qualitative research in sociology and anthropology was born "out of concern to understand the 'other'" (Vidich & Lyman, 2003, p. 2). Ellis (2004), Bochner (2002), and Richardson (2000) propose the following characteristics of qualitative research: verisimilitude, emotionality, evocation, ethics, political praxis, multivoiced texts, and narration. Autoethnography occupies the middle ground on the continuum between social science and language arts (Ellis). The term *ethnography* has been in use for a long time. It is "the process and product of describing and interpreting cultural behavior" (Schwandt, 2001, p. 80). Despite little consensus on the precise definition of culture itself, there is general agreement among scholars that culture is central to ethnography.

In this study, I strive to reenact the story of my life through the many memories, testimonials, and historical documents I have collected over time. I do not fictionalize or embellish my story. I make an effort to preserve the accuracy and authenticity of the narrative, relying on documented accounts of events. Yet, I also exercise my right as a writer to be selective in my stories in order to highlight their most significant moments. Thus, documents, memoires, artifacts, retrospective, introspective and self-reflective accounts, testimonies, and countless journals kept over the years constitute the data for this research. My purpose is to weave all the sources of data into a holistic account. Memories create stories, and stories reinforce memories. Ellis (2004) uses the metaphor of lenses to describe the work of autoethnographers. Their wide-angle lenses focus outward on social and cultural aspects of the personal experience. Zooming inward exposes the vulnerable, intimate self. Zooming backward and forward, moving inward and outward, an autoethnographer creates a multidimensional representation of history, social structures, and cultures through lived events, experienced feelings, thoughts, and language.

Autoethnography as Storytelling

As a narrator of my stories, I am a liaison between the reader, the writer, and the way in which the writer filters the idea through the prism of his or her mind. Why do we tell stories? Why do we listen? Stories are connective tissue of the human race; they are "our prayers, parables, history, and our soul ... stories make us human" (Banaszynski, 2007, p. 5). Every story involves a subjective person slamming into an objective world. Understanding both the subjective and the objective are "crucial to our knowing what happens" (Franklin, 2007, p. 128). How can we indeed encompass in our minds the complexity of some lived moments in life? "You don't do that with theories. You don't do that with a system of ideas. You do it with a story" (Coles, 1989, p. 179). Mine are the stories intended as histories and prayers capturing the complexity of the moments of my soul-searching and transformations.

Personal Narrative

Wedded to autoethnography is personal narrative that belongs to the poetic space. Brady (2000) conceives of the autoethnographic narrative as the alloy of anthropology and literature, as the *heart-full science*, reflecting the beauty of the world's tragedy by carefully chosen constructions and subjective understandings of the author. The narrative of oneself involves looking back at the past through the lens of the present. Stories give a "measure of coherence and continuity that was not available at the original moment of experience" (Bochner, 2002, p. 263). The purpose of narratives is to "extract meaning from experience rather than to depict experience exactly as it was lived" (p. 263). Stories are existential. We narrate to make sense of experience in all its dimensions and with all possible meanings.

In narrating my stories, I strived for self-empowerment and the empowerment of others. Through the art of narrative and coming to terms with the past of my ancestors and with my own past, I gained strength to move forward and meet life's new challenges. Narrative thus served me as both the tools of research and empowerment. I have lived through many experiences that were meant to undermine my sense of identity. Regardless of the circumstance, I never allowed myself to compromise my integrity. The past is certainly something that I cannot change. My intentions regarding this personal narrative are to affirm what and who I am as a person and professional today and what I aspire for the future. I am on a quest to transform my *self* as a "mode of being" through the "existential struggle for honesty and expansion in an uncertain world" (Lopate, 1994, p. 37).

Writing as a Method of Inquiry

I write, therefore, I am … The process of writing personal stories becomes a method of inquiry about ourselves. My personal knowing and telling about the world, in the way that I perceive it, is highly subjective: language does not "reflect social reality, but produces meaning, creates this social reality" (Richardson & Lockridge, 2004, p. 500). Language is the place where our sense of self, our subjectivity, is constructed. Our experiences and memories are open for interpretations at different periods. In our stories, we re-create our lived experiences, and by attending to our feelings and contradictions, ambiguities and uncertainties, we evoke emotional responses.

New ways of writing require new criteria for evaluating autoethnographic studies. Out of a number of metaphors for qualitative research—choreography (Janesick, 1998), triangulation (Denzin, 1997), and crystallization (Richardson, 1994)—I appropriate Richardson's imagery. Crystallization reflects on many facets of the story: personal, cultural, social, political, and historic. When we accept the metaphor of a crystal, we move into a multidimensional representation and validation of our findings. The crystal "combines symmetry and substance with an infinite variety of shapes, substances, transmutations, multidimensionalities, and angles of approach. Crystals grow, change, and alter, but are not amorphous" (Richardson & Lockridge, 2004, p. 8). What I see when I look at crystals depends upon my angle of repose and how I expose them to the light. Crystals reflect as does my narrative.

LOOKING BACK—MOVING FORWARD: MY STORY

I was leaving my students, my work, my archives, my paintings. I locked the door of my house (I still remember that sound of a click), and off I went.

A Boeing 747 was carrying me to the West, toward blinding sun. Covered by an iron shield of white clouds, down over there on the earth, were left endless miles of lazily stretching sandy beaches of Jirmala (the Riga seaside), the icy-cold water of the Baltics (even in August), the smell of pine trees (their sap sticky like honey), the charming romance of the narrow, crooked streets of Old Riga—everybody and everything that constituted my existence in Latvia.

I was leaving my mom. I could not take her with me. The best doctors and my brother were taking care of her. I promised to bring you here. I did not keep my word. At that time when I was saying it, deep in my heart, I was not sure if it was possible. You wanted to stay at home. You did not want to be a burden. There was a smile on your face, the smile of a mom who didn't want to discourage her son and deprive him of his cherished childhood dreams. "God bless you. Take care of yourself," you said.

I came to America with a briefcase of papers and a bunch of yellowed photos of my family . . .

The Best and the Worst of Times . . .

The reminiscences of my early childhood are imprinted in my memory and viewed through the prism of my parents' recollections and reflect their world outlook. I was born in the city of Harbin in the northern part of Manchuria, China. Tucked among Mongolia, Siberia, and North Korea, it was a small settlement. The Chinese Eastern Railway (CER), as a shortcut through Northern China, reached Harbin in 1898 and turned the village into a boomtown; it linked the Trans-Siberian Railway to Vladivostok. My grandparents settled in China at the turn of the nineteenth century and belonged to the Russian colony in Harbin. The Russian–Japanese War (1905), the First World War (1914–1918), and the October Socialist Revolution of 1917 added great numbers of new residents to the city of the White Russian emigration—all those Russians who opposed the Bolsheviks after the October Revolution and did not accept the new social order.

The Harbin diaspora continued, until the 1960s, to be the cultural center of the Russian emigration. If Red Petrograd (St. Petersburg) became the forefront of the new Soviet culture, Harbin remained the cradle of a genuine Russian spirit, customs, and traditions (Bakich, 2002). It sheltered those who were ousted from their native countries. The outcasts saw Manchuria as a sanctuary and the land of opportunities. In the first half of the twentieth century, when chaos, the October Revolution, two World Wars, and the Soviet Red Terror raged in a troubled world, this land was an enclave of relative political tolerance, diversity, and pluralism (Bakich). Consequently, the survival instincts forced the Harbiners to develop acute political flexibility and adapt themselves to ever-changing regimes of the region. Czarist Russia, Nationalist China, Imperial Japan, Communist China, and Soviet Russia all exerted control over this strategic and resource-rich area at some time. In general, the frequently changing governments encouraged business activities. Most people arrived in China penniless and worked hard to build life in exile. Their efforts and industriousness paid off, and active people became prosperous.

After the turmoil of the Revolution in 1917, the *New* Russia (the Soviet Union) took the path of proletariat dictatorship that crushed religious, spiritual, and moral values as well as thousands of years of history and culture (Service, 2003). Red Russia was being constructed with the collectivization of agriculture, industrialization, planned socialist economic systems accompanied by political repressions of the opponents, internal genocide, labor camps, and hunger. My parents had the good fortune to be born and raised in another dimension. They lived in a Russian colony, often quite isolated and insulated from any outside influence, which allowed them to preserve their cultural identity. Many of those who had lived in Harbin, once known as "the little Paris of the East," recalled with nostalgia a privileged life with a whirl of events and cold winters that reminded them a lot of Russia (Williams, 1991). Orthodox churches were erected, synagogues were opened, and vibrant cultural life flourished. Genuine Old Russian customs and traditions were strictly observed, nurtured, and preserved for the next generations, thereby exercising and intensifying the influence of the Russian culture on the Far East as time went on.

In 1949, after the Chinese communists under Mao Zedong came to power, everything changed. Russian Harbiners were pushed out by an increasingly unfriendly communist government wary of what they called imperialist capitalists (Moustafine, 2002). Rapid controversial changes in life made it difficult for the Russian diaspora to continue living there. Russians started immigrating to America, Canada, South Africa, and Australia.

After the death of Joseph Stalin and with the removal of the Iron Curtain, the borders of the Soviet Union were open for repatriation. There was a huge exodus of Harbin Russians throughout the early 1950s. Our family returned to the Soviet Union in 1954. My parents used to say that it was the call of the ancestors who had left China for Russia in 1936 that inflamed the desire for the family reunion. Yet, great personal losses awaited them. Their parents (my grandparents) and my uncle were promptly arrested and shot by the NKVD (Stalin's secret police), because they were suspected of being Japanese agents and participating in a Harbin-based spy ring.

When my parents stepped onto the soil of their ancestors, they found themselves being more "Russian" than the native Russians; they truly believed that the Russian diaspora abroad had preserved true Russian culture that, according to them, was essentially eradicated during the years of the Soviet regime. From a distance of immigration, my parents thought of Russia as a Holy Land. However, on their return, the Soviet Union appeared to be intolerably harsh and hostile to them. With their very first steps, as the family crossed the border of the USSR, their struggle for physical and economic survival began and lasted until their final breath. The image of the Soviet Holy Land evaporated like a mist. The Motherland of their dreams did not exist and they suffered emotionally, morally, and physically from the loss of the mirage they had created for themselves, lived in for many years, and prayed for.

My parents returned to the Soviet Union and discovered themselves being out of place and without a sense of time. They did not accept the socialist system. Russia was slowly recovering from Stalin's dictatorship, launched the first Sputnik, initiated the first manned space flight of Yuri Gagarin, and was entering the era of the Cold War.

The Soviet Union became my home country for several decades. Having experienced the life of a displaced person in the Kazakh steppe, I started my official schooling in the town of Kurgan, the place of Russian political exiles and convicts in Siberia and the center of the Soviet defense industry evacuated behind the Ural Mountains at the time of WWII (1941–1945) (the only place we were ever allowed to settle as nonreliable, untrusted, and alien foreign elements).

The 1960s found my family in the far west of the Soviet Union, in Latvia. Being occupied by Soviet troops as a result of the redivision of Europe between Stalin and Hitler in 1939, the Baltic republics—in spite of all the destruction brought by the Second World War—maintained their Western attractiveness for the Soviet people (Lieven, 1993; Service, 2003). At that time, it was extremely difficult, if not impossible, for the Soviet people to travel abroad, but they could travel to the Baltic Sea and the Baltic republics. Latvia, Estonia, and Lithuania (known as the Baltic republics of the former USSR) remotely resembled the West.

My parents moved to Latvia because they thought that it was the only place in the Soviet Union where they felt as if they could continue living like they did in Harbin. Russians constituted half of the Latvian population, so for my parents it felt like living in a "colony" again. Appreciating and sharing relatively high levels of culture and living standards in Latvia, we still found ourselves being aliens among aliens. The majority of Russians in Latvia perceived that they were treated like invaders and occupiers; a hostile attitude to everything that was Russian or connected with Russia had been displayed at all levels. In the Baltic republics, the bloody Red Purges of 1939 (occupation by the Russian troops with their political persecutions, executions, and the resettlement of almost a third of Latvia's residents) conducted by Stalin's order, caused irreparable and long-lasting hostile attitudes from the local population. Residing in Latvia, I sensed with all the fibers of my soul as if I was living on barrels of gunpowder; the time was ticking for this arsenal to explode, and it did.

In 1991, the Republic of Latvia separated from the Soviet Union and became an independent state. History made another turn on its spiral and the time for the Russians' departure arrived. Having received the status of political asylum, I moved my family to America in order to fulfill my family's dreams.

As I trace the memories of my life journey, I ask myself all over again: Who and what am I? Clearly, my personal identity is ultimately connected with the many facets of my cultural identifications. Yet, "culture is not simply a naturally occurring phenomenon, but it is a situation within and shaped by systems of political economy" (Yon, 2000, p. 9). The cultures, the socioeconomic and educational systems of Russia, China, the Soviet Union, Latvia, and the United States have been shaping, to a lesser or larger degree, my personal and professional identities.

My immigrant life is a unique track record of an émigré. My overall immigrant experiences did not signify feelings of loss, alienation, or confusion, and—in the end—were very positive. I have never been forced to "melt" into any specific culture, neither have I been forced to abandon my faith, values, and beliefs. For most people, immigration is a period of great stress. It is not easy to start life anew. However, it is much easier to adjust to new countries and situations when these changes are the result of one's own volition, as it was in my case. I chose to make a change in my life voluntarily and did it enthusiastically. I felt challenged in a good way by new opportunities. Most immigrants would not have decided to leave their lands if it were not for the extreme hardships experienced in their home countries. I left Latvia to escape chauvinistic nationalism against Russians and my own family. Economic reasons played an important role in my decision as well. Since that time, I have not had a single regret about the sacrifices I made for the sake of my family's and my own future.

As I look back at the years of my immigrant odyssey, I become more conscious of all the changes that occurred on the way, not only in terms of events but more so in terms of my growth as a person and an educational professional. Our global times are characterized by mobility and migrations. Mobility has become a part of the human condition in the contemporary world. The conceptualization of it is taking place not only in a changed spatial location, but it is occurring in shifted sociocultural and political contexts as well. In many ways, my life story is a testimony to these trends.

What Can I Share with Others?

Engaging in this autoethnographic study brought about many revelations, one of which was a deep realization that I have been reflexive throughout my career in education. For me, teaching has always been a very dynamic process. A lesson plan has never been scripted in its entirety and rarely has gone the way it was originally planned. As a teacher, the work of delivering academic material is more often than not intuitive.

Educators are accustomed to constantly monitoring themselves as every step of the teaching process unfolds. This ability becomes a natural habit after many years of teaching experience. While engaged in instruction, self-feedback instantaneously allows the teacher to make adjustments in response to the many factors at play and constantly changing situations. I noticed that while teaching, I exist in two dimensions: that of the teacher and that of the self-reflecting evaluator, who is permanently present in my classroom being aware of himself and others. My mind is constantly downloading information, overseeing the possibilities, and envisioning desirable results. When teaching, I am using not only feedback but also *feedforward*. The word *feedforward* was coined by Nagata (2005) to emphasize the importance of possible predictable assumptions. This entails looking ahead, self-reflecting, envisioning the final result, and averting any negative consequences that might occur. The process evokes reflexivity—a kind of *perpetum mobile* in teaching, self-observing, professional development, self-learning, and growth.

Having studied the teaching philosophies of two Russian pedagogues, Makarenko (1888–1939) and Sukhomlinsky (1918–1970), I believe that an educator exemplifies both the teacher and the "parent," in the sense of taking a full responsibility for nurturing and producing a "whole person" instead of a student as the "other." I see my task as an educator as that of striving to develop in students the joy of studying and working, thus laying the foundation for a lifelong desire to learn, to self-educate, and to grow. Interestingly, many of Makarenko's and Sukhomlinsky' ideas echo educational dispositions of Dewey (1859–1952).

Every morning I recite the Pledge of Allegiance with my students. Regardless the controversies surrounding the pledge, I ponder the importance of faith in our lives and the role that it can play in educating and leading others. I often say to myself, "God bless America," because I have faith in this country, in my future, and the future of America's children. My personal faith has sustained me throughout the many hardships and trials of my refugee, migrant, and immigrant experiences. I do not advocate for or privilege any specific religion or ideology. Yet, I strongly believe that most people need some version of faith to sustain their lives. I am also a strong believer in the principle of "walking the walk."

Faith gives us confidence and strength to move forward and create, hopefully, a better world. I am an optimist who has all the grounds, based on his lived experiences, to believe in the redemptive and constructive power of human beings to do the great things in this world. Faith inevitably entails hope, and hope is "grounded in the reality of faith"; it is the "essential ingredient necessary for hope to flourish.

Faith legitimizes hope. Faith gives courage for hope" (Dantley, 2005, p. 12). As an educator, I strongly believe that democracy, justice, and equity can bring a new hope in educational leadership. For students and teachers, the process of pursuing knowledge is never finished or complete. The learning community is always growing, evolving, and changing. The process of change starts with the visionary leader. Motivated by faith, the leader reflects on existing practices and makes decisions about change. From the very first steps, the visionary leader embraces the possibility of struggle. A leader who operates by faith "hopes through dialogue and problem posing for the learning community … to bring about a change" (Dantley, p. 15). The role of an educational leader, in my opinion, is in the transformation of learning communities through faith, regardless of its spiritual or secular nature.

An introspective journey into my life through this autoethnographic study has given me a greater sense of who I am and has led me to embrace my cultural roots and to reflect on my personal and professional transformations. My immigrant experience has tempered the resilience with which I walk my walk. The skills, attitudes, and behaviors that I acquired through life lessons have afforded me with the strength of character on which I can rely in the future chapters of my life journey. The most precious gift in my professional life comes from giving my best every day and trusting that I will somehow make an impact by empowering at least one student in my class to develop love for learning, a true sense of self, and the purpose of living a full and rewarding life.

Bibliography

Bakich, O. M. (2002). *Harbin Russian imprints: Bibliography as history, 1898–1961: Materials for a definitive bibliography*. New York: Norman Ross.

Banaszynski, J. (2007). Stories matter. In M. Kramer & W. Call (Eds.), *Telling true stories, a nonfiction writer's guide* (pp. 3–6). London: Penguin.

Berger, P., & Luckmann, T. (1966). *The social construction of reality*. Garden City, NY: Doubleday.

Bochner, A. P. (2002). Criteria against ourselves. In N. Denzin & Y. Lincoln (Eds.), *The qualitative inquiry reader* (2nd ed., pp. 257–265). Thousand Oaks, CA: Sage.

Brady, I. (2000). Anthropological poetics. In N. Denzin & Y. Lincoln (Eds.), *Handbook of qualitative research* (2nd ed., pp. 949–980). Thousand Oaks, CA: Sage.

Cleaver, J. (2002). *Immediate fiction: A complete writing course*. New York: St. Martin's.

Coles, R. (1989). *The call of stories: Teaching and the moral imagination*. Boston: Houghton Mifflin.

Dantley, M. (2005). Faith-based leadership: Ancient rhythms or new management. *International Journal of Qualitative Studies in Education, 18*(1), 3–19.

Denzin, N. K. (1997). *Interpretive ethnography: Ethnographic practices for the 21st century*. Thousand Oaks, CA: Sage.

Denzin, N. K., & Lincoln, Y. S. (Eds.). (2003). *Collecting and interpreting qualitative materials*. Thousand Oaks, CA: Sage.

Ellis, C. (2004). *The ethnographic I: A methodological novel about autoethnography.* Walnut Creek, CA: AltaMira.

Erickson, E. H. (1980). *Identity and the life cycle.* New York: W. W. Norton.

Franklin, J. (2007). The psychological interview. In M. Kramer & W. Louise (Eds.), *Telling true stories: A nonfiction writers' guide from the Nieman Foundation at Harvard University.* New York: Plume.

Gans, C. (2005). *The limits of nationalism.* Cambridge, UK: Cambridge University Press.

Gergen, M., & Gergen, K. (2002). Ethnographic representation as relationship. In A. Bochner & C. Ellis (Eds.), *Ethnographically speaking: Autoethnography, literature, and aesthetics* (pp. 11–33). Walnut Creek, CA: AltaMira.

Goossens, L. (2008). Dynamics of perceived parenting and identity formation in late adolescence. *Journal of Adolescence, 31*(2), 165–184.

Hall, S. (1996). Cultural identity and diaspora. In J. Rutherford (Ed.), *Identity: Community, culture, difference* (pp. 222–237). London: Lawrence & Wishart.

Hall, S., Held, D., & McGrew, T. (Eds.). (1992). *Modernity and its futures.* Cambridge, MA: Polity Press in association with Open University.

Janesick, V. (1998). *Stretching exercises for qualitative researchers.* Thousand Oaks, CA: Sage.

Lieven, A. (1993). *The Baltic revolution: Estonia, Latvia, Lithuania, and the path to independence.* Rayleigh, UK: Baskerville by SX Composing.

Lopate, P. (1994). *The art of the personal essay: An anthology of the form, from Seneca and Plutarch to present.* New York: Doubleday.

Moustafine, M. (2002). *Secrets and spies: The Harbin files.* Sydney, Australia: Vintage.

Nagata, A. L. (2005). Promoting self-reflexivity in intercultural education. *Journal of Intercultural Communication, 8,* 139–167.

Pratt, M. L. (1994). Transculturation and autoethnography: Peru 1615/1980. In F. Barker, P. Holme, & M. Iverson (Eds.), *Colonial discourse/postcolonial theory* (pp. 24–46). Manchester, UK: Manchester University Press.

Richardson, L. (1994). Nine poems: Marriage and the family. *Journal of Contemporary Ethnography, 23,* 3–14.

Richardson, L. (2000). Writing: A method of inquiry. In N. Denzin & Y. Lincoln (Eds.), *Handbook of qualitative research* (pp. 923–948). Thousand Oaks, CA: Sage.

Richardson, L., & Lockridge, E. (2004). *Travels with Ernest.* Walnut Creek, CA: Sage.

Schwandt, T. A. (2001). *Dictionary of qualitative inquiry.* Thousand Oaks, CA: Sage.

Service, R. (2003). *Russia: Experiment with a people.* London: Macmillan.

Vidich, A. J., & Lyman, S. M. (2003). Qualitative methods: Their history in sociology and anthropology. In N. K. Denzin & Y. S. Lincoln (Eds.), *Handbook on qualitative research* (2nd ed., pp. 37–84). Thousand Oaks, CA: Sage.

Williams, P. J. (1991). *The alchemy of race and rights: Diary of a law professor.* Cambridge, MA: Harvard University Press.

Yon, D. A. (2000). *Elusive culture: Schooling, race, and identity in global times.* New York: State University of New York Press.

CHAPTER FIVE

Sociocultural Perspectives of First-Generation Asian Indian Leaders in U.S. Higher Education

An Ethnographic Study

MATTHEW A. WOOLSEY

> What do I think of Western civilization? I think it would be a very good idea. In truth there are as many religions as there are individuals. (Suri, 2011)
>
> —MOHANDAS GANDHI

I have a nomadic spirit, an indelible curiosity to discover other walks of life unlike my own. Living to learn in another part of the state, country, and world has formed who I am today. Of these influences, none had a more profound impact on my life than the time I spent in India immersing myself in its culture. The people, aromas, food variations, music, religious festivals, chaotic but organized traffic, colors, elephants in the streets, and so much more triggered an indescribable passion within me to learn more. Subsequently, my India persuasion led me to this academic juncture of exploring the individual perspectives of Asian Indians in their interpretive journey that brought them to serve as leaders in what to them was a foreign country—the United States of America. While I have a desire and appetite to discover the ways of life of peoples in lands unlike mine, I wonder whether Asian Indians have the same compulsion with regard to the United States, with, moreover, a drive to become a leader.

What you think you become. (Suri, 2011)

—MOHANDAS GANDHI

Background of the Study

A striking feature of U.S. higher education is the high participation rate of Asian Americans as professionals in that employment sector. As of 2010, Asian American Pacific Islanders made up 7.2% of the total faculty population inclusive of Asian Indians (National Commission on Asian American and Pacific Islander Research in Education, 2010, p. 11). In terms of Asian Indians employed in U.S. higher education, there are more than 5,000 serving as faculty in U.S. post-secondary institutions (U.S. Census Bureau, 2004). With all this effort to attract Asian Indians to U.S. colleges and universities, less than 1% of all institutional presidents are of Indian descent (Yamagata-Noji, 2011). Why is this the case? And, for those Asian Indians who made it to higher education leadership roles, what were the contributing factors? What might the implications of these factors be for other Asian Indians who may aspire to similar positions of leadership?

Taking the Leap

History shows waves of Indian diaspora over time steadily manifesting into sizeable populations across the United States with recent reports of nearly three million Asian Indians in the country (U.S. Census, 2010). Indians who make the conscious decision to fully embrace the American way of life still find some link to their cultural roots (Kakar, 2007). As I reflect on my own experiences working in India as a team leader and trainer, I find it necessary to delve into the cultural nuances of Indian culture if I expect to achieve any level of success. In essence, making this cross-cultural leap requires recognition and effort to learn cultural norms and mores (Hofstede, 2001), incorporate a genuine willingness to learn the unspoken (tacit) culture (Li & Scullion, 2010), and embrace leadership competencies on both local and global dimensions (Cohen, 2007). What does this cross-cultural leap look like for Asian Indians coming to the United States?

Research Purposes and Questions

The study of leadership within the context of U.S. higher education covers the gamut from trait, contingency, and behavioral theories to modern frameworks, including transformational, collaborative, and social constructivism. Particular to Asian Indians in higher education, the bulk of research focuses on the influx of

Asian Indian students, and where focus on leaders does occur, studies tend to aggregate all Asians with Caucasian or Other designations (Teranishi, Behringer, Grey, & Parker, 2009). In fact, Museus states, "Asian Americans in the field of higher education … have been relatively excluded from higher education research and discourse" (Museus & Chang, 2009, p. 95).

The purpose of this study is to acquire an in-depth understanding of a complex world of sociocultural influences and interactions in which Indian expatriates pursue positions of leadership in U.S. higher education. I seek to answer the question: How do Indian expatriates view their highest professional attainments in U.S. higher education from their sociocultural perspectives? In an effort to unpack this main question, I am led to the following questions.

- What are the defining features of the Indian expatriates' backgrounds that sustain their *shakti* (life force) in India and especially in the United States?
- What ultimately motivates them to pursue higher education positions of leadership in the United States?

Leadership Inquiry into Asian Indians in U.S. Higher Education

> A man is but the product of his thoughts. (Suri, 2011)
> —MOHANDAS GANDHI

The stretch of general leadership research, defined as the Transactional age, harkens back to the Industrial Revolution (1830–1978) and focused on deliberate traits, the one-man, hero approach to defining leadership (Stogdill & Coons, 1957). Soon thereafter, the shape of leadership study began to explore the interchange between the leader and follower with the eminent goal for the leader to get the follower to achieve something under the headings of behavioral and contingency theories (Yukl, 2010). The late 1970s and early 1980s ushered in the Transformational leadership age recognizing the value of all working together toward a common goal, which is largely attributed to Burns's seminal book titled *Leadership* (1978). The debate about who plays the true influential role in this configuration continues with further examination. One thing is certain—leadership is no longer a title-honored concept, but rather one based on high moral standards, trust, devotion to followers, the ability for all to lead where social constructs influence self in relation to others, and the circumstances at play (Bass, 1990; Northouse, 2010).

Leadership studies of Asian Indian leaders migrating to the United States shows, from a business perspective, concerted effort required for leaders to make a successful leap. The work of Hofstede (1980, 2011) illustrates five cultural dimensions of difference—power distance, individualism, masculinity, uncertainty, avoidance, and long-term orientation—and Indian and U.S. cultures most notably differ in power distance and long-term orientation. Results from the Global Leadership and Organizational Effectiveness (Chhokar, Bordbeck, & House, 2008) initiative describe American and Indian leaders as action oriented with similar approaches to work, but they differ in the value Indian leaders put on self-reflection compared to their American counterparts. Studies indicate Indians migrating to the United States experience a shift in values (Budhwar, Woldu, & Ogbonna, 2008), while other research shows that Western tools for testing may have limitations in accurately measuring leadership style (Dalton & Wilson, 2000).

The U.S. higher education leadership inquiry landscape covers theoretical frameworks from trait to social constructivism (Bensimon, Neumann, & Birnbaum, 1989; Komives & Woodard, 2003). Recent trends indicate education leaders will need to demonstrate a set of nimble characteristics as technology and global influences pressure the academy. Contemporary research in U.S. higher education is beginning to focus on Asian leaders, though aggregated together with no discrimination between Asian origins (Teranishi et al., 2009).

> Truth is by nature self-evident. As soon as you remove the cobwebs of ignorance that surround it, it shines clear. (Suri, 2011)
>
> —MOHANDAS GANDHI

As a frequent visitor to India I became affectionately connected with and inquisitive about the Indian people, culture, and ways of life. I participated in religious activities and built relationships with locals, which led to home invitations. These relationships were based on trust with individuals whom I call my friends; trust is fundamental to relationship building in India. My personal disposition for a culture almost the opposite of my Western roots drives my desire for knowing, understanding, and interpreting the underpinning reasons that drive Asian Indians to lead in a world figuratively and literally opposite from their own.

Methodology

Qualitative Inquiry: Discovering Leadership Phenomenon Meaning

To examine the leadership phenomenon of a specific group of Asian Indians in U.S. higher education, I employed qualitative methodology, which deals with "multiple realities" and is flexible in nature to address the "shaping influences and value patterns experienced by the researcher" (Lincoln & Guba, 1985, p. 40). While describing the experiences of a group of Asian Indians as they see it, I attempted to create a holistic account and reconstruct the reality of cultural influences on their leadership journey (Creswell, 2009). Through these multiple forms of realities, the result was an emergent framework that renders this phenomenon meaningful and of practical value.

Qualitative research has been identified as a preferred method for leadership studies (Drath, 2001; Uhl-Bien, 2006; Yukl, 1989; Parry, 1998). The Relational Leadership Theory (RLT) approach posits a framework "for the study of leadership as a social influence process through which emergent coordination (e.g., evolving social order) and change (e.g., new approaches, values, attitudes, behaviors, ideologies) are constructed and produced" (Uhl-Bien, p. 668). With this premise, the discovery of context as it pertains to leadership further supports the need to deeply explore perceptions and interpretations through a qualitative approach.

Higher education is a unique, complex culture in which academic leaders fill a critical and influential role (Kezar, 2009; Rhoads & Tierney, 1992). To do this effectively, qualitative epistemology requires me to seek understanding that goes beyond making causal linkages. Lincoln and Guba (1985) state that dialogue between the research participants and me brings to the fore "myriad mutual shapings" where my understanding is reliant on an appreciation of the descriptive structures that emerge from our interactions (p. 152). I challenged myself to persist with genuine curiosity, to dig deeper opening myself to other "forms of order" about Asian Indian leadership in higher education (Shank, 2006, p. 208).

Ethnography: Depicting the Journey

In this study I utilized ethnography as the approach because it examines the human experiences of their journey to leadership as described by the participants. Extensive observation and field notes are required while collecting artifacts and representative cultural materials. Ethnographers are the recorders of life activities for those under study where inquiry is intimate, focusing on life influences like family, friends, socioeconomic structures, and religion (Hesse-Biber & Leavy, 2011).

Ethnography derives from the field of anthropology where researchers went "native" by immersing themselves in the foreign culture, seeking understanding of customs, cultural patterns, norms, beliefs, and behaviors. Since then the concept of *culture* has migrated to the study of *cultures* representing a group sharing common values, beliefs, and life experiences (McMillan, 2008). Flick (2009) emphasizes the criticality of the researcher "going native" to gain an inside perspective of the studied culture while systematizing "the status of the stranger at the same time" (p. 229). The common ground for this study is lived experience as a member of Indian culture and the impact these life experiences made on the selected individuals.

An ethnographic design is somewhat vulnerable given the interpretative and observational methods employed by the researcher. However, in cases where "interpersonal relationships, social structures, creative products, and so on . . . are under examination, quantitative methods simply are not appropriate" (Leedy & Ormrod, 2010, p. 135). Further, the ethnographic design is useful for educational research when it is incumbent on the researcher to collect "multiple sources of information and [spend] considerable time in the field" gathering information when evaluating the credibility of findings purported by the study (Creswell, 2008, p. 493).

Sociocultural Lens: Elucidating the Experiences

The process of finding meaning implies a learning process. Wertsch (1985) states that sociocultural perspectives take this a step further where "social contexts and interactions play in the construction of meaning . . . we cannot understand the individual without understanding the social and historical context in which he or she lives" (as cited in Lattuca & Stark, 2009, p. 156). Sense making, self-interpretation, and language are all influenced by culture where "cognitive processes are . . . cultural processes because they are situated in, and thus created by, relevant interpersonal, social, cultural, institutional, and historical contexts" (Lattuca & Stark, p. 156).

Sociocultural research tends to focus on the interpretation of identity formation after joining a community (Lewis & Moje, 2003, p. 1979). The intent of this project was to examine participant self-reflection and interpretation first from an Indian perspective, and then moving to their adjustment to American culture and their experience in U.S. higher education. By doing this, the discovery not only addressed past experiences but also explored "how they shape identities related to the conflict and tension that is always present in such communities" (Lewis & Moje, p. 1979).

The participants of this study were asked to reconstruct their life stories through a semi-structured interview. Throughout the inquiry, I continued posing these questions to myself: "What happens in the translation of reality into text? What happens in the retranslation of texts into reality or in inferring from texts to realities?" (Flick, 2009, p. 75). While the researcher is dependent on the subject's narrative, the aim is not to discern factual processes. This biographical narrative "becomes a mimetic presentation of experiences, which are constructed in the form of a narrative for this purpose—in the interview" (Flick, p. 81). Instead of mirroring reality, applying mimesis means interpretation happens from not only the subject's narrative but a construction by the researcher and reader as well.

Data Collection Strategies

INTERVIEWS

A major source of data collection for this study came from semi-structured interviews typical of ethnography (McMillan, 2008). Interviews provided me the advantage of asking the respondent to "reconstruct the past, interpret the present, and predict the future" (Lincoln & Guba, 1985, p. 273). The interviewer in a semi-structured approach uses open-ended questions to set the general direction of the dialogue, but the participant controls the discussion, requiring flexibility on the part of the interviewer (Cohen, Manion, & Morrison, 2008).

I interviewed five Asian Indian expatriate collegiate leaders at the vice presidential and presidential levels. Given the nature of this study where human interaction between the researcher and participant is necessary, a small sampling for in-depth analysis until reaching saturation is optimal (Creswell & Clark, 2011; McMillan, 2008). Creswell and Clark recommend four to ten participants typical of ethnographic research. The criteria stipulated participants must have:

- Grown up in India at least through their secondary education; and
- Served at the vice president level or higher in U. S. higher education.

A potential candidate list was generated from personal contacts combined with the snowball technique where additional participants were identified. Twelve individuals matched the criteria and seven were invited to participate, five individuals were subsequently interviewed. Interviews ranged from one to two hours each and took place within the participant's office space, except for one who was in-between positions at the time of data collection. Institutions were located in the East Coast and Midwest. Participant composition included a female at the vice president level, a female president, and three males at the president level.

FIELD NOTES

Field notes, in the form of journaling, "are the data that you gather to make sense of your research setting, and they serve as an aid in writing your research results" (Hesse-Biber & Leavy, 2011, p. 216). My journal entries contain both retrospective and most current memories. While in India, dating back to 2006, I witnessed a myriad of activities and celebrations transforming my perceptions and beliefs about the Indian way of life. I adopted Van Maanen's methodology (1988) called ethnographic impressionism. Van Maanen posits that time away from the field results in a more holistic and complete picture of experiences. My intent was to provide "thick descriptions" incorporating direct quotes, sensory observations such as smells and visuals, along with my feelings and emotions

(Hesse-Biber & Leavy, 2011), which contributes to the trustworthiness of this study (Lincoln & Guba, 1985).

DOCUMENTS AND ARTIFACTS

Ethnographic study lends itself to multiple forms of data, enriching the overall contextual interpretation of the phenomenon in question. Some argue there is not one way for recording field observations. Thus, pictures, documents, and video are considered elements of valid data collection (Hesse-Biber & Leavy, 2011). In addition to my journal entries, documents such as pictures, India Internet resources, a video I recorded featuring a typical drive to work each morning in India, and other leadership resources are contained on my website portal capturing my learning journey through this process.

Ethical Considerations of Ethnographic Research

With qualitative research, trustworthiness (credibility) is what gives the study merit. To be deemed trustworthy, the study must be transparent, have consistency-coherence, and communicability (Rubin & Rubin, 1995). Transparency relates to the manner in which data were collected; consistency references the extent the researcher investigated inconsistent responses, achieving coherence by describing conflicting points of view; and communicability means that the reader is able to contextualize the experiences as described by the subjects (Rubin & Rubin).

Qualitative research assumes multiple realities and it is the researcher's role to translate the interpretation of the subjects being studied (Merriam & Simpson, 1995). Internal validity guided my data analysis. The ultimate goal is to present that reality as accurately as possible by implementing various procedures. One way to ensure research credibility is through triangulating data sources and research techniques. Interviews, documents, and artifacts are meant to triangulate my data sources and to illuminate themes of discovery pertaining to events, facts, and interpretations about key factors and competencies for future Indian natives in pursuit of U.S. higher education leadership. Hesse-Biber and Leavy (2011) recommend looking for emergent themes within the text, then comparing artifacts and field notes to confirm consistency.

I made use of member checking after the interviews were transcribed and themes identified. Member checking is a common practice requiring the researcher to compile interview results and ask participants to confirm their reflections were accurately captured; in my case, one participant made minor revisions to the transcript (Creswell & Clark, 2011). Member checking is the most valuable approach to establishing credibility, and can be done in both formal and informal methods throughout the data collection process (Lincoln & Guba, 1985).

I sought feedback from a colleague, which proves to be an effective way to ensure credibility (Flick, 2009). I engaged a colleague to independently review the anonymous transcripts and that colleague subsequently confirmed my results (McMillan, 2008).

In an effort to maintain a balanced way of my own engagement in the study, of who I am, what I am experiencing, and my subsequent interpretations of the information before me, I maintained reflective dialogue; this approach is often termed *reflexivity* (Flick, 2009; Lincoln & Guba, 1985). Lincoln and Guba recommend the researcher engage in daily journaling, capturing logistical observations, reflecting on self in relation to values and areas for further exploration, and recording ongoing decision making about methodology. My personal reflections through the written word added to the collection of data for triangulation and illuminated places where I potentially may have been self-imposing my own sociocultural perspective on my participants.

Data Analysis: Making the Connections for Understanding

I began data analysis by transcribing the interviews and coding for themes and categories. I did my first round of descriptive coding manually by hand and then went back to adjust for consistency (Saldana, 2009). All 240 codes called *nodes* were transferred into NVivo9, a qualitative data analysis software tool designed specifically for qualitative research to assist in categorization of content. Digital audio recordings from participant interviews, field notes, and artifacts were subsequently uploaded, resulting in a multidimensional picture for analysis.

Information was categorized as either emic or etic data. The emic and etic data were then assembled into "families of codes" representing "setting and context subjects' definitions of a setting, subjects' perspectives about other people and aspects of a setting, process changes over time, activities, events, and techniques subjects use to accomplish things, and relationships and social structures" (McMillan, 2008, p. 284). The key here was to let the data form the codes, beginning from the specific and moving to the general as multiple layers of analysis were required for robust results (Creswell, 2009). Researcher interpretation required me to go beyond describing the complex themes and digging deeper for understanding.

The data analysis process yielded nine themes specific to this community of practice with seven particular to leadership and two others related to their journey alone and "going to the other side" while linking back to their roots. What follows is the description and representation of the research findings and results from the lives of Dr. Rajan, Dr. Gupta, Dr. Moorthy, Dr. Arora, and Dr. Agarwal.

There are times when you have to obey a call which is the highest of all, i.e., the voice of conscience even though such obedience may cost many a bitter tear, and even more, separation from friends, from family, from the state, to which you may belong, from all that you have held as dear as life itself. For this obedience is the law of our being. (Suri, 2011)

—MOHANDAS GANDHI

Exploring the Other Side Alone, Linking Back

Warren Bennis (2009) states, "Those who travel farther from home learn even more" (p. 84). Exploring "the other side" is a vital aspect with this group of Asian Indians. Filled with an inquisitive spirit, these individuals sought to reach a new land and soared in their new environment. Not only did they literally travel the expanse from East to West, they also embraced the American form of higher education and crossed the chasm from academic to administrative roles. Through each lived experience, the texture of each person's journey became vivid, revealing challenges and triumphs, testing and developing methods for navigation.

A number of participants used the word *alone* when describing elements about themselves whether it was their travels to America, leaving family as a child to attend school, or the work they enjoy as executives here in U.S. higher education. On the surface this makes sense, but in some ways it points to their ability to navigate between groups while preserving their individual identity. To move from where they were in their life required a strategy to permeate any perceived boundaries. A solo-spirit may just be one secret ingredient to their life success.

Hofstede (1980, 2001; Hofstede, Hofstede, & Minkov, 2010) describes India as a collectivist society where people help each other and do everything possible to save face. American culture is much more individualistic. Could there be an insight here for Asian Indians who describe themselves as "alone?" Perhaps this descriptor has been part of who they are from birth, which, even though living in a collectivist society as defined by Hofstede (1980, 2001), gave them the skills needed to navigate the Indian ways before moving to the United States. In essence, relocating to the United States provides the perfect entre for them to preserve the alone dimension, but successfully navigate boundaries to get things done. For them, becoming vulnerable, realizing skill strengths and gaps, and approaching the challenge with an eagerness to learn served a transformative platform into a new life construct.

Going to the other side has now mutated into a new career phase as some of the participants are now reconnecting with their India ethnic roots. Dr. Moorthy is forging academic agreements with Indian higher education institutions by which students may transfer to the United States and complete a baccalaureate degree within three years. Dr. Arora is increasing professional ties with Mumbai business leaders. In all cases, each participant makes it a priority to return to India for various reasons but is resolute in the proclamation that he or she is more American than Indian.

Immigrant Mentality: Asian Indian Self-Identity

In the beginning, self-actualization through acculturation and the refining of self-identity coalesced into an immigrant mentality of being American first. This insight bucks research findings asserting first-generation Asian Indians identify as Indian first (Farver, Narang, & Bhadha, 2002; Farver, Xu, Bhadha, Narang, & Lieber, 2007; Hickey, 2006). Born into a society with predetermined roles and a set of societal expectations, all formed an affinity for collectivism, maintained allocentric components in America "where the self and the family are integral, rather than separate, concepts" (Farver, Narang, et al., 2002, p. 340), but naturally absorbed elements of the individualistic American way of life. This assimilation into American culture netted the best of their Indian roots and positively impacted U.S. higher education leadership execution—leading with care for the home and family.

Work Hard: Pull to Serve and the Power of Encouragement

Working hard and responding to the "pull" gives these leaders the resolve that they are fulfilling their calling by not dwelling on the next strategic career move. This Gandhian approach links tightly back to Indian culture heavily influenced by Hindu constructs where one's role is assigned, all reinforced through ancient Indian teachings of heroism in the Ramayana and Mahabharata epics (Butt, 2004). Steeped in a life with values for doing the right thing, education was a catalyst for each person to elevate their role within society (Bhattacharya & Schoppelrey, 2004). Dr. Moorthy sees this "a calling from God to serve others…not as much aspirational, but something that sort of tends to pull you." By working hard and doing the right thing, all participants subscribed that the "pull" to the next life challenge presented itself, but all in one way or the other had to be encouraged before pursuing the next career move. This need for encouragement poses an incongruous paradigm since Asian Indians tend not to encourage others (Kakar, Kakar, Ketsde-Vries, & Vrignaud, 2002).

Education: Constant Learner

The genesis for academic achievement in each participant's story was fueled by external stimuli, namely his or her mother, who positioned education as a form of insurance toward a future of prosperity. Dr. Rajan said her "mother made it very clear to my sister and me ... that in order to have insurance of some kind ... and that insurance for us was our education." Wrapped in this motivation to succeed academically, education was a source credited for shaping their self-identity. This identity resulted in a search for truth as they migrated to the United States and becoming scholars in their academic fields. As life experiences synthesized, the "pull" factored into their work ethic, and education served as a catalyst by which each assumed formal administrative posts that led toward executive leadership positions with a drive to make a difference.

Credibility: Links to Teaching and Research

Leading U.S. higher education institutions demands leaders skilled across a portfolio of business-savvy competencies (Bolman & Gallos, 2011; Fullan & Scott, 2009; Waugh, 2003). This community of practice emphasized that while leadership roles can be taxing, maintaining credibility through continued scholarly actions was paramount. Dr. Gupta and Dr. Agarwal profess their admiration for learning and teaching and see these as critical parts of who they are. As president, Dr. Agarwal never really left teaching. Dr. Rajan blocks time on her calendar to meet with her laboratory research team. Dr. Rajan and Dr. Agarwal team-teach at their institutions while Dr. Moorthy remains engaged as a guest lecturer and publishes. The challenge is for leaders to strategically allocate time specific to scholarly activities.

Intolerance for Risk Aversion: Principles and Values

Asian Indian leaders are intolerant of academic leaders who avoid risk as the easy way out to evade potential public institutional scrutiny. Propelled by a spirit of exploration into new worlds, all participants spoke fondly of their formative years in India where they assumed their predestined role and achieved academic success while absorbing fundamental lessons shaping their values. "Entrepreneurial," "rebel," and "competitive" were some of the self-subscribed descriptors about who they are. In many ways, to explore in a highly rigid and structured society such as India is not commonplace since one typically lives within his or her birth role in a given community (caste) (Chhokar, Bordbeck, & House, 2008). This has changed considerably since the lifting of Licence Raj in 1991 (government laws established in 1947 composed of strict business regulations to control the economy), but for each of them, such exploration was rather novel in the 1960s and 1970s. Dr. Arora referenced Gandhi's essay on the Bhagavad Gita that explained while life may be predestined (dharma), all of us are still active participants and through good actions, actions will bring good. The implication here is that action requires risk taking, a concept strongly promoted by Gandhi's leadership during the liberation movement.

Research indicates people living in cultures with strict prescriptions for life activities and requirements for achieving favor with God, like Christianity in the United States, tend to be risk averse (Miller, 2000). Asian Indians come from a society where religion tends to be more fluid and one's religious journey offers more options about how to achieve a happy life on Earth and after (Bacon, 1999; Falk, Dunn, & Norenzayan, 2010). Taking risks is more acceptable as long as decisions are moral- and value-laden.

Permeate Boundaries: Relational Constructs

Living in a land interfacing with and engaging in customs and traditions of multiple faiths blurred boundaries for these Asian Indians, allowing for different religions and faiths to manifest together. The Hindi phrase, *Vasudheive Kutumbakam*, means the "whole world is my family." The consideration of the "whole world is my family" influences their perception about the concept of networked relations that extend beyond the immediate, nuclear construct. Dr. Rajan emphasized that "being an Indian you are used to larger groups, larger interactions and networks." Asian Indian executives consider all members of the academic community family—students, staff, faculty, alumni, neighboring community, and the board—no matter role, position, title, or any other designation.

Velvet Glove, Steel Hand: Communication with Action

Communicating with conviction, maintaining a tempered demeanor, fully listening to contrasting points of view, and making bold moves based on core principles is an earmark approach for this community of practice. To circumvent negative perceptions by others about his composed communication style, Dr. Arora said that leaders require a consciousness about the principles at stake as a gauge for implementing a firm communication style. He went on to say, "When people feel the velvet glove they think that you're going to be easy to push around . . . . But when it comes to the important things, you really have to stick to the principle and not be folding and compromising."

Going Forward

Be the change you want to see in the world. (Suri, 2011)

—MOHANDAS GANDHI

Asian Indians need to encourage others and pull them along. The message for all is to work hard in the moment and do so with a positive mindset. Likewise, Asian Indians need to seek out leadership training for constant refining, which can be done through internal institutional programs or external venues such as educational conferences and organizations. Time and energy must be devoted to sensemaking in a world of mixed messages about ethical leadership that will ultimately mitigate any unwarranted compromises.

People know when a person has their interests in mind no matter the given situation (Salovey & Mayer, 1990). Asian Indians have an opportunity to increase influence by collaborating with others, developing relationships, and doing so in overlapping places to incite positive change. Fostering these relationships requires a communication approach that works with Americans who tend to speak loudly and with emotionality (Varma, 2004).

Learning is a foundational dimension and the search for truth can only promote good in all leadership activities. When truth is at the core, Asian Indian leaders have the opportunity to not only discover new paradigms but also make positive differences in the lives around them and build an external network for support and guidance. Being a leader often causes one to compartmentalize and guard certain emotions, requiring time and a place for emotional venting without fear of reprisal to maintain balance.

My Journey, "On the Other Side"

Going to the other side is a metaphorical phrase descriptive of my life journey where the other side stimulated an unquenchable thirst to explore and learn. From my early years, education became a way for me to distinguish myself from the crowd, opening doors for opportunities unbeknown to me at the time. Primary education helped me hone leadership skills in student organizations while I dove into my studies and became skilled in communication and music.

My time at Washington State University (WSU), located on the other side of the state of Washington in relation to my hometown, nurtured this ongoing affinity for education and leadership development. WSU served as a catalyst to my venture in seeing the world, and from there I seized the opportunity to learn and help others, culminating in a career in student affairs. As I forged onward to West Virginia University on the other side of the country, I quickly learned that while part of the same country, a cultural shift came into play because life constructs and perceptions were different from my West Coast mindset. After six years of student affairs work, I made the choice to go to the other side and give the corporate world a chance.

Life on the other side of the planet struck a chord with me because my travels to India exceeded anything required as a work obligation. Education has always been about finding truth—truth as a result of learning about the world and the interpretations other human beings have about truth—and sorting through to create a holistic frame to guide how I live my life. My passion for working with others, my insatiable appetite for learning, and my affinity for cultural interludes have brought me to this intellectual exercise where India, leadership, and education converged.

Along the way, I have featured quotes from one of the most transformational leaders in the modern era, Mohandas Gandhi. Gandhi was heavily influenced by his readings of Hindu, Christian, Buddhist, and Muslim texts, as well as his experiences with racism in South Africa and with the British legal system, and then he developed it into the nonviolent movement after reading Tolstoy, Thoreau, and others. His life, his calling, his "pull" to serve literally changed the livelihood of an entire nation, inspiring people the world over since his walk on Earth to present day. Gandhi's voice had resonance, reaching all factions of Indian society, friend or foe, culminating in action for the greater good. As I continue along this life journey, I hope my voice and actions, big and small, somehow influence the world around me for the better.

Bibliography

Bacon, J. (1999). Constructing collective ethnic identities: The case of second generation Asian Indians. *Qualitative Sociology, 22*(2), 141–160.

Bass, B. M. (1990). *Bass and Stogdill's handbook of leadership: Theory research and managerial application.* New York: Free Press.

Bennis, W. (2009). *On becoming a leader: The leadership classic revised and updated.* Philadelphia: Perseus.

Bensimon, E M., & Neumann, A. (1993). *Redesigning collegiate leadership: Teams and teamwork in higher education.* Baltimore: Johns Hopkins University Press.

Bensimon, E. M., Neumann, A., & Birnbaum, R. (1989). *Making sense of administrative leadership: The "L" word in higher education* (ASHE-ERIC Higher Education Report No 1). Washington, DC: School of Education, George Washington University.

Bhattacharya, G., & Schoppelrey, S. L. (2004). Preimmigration beliefs of life success, postimmigration experiences, and acculturative stress: South Asian immigrants in the United States. *Journal of Immigrant Health, 6*(2), 83–92.

Bolman, L. G., & Gallos, J. V. (2011). *Reframing academic leadership.* San Francisco: John Wiley & Sons.

Budhwar, P. S., Woldu, H., & Ogbonna, W. (2008). A comparative analysis of cultural value orientations of Indians and migrant Indians in the USA. *International Journal of Cross Cultural Management, 8*(1), 79–105.

Burns, J. M. (1978). *Leadership.* New York: Harper & Row.

Butt, J. (2004). *Visions of service: An introduction to five of the world's great religions, with excerpts from the sacred writings and questions for study and reflection for those engaged in service.* New York: International Partnership for Service-Learning & Leadership.

Chhokar, J. S., Bordbeck, B. C., & House, R. J. (2008). *Culture and leadership across the world: The globe book of in-depth studies of 25 societies.* New York: Psychology.

Cohen, E. (2007). *Leadership without borders: Successful strategies from world-class leaders.* Singapore: John Wiley & Sons.

Cohen, L., Manion, L., & Morrison, K. (2008). *Research methods in education* (6th ed.). New York: Routledge.

Creswell, J. W. (2008). *Educational research: Planning, conducting, and evaluating quantitative and qualitative research* (3rd ed.). Upper Saddle River, NJ: Pearson.

Creswell, J. W. (2009). *Research design: Qualitative, quantitative, and mixed methods approaches.* Thousand Oaks, CA: Sage.

Creswell, J. W., & Clark, V. L. P. (2011). *Designing and conducting mixed methods research* (2nd ed.). Thousand Oaks, CA: Sage.

Dalton, M., & Wilson, M. (2000). The relationship of the five-factor model of personality to job performance for a group of Middle Eastern expatriate managers. *Journal of Cross-Cultural Psychology, 31,* 258.

Drath, W. (2001). *The deep blue sea: Rethinking the source of leadership.* San Francisco: Jossey-Bass.

Falk, C. F., Dunn, E. W., & Norenzayan, A. (2010). Cultural variation in the importance of expected enjoyment for decision making. *Social Cognition, 28*(5), 609–629.

Farver, J. M., Narang, S., & Bhadha, B. R. (2002). East meets West: Ethnic identity, acculturation, and conflict in Asian Indian families. *Journal of Family Psychology, 16*(3), 338–350.

Farver, J. M., Xu, Y., Bhadha, B. R., Narang, S., & Lieber, E. (2007). Ethnic identity, acculturation, parenting beliefs, and adolescent adjustment. *Merrill-Palmer Quarterly, 53*(2), 184–215.

Flick, U. (2009). *An introduction to qualitative research* (4th ed.). Thousand Oaks, CA: Sage.

Fullan, M., & Scott, G. (2009). *Turnaround leadership for higher education.* San Francisco, CA: Jossey-Bass.

Hesse-Biber, S. N., & Leavy, P. (2011). *The practice of qualitative research* (2nd ed.). Los Angeles: Sage.

Hickey, M. G. (2006). Asian Indians in Indiana. *Indiana Magazine of History, 102,* 118–140.

Hofstede, G. (1980). *Culture's consequences: International differences in work-related values.* London: Sage.

Hofstede, G. (2001). *Cultures' consequences: Comparing values, behaviors, institutions, and organizations across cultures.* Thousand Oaks, CA: Sage.

Hofstede, G., Hofstede, G. J., & Minkov, M. (2010). *Cultures and organizations: Intercultural cooperation and its importance for survival.* New York: McGraw Hill.

Kakar, S. (2007). *Indian-ness. Little India.* Retrieved from http://www.littleindia.com/news/142/ARTICLE/1730/2007-04-02.html

Kakar, S., Kakar S., KetsdeVries, M. F. R., & Vrignaud, P. (2002). Leadership in Indian organizations from a comparative perspective. *International Journal of Cross Cultural Management, 2*(2), 239–250.

Kezar, A. (2009). *Rethinking leadership in a complex, multicultural, and global environment: New concepts and models for higher education.* Sterling, VA: Stylus.

Komives, S. R., & Woodard, D. Jr. (Eds.). (2003). *Student services: A handbook for the profession* (4th ed.). San Francisco: Jossey-Bass.

Kouzes, J. M., & Posner, B. Z. (1995). *The leadership challenge*. San Francisco: Jossey-Bass.

Lattuca, L. R., & Stark, J. S. (2009). *Shaping the college curriculum: Academic plans in context*. San Francisco: Jossey-Bass.

Leedy, P. D., & Ormrod, J. E. (2010). *Practical research: Planning and design* (9th ed.). Upper Saddle River, NJ: Pearson.

Lewis, C., & Moje, E. B. (2003). Sociocultural perspectives meet critical theories: Producing knowledge through multiple frameworks. *International Journal of Learning, 10*, 1979–1995.

Li, W., & Scullion, H. (2010). Developing the local competence of expatriate managers for emerging markets: A knowledge-based approach. *Journal of World Business, 45*, 190–196.

Lincoln, Y. S., & Guba, E. G. (1985). *Naturalistic inquiry*. Newbury Park, CA: Sage.

McMillan, J. H. (2008). *Educational research: Fundamentals for the consumer* (5th ed.). Boston: Pearson.

Merriam, S. B., & Simpson, E. L. (1995). *A guide to research for educators and trainers of adults* (2nd ed.). Malabar, FL: Krieger.

Miller, A. S. (2000). Going to hell in Asia: The relationship between risk and religion in a cross cultural setting. *Review of Religious Research, 42*(1), 5–18.

Museus, S. D., & Chang, M. J. (2009). Rising to the challenge of conducting research on Asian Americans in higher education. *New Directions for Institutional Research, 142*, 95–105.

National Commission on Asian American and Pacific Islander Research in Education. (2010, December 20). *Reports & publications*. Retrieved from http://www.nyu.edu/projects/care/docs/2010_CARE_Report.pdf

Northouse, P. G. (2010). *Leadership: Theory and practice* (5th ed.). Thousand Oaks, CA: Sage.

Parry, K. W. (1998). Grounded theory and social process: A new direction for leadership research. *Leadership Quarterly, 9*(1), 85–105.

Rhoads, R. A., & Tierney, W. G. (1992). *Cultural leadership in higher education*. University Park, PA: National Center on Postsecondary Teaching, Learning, and Assessment.

Rubin, H. J., & Rubin, I. S. (1995). *Qualitative interviewing: The art of hearing data*. Thousand Oaks, CA: Sage.

Saldana, J. (2009). *The coding manual for qualitative researchers*. Thousand Oaks, CA: Sage.

Salovey, P., & Mayer, J. D. (1990). Emotional intelligence. *Imagination, Cognition and Personality, 9*(3), 185–211.

Shank, G. D. (2006). *Qualitative research: A personal skills approach* (2nd ed.). Upper Saddle River, NJ: Pearson.

Stogdill, R. M., & Coons, A. E. (1957). *Leader behavior: Its description and measurement*. Columbus: Ohio State University, Bureau of Business Research.

Suri, R. P. (2011). *Inspiring quotes of Mahatma Gandhi* [Kindle version]. Retrieved from Amazon.com.

Teranishi, R. T., Behringer, L. B., Grey, E. A., & Parker, T. L. (2009). Critical race theory and research on Asian Americans and Pacific Islanders in higher education. *New Directions for Institutional Research, 142*, 57–68.

Uhl-Bien, M. (2006). Relational leadership theory: Exploring the social processes of leadership and organizing. *Leadership Quarterly, 17*, 654–676.

U.S. Census Bureau. (2004). *Fact sheet for Asian Indian alone or in any combination and U.S. 2004 American community survey*. Retrieved from http://factfinder.census.gov

U.S. Census Bureau. (2010). Retrieved from http://2010.census.gov/2010census/

Van Maanen, J. (1988). *Tales of the field: On writing ethnography*. Chicago: University of Chicago Press.

Varma, R. (2004). Asian Americans: Achievements mask challenges. *Asian Journal of Social Science, 32*(2), 290–307.

Waugh, W. L. (2003). Issues in university governance: More "professional" and less academic. *The ANNALS of the American Academy of Political and Social Science, 585*(84), 84–96.

Wertsch, J. V. (1985). *Vyotsky and the social formation of mind*. Cambridge, MA: Harvard University Press.

Yamagata-Noji, A. (2011, July 6). *LEAP/APAHE leadership development program in higher education*. Paper presented at the annual Leadership Development Program for Higher Education, Kellogg West Conference Center, Pomona, CA.

Yukl, G. (1989). Managerial leadership: A review of theory and research. *Journal of Management, 15*(2), 251–289.

Yukl, G. (2010). *Leadership in organizations* (7th ed.). Upper Saddle River, NJ: Pearson.

CHAPTER SIX

Hermeneutics of Hispanic Parenthood

Reframing Conceptions through Personal Voices

MARIA E. HERNANDEZ-RODRIGUEZ

The Beginning of the Hermeneutical Journey

Based on my experiences of working with low-income Hispanic parents and school personnel, I have found that usually the faculty members have perceptions about Hispanic parents with regard to their lack of participation in their children's education, their indifference to their offspring's schooling, and their low expectations regarding education. These perceptions cause misconceptions, miscommunications, and judgmental attitudes that are noticeable when school personnel interact with these parents. Ultimately, these adverse perceptions affect the students because their teachers have lower expectations for them.

To my mind, it is unfortunate that these Hispanic parents, who are typically low-income, cannot comply with the school's expectations and demands. What is more disheartening is the negative opinions that some school personnel have about these parents' perceived lack of expectations for their children's education and the level of engagement that low-income Hispanic parents have with the schools. All personnel in a school have conceptions, opinions, and perceptions about how parents should participate in their children's education. These preconceived ideas have a significant influence on the way school professionals interact with Hispanic parents, specifically low socioeconomic Spanish-speaking parents. However, the question arises as to whether and how often school personnel communicate directly with parents regarding the expectations they have for their children and, more specifically, their children at the kindergarten level of education. How often do teachers, administrators, or staff members have direct and open conversations with Hispanic parents about the level of their engagement in school affairs? Developing and strengthening personal communication and listening to one another can significantly improve teacher–parent relations, which in turn may result in the better academic performance of these parent's children. The lack of direct communication automatically produces misconceptions and misunderstandings between parents and teachers. Non-Hispanic teachers may have negative emotions and opinions about Hispanic parents due to a sheer lack of knowledge about Hispanic cultural traditions and the realities of some Hispanic parents' daily lives. On the other hand, Hispanic parents often fail to convey their ideas and emotions to teachers and other school professionals because of the lack of knowledge of English and certain cultural, social, and economic conditions of their lives.

Within the microcosm of school culture, teacher–parent relations play a crucial role in assuring academic success and a dynamic and productive social life for students. It is imperative, therefore, for both parents and teachers, who could be representatives of different cultural traditions, to create spaces of mutual understanding and respect and to listen to and learn from one another. School personnel never ask these parents what their expectations are for their children's kindergarten education or ask them how they could participate in their children's schooling. Therefore, the purpose of the study was to allow for particular and authentic Hispanic parents' voices to be included in the dialogue on the value of education, the notion of success, and the shared responsibilities of parents and school professionals for children's educational attainment and advancement. In the context of this research, the dialogue is unfolding as a hermeneutic circle (Gadamer, 1998; Heidegger, 1962) of spiral movements of thoughts and experiences of scholars, researchers, practitioners, and the research participants that connects the past and the present and looks forward.

In particular, the study focused on Hispanic parents' interpretations of the academic expectations of their children's kindergarten education with the purpose of developing a deeper insight into the complexity of the relationship between school and parents and the need to improve this relationship. The intention of the study was to uncover the meaning of a variety of different and complex experiences that Hispanic parents lived through while rearing and educating their children. The research aimed at painting a picture of a micro "reality" of Hispanic parenthood that will illuminate the *Dasein* (Heidegger, 1962) of its experience and meaning. Consequently, the following were the research questions to be considered:

1. How did low-income Hispanic parents understand the expectations for their children's educational attainment?

2. What were these parents' conceptions of their role and responsibilities to-
    ward their child's education?
3. How did they view the role and responsibilities of the school towards
    their child's education?

Preparing the Journey

Qualitative Inquiry

Qualitative inquiry is an evolving design interested in the participants' point of view and in exploring how the participants make sense of experience from their own perspective. Therefore, the essence of this qualitative study relies on the participants' experiences and their interpretations (Creswell, 2003, 2007; Denzin & Lincoln, 2008; Patton, 2002). The qualitative researcher is able to get closer to the participants' interpretations and understandings through observations and interviews (Denzin & Lincoln) and by trying to reach this knowledge. The research takes place in a natural setting such as the school or parents' home. The aim of qualitative tradition is to understand multiple realities (Creswell, 2003, 2007; Lincoln & Guba, 2000) and to describe the nature of our everyday experiences and structures of the world in a narrative, expressive, and persuasive style (Creswell, 2003, 2007; Denzin & Lincoln; Patton, 2002). Describing the parents' interpretations of their participation and expectations for their children's education was a process of embroidering all their different or similar understandings and approaches together into a format that represents the parents' view of the educational world. Denzin and Lincoln provide the rationale for this position when they described the qualitative researcher as a quilt maker. Additionally, qualitative inquiry provides an interpretive and naturalistic approach to exploring Hispanic parents' interpretations of their educational expectations (Johnson & Onwuegbuzie, 2004), and this understanding is specific to each participant (Seidman, 1998).

Hermeneutics

Hermeneutics is defined as the art of interpretation. Its name is derived from Hermes, the Greek messenger whose endeavor was to bear knowledge and understanding between the gods and mortals. In the seventeenth century, hermeneutics was associated with the interpretation of text, specifically in the context of biblical studies. Early in the nineteenth century, Schleiermacher founded modern hermeneutics, moving beyond the interpretation of biblical texts to the illumination of human understanding. Afterward, Dilthey expanded the hermeneutics' field of interest by including cultural systems and organization (Kneller, 1984; Laverty,

2003; Moules, 2002; Polkinghorne, 1983). Hermeneutics as the art of interpretations unites the art of speaking and the art of understanding (Dilthey, 1992; Gadamer, 1998; Heidegger, 1962; Schleiermacher, 1992). As a result, the hermeneutic spirit arises from language and meaning. The researcher can access the participants' thoughts via language (Gadamer, 1998; Schleiermacher, 1992).

Hermeneutics is also a critique that brings to consciousness, in a reflective manner, experiences of social interactions with others through language (Habermas, 1992). Hence, interpretation is higher when people relate to language as a vehicle by which a person communicates his or her thoughts, and it adapts a psychological dynamic of intuition and empathy that occurs when the researcher is able to put him- or herself in the place of the participants (Rasmussen, 2002; Schleiermacher, 1992). Further, Dilthey (1992) indicates that understanding arises in the interest of practical life where people communicate with each other; one must know what the other wants. As a consequence, the most elementary form of understanding arises. The process of understanding becomes a process of self-reflection by becoming aware of unconscious presuppositions underlying accomplishments that people have taken for granted (Gadamer, 1998; Habermas). Hermeneutics is concerned with the human experience and with the world as we live in it. In this regard, Heidegger (1962) focuses on the *Dasein*, which is a German word used in hermeneutic tradition meaning "the mode of being human" or "the situational meaning of a human in the world." Dasein has a threefold structure: (1) attuning to the past, (2) interjecting the phenomena in the present, and (3) new possibilities for future understanding. The structure of Dasein conforms to the circle of understanding and the basis of this circle is the hermeneutics circle (Paterson & Higgs, 2005; Zweck, Paterson, & Pentland, 2008). Understanding is a basic form of human existence in terms of the way people are. Heidegger stressed that every experience involves an interpretation that is influenced by the person's background. Therefore, interpretation is a fundamental process of understanding; they are bonded (Dilthey; Gadamer; Heidegger; Schleiermacher).

Marking the Routes on the Map: Hermeneutic Circle

Schleiermacher viewed the hermeneutic circle as a movement according to the principle that parts of the speech (the participants' stories) are only intelligible in terms of the whole and the whole can be understood through its parts (Rasmussen, 2002). In order to travel from the parts to the whole and vice versa, the researcher must have comprehensive knowledge of the culture and language in which the study inscribes itself. In Gadamer's perspective (as cited in Rasmussen, 2002), the researcher shifts between his or her own horizon of understanding and the meaning of the text as well as between the researcher questioning the text and the questions that emanate from it. The fusion of horizons provides the bridge that brings together and connects the familiar and the unfamiliar (Gadamer, 1998). Metaphorically, this process is similar to the movements the waves make on the beach's shore. It is a constant and fluid back and forth dynamic in which the researcher challenges his or her understandings with the participants' stories, and this understanding is continuously revised on the basis of experiences attained by this movement and dynamic.

Coming to an understanding about something is coming to communality, consensus, or agreement (Gadamer, 1998). This sense of communality has embedded the concept of tradition (Rasmussen, 2002). The phenomena under study in the hermeneutic circle, in this case low-income Hispanic parents' expectations for their children's education, are presented first as blurry and unstructured where past experiences and knowledge are fused to become an enlightened understanding of the experience. This very enlightenment adds understanding to future events and completes the circle by adding new knowledge (Paterson & Higgs, 2005; Zweck, Paterson, & Pentland, 2008).

Lareau's (2003) natural growth theory added to the circle of conversations and understanding of Hispanic parents' expectations for their children's education. Lareau found that raising children from a natural growth perspective encompasses five spheres: (1) parents allow their children to grow and develop as they care about them; (2) the organization of daily life allows children to spend their time with relatives and peers; (3) communication is based on directives, which means that low-income parents tell the children what to do instead of trying to reason with them; therefore, children accept the directions and instructions and do not question or challenge adults; (4) the relationship with institutions such as the school is a dependent one since the school holds an authoritative status and low-income parents tend to expect educators and other professionals to take a leadership role. This can result in a sense of powerlessness and frustration, especially when there is a conflict between the school and the childrearing practices at home; (5) the consequences of feeling powerless can cause constraint as low-income parents feel they are less knowledgeable and less efficient, even though they are capable of challenging the decisions made by the institutions.

Central to this hermeneutic journey were the voices of Hispanic parents recorded during the extensive in-depth semi-structured interviews. Hermeneutic interviews are meant to help the participants explore the topics so as to facilitate further thoughts and reflection (Van Manen, 1997). Every element in the hermeneutic circle of this study maintained a dynamic dialogue in searching for understanding and taking the newfound meaning to the next cycle.

Experiencing the Hermeneutical Journey

The text of the interview transcripts provided existential space for a dialogue in which the participants and I sought to uncover the meaning of Hispanic parenthood. The dialogue transformed itself into fourteen themes:

1. a disciplined student with the ability to learn narrated the educational expectations that the participants' parents and teachers held for them when they were children;
2. positive experiences in the school based on interactions that the participants had with school personnel;
3. better education and more learning opportunities (the expressions about what the participants wished for their offspring);
4. the role of the school is to provide solid foundations (the academic content for kindergarten should be learned in depth by their children so the youngsters could be successful in first grade);
5. school teaches what it should teach (early language and literacy skills and early mathematics abilities, which represented what the kindergarteners ought to learn);
6. school does everything to support and advance education (this focused on specialized teachers, school personnel working collaboratively, the advantage of having bilingual staff, and the school staff taking a leadership role in the student's learning process);
7. school does its best given its available resources and the global economic situation;
8. more academic support after school hours opened dialogues about the possibility of parents receiving guidance from the school on how to help their children with schoolwork;
9. school wants my child to learn (participants described what they thought the school expected for their youngsters along with the participants' role in that matter);
10. school expects parents to encourage learning (parents conversed about what they perceived the school's expectations were for them as parents);
11. helping with schoolwork brought to light the participants' arrangements in order to assist their children with homework;
12. recognizing schooling's support (how the school personnel recognized the parental support in their children's schooling);
13. portal to a better future (participants utilized the metaphor *keys to a better future* to describe what education meant for them);

14. success comes with effort and patience and was described as being able to reach goals through hard work, patience, and effort.

As a person and researcher, I entered this study with an initial horizon that outlined my goal of listening to the parents' voices. In the process of inquiry, my knowledge and experiences have moved back and forth between my past and present horizons, infusing the participants' conversations and mine, reaching out to understand what lies ahead. The perspectives of the participants and my own views were presented from distinct vantage points with the purpose of arriving at the creation of new horizons and levels of understanding. The fusion of horizons does not necessarily mean full agreement among the participants. It is rather the search for what might be commonly understood and valued. As Gadamer (1998) reminds us, understanding through dialogue does not occur exclusively by asserting the participants' points of views, but by being transformed into a communion in which we do not remain what we are. Progressively, the dialogue between the parents' voices and my own voice became a special fusion that opened a window for me to experience the investigation from the inside and the outside in an uninterrupted synergy, and cleared a new passage to understand that I had found solace within the process.

Creating Knowledge Dynamically

Within the research questions' synergy, there were found common threads identified as a result of the analysis of the participants' descriptions of not only their perceptions of their parental role and responsibilities but also their vision of the role and responsibilities of school personnel with regard to their expectations. As the dialogue among the participants evolved, the whole unfolded. Once the whole came to light, it was revealed that Hispanic parents who participated in the study expected a better education for their children than the education they received when they were students themselves. They expected more learning opportunities for their children than what was available to them in their country of origin. These Hispanic parents immigrated to the United States with this hope in their hearts. On the surface, this seems to be a typical immigrant story, but there is much more to been seen. The parents revealed the subtleties and complexities of their unique views on life, education, culture, success, educational attainment, and what constitutes a happy and fulfilled life.

Understanding Expectations

The Hispanic parents who participated in the study expected a better education for their children than the education they received when they were students themselves. The participants' expectations toward their children's kindergarten schooling meant that their children were learning basic skills and building a strong academic foundation so as to be successful throughout grade school. It was the parents' expectation that their youngsters learned what teachers taught, as much as they could within their abilities, and that they behaved properly by paying attention to the teacher (*escuchar a la maestra*), showing respect (*respetar*), and not causing problems (*no dar problemas*). Being able to learn in school and behaving properly were signs of being a good student (*ser buen estudiante*). This conduct testified to the fact that the family's traditional values played an important role in rearing children. The participants described the expectations that their own parents had of them. The parents highlighted the importance of having a foundation for education, which in their view constituted early language and literacy (*las letras, el abecedario, empezar a leer y a escribir*), early math abilities (*los números, las cuentas*), and learning English. Acquiring English language skills was critical for their children because English guaranteed further success in education and life. Learning and maintaining their native language was important, but not as important as learning English.

Since parents were working from morning until night trying to provide for the family, they thought of education, and especially graduation, as the ultimate success for their children. Their children's future graduation could make these parents happy and feel personally successful as well. The participants viewed their children's kindergarten graduation as the first step of this success.

Parents Supporting Their Children's Education

Support of their children's education was paramount for the participants' understanding of their role as parents. Hispanic parents stated that ideally they would like school personnel to pay attention to their children's learning process, to be patient with them, and to help the parents help with homework. In order to support their children's schooling, the participants (1) encouraged their children to do the best that they could; (2) made sure that their children felt loved; (3) tended to their children's happiness in the school; (4) prepared their children to be ready for learning by teaching them to behave properly, pay attention to the teacher, and be respectful; (5) provided, first and foremost, for their offspring's basic needs; and (6) made sure that homework was completed. The participants taught their children good behavior and manners (*buen comportamiento*). This was considered by the parents to be providing educational support because they believed that when children behaved well they were ready to learn and, therefore, learning occurred. Additionally, it was crucial for the participants to make sure they attended to their children's basic needs (Delgado-Gaitán & Trueba, 1991; Delgado-Gaitán, 1992; Valdés, 1996).

There was a particular distinction between education at home (*educación en la familia*) and education at school (*educación en la escuela*). The parental mission was seen as providing moral support, food, shelter, and teaching proper behaviors; whereas, the school had the role of delivering academic content and academic support to their children (Drummond & Stipeck, 2004; Hoover-Demsey et al., 2005; Lareau, 2003; Quesada, Díaz, & Sánchez, 2003; Salinas, 1997; Valdés, 1996). The participants longed for the school to provide academic support after school hours for those students who needed it the most. The parents' understanding of their role in educating the child academically rested on their perceptions that they were not knowledgeable enough, or did not know the best approach to helping their youngsters (Hyson & DeCsipkes, 1993; Orozco, 2008; Zarate, 2007).

Parents' Circumstances

The participants of the study expressed their hopes to obtain a better education (*mejor educación*) and more learning opportunities for their children than the parents received in their education. The chance of their children receiving a better education translated into a better life and future for them. More important for some participants, their personal success was defined as being able to fully experience their children's success in kindergarten as well as their future graduations along the way. Because of the parents' financial situation, their main concern was to provide for the family and to take care of its basic needs (Brilliant, 2001; Delgado-Gaitán & Trueba, 1991). Yet, working toward maintaining the family was considered not only a gesture of supporting their children's education but also as their responsibilities and role (Lareau, 2003). Along the same lines, the participants commented on the importance of regularly sending their children to school clean and taken care of (*limpios y arreglados*). Regardless of their economic struggles, some parents mentioned the opportunity to modestly support the school financially when school personnel considered it necessary, or when they could contribute to something, even if it was a symbolic amount, if it was within their possibilities: *"Habrá veces que podremos cooperar con algo y con gusto lo haremos."* [There will be time when we could cooperate with something and we will do it with pleasure.]

The parents in the study were concerned about not knowing how to be helpful to their children with homework given their lack of English proficiency, and they wondered about the possibility of receiving additional support from the school, not only for their youngsters but also for themselves. Nonetheless, the participants did not communicate their suggestions about how to do this to school personnel because they were afraid of being imposing and impolite: *"No queremos molestar."* [We don't want to bother.] The participants' approach could be understood in the light of the natural growth model (Lareau, 2003). One example of this model is that school personnel were viewed by parents as the experts and authority figures. When school staff did not provide the expected support, the parents found it inappropriate to express their dissatisfaction to school authorities. The lack of English did not seem to be the problem. The Hispanic parents felt more comfortable expressing their opinions to bilingual staff members. They probably felt that it was disrespectful to ask questions or make suggestions (Brilliant, 2001; Gracia, 2000; Lareau; Trumbull, Rothstein-Fish, & Hernández, 2003; Vadés, 1996).

Conceptions of the Parents' Role and Responsibilities

The Hispanic parents in the study indicated that the school expected their children to learn what was taught every day, to behave properly, and to pay attention. The parents understood their function in the learning process as that of supporting their children's schooling. Hence, the role and responsibilities as viewed by the parents translated into (1) providing food, shelter, and comfort to their children; (2) making sure their children were ready to learn; (3) motivating and encouraging learning; and (4) supporting learning by teaching discipline or good manners (*buen comportamiento*).

It was the participants' understanding that school personnel knew that the parents were supporting their children's education and following up on their parental responsibilities when the parents sent their offspring to school ready to learn, which meant that their children were well rested, properly dressed, had their school materials, and behaved as their parents expected them to behave. The parents made efforts to help their children with their schoolwork but they did not know how to help in a way that would make their child's learning easier. Despite these difficulties, parents managed to overcome these obstacles by asking older siblings for assistance and making sure that the task was finished either by supervising the homework or by participating in the work by helping as much as they could with the knowledge they had.

The Twofold Process of Educating

The parents who participated in the study thought of education as a twofold process. On the one hand, education meant the key to a better future. These parents talked about education from the family in which parents taught good manners and good behavior, encouraged learning, and materially provided for the family so as to cover their basic needs. On the other hand, education was also perceived as a formal process that prepares a person academically to compete for a career or occupation. During conversations, the participants explained how an educated person (*persona educada*) was a person with good manners and respectful with others. Further, participants elaborated more on the definition by adding that a person could obtain the highest academic degree but at the same time not be educated in terms of having good manners or showing respect to others. The participants' interpretations of education from the family (*educación de la familia*) and education from the school (*educación de la escuela*) conveyed an understanding of the participants' perceived responsibilities and their parental traditions. When the participants' responsibilities and parental traditions were elements of the definition of education from the family, then it was the parents' goal to guide the children. The parents would then expect school personnel to practice their tradition as delineated in the definition of formal education from the school.

Conceptions of the School's Role and Responsibilities

The Hispanic parents who participated in this study asserted that the school's function was to provide a solid foundation for their children to learn language and literacy, mathematics, and English. The participants' youngsters would be prepared for the first grade by school personnel teaching and focusing on the above academic aptitudes. It was the participants' understanding that school personnel ought to pay attention to the children's learning process while focusing on teaching the academic content. The parents envisioned the school's expectations of their children to be for them to learn what was taught, to behave properly, and to pay attention. The parents admitted how well-prepared and knowledgeable school personnel were and they noticed how much their children were learning day after day. The participants perceived that the school was teaching what the school staff was supposed to teach, and they were doing the best they could with the resources available. Some of the elements from the school that impressed the parents were the staff working collaboratively, providing specialized teachers and bilingual educators, and providing a variety of activities such as cutting numbers and coloring animal-shaped letters so as to enhance students' learning.

From the parents' insights, one of the realities that prevented the school from doing its best was the general economic decline. The participants were referring to the loss of the at-risk program since it was state funded and there was not much that the school personnel could do. This educational program was offered to students from socioeconomically disadvantaged groups who needed intensive school experiences and more academic and social opportunities prior to enrolling in kindergarten.

School "Knows Best"

Intimately related to the natural growth model (Lareau, 2003) is the authoritative character that the school holds. *School knows best* reflected the school's responsibility to teach the academic content that the students were expected to acquire. Perspectives from the participants in this study revolved around interpretations about the school personnel being well prepared and being experts in their field (Lareau, 2003; Sheldon, 2002; Valdés, 1996). As a result, school staff knew what to teach at all times, understood the needs of the students, and worked diligently on the process of teaching and learning. Reliance on the expertise of the specialist and working cooperatively were aspects of the school that were well received and praised by parents. By appealing to the school staff's professionalism, the parents expected the school to practice its role properly and correctly, especially in those situations in which parents felt that they were being treated differently. As discussed in other conversations, this perception that the school knows best could be understood as the judgment the school applied when determining what was necessary or irrelevant at the time in which the discussion on this topic occurred. Examples of this would be the decision about whether or not to implement academic support programs for students and whether or not to provide parenting sessions regarding strategies that parents could use to assist their youngsters with schoolwork.

The dialogue with Hispanic parents revealed that school personnel and participants shared different expectations regarding education and parenting styles (Carlisle, Stanley, & Kemple, 2006; Coleman & Churchill, 1997; Deslandes, Royer, Turcotte, & Bertrand, 1997; Lareau, 2003). The participants in the study discussed what they thought school personnel ought to teach to their children. Their narrations about what was supposed to be taught in the classroom resembled direct instruction under which students would learn primarily academic skills. The Hispanic parents in the study wished to know about various forms of helping their children with their homework. They did the best they could with the knowledge they had. Conversing from a discipline angle, the Hispanic parents in the study perceived their good behavior system in a similar fashion that involved showing respect, being attentive, and behaving well. The Hispanic parents did not encourage their children to develop their own personal style since their children had to follow their parents' tradition. It seemed as if the children's own styles are shaped by the adults' expectations. For the Hispanic parents in the study, to know that their children were able to behave well and show respect testified to the fact that the parents were educating their children correctly.

Completing the Journey

Completing the hermeneutic circle enhances our understanding of low-income Hispanic parents and the expectations they have for their children's education. The voices of the participants of this study echo a great deal of what Lareau's (2003) natural growth model demonstrates. The dialogue with Lareau and other educational theorists indicate the possibility of the fusion of perspectives on the parents' expectations of children's educational success. Socioeconomic status with regard to childrearing and education seems to be of paramount importance (Hyson & De-Csipkes, 1993). Academic discussions that focus on parents from other ethnic and racial groups interwoven into the dialogues among Hispanic parents led to a new understanding of how parents view their children's success in school.

Understanding entails an evolution of thought and experience. It is never fixed or final (Gadamer, 1998; Moules, 2002). Parents' perspectives in the study are considered to be the horizons that provide a range of vision from the particular vantage points of the participants (Gadamer). Consequently, in the search for new horizons of understanding, the study involved primarily Hispanic parents. The perspectives of the parents from non-Spanish-speaking countries and different racial and ethnic groups were considered as part of the general discussion on the parental expectations of their children's academic attainment.

As a qualitative researcher, I have been intensely involved this investigation. The study was propelled by the time, effort, determination, and the complete devotion that I gave to it. The dialogues, conversations, experiences, and the hours of reading the transcriptions in search for understanding and meaning have developed into a new lens through which I now see these families. Their traditions, stories, and concerns offer me new horizons of understanding myself and the people of my own culture. The very experience of being involved in the study has been transformational for me as a person and as a professional. Hermeneutics entitles so much more than the fine art of interpretation. The hermeneutic circle allows for an introspective experience that brings to light forgotten memories from past experiences. As such, my past horizons have fused with the present, reaching out for new insights. I cannot remain in the shadow of this moment. As I look back at the beginning of the journey, I realize how the simple act of asking a question can initiate a study of a vast scope. What is clear in my mind is that there is a new understanding of who and what I was, and who and what I am now. I see myself as a person who has become more understanding, compassionate, and tender. The end of the research journey is always bittersweet. With sadness, I had to part ways with the participants. With excitement, I still wonder what lies beyond the next horizon.

References

Brilliant, C. D. G. (2001). Parental involvement in education: Attitudes and activities of Spanish-speakers as affected by training. *Bilingual Research Journal, 25*(3), 251–274.

Carlisle, E., Stanley, L., & Kemple, K. (2006). Opening doors: Understanding school and family influences on family involvement. *Early Childhood Educational Journal, 33*(3), 155–162.

Creswell, J. W. (2003). *Research design: Qualitative, quantitative, and mixed methods approaches* (2nd ed.). Thousand Oaks, CA: Sage.

Creswell, J. W. (2007). *Qualitative inquiry and research design: Choosing among five approaches* (2nd ed.). Thousand Oaks, CA: Sage.

Coleman, M., & Churchill, S. (1997). Challenges to family involvement. *Childhood Education, 73*(3), 144–148.

Delgado-Gaitán, C. (1992). School matters in the Mexican-American home: Socializing children to education. *American Educational Research Journal, 29*, 495–513.

Delgado-Gaitán, C., & Trueba, H. (1991). *Crossing cultural borders: Education for immigrant families in America*. London: Falmer.

Denzin, N. K., & Lincoln, Y. S. (2008). *The discipline and practice of qualitative research*. In N. K. Denzin & Y. S. Lincoln (Eds.), *Strategies of qualitative inquiry* (3rd ed., pp. 1–43). Thousand Oaks, CA: Sage.

Deslandes, R., Royer, E., Turcotte, D., & Bertrand, R. (1997). School achievement at the secondary level: Influence of parenting style and parent involvement in schooling. *McGill Journal of Education, 32*, 191–207.

Dilthey, W. (1992). The hermeneutics of the human science. In K. Mueller-Vollmer (Ed.), *The hermeneutics reader: Texts of the German tradition from the enlightenment to the present* (pp. 148–164). New York: Continuum.

Drummond, K., & Stipek, D. (2004). Low-income parents' beliefs about their role in children's academic learning. *Elementary School Journal, 104*(3), 197–213.

Gadamer, H. (1998). *Truth and method* (2nd ed.). New York: Continuum.

Gracia, J. J. E. (2000). *Hispanic/Latino identity. A philosophical perspective*. Malden, MA: Blackwell.

Habermas, J. (1992). Hermeneutics and the social science. In K. Mueller-Vollmer (Ed.), *The hermeneutics reader: Texts of the German tradition from the enlightenment to the present* (pp. 293–319). New York: Continuum.

Heidegger, M. (1962). *Being and time*. New York: Harper

Hoover-Demsey, K. V., et al. (2005). Why do parents become involved? Research findings and implications. *Elementary School Journal, 106*(2), 105–130.

Hyson, M., & DeCsipkes, C. (1993). *Educational and developmental beliefs systems among African America parents of kindergarten children*. Retrieved November 11, 2009, from ERIC database.

Johnson, R. B., & Onwuegbuzie, A. J. (2004). Mix methods research: A research paradigm whose time has come. *Educational Researcher, 33*(7), 14–26.

Kneller, G. F. (1984). *Movements of thought in modern education*. New York: Macmillan.

Lareau, A. (2003). *Unequal childhood: Class, race, and family life*. Los Angeles: University of California Press.

Laverty, S. M. (2003). Hermeneutic phenomenology and phenomenology: A comparison of historical and methodological considerations. *International Journal of Qualitative Methods, 2*(3), article 3. Retrieved from http://www.ualberta.ca/~iiqm/backissues/2-3final/pdf/laverty.pdf

Lincoln, Y. S., & Guba, E. G. (2000). Paradigmatic controversies, contradictions, and emerging confluences. In N. K. Denzin & Y. S. Lincoln (Eds.), *Handbook of qualitative research* (2nd ed., pp. 163–188). Thousand Oaks, CA: Sage.

Moules, N. J. (2002). Hermeneutic inquiry: Paying heed to history and Hermes. An ancestral, substantive, and methodological tale. *International Journal of Qualitative Methods, 1*(3), article 1. Retrieved from http://www.ualberta.ca/~ijqm/

Orozco, G. (2008). Understanding the culture of low-income immigrant Latino parents: Key to involvement. *School Community Journal, 1*(18), 21–37.

Paterson, M., & Higgs, J. (2005). Using hermeneutics as a qualitative research approach in professional practice. *Qualitative Report, 10*(2), 339–357. Retrieved from http://www.nova.edu/sss/QR/QR10-2/paterson.pdf

Patton, M. Q. (2002). *Qualitative research and evaluation methods* (3rd ed.). Thousand Oaks, CA: Sage.

Polkinghorne, D. (1983). *Methodology for the human sciences. Systems of inquiry.* Albany: State University of New York Press.

Quezada, R., Díaz, D., & Sánchez, M. (2003). Involving Latino parents. *Educational Leadership, 1*(33), 32–38.

Rasmussen, J. (2002, April). *Textual interpretation and complexity—radical hermeneutics.* Paper presented at the American Educational Research Conference, AERA SIG Chaos & Complexity, New Orleans, LA.

Salinas, A. (1997). Involving Hispanic parents in educational activities through collaborative relationships. *Bilingual Research Journal, 2*(21), 1–8.

Schleiermacher, F. (1992). Foundations: General theory and art of interpretation. In K. Mueller-Vollmer (Ed.), *The hermeneutics reader: Texts of the German tradition from the enlightenment to the present* (pp. 72–97). New York: Continuum.

Seidman, I. (1998). *Interviewing as qualitative research: A guide for researchers in education and the social sciences* (2nd ed.). New York: Teachers College Press.

Sheldon, S. B. (2002). Parents' social networks and beliefs as predictors of parent involvement. *Elementary School Journal, 102*(4), 301–316.

Trumbull, E., Rothstein-Fish, C., & Hernández, E. (2003). Parent involvement in schooling: According to whose values? *School Community Journal, 13*(2), 45–72.

Valdés, G. (1996). *Con respeto: Bridging the distances between culturally diverse families and schools.* New York: Teachers College Press.

Van Manen, M. (1997). *Researching lived experience: Human science for an action sensitive pedagogy* (2nd ed.). London: Althouse.

Zarate, M. (2007). *Understanding Latino parental involvement in education.* Irvine: University of Southern California Press.

Zweck, C., Paterson, M., & Pentland, W. (2008). The use of hermeneutics in a mixed methods design. *Qualitative Report, 13*(1), 116–134. Retrieved from http://www.nova.edu/sss/QR/QR13-1/vonzweck.pd

CHAPTER SEVEN

In Pursuit of Change

A Study of a Principal's Application of Transformational Leadership Strategies

CHRISTINE L. KRAMP PFAFF

Introduction

From the positive perspective, which is where I prefer to place myself, the word *transformation* evokes for me an image of someone or something morphing itself into something beautiful, positive, or successful from a previous state that may have not been its best or very appealing. Take, for example, the butterfly that starts its existence as a common caterpillar but transforms itself into a creature of beauty and grace. This inspiring transformation evokes images of strength and instills hope for a better future in that one so delicate can be so strong.

When I look at my life in the rearview mirror, I see twists and turns and, thankfully, lengths of straight road where I was able to find my footing and make the necessary transformations in my life that have assisted me in finding success. In my rearview mirror, I remember that I was a nurtured child, loved, and well cared for, as were my two brothers, but I also see a home environment that was full of twists and turns. Sometimes we were out on the straight-away for a pleasant drive through rolling picturesque hills enjoying our time together around the dinner table, at family functions, or supporting each other in our endeavors. At other times, though, our drive was unstable as if we were traveling through a bad storm and fearing a spinout. My parents loved each other but often their passion turned to heated arguments. The intensity of their voices could shake the house and the aftermath of their silence was unnerving.

As our environments shape who we are, my environment left upon me a spectrum of esteem, ranging from confidence to diffidence. Sometimes in my youth, this led me to make poor decisions. I wasn't sure where I was going or if I had what it took to get there. I was fortunate to have many people in my life that cared about me and who helped me get back on track. And thankfully, my parents highly valued education and modeled exceptionally strong work ethics. With these supports behind me, I entered the college environment with a spectrum of belief in myself and was beginning to see the possibilities for my future through the range of new experiences and relationships that entered my life. As my journey through college continued, I settled upon a career choice, education. I wanted to be in a position where I could be an encouraging force in children's lives and, hopefully, be that change agent that others were for me.

I have been blessed with a rewarding and exciting career. Much of my happiness comes from the fourteen years I spent as a classroom teacher, instructing math and language arts to middle school students. In the classroom, I had the joy of working with curriculum that was interesting and fulfilling, providing endless opportunities for creativity. More important, I worked with children, helping to expand their academic knowledge and build their confidence.

In existentialism, individuals are viewed as being responsible for the meaning of their own existence and creating their own essence or self-definition. If this is the case, I am where I am supposed to be as this is how I have defined myself thus far. In that I am responsible for creating my own self-definition and driving my own future, what road will I take next? As my education career shifts from the classroom to administration, I am considering how I can be a change agent for my staff, students, and school community. What can I do to help others succeed? How can I best lead?

As with my childhood experiences, my early administrative experiences helped shape who I am today. My four-year assistant principalship at Cottage Hill Junior High School, the only junior high school in the Fairfield Consolidated Unit District 56, afforded me many opportunities to further my skills and gain knowledge on the managerial components of administration. I learned how to evaluate faculty effectively and offer guidance to struggling teachers. I sharpened my skills of working with challenging parents and working through difficult faculty issues. I assisted in leading, along with dynamic teacher leaders, the planning of several small- and large-scale events. I planned and executed school- and disrictwide committee meetings. I was fortunate to have wonderful learning opportunities that expanded my knowledge of special education law and procedures.

I also met regularly with grade-level teams where discussions focused on student concerns and sharing of current instructional units. Periodically, teams would plan interdisciplinary units where discussion of best practice arose. At these meetings, I was able to share my curricular knowledge and math content area expertise, but this type of meeting was infrequent. With all of these assistant principal experiences, I did not, however, have an extended opportunity to work with faculty on curriculum and instruction development, nor did I have an opportunity to drive schoolwide change initiatives. Moving into the principalship, this underexposure in my early administrative work, coupled with my junior high–level teaching experiences, has left me questioning how to best approach leading the Fairfield Elementary School (FES) staff toward positive school change. Specifically, I am exploring how I can steer my new elementary level staff forward.

At the time of my promotion, two elementary positions were available in the district. I was placed at Fairfield with a complimentary statement from district level administrators that I had the strength to work with an equally strong and confident staff whose culture has the reputation as one of the most stringent in the district. Fairfield teachers are known for practicing a by-the-book adherence to contractual language. With this being the case, I reflected on what approach I would take in guiding a cultural change with teachers toward greater professionalism and beyond self-interests. I did this in order to benefit students and to steer away from the current constraining labor mind-set that restricts some teachers from expanding their professional practice and rebukes other teachers who dare to put students before the Fairfield Teachers' Association Negotiations Agreement. My desire to expand my knowledge and advance my leadership skills led me to investigate different leadership styles.

Leadership Styles

Leadership is a topic that is broad and well-studied and focuses on various styles as well as successful individuals and organizations. In education, leadership styles such as instructional, transactional, and transformational are prominent in contemporary literature. Being a new principal, I searched for the best manner to lead my staff and school community. I had confidence in my management abilities as I had many opportunities during my assistant principalship to hone these skills. But I felt inexperienced in the skills necessary to lead staff toward the positive school change that would create an environment of teaching for learning with a momentum of engagement and improvement to get us there (Wagner & Kegan, 2006).

With teaching as my passion, I was initially drawn to instructional leadership in that it has a strong focus on curriculum and instruction from the principal (Hallinger, 2003). Upon further study, however, I learned that instructional leadership focused on the principal coordinating and controlling school operations while developing curriculum, instruction, and goals independently of staff input (Hallinger, Murphy, & Peterson, 1985; Hallinger, Bickman, & Davis, 1996). Daresh (2006) disagrees with this representation of instructional leadership by sharing a statement from the Association of Supervision and Curriculum Development (ASCD, 1989) and notes that instructional leaders encourage a better organizational climate by allowing teachers to participate meaningfully in making decisions of substance. Though research opinions vary regarding this leadership style and being an instructional leader was very appealing to me, this style of leadership in and of itself did not encompass the leadership qualities I sought to apply.

By exploring further research on leadership styles, I discovered transactional leadership. Transactional leadership, often described as managerial in nature, encourages employees to vie for positions of power under a highly regulated system (Bass, 1997) with things being exchanged that are of value to both leader and follower (Burns, 1978). As with instructional leadership, I rejected this leadership style as the right fit for me. I viewed my role as principal to be an encouraging and supportive leader for faculty. I wanted to foster growth in my teachers rather than create an environment of competition. Finally, my research led me down the path toward transformational leadership. I found terms that began to coincide with my drive: collaboration, motivation, distributive, shared vision, and commitment. Transformational leadership strives to encourage individuals within an organization to motivate each other to rise to higher levels of performance (Burns). As Bass proposes, authentic transformational leaders motivate followers to work toward goals that go beyond immediate self-interests. This was it! Transformational leadership was the right fit for me. This complemented who I am and led me to the question: How do I get started?

Research Purposes and Questions

The search for effective leadership strategies to employ at Fairfield Elementary School came from my early principalship experiences and concerns that arose from them. For example, I was concerned about a school culture that was, at times, inflexible toward change and staff who were unforgiving to colleagues who went the extra mile. I was concerned that some staff felt an 8:30 a.m., fifteen-minute faculty meeting, was ample time to complete tasks with fidelity. I was concerned that some teachers were unwilling to implement research-supported instructional interventions because of the extra planning time it would require during the initial implementation process. I needed to determine the best leadership behaviors to implement that would allow me to maintain the positive relationships I had created with my staff and produce the needed changes at FES.

Educational research supports positive outcomes for schools when transformational leadership behaviors are applied in making progress toward the education profession working collaboratively as a community. School reformers cannot work alone any better than the teacher can work alone behind a closed classroom door (Barth, 2001). I set it as the purpose of this study to determine whether transformational leadership strategies, when applied at FES, can enhance my leadership capabilities, expand the instructional practices of teachers, and establish a more effective professional school culture with greater focus on students as the priority during my second year in the principalship. I was ultimately guided by the notion of transformational leadership as identified by Leithwood and Jantzi (2005). Resulting from this research are my perspectives on the implementation of transformational leadership strategies that were intended to move the school beyond traditional practices, as well as the perspectives of faculty regarding their experiences and view points during the implementation effort.

The overarching research question was, "As a new principal, what transformational leadership qualities can I further develop and employ to affect change in self, instructional practices, and school culture?" The following were the supporting research questions:

- How can applying transformational leadership strategies in my professional practice enhance my leadership capabilities?
- How can applying transformational leadership strategies expand the instructional practices of teachers?
- How can applying transformational leadership strategies establish a more inclusive and participative culture?
- In what ways is transformational leadership an effective leadership style to partner principals and teachers together to improve instruction?

Moving into the Principalship

Being in the field of education for more than twenty years, I have developed many strong relationships with peers and supervisors. As I transitioned through various positions and school districts throughout my career, colleagues frequently provided me with advice for success. Moving into the principalship was no different and perhaps even more prolific. As soon as my promotion from assistant principal to principal was announced, the advice started pouring in on how to get off to a good start as a principal.

The suggestions I received were founded in both common sense and good leadership practices. From principal colleagues I heard: spend your first year developing relationships and remember the secretary and custodian are your right-hand helpers. From the superintendent and assistant superintendents I heard: get to know every kindergartener by name, this will bring you closer to the families and you'll have formed strong bonds that will last for six years; make sure you are visible, teachers and students need to see that you are interested in their teaching and learning. The most frequently heard piece of advice from everyone was don't make any changes your first year unless the teachers are requesting them. Having observed my colleagues successes over the years, I took their advice seriously and adhered to it.

I did not make any major changes during my first year with the exception of a greater focus on improving student behavior. Attention to student behavior was a direct request from the faculty as conveyed to me through the Getting to Know You survey I sent to staff in their 2007–2008 Welcome Back to School letter. I asked, "On what should I focus my attention this year?" The response was nearly unanimous: student discipline. With discipline, managerial tasks, and expanding my knowledge of the elementary curriculum and culture as my necessary foci, I devoted much of my time to developing relationships and increasing my knowledge and comfort level in the elementary setting.

Intentionally spending my first year as principal in the role of observer and gentle guider, I had the opportunity to note the strengths and weaknesses of the school culture, instructional practices, and the professional learning environment of which I had become a part. The culture at Fairfield was traditional in nature where the majority of teachers were veteran faculty members. Many faculty members were enthusiastic and quickly surfaced as teacher leaders. Because of this, I was able to quickly assemble a discipline committee to focus upon the discipline concerns the teachers noted in the survey. On the other hand, however, there were times when inflexibility was observed and a by-the-book adherence to following the teachers' contract was a grounded cultural norm for some. Teachers who desired to put forth extra efforts were, at times, convinced to withdraw their enthusiasm through peer pressure for stated reasons such as "you shouldn't put in time outside of the contractual work day."

Instruction in some classrooms was meeting the needs of twenty-first-century life as described by Brandt (2010) through emphasizing skills like critical thinking and problem solving to meet the obvious needs of society's demands. This instruction was observed through the use of guided reading implementation, differentiation, hands-on activities, problem-solving opportunities, and technology use. This type of classroom addressed the needs of twenty-first-century students who are growing up, as Wagner (2008) claims, in an environment that is radically different from previous generations. Classrooms of this nature meet students' needs for more intellectually challenging or creative work. Other classrooms at Fairfield could be described as traditional in nature with Industrial Revolution era teaching practices dominating lessons such as whole group and basal-based instruction coupled by independent seat work.

At this time, data were not being utilized to drive instruction. A complicating factor in addressing instructional practices and the need for data-based decision making was the high performance of FES students on the ISAT exam and the yearly attainment of AYP. In 2008, 81% of 3rd graders, 88% of 4th graders, and 93% of 5th graders met or exceeded expectations in reading. For the same testing year in math, 97% of 3rd graders, 96% of 4th graders, and 94% of 5th graders met or exceeded standards (http://iirc.niu.edu). What the data did not reflect were the students whose home schools differed from FES due to special education program placements. These special education students had their scores reported out at their residential school per state guidelines, thus making the residential school on state reports responsible for their scores. The overall high ISAT scores fostered an unrealistic picture of individual student performance. These high averages contributed to an unrealistic sense of security for some faculty members and refuted any immediacy for change in instructional practices. Fairfield's content area averages failed to communicate individual student shortcomings and though teachers received individual student test scores, applying the annual summative data purposely to differentiate instruction was a challenge at best.

During this first year, I also noted areas for improvement that fell both under the managerial and transformational leadership aggregates. One of the most glaring weaknesses was the lack of common planning time for grade-level teachers. Providing this common time would be the starting point for promoting greater collaboration and incorporating data discussions to drive instruction. Luckily, the faculty had expressed to me their desire for more planning time with colleagues. With the exception of faculty who had, within the past five years, undertaken graduate work, I had also observed a lack of current professional knowledge.

As with many schools, there is a need for change at FES, and therefore I chose to focus my efforts on implementing the strategic plan that was created, in part, collaboratively with staff by applying transformational leadership theory and practice. Transformational leadership lent itself well to job satisfaction, commitment, effectiveness, organizational learning, school culture, teacher morale, and student literature (Sahin, 2004).

Research Methodology

I found qualitative methodology best suited to address the research purposes and questions of this study. Qualitative inquiry seeks honest, meaningful, credible, and empirically supported findings (Patton, 2002). Since qualitative inquiry approaches "often cover a wide terrain of perspectives, beliefs, and methods" (Shank, 2006, p. 10), I employed a variety of techniques common to several qualitative designs such as ethnography, autoethnography, and narrative. I presented my own story and the stories of teachers in my school in order to identify actual and potential forces that moved my school's culture beyond conventional practices toward more visionary and transformational endeavors.

The story of my life was interwoven in the narrative of this study. It conveyed the elements of ethnography and autoethnography within a larger framework of interpretive research. Autoethnography is a form of interpretive research that does not seek to explain or prove, but rather to open spaces for description of individual lived experience and create meaning for that experience (Goodall, 2000; Patton, 2002). Autoethnographic writing allowed me to express myself in first-person and to make personal statements about myself in profound ways (Chang, 2008; Denzin, 1989; Polkinghorne, 2005; Ellis & Bochner, 1999). McAtee (2006) considers ethnography as "useful in the area of educational administration because it helps surface a missing understanding of leadership. An ethnographic approach to leadership not only brings about greater understanding of leaders but also the factors that influence that understanding" (p. 67). Merriam and Simpson (1995) state that the term *ethnography* has recently been used interchangeably with field study, case study, qualitative research, and participant observation. Chambers (2000) recognizes cultural relevance in ethnography as well and notes the cornerstone of "applied ethnography" is the importance of understanding culture especially in relation to change efforts. To gain further understanding of staff experiences and school culture and to add detail to my lived experiences during this time frame, four ethnographic interviews were conducted with FES certified staff to increase the breadth of perspectives about the implemented changes during the 2008–2009 school year.

Case Study

A broad range of theoretical and methodological perspectives, along with their corresponding strategies of data collection and analysis, necessitated the choice of a case study, which is a "decision about what is to be studied, not a methodological decision" (Hesse-Biber & Leavy, 2011, p. 255). The term *case study* is not used in a consistent way in research literature (Hesse-Biber & Leavy, 2011), and researchers who do case studies "often refer to their work by the methods they employed within the case study, such as ethnography or oral history" (Hesse-Biber & Leavy, p. 255). Case study approach provides researchers with a "holistic understanding of a problem" and conducting case study research involves "more than one method to collect extensive data about the case" (Hesse-Biber & Leavy, p. 256).

Case studies in education draw upon concepts, theory, and research techniques from anthropology, history, sociology, and psychology with such a sociocultural analysis of a single unit producing an ethnographic case study (Merriam & Simpson, 1995). The ethnographic case study, as applied to this research, involved several individuals and focused upon studying the results of the ten implementation goals designed to hone in on transformational leadership behaviors.

As the researcher in this study, I was a participant observer where I engaged in the activities I set out to observe. Bailey (1994) identifies advantages in the participant observer approach noting: observation studies are superior when data is being collected on nonverbal behavior; researchers are able to make appropriate notes regarding nonverbal behavior as it occurs; that case study observations occur over an extended period of time, researchers can develop more intimate relationships with those they are observing; and case study observations are less reactive than other types of data-gathering methods (as cited in Cohen, Manion, & Morrison, 2008, p. 260).

Data Collection and Analysis Strategies

Data collection strategies employed in this case study drew on multiple sources of information: extensive observational and self-reflective notes, ethnographic interviews, institutional documents, artifacts, and an exploratory survey (Creswell, 2007; Lincoln & Guba, 2000; Yin, 2003; Leedy & Ormrod, 2010).

Observational Notes

Throughout the study, I maintained near daily field notes chronicling the implementation of the components of transformational leadership strategies and reflecting on a myriad of experiences along the way. My observational notes also included staff meeting agendas, memos, applicable email communications, weekly staff bulletins, bimonthly school newsletters, and student discipline records. I maintained a log of informal classroom visits and a log of accolades awarded throughout the course of the school year to staff and students. Grade-level teams' meeting minutes that reflect collaborative efforts were also included. Evidence of celebrations was included in pictorial format.

Ethnographic Interviews

Ethnographic interviews with the four faculty members were essential to this research. The interviews were semi-structured with open-ended questions, many of which were fashioned after Leithwood and Jantzi's (2005) transformational leadership framework. Although the same questions were presented to each participant, there were natural segues in their answers during the interview process. The participants clearly demonstrated a desire to share a greater breadth of information. Data from these interviews shed incredible light on the study of faculty members' perspectives regarding attempted transformations to instructional practices and school culture at FES, as well as an understanding of the process and success of my implementation of the leadership strategies that fall under the transformational leadership behavior aggregates.

Survey

An exploratory online survey (Creswell, 2007) was employed in this study to assist me in describing the practices and attitudes of the participants. The survey was administered to all staff members and focused on transformational leadership qualities categorized by Leithwood and Jantzi (2005), which are: setting directions, helping people, redesigning the organization, and the managerial aggregate. Seventy percent of certified staff completed the survey with 21 surveys finished completely and one survey completed partially. The data obtained from the survey provided important insights in the nature of transformational leadership and contributed a great deal to the creation of a holistic description of transformational strategies.

Reflexivity

Subjectivity is a pathway to deeper understanding of the human world in general as well as whatever specific phenomena they are examining (Patton, 2002). Subjectivity plays a role in qualitative research by allowing for a focus on the nature of the *Self* (Gonzalez, 2001). I am acutely aware of the fact that, as a researcher, I cannot be a neutral spectator (Denzin, 1997). As an ethnographic researcher, my personal experiences were essential to this study. Throughout the study, I kept a journal of my observations and self-reflections, whereby acknowledging and disclosing my own self in the research, and seeking to understand my part in or influence on the research (Cohen, Manion, & Morrison, 2008). My reflections were full of emotion about my leadership experiences whether they were pleasant, frustrating, or benign. I often found myself analyzing my feelings on a situation or attempting to diagnose why a staff member conducted herself or reacted in a particular way to a situation. This daily reflection assisted me in working through, what were at times, my private knee-jerk responses to situations, particularly frustrating ones, and afforded me the opportunity to consider the situation and staff member's response from her worldview and perceptions of me. Combating reactivity through reflexivity "requires researchers to monitor closely and continually their own interactions with participants, their own reaction, roles, biases, and any other matters that might affect the research" (Cohen, Manion, & Morrison, p. 172).

Conclusions

Central to this research is an investigation of my unique experiences as a second-year principal and the school culture of which I was a part. Looking at these experiences autoethnographically revealed my innermost personal beliefs and feelings. This reflective journey assisted me in identifying my own successful leadership skills, provided me with areas for growth, and framed the future of my leadership strategies. It is my hope that my personal reflections will be of assistance to others striving to be excellent leaders.

The ethnographic interviews were conducted in a manner to allow each participant to share their knowledge about and observations of the implementation goals rooted in transformational leadership. Opportunities were provided for the participants to reflect on their personal experiences at FES that were not scripted into interview questions. The candidness of the participants' stories brought to life for me their daily experiences, which were not readily available to me as the school principal. The survey given to staff allowed them to express their perceptions of my leadership skills and school culture in a nonthreatening, anonymous manner.

Finally, as I continue to reflect on my own experiences and the experiences of the participants during the course of this study, I consider their impact on my leadership journey. The depth of knowledge that I gained from my own and my research participants' experiences have provided the foundation for further growth in my leadership skills. These experiences taught me to always ask questions because the answers will always provide me with the next leg of my journey.

Bibliography

Association for Supervision of Curriculum and Development. (1989). *Instructional leadership* (Videotape). Alexandria, VA.

Bailey, K. (1994). *Methods of social research.* New York: Free Press.

Barth, R. (2001). *Learning by heart.* San Francisco: Jossey-Bass.

Bass, B. M. (1997). Does the transactional-transformational leadership paradigm transcend organizational and national boundaries? *American Psychologist, 52*(2), 130–139.

Brandt, R. (2010). Preface. In J. Bellanca & R. Brandt (Eds.), *21st century skills: Rethinking how students learn* (p. ix). Bloomington, IN: Solution Tree.

Burns, J. M. (1978). *Leadership.* New York: HarperCollins.

Chambers, E. (2000). Applied ethnography. In N. Denzin & Y. Lincoln (Eds.), *Handbook of qualitative research* (pp. 851–869). Thousand Oaks, CA: Sage.

Chang, H. (2008). *Autoethnography as method.* Walnut Creek, CA: Left Coast.

Cohen, L., Manion, L., & Morrison, K. (2008). *Research methods in education.* New York: Routledge.

Creswell, J. (2007). *Qualitative inquiry and research design: Choosing among five approaches.* Thousand Oaks, CA: Sage.

Daresh, J. C. (2006). *Leading and supervising instruction.* Thousand Oaks, CA: Corwin.

Denzin, N. (1989). *Interpretive biography.* Newbury Park, CA: Sage.

Denzin, N. (1997). *Interpretive ethnography: Ethnographic practices for the 21st century.* Thousand Oaks, CA: Sage.

Ellis, C., & Bochner, A. (1999). Autoethnography, personal narrative, reflexivity: Researcher as subject. In N. K. Denzin & Y. S. Lincoln (Eds.), *Handbook of qualitative research* (pp. 733–768). Thousand Oaks, CA: Sage.

Gonzalez, K. P. (2001). Inquiry as a process of learning about the other and the self. *Qualitative Studies in Education, 14,* 543–562.

Goodall, H. L. (2000). *Writing the new ethnography.* Walnut Creek, CA: Alta Mira.

Hallinger, P. (2003). Leading educational change: Reflections on the practice of instructional and transformational leadership. *Cambridge Journal of Education, 33*(3), 329–351.

Hallinger, P., Bickman, L., & Davis, K. (1996). School context, principal leadership and student achievement. *Elementary School Journal, 96,* 498–518.

Hallinger, P., Murphy, J., & Peterson, K. (1985, October). Assessing the instructional leadership behaviors of principals. *Elementary School Journal,* 217–248.

Hesse-Biber, S. & Leavy, P. (2011). *The practice of qualitative research.* Thousand Oaks, CA: Sage.

Leedy, P., & Ormrod, J. (2010). *Practical research: Planning and design.* Boston: Pearson.

Leithwood, K. A., & Jantzi, D. (1999). Transformational leadership effects: A replication. *School Effectiveness and School Improvement, 10*(4), 451–479.

Leithwood, K. A., & Jantzi, D. (2005). A review of transformational school leadership research 1996–2005. *Leadership and Policy in Schools, 4,* 177–199.

Lincoln, Y., & Guba, E. (2000). Paradigmatic controversies, contradictions and emerging confluences. In N. K. Denzin & Y. S. Lincoln (Eds.), *Handbook of qualitative research* (2nd ed., pp. 163–188). Thousand Oaks, CA: Sage.

McAtee, K. A. (2006). Women leaders in education: An autoethnography, ethnographic interviews, and focus group of women's journey to leadership. *Dissertation Abstracts International* (UMI No. 3241407).

Merriam, S., & Simpson, E. (1995). *A guide to research for educators and trainers of adults.* Malabar, FL: Krieger.

Patton, M. Q. (2002). *Qualitative research and evaluation methods.* Thousand Oaks, CA: Sage.

Polkinghorne, D. (2005). Language and meaning: Data collection in qualitative research. *Journal of Counseling Psychology, 52*(2), 137–145.

Sahin, S. (2004). The relationship between transformational and transactional leadership styles of school principals and school culture. *Educational Sciences: Theory & Practice, 4*(2), 387–396.

Shank, G. D. (2006). *Qualitative research: A personal skills approach.* Columbus, OH: Pearson.

Wagner, T. (2008). *The global achievement gap.* New York: Basic.

Wagner, T., & Kegan, R. (2006). *Change leadership: A practical guide to transforming our schools.* San Francisco: Jossey-Bass.

Yin, R. (2003). *The art of case study research.* Thousand Oaks, CA: Sage.

CHAPTER EIGHT

Is There a Model for Success?

Exploring Sustainable Professional Employment among Clinical Exercise Physiology Program's Graduates

REGINA SCHURMAN

When I say that I am a clinical exercise physiologist, people usually think I am either a personal trainer or a physical therapist. While there is some overlap between the skill sets of clinical exercise physiologists, personal trainers, and physical therapists, there are important differences that set clinical exercise physiologists apart. Personal trainers and clinical exercise physiologists assess various indices of physical capability of their clients and develop exercise programs to improve deficiencies; however, only clinical exercise physiologists possess the training necessary to work with individuals who have a variety of chronic health conditions. Physical therapists work with a broad range of conditions that limit mobility (American Physical Therapy Association [APTA], n.d.) but usually do not work with a patient until an event has occurred whereas clinical exercise physiologists utilize exercise as a means of chronic disease prevention (CEPA, n.d.; Potteiger, 2011).

Unlike other healthcare professions such as nursing or physical therapy, clinical exercise physiology is relatively new. The work of Levine, Lown, and Hellerstein, who used exercise in the rehabilitation of cardiac patients, led to the establishment of cardiac rehabilitation programs in hospitals in the 1970s (Potteiger, 2011). Despite several decades of practice, it was not until 2010 that the Bureau of Labor Statistics finally created a separate Standard Occupation Code (SOC) for exercise physiologists (U.S. Department of Labor, 2010). Between the confusion over what clinical exercise physiologists do and the delay in receiving government recognition, it is no wonder that the general public does not understand the scope of practice for clinical exercise physiologists.

Why would someone go into the field of clinical exercise physiology given all the challenges that the profession is facing? Clinical exercise physiology has its origins in anatomy, physiology, and medicine and thus appeals to students who want to better understand both the human body's response to exercise as well as the power of exercise to improve health (Potteiger, 2011). The practice of clinical exercise physiology is broader than that of personal trainers who typically only work with healthy individuals. While physical therapists are typically limited to treating a specific body part, clinical exercise physiologists look at the whole person as they work to manage chronic disease and promote lifestyle habits that enhance health.

The students who enter our master's clinical exercise physiology program at Benedictine University usually have the goal of obtaining full-time employment in the field after graduation. Most of them seek employment in cardiac rehabilitation or cardiac diagnostics departments at hospitals. Several of the adjunct faculty who teach in our program have full-time positions as managers of these types of departments at local hospitals. These individuals serve as exemplars when prospective students inquire about their prospects for finding employment post-graduation. How these individuals attained their career success despite competition from other professions as well as the lack of licensure for clinical exercise physiologists is unclear.

It is apparent that more than a master's degree is needed to be successful in the competitive job market in the field of clinical exercise physiology. Graduates face many challenges in securing positions due to the economy, healthcare reform, and a lack of license for their profession. However, in spite of these challenges, some students are able to secure professional employment with opportunities for future advancement. There seem to be other factors involved that allow these students to succeed in an adverse job market.

This study was needed since the profession of clinical exercise physiology does not have a clear career path like physical therapy or nursing. Marketing materials for clinical exercise physiology graduate programs state that exercise physiologists can be found in leadership roles in cardiac rehabilitation programs, fitness centers, and agencies. However, it is left up to the students to determine the best way to secure their desired career post-graduation.

The flash of insight that focused me on the substantive area of this study was the realization that there were several clinical exercise physiologists in the Chicago area who held management positions in hospitals. This was interesting because clinical exercise physiologists are not licensed, except in the state of Louisiana. However, this lack of licensure had not held back these individuals from achieving positions as managers in cardiac rehabilitation and cardiac diagnostic departments. The departments these clinical exercise physiologists manage have a mix of healthcare professions, including nurses, respiratory therapists, echocardiography technicians, and other licensed professionals. This insight led me on a process of abduction to form a hypothesis of how this was possible and to conduct a research study in a manner that generated a substantive theory to explain my observations.

The purpose of this study was twofold: (1) to describe the clinical exercise physiology profession from the perspective of its practitioners and the graduates of clinical exercise physiology programs; and (2) to develop a model of sustainable professional employment that exhibits the processes that allow graduates from clinical exercise physiology programs to attain management positions in a healthcare system dominated by licensed professionals.

This study was guided by the following questions:

- What are the graduates' perceptions on sustainable professional employment within the clinical exercise physiology profession and the path to its highest attainment?
- What are the perspectives of clinical exercise physiology professionals on sustainable professional employment and what is the career path toward their highest professional attainment?
- What is the model that exhibits the processes that allow clinical exercise physiologists to obtain sustainable professional employment and to attain management positions in a healthcare system dominated by licensed professionals?

Theoretical Positioning of the Study

Pragmatism provided the foundation of this study in terms of methodological and epistemological assumptions. Pragmatism was selected because this study seeks to provide "practical solutions to practical problems" (Ozmon & Craver, 2003, p. 138). Clinical exercise physiology students seek guidance on how to best prepare themselves to attain sustainable professional employment in today's competitive job market. Identifying the factors that contribute to securing employment in the field and thus creating a model of sustainable professional development is one of the solutions offered by this study. Wedded to my pragmatic goals is the choice of a qualitative grounded theory that is rooted in the philosophical tradition of pragmatism. Qualitative methodology would allow the experiences of clinical exercise physiology practitioners to be captured and provide the opportunity to probe more deeply into themes that may be revealed during interviews.

Grounded theory method originated with Glaser and Strauss's 1965 publication of their research in *Awareness of Dying*. At the time of the development of grounded theory method, qualitative methods were viewed as inferior to quantitative ones (Glaser & Strauss, 1967). Therefore, Glaser and Strauss wanted to prove that there were forms of qualitative research that could have as much rigor as quantitative research (Bryant, 2009). In the publication of the grounded theory method their philosophical worldview was never explicitly defined, which perplexed many, including Bryant, since Strauss had a pragmatist background being from the Chicago School of Sociology.

The two founders of grounded theory method parted ways when Strauss published *Basics of Qualitative Research* with Corbin in 1990, a book which Glaser rebutted in his book *Emergence vs. Forcing: Basics of Grounded Theory Analysis* in 1992. Despite this split, the use of the method grew in popularity. In the 1990s, those using the method realized that the issues of the role of the researcher, induction, and prior knowledge needed to be addressed, and thus many argued that grounded theory method was based on interpretivism or constructivism (Bryant, 2009). However, using constructivism does not solve the criticisms of grounded theory method since constructivism has as its basis that knowledge depends on the participants' meanings rather than on an objective view of reality (Bryant; Creswell & Clark, 2011; Mills, Bonner, & Francis, 2006). A researcher's view of truth and reality can influence him or her to justify study outcomes based on the belief that knowledge was provisional and dependent on the participant's perspectives (Bryant). However, researchers are part of the research process and their humanness will influence the construction of knowledge (Mills et al., 2006).

Positioning grounded theory method in the framework of pragmatism resolves this lack of a solid epistemological footing (Bryant, 2009). Despite a lack of an explicit reference to American pragmatism in the writings of Glaser and Strauss, Strauss did stress that it was a key part in his intellectual formation because he was exposed to the writings of Dewey and James when a student in the 1930s (Bryant). Strauss referred to the influence of pragmatism on his work as "a red thread running through my work" (Bryant, para. 51). Bryant's reconsideration of grounded theory method in the worldview of pragmatism leads to a more cohesive method that can be defended and that turns "the red thread into a lifeline" (para. 58). When taking the pragmatist view that any theories or concepts developed should be judged by their "usefulness rather than their truthfulness," the features of grounded theory become more understandable in terms of generating substantive theory (Bryant, para. 61).

In selecting a method to perform the inquiry for this study, it was important that I choose one based on the scientific method in order to generate the substantive theory for my model. What Glaser and Strauss (1967) mean by substantive theory is that it was developed for a particular "area of sociological inquiry, such as patient care, race relations, professional education," as opposed to a conceptual area of sociological inquiry, such as "stigma, deviant behavior, formal organization" (p.

32). Glaser and Strauss (1967) label these theories as "middle-range" because they "fall between the 'minor working hypothesis' of everyday life and 'all-inclusive' grand theories" (pp. 32–33).

Clinical exercise physiology is a scientific field; therefore, the primary audience for this study is those accustomed to reading research articles that use solid quantitative research. This audience typically values hard numbers higher than the softer qualitative research often used in social sciences. Some of the problems associated with the use of qualitative data include producing a study full of "undisciplined speculation laced with interesting anecdotes" (Mullen, 1996, p. 63). By utilizing a method guided by pragmatism, it was possible to generate substantive theories and a model that can be judged by its practicality in helping subjects resolve their main concern (Bryant, 2009). This aligns with Dewey's view of knowledge as instrumental, which allows theories to best be considered as tools (Bryant). The theoretical model generated by this study is a tool for future practitioners in the field to guide them onto a path to sustainable professional employment.

Grounded theory method consists of the typical stages of analysis employed in traditional scientific inquiry. However, the process of inquiry begins with abduction, or that "flash of insight" (Bryant & Charmez, 2007). Founder of pragmatism C. S. Peirce (1839–1914) believed that abduction was the only type of inference that would allow the creation of new knowledge since both induction and deduction were rooted in the development of existing knowledge. Peirce "always saw abduction as a form of reasoning that develops from surprise or sudden flashes of insight" (Bryant, 2009, para. 93).

Glaser and Strauss were considered radical by positioning grounded theory method as an open-minded, inductive model. In the ensuing years, this has led to criticism of the method when researchers do not explicitly position the method in an appropriate worldview. Utilizing pragmatism as the philosophical worldview for this study, in conjunction with grounded theory method for data collection and analysis, yielded a model that is robust and truly grounded in the data (Merriam & Simpson, 1995).

Grounded Theory Method

Grounded theory method is intended to develop new theories, but what "a theory" means is ambiguous (Bryant, 2009). Theories span the range of those based on conjecture to those that have been extensively tested and challenged and yet still hold up (Bryant). By adopting an instrumental view of theories, it can be shown the ways a particular theory holds up in practice (Bryant). Theories developed with the grounded theory method are tied to the context in which the research is based, thus becoming substantive (Bryant). Glaser and Strauss (1967) explain that "generating a theory from data means that most hypotheses and concepts not only come from the data, but are systematically worked out in relation to the data during the course of the research" (p. 6).

A test of a theory or model generated with qualitative methodology is whether the findings will be applicable beyond the specific research subjects and setting (Bogdan & Biklen, 2007). I expect my model to hold up and be reproducible since it is grounded in the data due to the use of the scientific method as described by Peirce and Dewey. The relationship between theory and practice in a worldview of pragmatism lies in the utility of the theory in practice (Bryant, 2009). If the theory that is generated makes a difference in people's understanding and actions, then it is substantive (Bryant). The ultimate goal of this study was to make a difference in the career outcomes of the graduates of clinical exercise physiology programs.

Data Collection and Analysis Techniques

Grounded theory is unique because analysis of the data is done concurrently with data collection. The primary data for analysis were gathered through semi-structured and unstructured interviews with the participants—graduates from clinical exercise physiology programs practicing in the field. The codes that emerged from each interview were compared with previous interviews in order to guide the collection of additional data as well as to identify when enough data had been gathered (Merriam & Simpson, 1995). The goal of the data collection process was to gather sufficient information in order to identify common themes and generate a model of sustainable professional employment. I felt this method best revealed the factors that were involved in my study's participants achieving career success.

Qualitative semi-structured and unstructured interviews provided my main source of data because I wanted to understand my participants' unique journeys to their career success. An open-ended question asking the participants to describe their experiences from the time they started college to their current position began each interview. Questions were added to the later interviews to provide insight on themes that were revealed earlier in data collection, which is consistent with constant comparative analysis. Grounded theory method mandates that the researcher remain open to what is being said in order to observe and determine the main concern of the interviewees and how they were able to resolve it (Glaser & Holton, 2004).

A total of 21 interviews were conducted. Seventeen interviews were conducted with veterans in the field and four interviews were conducted with recent graduates of Benedictine University's program who aspired to higher positions within the healthcare system. By the time of the last few interviews, I felt I had gathered enough data since very little new information was revealed. This is consistent with Glaserian grounded theory method in that it proscribes interviews be conducted until saturation of the categories is achieved (Glaser, 1992, 1998).

Grounded theory method begins with Glaser's concept of *theoretical sensitivity*, which is essential to being able to generate concepts from data and turn them into theory. Glaser writes extensively on emergence, meaning concepts emerge from the data that in turn lead to the development of theories from the concepts that are identified. Development of grounded theory is based on taking the data collected and turning it into concepts referred to as *codes*. Theoretical coding begins with examining the data collected and grouping incidents into substantive categories. Substantive categories refer to particular aspects of the area being studied. These substantive categories are then examined to see how they might relate to each other in order to begin to develop the hypotheses that will eventually be turned into theory. Theoretical codes can be thought of as giving the big picture or a new perspective of what is occurring (Glaser & Holton, 2004, para. 47).

During open coding, the data are looked over carefully or line-by-line in order to determine what substantive codes can be found. Open coding can be thought of as the step where the story is broken apart so that the descriptive material can be reorganized into concepts (Mullen, 1996). The constant comparative method is one of the two foundational concepts of grounded theory, the other being theoretical sampling, which drives the development of the theory that emerges from the data. This is often referred to as a method to "tease out the similarities and differences in order to refine concepts" (Bryant & Charmez, 2007, p. 607).

Because grounded theory involves the simultaneous collection and coding of data, certain categories will become saturated earlier and this will help prevent the researcher from collecting redundant data (Holton, 2010). Saturation refers to the point at which "no new conceptual properties or dimensions are emerging" (p. 27) and, therefore, no additional data need to be obtained for that category since one more indicator or incident will not expand on the theory being developed. Glaser describes the core variable as the category that emerges and can explain most of the variation surrounding the main concern of the study. The core variable serves the function of linking together as many other categories as possible. It is what provides "grab" for the formal theory that is being developed (Glaser & Holton, 2004, para. 54).

Memo writing is important in capturing the analyst's thoughts, hunches, and impressions about the data as they are coding or just after an interview. Memos provide a way to help bring out the emerging theory. These memos are not detailed notes; rather, they are theoretical descriptions. Upon reaching the point of theoretical saturation, the analyst takes the memos and sorts them. This is how the data that have been broken apart during all the coding processes can be put together to form a cohesive theory. Because there are no preconceived notions with classic grounded theory, this allows for a richer and more robust theory. The relevant literature is brought into the theory during this process. Parsimony is the key here—what is the simplest explanation of the resolution of the core concern expressed by the participants (Glaser & Holton, 2004, para. 66–70)?

The next step is sorting the memos in order to explain the most variation in the data with the least number of concepts. According to Glaser and Holton (2004), this will result in a theory that will be able to explain how the subjects are able to resolve "their main concern with concepts that fit, work, have relevance and are saturated" (para. 71–74). This goes back to the pragmatist view that theories should be viewed as tools and they should be judged by how well they help people resolve their main concerns (Bryant, 2009, para. 103).

I concur with Bryant that when grounded theory is based on a worldview of pragmatism, the theories and concepts generated are evaluated based on how applicable they are to certain situations (Bryant, 2009). Being able to generate a model out of my research that can be used to help counsel students to sustainable professional employment in the clinical exercise physiology profession reflects the pragmatic orientation of this study.

Turning Words into Theory

Classic grounded theory utilizes the participant's own words to derive the theory, therefore, generating an inductive, substantive theory. The process of analysis began with line-by-line coding that entailed examining the words of the participants and assigning codes to concepts conveyed. No predefined list of codes was used so as to avoid preconceiving what would be found in the data (Glaser, 1992). This first pass of coding the interview transcripts yielded numerous codes, many of them repetitious. These codes were compared and those that were very similar in terms of the concept they were trying to describe were combined. Then the categories were examined for their relationships with each other and how accurately they represented the participants' concerns. Codes were also examined to determine their best fit within the categories that were identified. This was an iterative process, and numerous additional passes of the data were made until it was felt that the categories derived accurately described the participants' observations.

It was during this interactive process that a core category appeared to emerge that represented the main concern of the study participants. Other categories also emerged that supported this core category. Eventually this process yielded 11 main categories as follows: *academic preparation, competitive job market, professional devel-*

opment, career satisfaction, professional identity, credentials, compensation, licensure, scope of practice, boundaries of expertise, and *recognition of the expertise of clinical exercise physiologists.* The relationships among these categories were examined in order to produce a model that explains the key factors involved in the attainment of sustainable professional employment in the clinical exercise physiology field.

The development of the model of sustainable professional employment for clinical exercise physiologists has been central to my research purposes. The model reflects the processes involved in the journeys of successful clinical exercise physiologists, starting with their academic careers and culminating in an understanding of their current level of career satisfaction. In addition to deriving the factors that influenced their success, the challenges encountered in the practice of clinical exercise physiology were examined and are represented in the model.

The model created as a result of this study is pragmatic in the sense that it is a tool that can be used by others to address the concerns faced in practicing the profession of clinical exercise physiology (Bryant, 2009, para. 103). These categories form two main components of the model: (1) *the path to employment in cardiac rehabilitation and diagnostics environment,* and (2) *recognition of the expertise of clinical exercise physiologists.*

The Path to Employment

The bottom portion of the model shown in figure 8.1 describes the process of becoming a successful practitioner in the field. The information derived from the interviews spanned many years. No matter the length of their journeys, all participants went through a process of transformation in order to become the successful practitioners they are today. No two participant's journeys were the same; however, there were many commonalities among them. All of the participants' journeys, *the path to employment in the cardiac rehabilitation and diagnostics environment,* consisted of four main categories: (1) *academic preparation,* (2) *competitive job market,* (3) *professional development,* and (4) *career satisfaction.*

Academic Preparation

In the Chicago area, a master's degree is usually required to secure a position in cardiac rehabilitation and diagnostics departments. Key components of academic preparation are clinical internships as well as the program of study's rigor. Nearly all of the study's participants felt that their internships were a critical component of their academic preparation (Ives & Knudson, 2007). The participants agreed that internships are a form of anticipatory socialization that allows a student to try on a career (Callanan & Benzing, 2004). It was through clinical internships that several of the participants discovered how much they loved the field of cardiac rehabilitation.

Hennemann and Liefner (2010) stress that an important component of an academic program is the development of competence. The goal of my participants when they have student interns is to have them as competent as regular staff by the end of their internship. *Academic preparation* is linked with the *competitive job market* through the networks that students begin to develop when they perform their internships. Many of the participants attained their first positions in the field through their internships.

Competitive Job Market

The next step in the path is entering the job market. The cardiac rehabilitation and diagnostics environment is very competitive in the Chicago area; thus, enhancing one's employability is key. Employability encompasses the "skills, understandings, and personal attributes" (Atlay, 2010, p. 19) that improve the chances that graduates will obtain employment in the occupation of their choice. Internships serve as a means for students to demonstrate their employability to potential employers.

My participants constantly emphasized the importance of networking, not only to enter the field but also their ability to advance within the field. Networking is a critical component in securing employment in addition to internships since both provide a means for students to demonstrate their competencies to potential employers (Sherman & Dyess, 2010). Henley's (1999) comment that "what you know counts, but who you know counts, too" was reflected in the number of instances where practitioners in this study obtained positions before they were even advertised.

Professional Development

Attainment of a position in the field is not the final step; those who hope to advance need to continue to invest in professional development. It is important to keep up with the changes in healthcare in terms of treatments, patient demographics, and insurance reimbursements that have a direct impact on participants' departments and, in turn, their job security. Continuing education is a means of lifelong learning and a way to develop professionalism (Garman, Evans, Krause, & Anfossi, 2006). This study's participants utilized different approaches toward continuing education. Educational opportunities offered through professional societies are a common way that practitioners stay current in the field. *Professional develop-*

ment is linked with the *competitive job market* primarily through the networks participants built through service in professional organizations.

Career Satisfaction

The culmination of *the path to employment in cardiac rehabilitation and diagnostics environment* is achieving satisfaction with your career choice. The vast majority of this study's participants had engaged in internships in the area in which they are currently employed. The awareness of the work environment produced by internships contributed to students making a commitment to the profession (Callanan & Benzing, 2004; Cranmer, 2006). Career success and fulfillment are a "function of the individual optimizing the 'fit' between their personal characteristics and their work environment" (Callahan & Benzing, p. 82). This was reflected in the passion that the successful practitioners exhibited when they spoke of their work with patients, which is also consistent with the findings of Ng and Feldman (2010) regarding the factors that contribute positively to a sense of well-being.

It Is a Profession! Recognition of the Expertise of Clinical Exercise Physiologists

A key concept in the development of grounded theory is that the researcher is to determine the main concern of the interviewee and how the person was able to resolve it (Glaser & Holton, 2004). This study's participants shared much information about their journeys, but the one key concern that kept emerging was the difficulty of having their expertise recognized by other healthcare practitioners. This main concern, or core category, is positioned in the center of the top section of the model presented in figure 8.1. Surrounding the core category are the categories, or factors, that influence it. These supporting categories include *professional identity, credentials, compensation, licensure, scope of practice*, and *boundaries of expertise*. The model represented in figure 8.1 also portrays the interrelationships between these categories and those that comprise *the path to employment in the cardiac rehabilitation and diagnostics environment*.

Professional Identity

Even though Brown (2000) argues that exercise physiology is not a profession, this study's participants felt that it *was* a profession. As part of the push for licensure to further establish exercise physiology as a profession, academic programs in clinical exercise physiology are being encouraged to attain accreditation. As part of accreditation, academic programs must demonstrate that their curriculum will ensure their graduates will possess a defined set of knowledge, skills, and abilities. Without this standardization it is hard for others to know what expertise a clinical exercise physiologist should possess. This results in a lack of a clear professional identity that works against attaining the *recognition of the expertise of clinical exercise physiologists* among those in the healthcare community.

In addition, clinical exercise physiologists are not united behind a single professional organization unlike other professions such as physical therapy. Only some of this study's participants were members either of the American Association of Cardiovascular and Pulmonary Rehabilitation (AACVPR) or the Illinois Society for Cardiopulmonary Health and Rehabilitation (ISCHR). However, these organizations do not represent those practitioners who work outside of cardiac rehabilitation. The lack of a single organization that actually represents all of clinical exercise physiologists hinders the attainment of the *recognition of the expertise of clinical exercise physiologists*.

Credentials

One way to address the current lack of a standardized curriculum is for practitioners to take certification examinations to prove that they do have the knowledge, skills, and abilities required of those who desire to work in the cardiac rehabilitation and diagnostics environment. Despite Keteyian's (1999) findings that certification examinations help address concerns from other healthcare professions regarding the academic preparation of exercise physiologists, this study's participants felt that examinations were of limited value because they only tested book knowledge. In addition, there was much confusion over what the differences were between the Exercise Specialist (ES), Clinical Exercise Specialist (CES), and Registered Clinical Exercise Physiologist (RCEP) certifications offered by the American College of Sports Medicine (ACSM).

Compensation

This study's participants are frustrated because they are paid less than nurses even though they have a higher level of education; they do not feel that their compensation reflects their expertise (Davis, Jankovitz, & Cooper, 2001). Although Davis and colleagues and Ives and Knudson (2007) suggest that the employment of exercise physiologists might be favored over other licensed professionals such as nurses because of the salary differences, this was not consistent with what this study's participants reported. Due to the limits on scope of practice, nurses were still needed and, in fact, it was the versatility of nurses that made utilizing them preferable in cardiac rehabilitation and diagnostics departments despite their higher wages. Some of this study's participants suggested that licensure would increase the utilization of exercise physiologists.

Licensure

The lack of licensure for clinical exercise physiologists poses several problems. Of biggest concern to this study's participants is the lack of professional equality they feel when compared with other healthcare professionals. On a microlevel, they reported excellent working relationships with the other professions in their department, but on a macrolevel, there were concerns about the discrepancy in pay as well as limitations on what they could do as part of their jobs.

Related to *licensure* is *professional identity*. As a profession, we have not done a good job defining who we are and what we do since there are so many different career paths that clinical exercise physiologists can pursue. Berry and Verrill (2012) argue that "achieving licensure will finally enable the CEP to be viewed in the same light and with the same respect as other licensed health care professionals who work in the rehabilitation fields" (p. 37). Foster and Porcari (2012) outline the great difficulty involved in convincing legislators to support licensure due to the lack of evidence showing that large numbers of the general public are being harmed by the activities of unqualified practitioners. The points made by Foster and Porcari echo what this study's participants have mentioned—that we in the profession are not coming together to present a unified front in terms of minimal educational standards as well as working together with larger organizations, such as the physical therapists, to better define how our profession can work effectively with other professions in delivering patient care.

Scope of Practice

This category is related to *licensure* as part of the process of creating a practice act for a profession that defines those activities practitioners are permitted to engage in and what is prohibited. This study's participants repeatedly related how they were not able to perform certain activities, such as giving medications to a patient or taking orders from a doctor, due to the restrictions of the Nurse Practice Act. Several expressed frustration over how these restrictions limited their ability to service their patients. *Scope of practice* affects compensation because exercise physiologists are not able to function independently in cardiac rehabilitation. For smaller cardiac rehabilitation outreach sites, this often means that a registered nurse will be utilized since they are more versatile, thus keeping staffing to a minimum. Several of this study's participants suggested an expansion of scope of practice for clinical exercise physiologists could result in need for fewer nurses. This, in turn, could have a positive impact on *competitive job market*.

Boundaries of Expertise

Nancarrow and Borthwick (2005) found that professional boundaries are dynamic due to staffing shortages caused by changes in healthcare policies. Many of this study's participants reported a high degree of role sharing between exercise physiologists and nurses. The ability of clinical exercise physiologists to perform a wide variety of roles in the cardiac rehabilitation and diagnostics environment demonstrates their broad expertise. *Scope of practice* is related to *boundaries of expertise* since the scope of practice helps to define what should be expected of each profession. Regarding the scope of practice for exercise physiologists, ACSM mentions the use of exercise as a means of therapy for clinical situations such as those found in cardiac rehabilitation and diagnostics environments (Verrill & Keteyian, 2010). This study's participants felt that exercise prescription was best left to clinical exercise physiologists. Several participants believed patients were not being served well when cardiac rehabilitation programs only utilized registered nurses. They felt the lack of training for nurses in exercise prescription was a disservice to the patient.

Recognition of the Expertise of Clinical Exercise Physiologists

The main concern of this study's participants was earning recognition of their unique expertise from the other healthcare professionals. Many of this study's participants felt that they were being held back because they are not licensed professionals like nurses or physical therapists. As was previously discussed, there are several facets to this perception of a lack of recognition of expertise. A strong *professional identity*, such as that possessed by other professions, can help practitioners earn respect because it clarifies the role that the practitioner serves on the healthcare team. However, as was previously discussed, clinical exercise physiology practitioners are not unified behind one organization.

An acknowledgment of a practitioner's expertise is often demonstrated when they are paid in accordance with their *credentials*. However, the reality that a nurse with only an associate's degree has a higher starting salary than a clinical exercise physiologist with a master's degree makes some question their career choice. Other practitioners in this study take a more philosophical view—that it is more important to do something you are passionate about rather than earn a higher salary but not enjoy your work.

Licensure, despite being touted as a means to gain credibility and recognition, does not appear to be anywhere close to becoming a reality in the majority of states.

Furthermore, this study's participants were mixed in their feelings regarding the benefit they would actually derive, and they questioned whether it would cause an additional burden, not only in terms of limits on the activities they could perform but also the expense practitioners would have to assume in attaining and maintaining a license.

Practitioners often feel that their unique expertise is not recognized due to the limitations imposed on their *scope of practice* by the Nurse Practice Act. This goes along with establishing *boundaries of expertise*. Clinical exercise physiologists have a significant investment in acquiring expertise in exercise prescription and the body's responses to the stress of exercise. They desire to utilize their expertise to provide better outcomes for their patients. While some of this study's participants feel that their expertise is recognized and sought out by other professions, it was not a sentiment that was shared by all.

The model of sustainable professional employment for clinical exercise physiologists generated by this study reflects the processes by which this study's participants have achieved their career success in addition to presenting their main concern of achieving recognition of the expertise of clinical exercise physiologists. This model shown in figure 8.1 has been developed out of the analyses of the interviews that were conducted and has been further substantiated by relevant literature in the field. Arrows are used to represent how *the path to employment in the cardiac rehabilitation and diagnostics environment* interacts with *recognition of the expertise of clinical exercise physiologists*.

This model represents a pragmatic and inspiring tool to be used by practitioners in the field as well as those who hope to pursue new levels of career attainment. The inclusion of the perspectives of recent graduates into the creation of this model helps to strengthen its applicability to those students who seek to enter the field.

The original idea for this study started with a flash of insight when I observed so many exemplars in the field that had inexplicably overcome the challenges of the profession of clinical exercise physiology and attained career success. The use of grounded theory method revealed much about the preparation and practice of clinical exercise physiologists employed in the cardiac rehabilitation and diagnostics environment. I gained insight into the importance of clinical internships and the development of professional networks in attaining employment. I was dismayed to discover how widespread the lack of name recognition is for clinical exercise physiologists, even in a healthcare setting. Clinical exercise physiologists make significant contributions in cardiac rehabilitation due to their extensive master's level academic preparation that is the equivalent of nurses, dieticians, and physical therapists. Clinical exercise physiologists often work side-by-side with these professions, yet lack the recognition of expertise that licensure conveys. I

Figure 8.1. Model of Sustainable Professional Employment for Clinical Exercise Physiologists

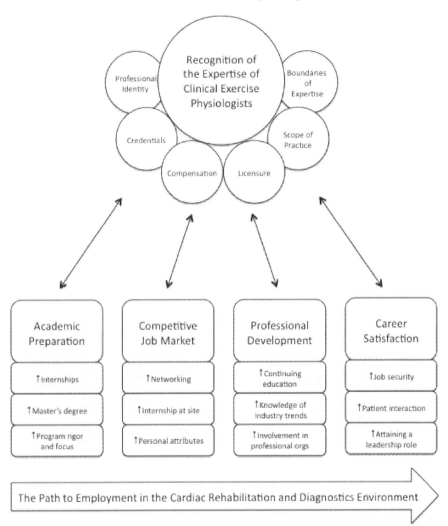

was saddened to learn they are treated as the odd duck in the clinical environment because they do not exist independently despite being highly skilled (Foster & Porcari, 2012). Much work remains to unite our profession and elevate its standing in the healthcare setting.

References

American Physical Therapy Association. (n.d.). *Who are physical therapists?* Retrieved from http://www.apta.org/AboutPTs/

Atlay, M. (2010). *Introducing CRe8—The Curriculum Review 2008.* Retrieved from http://www.beds.ac.uk/__data/assets/pdf_file/0017/26702/creatingbridges-new.pdf

Berry, R., & Verrill, D. (2012). POINT: Licensure for clinical exercise physiologists—An argument in favor of this proposal. *Journal of Clinical Exercise Physiology, 1*(1), 35–38.

Bogdan, R. C., & Biklen, S. K. (2007). *Qualitative research for education: An introduction to theory and methods.* Boston: Pearson.

Brown, S. P. (2000). Profession or discipline: The role of exercise physiology in allied health. *Clinical Exercise Physiology, 2*(1), 52.

Bryant, A. (2009). Grounded theory and pragmatism: The curious case of Anselm Strauss. *Forum: Qualitative Social Research, 10*(3). Retrieved from http://www.qualitative-research.net/index.php/fqs/article/view/1358

Bryant, A., & Charmaz, K. (Eds.). (2007). *The Sage handbook of grounded theory.* London: Sage.

Callanan, G., & Benzing, C. (2004). Assessing the role of internships in the career-oriented employment of graduating college students. *Education & Training, 46*(2), 82–89.

Clinical Exercise Physiology Association. (n.d.). *Consumer information: Clinical exercise physiology.* Retrieved from http://www.acsm-cepa.org/i4a/pages/index.cfm?pageid=3393

Cranmer, S. (2006). Enhancing graduate employability: Best intentions and mixed outcomes. *Studies in Higher Education, 31*(2), 169–184.

Creswell, J. W., & Clark, V. L. (2011). *Designing and conducting mixed methods research* (2nd ed.). Thousand Oaks, CA: Sage.

Davis, S., Jankovitz, K., & Cooper, J. (2001). California cardiac rehabilitation practitioners and their staff preparation preferences. *Clinical Exercise Physiology, 3*(2), 94.

Foster, C., & Porcari, J. P. (2012). COUNTERPOINT: Licensure for clinical exercise physiologists—A desirable goal with an elusive outcome. *Journal of Clinical Exercise Physiology, 1*(1), 38–40.

Garman, A. N., Evans, R., Krause, M., & Anfossi, J. (2006). Professionalism. *Journal of Healthcare Management, 51*(4), 219–222.

Glaser, B. G. (1992). *Emergence vs. forcing: Basics of grounded theory analysis.* Mill Valley, CA: Sociology.

Glaser, B. G. (1998). *Doing grounded theory: Issues and discussions.* Mill Valley, CA: Sociology.

Glaser, B. G., & Holton, J. (2004). Remodeling grounded theory. *Forum Qualitative Social Research, 5*(2). Retrieved from http://www.qualitative-research.net/index.php/fqs/article/view/607

Glaser, B. G., & Strauss, A. L. (1965). *Awareness of dying.* Hawthorne, NY: Aldine de Gruyter.

Glaser, B. G., & Strauss, A. L. (1967). *The discovery of grounded theory: Strategies for qualitative research.* Hawthorne, NY: Aldine de Gruyter.

Henley, R. J. (1999). Enhancing what you know through who you know. *hfm (Healthcare Financial Management), 53*(12). Retrieved from http://findarticles.com/p/articles/mi_m3257/is_12_53/ai_58185737/

Hennemann, S., & Liefner, I. (2010). Employability of German geography graduates: The mismatch between knowledge acquired and competences required. *Journal of Geography in Higher Education, 34*(2), 215–230.

Holton, J. A. (2010). The coding process and its challenges. *Grounded Theory Review, 9*(1), 21–40.

Ives, J. C., & Knudson, D. (2007). Professional practice in exercise science. *Sports Medicine, 37*(2), 103–115.

Keteyian, S. J. (1999). Trained in a discipline and practicing as a professional…Who we are, revisited. *Clinical Exercise Physiology, 1*(2), 55.

Merriam, S. B., & Simpson, E. L. (1995). *A guide to research for educators and trainers of adults.* Malabar, FL: Krieger.

Mills, J., Bonner, A., & Francis, K. (2006). The development of constructivist grounded theory. *International Journal of Qualitative Methods, 5*(1), 1–10.

Mullen, P. D. (1996). Cutting back: Life after a heart attack. In B. G. Glaser (Ed.), *Gerund grounded theory: The basic social process dissertation* (pp. 60–72). Mill Valley, CA: Sociology.

Nancarrow, S., & Borthwick, A. M. (2005). Dynamic professional boundaries in the healthcare workforce. *Sociology of Health & Illness, 27*(7), 897–919.

Ng, T., & Feldman, D. (2010). Human capital and objective indicators of career success: The mediating effects of cognitive ability and conscientiousness. *Journal of Occupational & Organizational Psychology, 83*(1), 207–235.

Ozmon, H. A., & Craver, S. M. (2003). *Philosophical foundations of education.* Upper Saddle River, NJ: Merrill Prentice Hall.

Potteiger, J. A. (2011). *ACSM's introduction to exercise science.* Baltimore: Lippincott Williams & Wilkins.

Sherman, R. O., & Dyess, S. (2010). New graduate transition into practice during turbulent economic times. *Journal of Nursing Education, 49*(7), 367–368.

Strauss, A., & Corbin, J. (1990). *Basics of qualitative research.* Newbury Park, CA: Sage.

U.S. Department of Labor, Bureau of Labor Statistics. (2010). *Standard occupational classification: 29–1128 exercise physiologists.* Retrieved from http://www.bls.gov/soc/2010/soc291128.htm

Verrill, D. E., & Keteyian, S. J. (2010). Evolution of the clinical exercise physiologist. In J. Myers & D. C. Nieman (Eds.), *ACSM's resources for clinical exercise physiology: Musculoskeletal, neuromuscular, neoplastic, immunologic, and hematologic conditions* (pp. 280–287). Philadelphia: Lippincott Williams & Wilkins.

CHAPTER NINE

The Impact of Cognitive Information Processing on the Career Decision Making of First-Year College Students

ANNE PERRY AND NANCY W. BENTLEY

Introduction

This chapter presents an experimental research study that examines the impact of an intervention strategy in the thought processes of first-year college students toward career problem solving and decision making. The study used the Career Thoughts Inventory (CTI) (Sampson, Peterson, Lenz, Reardon, & Saunders, 1996a), a standardized career assessment tool that categorizes participants into a specific construct area, and an intervention based on Cognitive Information Processing theory (Sampson, Lenz, Reardon, & Peterson, 1999) using a related CTI workbook, *Improving Your Career Thoughts: A Workbook for the Career Thoughts Inventory* (Sampson, Peterson, Lenz, Reardon, & Saunders, 1996b).

Theoretical Framework

The cognitive information processing (CIP) approach to career development and services is intended to help individuals learn improved problem-solving and decision-making skills needed for career choices (Sampson, Peterson, Lenz, Reardon, & Saunders, 1998). Sampson and his colleagues made two determinations from their review of literature: "First, dysfunctional career thinking compromises the effectiveness of career problem solving and decision making. Second, effective cognitive restructuring strategies exist for identifying, challenging, and altering dysfunctional career thinking" (p. 116). They based their theory on cognitive therapy and the theoretical approach to (1) problem solving and decision making; (2) understanding the positive and negative impact of metacognitions on career problem solving and decision making; and (3) a conceptual basis for instruction designed to enhance skills in career problem solving and decision making (Sampson et al., 1996a, p. 4). The underlying rationale for cognitive therapy is that an individual's behavior is largely determined by his or her cognitions. Cognitions are based on beliefs formed from past experiences, and they can become damaging if incoming stimuli is distorted to fit one's systematic thinking. Impaired thinking over time leads to faulty information processing and errors in reasoning.

In their approach, the Florida State researchers apply cognitive therapy to monitor and restructure negative thoughts by outlining four information-processing domains that students encounter during the decision-making process. They then conceptualized these as the pyramid of information processing domains, or the *knowing* element of decision making.

There are three levels of domains within the pyramid. At the bottom of the pyramid are the knowledge domains—self-knowledge and occupational knowledge. In the middle is the decision-making skills domain, and at the top is the executive-processing domain, which controls metacognitions such as self-talk and self-awareness. Within the *self-knowledge domain*, the individual answers questions relating to knowledge of self (values, interests, skills). Within the *occupational knowledge domain*, the individual answers questions relating to knowledge of occupations (programs of study, job-training requirements, and categories of employers). Within the *decision-making skills domain*, the individual answers questions related to the steps required to choose an occupation, programs of study that will meet individual needs, and the process for making important decisions. Within the *executive processing domain*, the individual investigates metacognitions such as self-talk and self-awareness, and the amount of assistance needed to make a decision. Through improved self-awareness, individuals can learn to reframe negative self-talk into positive self-talk, freeing themselves to apply their own effective problem-solving and decision-making skills, and in the process, enhance self-knowledge and occupational knowledge (Sampson et al., 1996a).

By improving decision-making skills, students can increase the likelihood of making effective career choices; therefore, the researchers focused on the decision-making skills domain. CASVE is an acronym for five stages of information processing that should be used by career counselors when assisting students. The first is the *Communication phase*, where an awareness of the gap between the existing and desired state of affairs is identified. The next phase is the *Analysis phase*, where a mental model of the problem and perceived relationships among the elements is created (such as relating self-knowledge with their knowledge of options). Soon students move into the *Synthesis phase*, where options are expanded (elaborate) and narrowed (crystallize). The fourth phase is called the *Valuing phase*, when the costs and benefits of options, to themselves and to others, is analyzed. Finally, students experience the *Execution phase*, where the creation of and commitment to an implementation plan for the tentative choice is made. Upon completion of the execution phase, students resume the communication phase to find out if there is still a gap between where they are and where they want to be, and if so, they repeat the CASVE cycle.

This cycle is intended to make a relatively complex process simple so that it is less overwhelming to students. External variables may influence the student's progression through the CASVE cycle; however, successful application of the approach requires assistance from career-counseling sources. By reducing negative career thinking, students will be more likely to process information related to career decision making successfully. Negative thinking does not just occur in the executive processing domain though; it is possible across all elements of the pyramid of information processing and CASVE combined. For the purpose of developing an assessment tool and workbook to implement the concepts in the theory, the four domains and CASVE subcomponents were organized into eight cognitive information processing dimensions: self-knowledge, occupational knowledge, communication, analysis, synthesis, valuing, execution, and executive processing (Sampson et al., 1996a, p. 11). The cognitive restructuring process in the workbook is designed to have the user identify, challenge, and alter negative career thoughts, then follow up with action (p. 16).

Negative thinking compromises the cogency of problem solving and decision making, and can hinder students from setting goals. Understanding how information is processed is essential in identifying, challenging, and reframing negative thoughts, setting appropriate goals, and creating an action plan to achieve those goals. Through the use of the pyramid of information processing and the CASVE cycle, counselors and students can work together to apply cognitive restructuring.

Methodology

An experimental design was used to examine the impact of an assessment and intervention process on 116 college students enrolled in freshman-level core college courses at an open-enrollment, career-oriented, regionally accredited, Midwestern proprietary university. The courses were divided into two different groups, one group of participants that completed an intervention using an accompanying CTI workbook, and a control group. All students were assessed using the CTI. The intervention workbook was designed to use the eight cognitive information processing content dimensions to categorize participants using three different constructs: decision-making confusion (DMC), commitment anxiety (CA), or external conflict (EC). The participants who completed the workbook were then led through methods to overcome barriers to career problem solving and decision making, and take action steps to implement a career choice.

The following research question was identified for this study: Will a workbook intervention based on Cognitive Information Processing theory help improve CTI scores of first-year college students when used in a non-career development classroom setting?

The hypothesis is CTI scores for subjects who complete the workbook intervention will be lower than for those who do not.

Data Collection

Freshman-level core college courses were selected for the study and randomly divided into two groups, an intervention group and a control group. The CTI and the workbook intervention were administered during regular scheduled classes, and because the workbook intervention is based on the results of the CTI total score and content scores, the groups completed both a pre-test and a post-test. A comparison of post-tests for each group was made.

Figure 9.1 illustrates the structure that was used throughout the study.

Participants

The participant sample was comprised of 116 first-year college students enrolled in freshman-level courses at an open enrollment for-profit university in Illinois. Students 18 years of age or older participated in the study via their mandatory core coursework, and all were informed that the results of the study were intended to

Figure 9.1: Data Collection Structure

GROUPS	PRE-TEST	INTERVENTION	POST-TEST	DATA ANALYSIS
TEST GROUP IG	CTI total score and breakdown of content scores: DMC, EC, CA	Intervention	CTI total score and breakdown of content scores: DMC, EC, CA	Pre-test vs. post-test results for IG
CONTROL GROUP CG	CTI total score and breakdown of content scores: DMC, EC, CA	No Intervention	CTI total score and breakdown of content scores: DMC, EC, CA	Pre-test vs. post-test results for CG
				IG vs. CG post-test results

evaluate the effectiveness of using an intervention in improving career decision making and career readiness. They were also informed that all data would be reported as aggregate data.

Variables in the Study

1. Independent Variables: (1) CTI workbook intervention; (2) Student questionnaire
2. Dependent Variables: (1) CTI Total scores; (2) CTI construct scores—decision-making confusion (DMC), commitment anxiety (CA), and external conflict (EC)

Instrument

The Career Thoughts Inventory (CTI) was chosen because it is both a diagnostic and a treatment product designed to help individuals identify, challenge, and alter negative thinking that impairs their ability to solve career-related issues successfully. It can serve as a screening measure for individuals experiencing career choice problems, as a needs assessment to identify the specific nature of individuals' negative thinking, and as a learning resource to challenge specific thoughts that prevent them from making proper career choices. The inventory, answer sheet, and profile form were included in a booklet, and the first three pages contained a brief explanation of the purpose of the inventory, instructions for the participant, and spaces for entering demographic information. The CTI readability level is 7th grade, and it is intended for use with 11th and 12th grade high school students, college students, and adults choosing a field of study, seeking employment, reentering the labor market, or considering an occupational change. It is self-administered, uses paper and pencil, and contains 48 items that are objectively measured. Items were scored using a 4-point Likert scale ranging from strongly agree (3.00) to strongly disagree (0.00), and the CTI can be completed in 7 to 15 minutes (Sampson et al., 1996a, p. 22).

Each item on the CTI addressed at least one of the eight cognitive information processing content dimensions: self-knowledge, options knowledge, communication, analysis, synthesis, valuing, execution, and executive processes. The CTI yields a total score as well as scores in three construct scales: 14 items are assigned to Decision-Making Confusion Scale, 10 items are assigned to Commitment Anxiety Scale, and 5 items are assigned to External Conflict Scale. Decision-making confusion (DMC) refers to inability to initiate or sustain the decision-making process as a result of emotions that deter decision making and/or a lack of understanding about the decision-making process itself. Commitment anxiety (CA) reflects inability to make a commitment to a specific career choice, accompanied by general-ized anxiety about the outcome of the decision-making process that perpetuates indecision. External conflict (EC) reflects inability to balance the importance of one's own self-perceptions with the importance of input from significant others, re-sulting in a reluctance to assume responsibility for decision making (Sampson et al., 1996a, pp. 28–29). The CTI workbook, *Improving Your Career Thoughts: A Work-book for the Career Thoughts Inventory* (Sampson et al., 1996b), is used to facilitate an individual's understanding of the nature of his or her negative thoughts based on construct score results.

Reliability of the Instrument

Since the survey instrument has several constructs consisting of sub-items that are included in a composite score or summated scale for the specific construct, the most commonly used and appropriate type of measure to determine internal con-sistency is Cronbach's coefficient alpha for each assessment construct (Leech, Bar-rett, & Morgan, 2005). Gliner and Morgan indicate that this measure of reliability takes only one administration, and it is a suitable method for multiple-choice in-struments such as the Likert scales used in my research. According to Fontain (2010) at the Buros Institute of Mental Measurements who evaluated the CTI in-strument adopted in my research, the Cronbach's alphas for CTI total score range from .93 to .97; the Cronbach's alphas for DMC range from .90 to .94; the Cron-bach's alphas for CA range from .79 to .91; while the Cronbach's alphas for EC range from .74 to .81, showing that all instrument items have good to very good in-ternal consistency reliability.

Stability of the CTI total score and construct scales was determined by the CTI authors by having 73 college students and 48 high school students complete the CTI twice over a four-week period. For the college student sample, test-retest CTI total score was high ($r = .86$), indicating there was little change in responses over a four-week period. The same pattern was observed for the high school student sam-ple, with the CTI total at ($r = .69$) and the construct scales ranging from .72 for DMC, .70 for CA, and .52 for EC, showing that adequate stability exists (Samp-son et al., 1996a, p. 51).

Validity of the Instrument

Content validity was built into the development strategy for the CTI items and scales. Individual items and construct scales are directly linked to CIP theory through content dimensions. Because the test authors are also the developers of the CIP theory, expert content analysis is adequate (Fontain, 2010).

Evidence of construct validity (DMC, CA, and EC) for the instrument was established through a series of factor analyses. The CTI total score is highly correlated ($r = .89$ to $.94$) with DMC for all groups. These correlations suggest that a general predisposition toward negative thinking strongly influences subsequent aspects of negative career thinking such as commitment anxiety. External conflict (EC) appears to be less related to general negative thinking as represented by the lower correlation of EC with the CTI total score ($r = .23–.80$) (Sampson et al., 1996a, p. 52).

The authors of the CTI established evidence of convergent validity by administering four other instruments with similar concepts to 50 adults, 152 college students, and 151 11- and 12-grade high school students. Assessments included *My Vocational Situation* (Holland, Daiger, & Power, 1980), *The Career Decision Scale* (Osipow, Carney, Winer, Yanico, & Koschier, 1987), *The NEO PI-R* (Costa & McCrae, 1992), and *The Career Decision Profile* (Jones, 1989). CTI scales were directly correlated with indecision, and consistently inversely correlated with positive constructs such as career goals. The CTI total score was consistently directly correlated with neuroticism and vulnerability. As was expected, only career choice importance exhibited inconsistency in relationships across groups (Sampson et al., 1996a, p. 58).

Description of Research Findings

Data were analyzed using linear regression, to determine the degree of relationship between CTI total scores and content scores from pre-test to post-test for each individual group, and one-way analysis of variance (ANOVA), to determine if there was a significant difference between the post-test CTI total, DMC, CA, and EC mean scores of the intervention group (IG) and the control group (CG). The results of the analysis of variance would determine if the hypothesis was correct.

Comparison between Groups

This section presents the results of the statistical analysis using a significance level $p = .05$ and shows pre-test comparisons between groups, pre-test to post-test comparisons within each group, and post-test comparisons between groups to show the impact of the intervention. Scores represent the level of dysfunctional thinking.

Pre-test Comparisons between Groups

Using one-way Analysis of Variance (ANOVA), pre-test comparisons were made between the group dependent variables, the CTI total score, and the three content area scores: Decision-Making Confusion (DMC), Commitment Anxiety

(CA), and External Conflict (EC). The analysis of pre-test data showed there were no significant differences ($p \leq .05$) between group means for any of the variables.

Pre-test to Post-test Comparisons

Using linear regression, comparisons were made to determine the impact of the intervention on the total score and content area scores for each group. The post-test scores for the intervention group were significantly lower than the control group, supporting the hypothesis that CTI scores for subjects who complete the workbook intervention will be lower than for those who do not. For the intervention group, the CTI total score mean decreased from 37.79 (SD = 22.06) at pre-test to a mean of 27.34 (SD = 22.22) at post-test. The Decision-Making Confusion mean decreased from 6.90 (SD = 5.76) at pre-test to a mean of 5.17 (SD = 6.24) at post-test. The Commitment Anxiety mean decreased from 10.64 (SD = 6.44) to a mean of 7.94 (SD = 6.53) at post-test, and it is interesting to note that the CA score for the control group actually increased from pre-test to post-test, although it was not significant. Finally, there was a significant decrease in the External Conflict mean from 4.18 (SD = 3.19) at pre-test to 2.51 (SD = 2.69) at post-test. All content areas contributed significantly to the total score; however, regression analysis revealed that Commitment Anxiety had the greatest impact, with Decision Making Confusion following, and External Conflict contributing the least.

With regard to the group mean comparisons, while the control group shows a slight change from pre-test to post-test, it is not statistically significant, as compared to the intervention group whose scores show a significant decrease from pre-test to post-test.

Post-test Comparisons between Groups

Using one-way Analysis of Variance (ANOVA), post-test comparisons were made between the group CTI total scores and the content area scores. Results of the analysis support the hypothesis, with statistically significant differences in the mean post-test scores for the intervention group versus the control group. Post-test scores for the group that completed the intervention are significantly lower, showing a decline in negative thinking toward career decision making.

Career Questionnaire

All student participants filled out a questionnaire designed to determine the level of occupational preparation experienced prior to the study. Both the intervention group and the control group had similar results, ranging from 6 to 7% of group participants stating that they had clearly established goals that met their occupational interests, and 32–34% had considered changing their major. None of the participants had been enrolled in a career development course, had met with a career services staff member for the purpose of discussing career goals, or completed an assessment to help determine possible careers.

Conclusions

At the start of the study, there were 61 students in the intervention group and 55 students in the control group. At the time the post-tests were administered, through attrition, the groups were reduced to 47 students in the intervention group, and 53 students in the control group. The groups began the study with no significant differences between their pre-test scores; however, post-test result comparisons between the groups exhibited statistically significant improvements ($p \leq .05$) in every area for the intervention group. All data were compiled as aggregate group data in an effort to maintain student anonymity and, therefore, individual participant comparisons could not be made.

The results of this study suggest that the CIP intervention reduced negative career thoughts of college students enrolled in freshman-level coursework. Individual content area results for the intervention group also verified that using an assessment and intervention process during the first year of college can improve how students feel about areas of personal concern such as career opportunities, conflicts that interrupt their studies, and personal anxieties related to setting career goals. Results for the control group showed only a slight decrease in negative thoughts, except for the content area that focused on conflicts that interrupt their studies and results showed an increase in negative thoughts. This increase may be attributed to various external factors related to student demographics, work status, or family issues.

Bibliography

Costa, P. J., & McCrae, R. (1992). *Revised NEO personality inventory.* Odessa, FL: Psychological Assessment Resources.

Fontain, J. (2010). Review of the career thoughts inventory. *Buros Institute Mental Measurements Yearbook.* Lutz, FL: Psychological Assessment Resources.

Gliner, J. A., & Morgan, G. A. (2000). *Research methods in applied settings: An integrated approach to design and analysis.* Mahwah, NJ: Psychology.

Holland, J., Daiger, D., & Power, G. (1980). *My vocational situation.* Palo Alto, CA: Consulting Psychologists.

Jones, L. (1989). Measuring a three-dimensional construct of career indecision among college students: A revision of the vocational decision scale—the career decision profile. *Journal of Counseling Psychology, 36,* 477–486

Leech, N. L., Barrett, K. C., & Morgan, G. A. (2005). *SPSS for intermediate statistics: Use and interpretation.* Mahwah, NJ: Lawrence Erlbaum.

Osipow, S., Carney, C., Winer, J., Yanico, B., & Koschier, M. (1987). *Career decision scale.* Odessa, FL: Psychological Assessment Resources.

Peterson, G.W., Sampson, J. P., Reardon, R. C., & Lenz, J. G. (2003). *Core concepts of a cognitive approach to career development and services.* Tallahassee, FL: Center for the Study of Technology in Counseling and Career Development.

Sampson, J. P., Lenz, J. G., Reardon, R. C., & Peterson, G. W. (1999). A cognitive information approach to employment problem solving and decision making. *Career Development Quarterly, 48,* 3–18.

Sampson, J., Peterson, G., Lenz, J., Reardon, R., & Saunders, D. (1996a). *Career Thoughts Inventory professional manual.* Lutz, FL: Psychological Assessment Resources.

Sampson, J. Peterson, G., Lenz, J., Reardon, R., & Saunders, D. (1996b). *Improving your career thoughts: A workbook for the Career Thoughts Inventory.* Odessa, FL: Psychological Assessment Resources.

Sampson, J., Peterson, G., Lenz, J., Reardon, R., & Saunders, D. (1998). The design and use of a measure of dysfunctional career thoughts among adults, college students, and high school students: The Career Thoughts Inventory. *Journal of Career Assessment, 6*(2), 115–134.

CHAPTER TEN

Greek Parents' Perceptions and Experiences Regarding Their Children's Learning and Social-Emotional Difficulties

EIRINI ADAMOPOULOU

Introduction

A major issue confronting the mental health service system for children and adolescents worldwide is the role of the family. Children, for the most part, cannot access services on their own; parents must provide permission, transportation, knowledge of available sources, and financial resources for a child to receive care (Farmer, Burns, Angold, & Costello, 1997). Cultural and ethnic differences are associated with differences in parents' beliefs about children's problems, the pathways that lead youngsters into mental health care, the kinds of referral problems identified by parents when they do seek help, and the kinds of interventions for those problems preferred by parents (McMiller & Weisz, 1996). Therefore, efforts to advance mental health services for children and adolescents in a particular country should include an examination of parents' distinct cultural differences and perceptions regarding their children's mental health.

Greece is one of the countries with the smallest changes in the family system and one of the most traditional countries in the European Union (EU). This is evident by the numbers of marriages, divorces, single-parent families, families with three generations, and interactions with relatives compared to other European countries (Georgas, Gari, & Mylonas, 2004). Studies of the functional elements of the Greek family indicated that the family functions expand to a larger kinship network of extended family members and close relatives (grandparents, uncles, in-laws, aunts, and cousins) with very frequent visits and telephone contacts (Georgas, 1997, 1999a, 1999b; Georgas et al., 2004). At the same time, the family institution continues to be the most important kinship group for Greeks (Georgas et al., 2004; Giotsa, 1999; Sutton, 2001). The Greek nuclear family and the traditional extended family have strong expectations for social uplifting and enhancement of family prestige through the academic success of their children (Georgas, 1988; Kataki, 1998; Madianos, 1989). Even though Greek parents seem to be very involved in anything that has to do with their children's schooling, there is limited research on their perceptions and experiences regarding their children's learning and social-emotional difficulties.

At the same time, there has been a general reluctance among Greek parents to acknowledge their children's psychological problems and seek professional help due to prejudice and lack of adequate information (Bouhoutsos & Roe, 1984; Tsiantis, 1993b). Tsiantis (1993c) notes that referrals for mental health services were usually made around serious incidents as children were brought to the mental health providers after they had experienced severe health or social-emotional episodes. Additionally, Greek parents of students with disabilities often denied the need for special education services because they did not want their child in a special school or class (Kassotakis, Papapetrou, & Fakiolas, 1996; Vardis, 1994). One reason for this rejection might be that Greek society viewed special schools with prejudice because of their history, as students with severe disabilities were secluded and mar-ginalized in special schools in the recent past (Zoniou-Sideri, 2000). Nevertheless, the number of special classes in mainstream schools has dramatically increased in the past two decades due to the special attention that has been given in the development of special education (Kassotakis et al., 1996; Nikodemos, 1994). Despite the recent educational laws concerning special education services and psychological services in Greek schools, the vast majority of the student population with special educational needs attends regular schools and programs, and could benefit from special education services (Hatzichristou, 1998; Kassotakis et al.; Nikodemos; Υπουργείο Εθνικής Παιδείας και Θρησκευμάτων, 2008). Koliadis (1994) notes that even though there has been an emphasis on learning difficulties in recent years in Greece, teachers and parents frequently viewed the weak student in reading and spelling, who might have also failed in other academic subjects, as a "bad and lazy student." Thus, it is imperative to explore how parents are evaluating their children's academic and social-emotional functioning in contemporary Greece. Additionally, it is important to explore the significance that Greek parents attribute to their children's problematic behavior in relation to the interventions they adopt to support their children's needs.

Furthermore, the particular geographical composition of Greece has favored the creation of distinct residential, demographic, and cultural features. There is an inequality in the available mental health services and school special education services because of the geographic remoteness, overcentralization of services, and lack of efficient coordination and personnel (Bouhoutsos & Roe, 1984; Dellassoudas, 1994; Gari & Sofianidou, 2000; Hatzichristou, Polychroni, & Georgouleas, 2007; Mazi, Nenopoulou, & Everatt, 2004; Tsiantis, 1993a, 1993b, 1993c; Vardis, 1994). Hence, not all Greek families have access to the same level of state resources and services. The availability of community-based resources can impact how Greek parents identify and what type of services they prefer to address their children's learning and social-emotional difficulties.

Purpose of the Study and Research Questions

The purpose of this study was to explore the perceptions and experiences of Greek parents whose children experience learning and social-emotional difficulties. Seven research questions were addressed by this study. The research questions were as follows:

1. What are the parents' perceptions of their children's learning and social-emotional difficulties?
2. What children's behaviors are the parents most concerned about?
3. What do the parents perceive as the causes of their children's learning and social-emotional difficulties?
4. Who do the parents consider as responsible for solving their children's learning and social-emotional difficulties?
5. What is the perceived burden that the parents experience due to their children's learning and social-emotional difficulties?
6. What are the parents' actions to support their children's learning and social-emotional difficulties?
7. What are the parents' views and experiences with the available community services to support their children's needs?

Research Methodology

Conceptual Framework

This study design was guided by an ecologic understanding of parents' perceptions and experiences, suggesting that a myriad of factors at the child, family, and environmental levels simultaneously impact Greek parents' understanding of their children's problems and what they do to try to solve them. As Bronfenbrenner (1979, 1989) points out, influences on children's behavior and development extend from the immediate family to schools, friendship networks, relatives, neighborhoods, communities, and geographical locations. These influences need to be conceptualized in terms of both individuals and the nested set of ecosystems within which they develop and function. Following an ecological perspective, this study examined Greek society's limiting factors and resources, constraints and opportunities, and the general environment, which can promote or undermine students' well-being and academic competence in regular Greek schools.

Specifically, this study assumed that Greek parents' decision to seek and utilize help for their children was based on their perceptions of the nature of their children's problems, the causes, and responsibility for solving their children's learning and social-emotional difficulties, as well as the cultural norms of Greek society. Even though one can imagine a plethora of possible causes inducing children's learning and social-emotional difficulties, this study included four causes: child, family, school, and sociocultural factors. Using an ecological perspective, an attempt was made to explore factors not only deriving from the child him- or herself, but also factors deriving from his or her immediate environment such as the family, his or her wider environment formed by teachers, educational system, neighborhood, and even possible immigration from another country. In addition, the proposed responsible persons for solving children's difficulties were the child, family members, school professionals, and specialists. These persons emerge from the child's immediate environment to broader dimensions of his or her surroundings.

An additional important variable is the perceived burden that Greek parents might experience due to the child's learning and social-emotional difficulties. The parental perceived burden was measured in three aspects: personal experience, relationships with family members and friends, and the family's finances and everyday activities. This study also examined the parents' actions to support their children's learning and social-emotional difficulties beginning with their personal efforts and extending to the supporting sociocultural environment in terms of the informal sources (e.g., family) and formal sources (e.g., community services) available for receiving help.

Research Design

Traditional educational and psychological research has commonly followed one of the two research paradigms: empirical-analytic versus interpretive. This study used primarily a quantitative method, which is derived from empirical-analytic research paradigm. Although in this conception, knowledge comes from systematic testing of hypotheses through experimentation (or quasi-experimentation), this study was primarily exploratory and was not drived from systematic testing of hypotheses. Measurement (including psychological testing) provides an objective, interpretation-free record of empirical regularities (Maxim, 1999).

In quantitative research, inquiry begins with a specific plan, a set of detailed questions and/or hypotheses. Researchers seek facts and causes of human behavior and want to know a lot about a few variables so differences can be identified. They collect data that are primarily numerical, resulting from surveys, tests, experiments, and so on (Maxim, 1999). Most quantitative approaches manipulate variables and control the research setting. Quantitative research allows the researcher to generalize research findings, and provides precise, quantitative, and numerical data. In addition, the research results are relatively independent of the researcher, and it is useful for studying large numbers of people (Johnson & Onwuegbuzie, 2004).

This study used a descriptive survey design that involves the collection of data from the population of interest on a particular problem or issue (Ravid, 2005). Specifically, this is a nonexperimental quantitative research that used questionnaires with categorical and quantitative variables. This method was selected because it is a means to describe systematically, factually, and accurately the characteristics of an existing phenomenon or to document its characteristics (Belli, 2008; Maxim, 1999). In this study the phenomenon included Greek parents' perceptions and experiences regarding their children's learning and social-emotional difficulties in elementary schools. As there has been limited research in this field of inquiry, I selected a quantitative methodological approach to summarize large amounts of data and reach conclusions and generalizations based on numerical descriptions (Roberts, 2004). Studying a larger sample of parents provided an opportunity to explore trends from a diverse population from different areas of Greece. The quantitative methodology and, specifically, the completion of surveys, also addressed the issues related to the time constraints of conducting research in another country. Specifically, I was able to travel only for a two-week period during January 2009 to Greece to collect the data, which were later analyzed through the SPSS version 16.0 for Windows in order to derive the numerical findings. Thus, there were time economics gained in this approach during the collection of the data and the use of accepted statistical analysis methods. Another advantage of this method is that it offered the possibility of collecting data anonymously.

However, quantitative research cannot capture the meanings people attach to the activities and events in their world as qualitative research can (Roberts, 2004). To offset this limitation, I included narrative data (open-ended questions and open responses) in the quantitative study. I collected the quantitative data using a Likert scale on two structured questionnaires about parents' perceptions and experiences regarding their children's learning and social-emotional difficulties. The qualitative data included two open-ended questions and open responses on the same questionnaire completed by the same number of participants (parents) who completed the quantitative items. The quantitative data and their analysis enabled further exploration of the research questions. The embedded qualitative responses enhanced our understanding of Greek parents' perceptions and experiences regarding their children's learning and social-emotional difficulties. Thus, using the qualitative methods complementary to quantitative method I was able to validate and expand on the quantitative findings of the survey (Creswell & Plano Clark, 2007).

For the purposes of this research, the parents completed the Test of Psychosocial Adaptation of Preschool and Elementary Children (Test of Psychosocial Adaptation), where they evaluated their children's learning and social-emotional functioning, and the Parent Survey, which explored their perceptions and experiences regarding their children's learning and social-emotional difficulties. The Test of Psychosocial Adaptation of Preschool and Elementary Children is a rating scale that was developed recently in Greece to identify the skills or deficits in the social and emotional domains, and the personal, interpersonal, and school adaptation of a child (Hatzichristou, Polychroni, Besevegis, & Mylonas, 2008). The Parent Survey was created based on the themes identified by the literature review. A pilot study was conducted to explore the use of the Test of Psychosocial Adaptation with Greek parents, to ensure and develop the questions of the Parent Survey, and examine the procedures of the study.

Procedure

With the permission of the the the Greek Ministry of Education and Religious Affairs, 30 primary schools were asked to participate in the study from five different areas of Greece. Primary schools in Greece covers 6 years of elementary education between the ages of 6 to 12 (Georgas, 1988; Hatzichristou et al., 2007; Vlachos, 2004). Nineteen primary schools from four different areas of Greece agreed to participate in the study resulting in a 61.29% permission rate. These areas represent different population densities and cultural and socioeconomic diversity. Parents were asked to complete the Test of Psychosocial Adaptation and the Parent Survey and return it to the school. The questionnaires were self-administered by parents.

Of the 1,000 questionnaires that were distributed to parents through their children's schools, 298 were returned, which resulted in a 29.8% response rate. The majority of the questionnaires ($N = 209$; 70.1%) were gathered from 15 schools in the capital city region of Athens. The schools in the area of Athens belong predominately to the northeast suburban school district (63.7%). Eighty-nine questionnaires (29.9%) were returned from three rural areas: one school from a city in the northeast part of Greece, one school from a small town in the south of Greece, and two schools from an island in southeast Greece.

Participants

The sample of this study consisted of 298 parents of elementary students aged 6 to 11 years old. The majority of parents were female (N = 235; 78.6%) and in 25 cases both parents completed the questionnaires. The majority of the participants' ages ranged from 30–39 years (N = 129; 43.1%) to 40–49 years (N = 144; 48.2%). In terms of education, 134 mothers (44.9%) completed lyceum/college or technical school and 122 mothers (40.9%) held an undergraduate/graduate degree. Forty-eight percent of the fathers graduated from lyceum/college or technical school (N = 143) and 95 held a undergraduate/graduate degree (31.9%). Compared with the monthly minimum wage in Greece, the majority of the participants had a middle- to upper-class monthly income (Eurostat, 2009). With regard to housing, the majority of participants owned their house or apartment.

Model for Data Collection and Analysis

This study included two phases of data analysis. In the first phase of the data analysis, the responses of 298 Greek parents of elementary school students, aged 6 to 11 years, on the Test of Psychosocial Adaptation and on the first part of the Parent Survey were analyzed. Data from these two measures assessed children's learning and social-emotional difficulties and Greek parents' concerns and accessed services.

In the second phase of the analysis, 105 of the 298 Greek parents' responses on the second part of the Parent Survey were examined. The sample of the 105 parents was selected because their ratings on the Test of Psychosocial Adaptation identified their children with significant behaviors at least 1 SD below or above the mean. In this part of the Parent Survey, parents reported (1) the causes and responsibility for solving their children's difficulties; (2) parental perceived burden; and (3) actions, as well as (4) the use, likelihood to use, and barriers in accessing community services regarding their children's learning and social-emotional difficulties.

Discussion of Research Findings and Results

Prevalence and Types of Children's Learning and Social-Emotional Difficulties

Based on parents' ratings on the Test of Psychosocial Adaptation, 35.2% of Greek elementary students aged 6 to 11 years experienced significant learning and social-emotional difficulties. Greek parents rated higher those behaviors that are more obvious and noticeable, especially in interpersonal relationships and groups on the Test of Psychosocial Adaptation. By contrast, parents had the tendency to rate the internalized behaviors of their children as significant when they were accompanied by externalized behaviors. Consequently, results from the Test of Psychosocial Adaptation suggest that Greek parents gave importance to children's social aspect of behavior and underreported introvert behavior.

Greek Parents' Concerns and Accessed Services

Almost one-third of Greek parents from the total sample of participants reported having concerns over their children's behavior and only 13.1% responded in the Parent Survey that they have accessed services. Even though parents reported mostly concerns over their children's social-emotional difficulties (e.g., anxiety, socialization, anger, and low self-esteem), the majority of their accessed services included support for their children's learning difficulties (e.g., dyslexia). From the parents who accessed services, only a small number reported a variety of other types of services for their children (e.g., occupation and play-based therapy).

Child's Responsibility

About a half of the parents appeared to consider their children's character as an important cause of their children's learning and social-emotional difficulties. This finding suggests that when parents attribute responsibility to their children for their problematic behavior, they consider these difficulties as part of their temperament, an innate characteristic. This was also reflected in parents' responses regarding who is responsible for solving their children'difficulties in these areas, where almost 60% of the parents attributed responsibility to their children for improving their behavior. This indicates that some parents regard children as responsible both for causing their learning and social-emotional difficulties and for solving these problems. In conclusion, when Greek parents believed that children's character caused their behavior, they held children accountable for changing and ameliorating their learning and social-emotional difficulties.

Parents' Role

More than half of the parents did not believe they were mainly responsible for children's learning and social-emotional difficulties. The role of parents was more important in parents' opinions about who is responsible for solving or improving their children's problems. Around 80% of parents indicated that both parents should have the responsibility for solving or improving their children's behavior. Furthermore, in accordance with their perceptions about the responsibility for solving children's learning and social-emotional difficulties, parents indicated a greater preference for the use of personal actions and positive incentives to support their children over other interventions. Parents also did not ask the recommendations or support of their extended family for their children's challenges. The level of personal burden Greek parents experience due to their children's learning and social-emotional difficulties might also explain their preference for personal actions to support their children's needs. Specifically, almost half of the parents indicated a significant general level of family impact, especially on their personal competence as parents, as a results of their children's learning and social-emotional difficulties. Hence, the high level of these parents' personal and family burden can influence their actions and type of intervention implemented—in this case their preference for personal efforts.

Educational System

Another important finding is that more parents (n = 40%) attributed responsibility of their children's learning and social-emotional difficulties to the current structure of the Greek educational system than to the teachers' methods (n = 26.7%). One other interesting aspect was that even though 60% of parents indicated teachers or school personnel as responsible for improving their children's behavior, only one-third of Greek parents reported that they had consulted a teacher or other school personnel to support their children's needs.

Mass Media

It is notable that half of the participants indicated that television, movies, and video games were significant causes of their children's learning and social-emotional difficulties. For some parents these ratings might be an indication of their concerns about their children's overexposure to these programmings. This finding also underlines the important role of parents in limiting the amount of exposure their children have to television, movies, and video games to improve their children's behavioral challenges.

Sociocultural Factors

Greek parents did not attribute their children's learning and social-emotional difficulties to sociocultural and environmental factors such as low family income, type of neighborhood, speaking a second language, or recent immigration from another country. It should be noted that the majority of parents had children who were born in Greece (98%) and had not experienced immigration and second language acquisition challenges. In terms of the neighborhood, the majority of participants came from the northeastern suburban area of Athens, which includes mainly middle- and upper-class families who owned their house or apartment. Thus, the majority of the parents in this study appeared not to consider the socioeconomic conditions in which they live to have a negative impact on their children's behavior or the reverse.

Community Services

Overall, a very small number of Greek parents indicated that they had accessed community services to support their children's learning and social-emotional needs (responses ranged from 1% to 5%). Of these community services, private clinicians appeared to be the preferred service for parents (n = 13.3%). At the same time, parents reported an increased likelihood to use community services. Private clinicians were again the service with the highest future utilization based on parents' reports (n = 21.9%). It is significant that almost one-third of the parents reported that the lack of knowledge about the services, the time it takes to initiate services and long waiting lists, and the lack of specialists were barriers in the access of community services. These numerous barriers can limit children's access to community mental health care.

Conclusions

The results of this study are subject to the limitations of any self-report survey. Despite the limitations, this study provided useful information as there is little evidence and research in this domain. These research findings can provide professionals with information regarding the help Greek parents prefer when conducting assessment and implementing interventions. Finally, this information can contribute to a model of mental health delivery system that includes parents and provides culturally sensitive and effective services to Greek children.

References

Belli, G. (2008). Nonexperimental quantitative research. In *Lapan*. Retrieved from http://media.wiley.com/product_data/excerpt/95/04701810/0470181095-1.pdf

Bouhoutsos, J. C., & Roe, K. V. (1984). Mental health services and the emerging role of psychology in Greece. *American Psychologist, 39*, 57–61.

Bronfenbrenner, U. (1979). *The ecology of human development: Experiments by nature and design.* Cambridge, MA: Harvard University Press.

Bronfenbrenner, U. (1989). Ecological systems theory. In R. Vasta (Ed.)., *Annals of child development* (Vol. 6, pp. 187–251). Greenwich, CT: JAI.

Creswell, J. W., & Plano Clark, V. L. (2007). *Designing and conducting mixed methods research.* Thousand Oaks, CA: Sage.

Dellassoudas, L. G. (1994). Ειδική επαγγελματική κατάρτιση: Προτάσεις για την αναβαθμισή της [Special professional development: Recommendations for its advancement]. In M. Kaila, N. Polemikos, & G. Filippou (Eds.), *Άτομα με ειδικές ανάγκες* (Vol. 1, pp. 206–221). Athens: Ελληνικά Γράμματα.

Eurostat. (2009). *Population and social conditions: Minimum wages in January 2009.* Eurostat, Beate CZECH.

Farmer, E. M. Z., Burns, B. J., Angold, A., & Costello, E. J. (1997). Impact of children's mental health problems on families: Relationships with service use. *Journal of Emotional and Behavioral Disorders, 5,* 230–238.

Gari, A., & Sofianidou, E. (2000). Δομή και λειτουργία φορέων διάγνωσης και αντιμετώπισης διαταραχών παιδικής και εφηβικής ηλικίας. Παρουσιάση, σχολιασμός, και σύνθεση προτάσεων ομάδων εργασίας [Structure and function of providers of diagnosis and care of child and adolescent disorders: Presentation, comment, and synthesis of recommendations from working teams]. In A. Kalantzi-Azizi & I. Besevegis (Eds.), *Θέματα επιμόρφωσεις ευαισθητοποίησης στελεχών ψυχικής υγείας παιδιών και εφήβων* (pp. 105–112). Athens: Ελληνικά Γράμματα.

Georgas, J. (1988). An ecological and social cross-cultural model: The case of Greece. In J. W. Berry, S. H. Irvine, & E. B. Hunt (Eds.), *Indigenous cognition: Functioning in cultural context* (pp. 105–123). Dordrecht, the Netherlands: Martinus Nijhoff.

Georgas, J. (1997). Ψυχολογικές και οικολογικές διαστασείς στη δομή και τη λειτουργία της οικογένειας [Psychological and ecological dimensions in the structure and function of family]. In J. Tsiantis (Ed.), *Βασική Παιδοψυχιατρική. Εφηβεία* (Vol. 2, pp. 101–143). Athens: Εκδόσεις Καστανιώτη.

Georgas, J. (1999a). Ecological theory in social psychology. *Psychology, 6*(2), 111–123.

Georgas, J. (1999b). Family in cross-cultural psychology. In J. Adamopoulos & Y. Kashima (Eds.), *Social psychology and cultural context* (pp. 163–175). Thousand Oaks, CA: Sage.

Georgas, J., Gari, A., & Mylonas, K. (2004). Σχέσεις με συγγενείς στην ελληνική οικογένεια [Relationships with relatives in the Greek family]. In L. M. Mousourou & M. Etratigaki (Eds.), *Ζητήματα οικογενειακής πολιτικής: Θεωρητικές αναφορές και εμπειρικές διερευνήσεις* (pp. 189–225). Athens: Gutenberg.

Giotsa, A. (1999). Ο προσωπικός χώρος και η γειτονιά: Διαπολιτισμική έρευνα σε γειτονιές της Γενεύης, της Αθήνας και της Κεφαλλονιάς [Personal space and neighborhood: Cross-cultural research in neighborhoods of Geneva, Athens and Kefallonias]. *Psychology, 6*(2), 124–136.

Hatzichristou, C. (1998). Alternative school psychological services: Development of a data-based model in the Greek schools. *School Psychology Review, 27*(2), 246–259.

Hatzichristou, C., Polychroni, F., Besevegis, G., & Mylonas, K. (2008). Εργαλείο Ψυχοκοινωνικής Προσαρμογής Παιδιών Προσχολικής και Σχολικής Ηλικίας [Test of psychosocial adaptation of preschool and elementary children]. Athens: Υπουργείο Εθνικής Παιδείας και Θρησκευμάτων-ΕΠΕΑΕΚ.

Hatzichristou, C., Polychroni, F., & Georgouleas, G. (2007). School psychology in Greece. In S. R. Jimerson, T. D. Oakland, & P. T. Farrell (Eds.), *The handbook of international school psychology* (pp. 135–145). Thousands Oaks, CA: Sage.

Johnson, R. B., & Onwuegbuzie, A. J. (2004). Mixed method research: A research paradigm whose time has come. *Educational Researcher, 33*(7), 14–26.

Kassotakis, M, Papapetrou, S., & Fakiolas, N. (1996). Φραγμοί στην εκπαίδευση και την επαγγελματική αποκατάσταση των ατόμων με ειδικές ανάγκες [Barriers in the education and professional development of people with special needs]. *Διαστάσεις του κοινωνικού αποκλεισμού στην Ελλάδα: Κύρια θέματα και προσδιορισμός προτεραιοτήτων πολιτικής* (Vol. 1, pp. 449–473). Athens: Εθνικό Κέντρο Κοινωνικών Ερευνών.

Kataki, C. (1998). *Οι τρεις ταυτότητες της ελληνικής οικογένειας* [The three identities of the Greek family] (8th ed.). Athens: Ελληνικά Γράμματα.

Koliadis, M. (1994). Οργανωτικά-διοικητικά σχήματα και ψυχοπαιδαγωγικά μοντέλα αντιμετώπισης των μαθησιακών δυσκολιών στο χώρο του σχολείου [Structural-administrative schemas and psycho-pedagogic models for the intervention of learning difficulties at school]. In M. Kaila, N. Polemikos, & G. Filippou (Eds.), *Άτομα με ειδικές ανάγκες* (Vol. 1, pp. 290–301). Athens: Ελληνικά Γράμματα.

Madianos, M. J. (1989). *Κοινωνία και ψυχική υγεία* [Society and mental health]. Athens: Εκδόσεις Καστανιώτη.

Maxim, P. S. (1999). *Quantitative research methods in the social sciences*. Oxford, UK: Oxford University Press.

Mazi, M. S., Nenopoulou, S., & Everatt, J. (2004). Dyslexia in Greece. In I. Smythe, J. Everatt, & R. Salter (Eds.), *International book of dyslexia: A guide to practice and resources* (pp. 103–108). Hoboken, NJ: John Wiley & Sons.

McMiller, W. P., & Weisz, J. R. (1996). Help-seeking preceding mental health clinic intake among African-American, Latino, and Caucasian youth. *Journal of the American Academy of Child & Adolescent Psychiatry, 35*, 1086–1094.

Nikodemos, S. (1994). Αγωγή και εκπαίδευση των παιδιών με ειδικές ανάγκες στην Ελλάδα: Γενικές διαπιστώσεις, σύγχρονες τάσεις-προοπτικές [Education of children with special needs in Greece: General findings, contemporary tendencies-expectations]. In M. Kaila, N. Polemikos, & G. Filippou (Eds.), *Άτομα με ειδικές ανάγκες* (Vol. 2, pp. 623–631). Athens: Ελληνικά Γράμματα.

Ravid, R. (2005). *Practical statistics for educators* (3rd ed.). Lanham, MD: University Press of America.

Roberts, C. M. (2004). *The dissertation journey: A practical and comprehensive guide to planning, writing, and defending your dissertation*. Thousand Oaks, CA: Sage.

Sutton, S. B. (2001). Greece. In M. Ember & C. R. Ember (Eds.), *Countries and their cultures* (Vol. 2, pp. 887–899). New York: Macmillan Reference.

Tsiantis, J. (1993a). Η εκπαίδευση για την ψυχική υγεία του παιδιού [Education for the mental health of the child]. *Ψυχική υγεία του παιδιού και της οικογένειας* (pp. 229–241) Athens: Εκδόσεις Καστανιώτη.

Tsiantis, J. (1993b). Προτάσεις για την παιδοψυχιατρική περίθαλψη στην Ελλάδα [Recommendations for child psychiatric care in Greece]. *Ψυχική υγεία του παιδιού και της οικογένειας* (pp. 242–271). Athens: Εκδόσεις Καστανιώτη.

Tsiantis, J. (1993c). Ψυχοθεραπεία στο γενικό παιδιατρικό νοσοκομείο [Psychotherapy in the general children's hospital]. *Ψυχική υγεία του παιδιού και της οικογένειας* (pp. 242–271). Athens: Εκδόσεις Καστανιώτη.

Vardis, P. (1994). Η ενσωμάτωση των παιδιών με ειδικές ανάγκες: Περιεχόμενο και φιλοσοφία ενσωμάτωσης [Integration of children with special needs: Content and philosophy of integration]. In M. Kaila, N. Polemikos, & G. Filippou (Eds.), *Άτομα με ειδικές ανάγκες* (Vol. 2, pp. 740–751). Athens: Ελληνικά Γράμματα.

Vlachos, A. (2004). *Οδηγός του ελληνικού εκπαιδευτικού συστήματος* [Guide of the Greek educational system]. Athens: Βιβλιοσυνεργατική ΑΕΠΕΕ.

Zoniou-Sideri, A. (2000). Η εξέλιξη της ειδικής εκπαίδευσης: Από το ειδικό στο γενικό σχολείο [The evolution of special education: From special to general school]. In A. Zoniou-Sideri (Ed.), *Άτομα με ειδικές ανάγκες και η ενταξή τους* (pp. 22–38). Athens: Ελληνικά Γράμματα.

Υπουργείο Εθνικής Παιδείας και Θρησκευμάτων. (2008). Ειδική αγωγή και εκπαίδευση ατόμων με αναπηρία ή με ειδικές εκπαιδευτικές ανάγκες [Special education of individuals with disabilities or special educational needs]. *Εφημερίς της Κυβερνήσεως της Ελληνικής Δημοκρατίας, 199*(1), 3499–3520.

CHAPTER ELEVEN

Successful Practices and Models of Enrollment Management in Illinois Community Colleges

An Explanatory Mixed-Methods Research Case Study

ANDREA LEHMACHER

Introduction

Background of the Study

In 2006, the U.S. Department of Education assembled a commission to examine the challenges facing the U.S. higher education system under the leadership of Secretary of Education Margaret Spellings. The outcome was a report titled *A Test of Leadership: Charting the Future of U.S. Higher Education*, which has been commonly referred to as the Spellings Report. When the Spellings Report was published, it described a nation that had dramatically changed in just four decades due to globalization, competition for scarce resources, new technologies, decreases in manufacturing capacities, and increasingly fluctuating unemployment rates (Spellings Commission, 2006).

As the Spellings Report notes, the U.S. higher education system is also experiencing rapid change. Today's colleges and universities are experiencing the challenges of rising tuition costs, high student indebtedness and default rates, state budget crises, and low graduation rates for historically underrepresented groups such as first-generation and ethnic minority students. Colleges are also challenged to demonstrate accountability by identifying the learning outcomes of students, demonstrating transparency, ensuring graduates have the requisite skills and knowledge for today's society, and that they are graduating students successfully and on time.

The Obama administration has called on community colleges to help the nation compete in today's global economy and graduate more than five million new community college graduates by 2020. Community colleges are being asked to link curriculum to the needs of the business community, focus on results, develop a means for measuring success, improve aging facilities, ensure students have access to college, and graduate students in a timely manner (Pulley, 2009). In April 2010, the American Association of Community Colleges (AACC) confirmed their commitment toward completion by establishing a *Call to Action* pledge for all community colleges (AACC, 2011). This pledge reaffirms an institution's commitment to improving the completion rates of its students who are earning degrees and certificates as well as its commitment to access and quality.

Illinois Community Colleges: Enrollment Growth and Funding Challenges

The community college landscape of Illinois is a large part of the state's postsecondary environment and has seen significant enrollment growth over the last 10 years (1999–2009). According to the Illinois Community College Board (2010), Illinois community colleges enrolled approximately 65% of all public and private postsecondary students. Illinois community colleges have experienced an 11% enrollment growth between fall 2000 and fall 2009, with an 8% enrollment growth just within the last five years. Illinois community colleges will need to manage enrollment growth and demographic shifts as well as employ retention strategies that lead to successful completion of associate degrees and certificates. Currently, only 41% of working-age adults in the state of Illinois have an associate's degree or higher; by 2020, it is estimated 60% of jobs will require some form of postsecondary education (Higher Education Finance Study Commission, 2010). Illinois needs to graduate 600,000 more students with degrees and career certificates, which means that by 2025, Illinois will need to graduate 70,000 more students each year. Illinois community colleges will need to increase the number of students earning degrees and certificates by 70%.

Today, the cost burden of a college education is increasingly falling upon the student. According to the Higher Education Finance Study Commission (2010), Illinois community college budgets in 2010 are at the same level as they were in 1999; Illinois community colleges rank 46th in the nation in spending on education; and since 1996, the state's support for community college spending has fallen from 28% to 17%. The Higher Education Finance Study Commission also notes that since 1996, the portion of student tuition covering expenses has risen from 28% to 40%, which means student tuition covers nearly 53% of institutional expenses.

Statement of the Problem and Research Purposes

The effectiveness of community colleges ultimately depends on a collaborative enrollment management approach that aligns enrollment management, student services, marketing, and academic initiatives to address societal changes that are impacting today's community colleges. Illinois community colleges will need to identify best practices and implement enrollment management initiatives to address federal and state policy, societal and economic changes, and the state public agenda, all of which impact Illinois community colleges. A collaborative enrollment management structure not only addresses demographic and economic shifts but is also a strategy to address accountability and manage strained resources (Bontrager, 2004). The following areas require particular attention within the Illinois community college system: an institution's comprehensive approach to enrollment management, how community colleges implement enrollment management from a concept to an integral process, and how collaboration impacts the alignment of key functional areas within the community colleges.

The purpose of this study was to explore enrollment management practices of two Illinois community colleges and to identify factors that contribute to or impede the successful implementation of enrollment management. This study focused on exploring and addressing the following questions:

1. What role does campus leadership play in the process of implementation of enrollment management practices?
2. In what ways does enrollment management encourage collaborative planning among internal units within the institution?
3. What factors contribute to successful implementation of enrollment management practices?
4. What barriers limit successful implementation of enrollment management practices?
5. What is needed to ensure enrollment management is an integral function throughout the entire community college?

Research Methodology

Theoretical Framework for the Study

The theoretical framework for this study includes the following three positions: (1) community colleges are open systems and are thus constantly adapting to the internal and external environment; (2) enrollment management should become an integral process throughout the community college system; and (3) collaboration among internal departments is critical for successful implementation of enrollment management and institutional health.

COMMUNITY COLLEGES: OPEN SYSTEMS AND COLLABORATION

Community colleges are open systems that interact and react with the changing external environment (French & Bell, 1999; Hossler et al., 1990; Hossler & Kalsbeek, 2008). This dynamic affects how the instituion performs, determines which academic programs and certificates are offered, and how student learning and programs are assessed. Because community colleges are constantly interacting with the environment, they should create an organizational culture that supports collaboration and continuous learning and empowers the campus community to create change (French & Bell, 1999). Research suggests that successful community colleges take a systematic and holistic approach to the alignment of their institution's processes, practices, infrastructures, and external environment (Cummings & Worley, 2009). Collaborative and open community colleges align departmental and academic planning initiatives such as offering degrees and short-term certificates that lead to employment, implementing technology to assist faculty with at-risk students, and offering support programs for local businesses within the community.

ENROLLMENT MANAGEMENT: A DRIVER FOR CHANGE

Colleges and universities began implementing enrollment management as a strategy to respond to demographic shifts in the 1970s (Bontrager, 2004; LoBasso, 2005; Harris, 2009). Today, enrollment management is a comprehensive concept and a process that is focused on much more than new student enrollment. As defined in the literature, enrollment management addresses the mission and goals of the institution through a collaborative approach. As a process, enrollment management defines intentional efforts and strategies to manage enrollment and resources where faculty and staff have an informed view of the challenges and opportunities facing the institution (Hossler & Kalsbeek, 2008). Bontrager (2004) states, "Colleges and universities began to employ more comprehensive approaches to enrollment, which moved beyond marketing, recruitment, and financial aid to include sophisticated financial aid strategies, institutional research, and retention efforts" (p. 11). When implemented successfully, Penn (1999) explains enrollment management as a driver to create change that shapes institutional decision making and provides an opportunity for the involvement of campus constituents. Huddleston's (2000) research describes the integration of the identified key functional areas, which not only strengthen institutional success but also are vital to the success of enrollment management. Hossler and Kalseek (2008) concur that enrollment management is more than a passing fad in higher education and state that "even if its core principles and optimal structures have evolved over the past 30 years and its scope and purposes still evade simple definition, there is no question that enrollment management is now and will continue to be a fixture in higher education administration" (p. 3).

In agreement with the above mentioned theoretical positions grounded in an understanding that enrollment management, through a collaborative approach, addresses institutional accountability and plans for resource management that can be a campus-wide initiative, I have developed my own theoretical model that integrates open systems theory and enrollment planning through a comprehensive, holistic, and collaborative approach among enrollment management, student services, marketing, and academic initiatives.

Research Design

An explanatory mixed-methods case study research design was selected because enrollment management is regarded as both the concept and the process that involves campus-wide collaboration and, thus, needs to be looked at as a many-faceted phenomenon. Case studies are intended to gain an understanding of the phenomena through detailed descriptions (McMillan, 2008). McMillan describes case studies as "an in-depth analysis of one or more events, settings, programs, social groups, communities, individuals, or other 'bounded systems' in their natural context" (p. 288). Mixed-methods design is "an approach to inquiry that combines or associates both qualitative and quantitative forms of research. It involves philosophical assumptions, the use of qualitative and quantitative approaches, and the mixing of both approaches to the study" (Creswell, 2009, p. 230).

An explanatory mixed-methods approach has two distinct and interactive phases for data collection and analysis that will benefit this study since the research intends to explore and describe enrollment management practices and models in two Illinois community colleges (Creswell & Clark, 2011). An explanatory mixed-methods design includes quantitative and qualitative components and employs the use of mixing different approaches to data collection and analysis (Creswell, 2009). The purpose of this design is to use a "qualitative strand to explain initial quantitative results" (Creswell & Clark, p. 82).

This study brought together data regarding enrollment management and the voices of the participants. The research design included four phases for gathering data and interpretation as it relates to successful implementation of enrollment management within two Illinois community colleges. The research design was grounded in open systems theory as it relates to community colleges. The role of collaboration and enrollment management should become an integral process throughout the community college system.

Site and Participants

The following were the criteria for the site selection: (1) the two community colleges should be similar in size; (2) they should have full-time enrollment; (3) they should have an enrollment management structure in place; (4) and they should be chosen based on the benchmark survey results from the Community College Survey of Student Engagement (CCSSE). Bontrager and Clemetsen (2009) indicate that there are five benchmarks from the CCSSE survey that are important to successful implementation of SEM: active and collaborative learning, student effort, academic challenge, student-faculty interaction, and support for learners. An important component of this study is the alignment of academic planning within an enrollment management framework. The benchmarks from CCSSE can become a tool for enrollment management programs and services to support the academic endeavor of the institution.

This study required participants to have knowledge and experience within enrollment management; therefore, the participants were selected purposefully. I selected particular individuals because they were "particularly informative about the topic" (McMillan, 2008, p. 119). Creswell and Clark (2011) note that the value of purposeful sampling allows different perspectives to be brought into the research. The participants' familiarity with an enrollment management structure, terminology, concepts, and principles was important to consider in the process of selection. The participants included the persons whose support and collaboration were instrumental to successful implementation of enrollment management: president, VP of academic affairs, VP of student development, faculty members, dean of enrollment management or chief enrollment officer, director of admissions/recruitment, dean of student success (retention), director of financial aid, director of marketing, director of institutional research, registrar, and director of counseling.

Data Collection Strategies

In the first quantitative phase of the study, the Strategic Enrollment Management (SEM) Health Assessment Survey data were collected from enrollment management, student services, and marketing and academic affairs administrators at two Illinois community colleges to assess whether the implementation of enrollment management relates to administrator support and a collaborative enrollment management approach that aligns enrollment management, student services, marketing, and academic initiatives. The second qualitative phase was conducted as a follow-up to the quantitative data to help explain the quantitative results. Semi-structured individual interviews with enrollment management, student services, marketing, and academic staff from the two community colleges generated the qualitative data. The qualitative data analysis and interpretation were intended to amplify the description of enrollment management successful practices and models.

SURVEY INSTRUMENT

The SEM Health Assessment survey was administered as a web-based survey to the administrators and faculty involved in enrollment management at the two Illinois community colleges. This survey was intended to assess an institution's enrollment management development in the following areas: as a comprehensive system, academic program innovation, marketing, recruitment, retention, and student services practices. The survey data were analyzed through descriptive statistics within SPSS software. The results from the survey helped identify an institution's perception and institutional strengths and weaknesses within enrollment management, which is important since the study attempted to identify successful practices and models of enrollment management.

Analysis of Results and Findings

The results from the survey identified the community college's perception, along with institutional strengths and weaknesses within enrollment management. The survey results are organized in the following six categories: a comprehensive system, academic program innovation, marketing, recruitment, retention, and student services practices. The community colleges were identified as Community College A and Community College B. Community College A had a total of 9 purposefully selected participants and Community College B had a total of 12 purposefully selected participants. A total of 95% of the targeted participants ($n = 20$) completed the web-based survey from the two Illinois community colleges. The president from Community College A did not respond to the survey. The original study included the mean, weighted score, and standard deviations. The participants were instructed to use the following Likert scale: 1 = poor or nonexistent; 2 = functional but needs significant improvement; 3 = average in relation to professional practices in SEM; 4 = above average and meets current institutional needs; 5 = a professional model or best practice.

In addition to the 50 questions on the survey, I asked the following open-ended question at the end of the survey to help generate the follow-up questions for the qualitative phase: What other ideas do you have to ensure enrollment management is an integral function throughout the campus community? The qualitative phase included individual interviews with enrollment management, student services, marketing, and academic staff from the two community colleges that participated in the SEM Health Assessment survey. The participants were identified as Community College A administrator 1, 2, 3, 4, and as Community College B administrator 1, 2, 3, 4.

Community College A: Findings

Nine administrators, including the president, were sent the web link to the SEM Health Assessment survey at Community College A and a total of eight administrators completed the survey. As I collaborated with administration at Community College A, it was identified that there is disconnect with the role of faculty within the current enrollment management structure. Some faculty is involved with various student success initiatives at the college; however, according to the administrator, "none of the faculty would associate that work with enrollment management." Therefore, it was determined to not include faculty in the survey.

Since 2006, Community College A has had an annual new student enrollment plan and has attempted to implement an overall enrollment management structure under the student services division. The structure included identifying a few key functional areas, such as marketing, admissions, the recruitment office, and student life, where key administrators began to have cross-functional input conversations. In 2009, Community College A was invited to participate in an external initiative called Achieving the Dream. Participation in this external initiative, according to administrator 2:

> gave us the opportunity to kind of set down this strategic enrollment management structure that wasn't really working for us because Achieving the Dream was also going to require broad, cross-functional committees and structures. We essentially put our strategic enrollment management groups on hiatus.

Administrator 2 explained that the Achieving the Dream initiative helped the institution look at data intentionally, set directions, and include people in broad and cross-functional ways, which is the principle of enrollment management.

During the time of this study, Community College A was in the midst of reorganizing the enrollment management structure from student services to academic affairs. The college felt this change was strategic and purposeful and would eventually help the institution set the overall direction regarding processes and programs, including the use of data and the assessment of both co-curricular and curricular initiatives within the enrollment management framework.

SEM AS A SYSTEM

The participants believe SEM is a core set of values that the institution embraces and feel they have a quality work environment to serve students. While the participants are committed to the institution, the results of this survey seem to indicate the participants do not feel support for SEM efforts by key decision makers on campus, or that there is adequate training and staff development to understand the needs of students. When asked about the current enrollment management structure and enrollment management plan at Community College A, the response was consistent among the four administrators who were interviewed; the structure and plan is not clearly defined or understood. For instance, Administrator 1 said:

> Most people don't understand enrollment management here and I think that it just means that admissions recruits someplace else. And the way that we are organized, it really requires a lot of lateral collegial cooperation in order to put together anything that looks like enrollment management.

The participants believe courses offered meet individual student learning styles and promote student and faculty interaction. While the participants believe course offerings provide an active learning experience with faculty, the results of this survey seem to indicate the participants do not feel the current course schedule provides flexibility for students to meet their educational goals, and the decisions and use of data to add, revamp, or delete academic programs are not driven by market demand. One of the focuses of this study is the alignment of curriculum planning and data-driven decision making within the enrollment management structure. Administrator 4 said:

> It really is, the bottom line, about meaningful data...when we give information to our faculty to then report on, which we do through our assessment office, one of the things we want to see is then, what are the priorities that come out of the program review that could inform marketing and what we need to do....I don't think we're doing a good enough job of a needs analysis piece as we could. What we do is we decide we're going to go in a direction, and then find the data to support that direction. What we need to do is find the data and then find what programs would be best to support the direction. We don't do that, so we have to teach people how to do that.

SEM AND MARKETING

The participants believe the current marketing efforts are consistent, distinct, targeted at key student audiences, and have an appropriate marketing mix to reach students. While the participants believe they have a robust marketing program, the results of this survey seem to indicate the participants do not feel marketing efforts are regularly assessed for effectiveness. Administrator 3 describes the marketing alignment within the enrollment management framework as the following:

> We have a committee that gets together. The five of us meet every three weeks and we also have met separately to devise a better communication plan overall. Separate from event related or deadline related marketing, we have been building a plan where seniors in high school will need messages and anyone who's inquired at all will be on this track, and we build tracks together.

However, a key focus of this study is the alignment of curriculum planning and marketing within the enrollment management structure. Administrator 3 describes this process as:

> If anyone, a program or a class, has a problem it's a marketing problem. We'll sit down with them and figure out if no one needs that certificate anymore to get that job, and maybe that's really the problem. So, we pushed this whole concept back to the Teaching/Learning and Student Development head...to come up with a process to define what programs need to be marketed for enrollment, and they are trying to start that.

SEM AND RECRUITMENT

The participants believe current recruitment efforts to students are immediate and the communication moves students through an enrollment funnel (inquiry, applicant, admit, and enrolled). While the participants believe they have an active recruitment process, the results of this survey seem to indicate the participants do not feel data are used to identify potential students, award scholarships appropriately, or communication with students is consistent college-wide.

SEM AND RETENTION

The participants believe the conditions for student success have been identified and the orientation process prepares students for success in the institution. While the participants believe they have an orientation process to prepare students to enter college, the results of this survey seem to indicate the participants do not feel the college provides accurate mentoring or advising for students, or that there are strategies in place to identify at-risk students. When asked to describe the retention function within the enrollment management framework, Administrator 1 states:

> Retention reports in a different direction and both everyone and no one is responsible for retention and I think we may have an opportunity...it's my goal to provide some of the linkages that are retention related in a reactive process. And if we can link the reactive pieces, then I think the proactive

pieces, which would really predominantly help with the huge mass of deciding, like undecided students get a glimpse of what their future might be, and to use that in an action form to identify a program of study, and if it's a transfer program, to identify an institution and a major, that we will come a long way to identifying some of the inputs to retention.

SEM AND SERVICE DELIVERY

The participants believe students are serviced through the use of technology. The results of this survey seem to indicate the participants do not feel current processes are intuitive for students and service providers do not understand the needs of students. Administrator 4 describes the service delivery component within enrollment management as: "Everything we do at the college is about enrollment management. Everything we do. It's bringing them in, retaining them, prioritizing what programs are best for our community, what are the services best for them to stay." All the administrators at Community College A agree that collaboration is important in order for enrollment management to be successful. However, campus leadership may not understand or explain how individual roles, policies, and procedures integrate into an enrollment management framework that serves students across the institution.

Community College B: Findings

Community College B had 12 administrators, including the president, who were sent the web link to the SEM Health Assessment survey, and a total of 12 administrators completed the survey. As the results demonstrate, Community College B has an active president within the college-wide enrollment management team (EMT) and the president communicates data and enrollment management updates to the board of trustees. In addition, to enrollment management offices, the vice president of students services, the vice president of academic services, faculty, academic and non-academic deans, information technology, and even public safety are members of the EMT, which meets monthly. The EMT was described as a group that shares information rather than a group that develops action plans and strategies for issues. Within the larger EMT, subgroups have formed. For example, a subgroup has been formed to address the recruiting and retention of Latino students. So, the EMT is somewhat decentralized in its structure.

SEM AS A SYSTEM

The participants feel committed to the institution and the SEM efforts are embraced, supported, and facilitate open communication. While the participants believe they have supported SEM efforts, the results of this survey seem to indicate the participants do not feel their decisions are data driven and the college lacks measures in place to assess the enrollment management plan. All of the participants agree enrollment management principles are embedded within the institution. Administrator 1 describes this:

> If there's something else that comes up in enrollment management that we know is an issue, which plays into how each department goes. It influences and develops their individual plans, too. I guess it almost becomes part of our management conscience.

However, Community College B does not have a formalized enrollment management plan. Administrator 3 states:

> I think it needs to be a much more broad-based look at what we are doing because sometimes enrollment management can evolve into "What is headcount and FTE?"…I want to move the conversation to strategic planning in terms of students reaching the crucial momentum points. I want to see that as the basis for looking at retention, not whether we have a good fall to fall.

SEM AND ACADEMIC PROGRAM INNOVATION

The participants believe current course offerings meet the needs of the community and student-learning preferences. The results of this survey seem to indicate the participants feel there is room for improvement when it comes to offering a schedule that is flexible for students and the institutional capacity to meet student demands. One of the focuses of this study is the alignment of curriculum planning and data-driven decision making within the enrollment management structure. Administrator 4 agrees that using data to drive enrollment management decisions within academic planning is critical. For example, this is demonstrated within academic programs through the career and technical area, course section management, dual credit strategies, and the first-year student experience program.

SEM AND MARKETING

The participants believe current marketing efforts are targeted, frequent, and an appropriate mix of marketing channels is utilized to reach students. While the participants believe they have an active marketing program, the results of this survey seem to indicate the participants do not feel there are written objectives for marketing activities, and improvement can be made to assess marketing efforts. Administrator 1 described the marketing alignment within enrollment management as connected and collaborative:

Enrollment management is from a very broad perspective. I give a report to the group, but we also have a department chair that represents the department chairs on the panel. We come together every month in the academic year and we talk about the issues, talk about what enrollment is, what the terms are, what we think about the terms...I think we're evolving from that now to talk about more strategic directions.

SEM AND RECRUITMENT

The participants believe current recruitment efforts and the awarding of scholarships to students is proactive, and communication moves students through an enrollment funnel (inquiry, applicant, admit and enrolled). While the participants believe they have a proactive recruitment program, the results of this survey and interviews seem to indicate the participants feel there is room for improvement in the evaluation of recruitment activities due to a lack of an enrollment management plan.

SEM AND RETENTION

The participants believe the current retention efforts orientate students to the college, policies, and procedures are student centered, and conditions for student success have been identified. While the participants believe they have proactive retention efforts, the results of this survey seem to indicate the participants do not feel the college uses retention data strategically during critical points throughout a semester. When asked to describe the retention alignment within the enrollment management framework, Administrator 3 states:

> Because our EMT is chaired by the operator of admissions, it has the flavor of a student services piece. So, those of us that come through the instructional side of the house may or may not know of anything that EMT is doing. Many of our programs and initiatives to keep students successful have never been directly in conversation with the EMT.

Even though retention initiatives were discussed by the administrators who were interviewed, the planning and implementation is performed through subgroup work, not EMT.

SEM AND SERVICE DELIVERY

The participants believe students are serviced through the use of technology, and processes to access services and the campus community reflect understanding and respond to the needs of students. The results of this survey seem to indicate the participants do not feel current processes are intuitive for students.

Conclusions

The findings of this study suggest that community colleges are complex and multidimensional institutions. There is not one ideal enrollment model, but rather community colleges will need to modify models and practices to fit their distinctive institutional culture, mission, and strategic goals. Therefore, community college leadership will need to view the principles of enrollment management through a multidimensional approach and understanding that includes the role of campus leadership, institutionalization of enrollment management, a created and shared understanding of enrollment management, data-driven decision making, integrated assessment and evaluation principles, and campus collaboration and communication. The findings of this study strongly indicate that the above principles of enrollment management should be taken into serious consideration by those community colleges who are attempting to implement an enrollment management framework. Illinois community colleges will need to identify best practices and implement enrollment management initiatives to address federal and state policies, societal changes, and the state public and completion agenda, all of which are impacting Illinois community colleges. Creating and implementing a collaborative multidimensional enrollment management approach and plan allows community colleges to not only fulfill their mission but also ensure the institution is poised to address the challenges and opportunities of the twenty-first century and meet the needs of the modern community college student (Simon, 2012).

References

American Association of Community Colleges (AACC). (2011). *Rebalancing the mission: The community college completion agenda.* Retrieved from http://www.aacc.nche.edu/Publications/Briefs/Pages/rb06152010.aspx

Bontrager, B. (2004). Enrollment management: An introduction to concepts and structures. *College and University Journal, 79*(3), 9–15.

Bontrager, B., & Clemetsen, B. (2009). *Applying SEM at the community college.* Washington, DC: American Associate of Collegiate Registrars and Admissions Officers.

Creswell, J. W. (2009). *Research design: Qualitative, quantitative and mixed methods approaches.* Los Angeles: Sage.

Creswell, J. W., & Clark, V. L. (2011). *Designing and conducting mixed methods research.* Los Angeles: Sage.

Cummings, T. G., & Worley, C. G. (2009). *Organization development & change.* Mason, OH: South-Western/Cengage Learning.

French, W. L., & Bell, C. H. Jr. (1999). *Organization development: Behavioral science interventions for organization improvement.* Upper Saddle River, NJ: Prentice Hall.

Harris, T. (2009). Influence of orientation coursework on enrollment persistence. *Enrollment Management Journal, 3*(2), 10–25.

Higher Education Finance Study Commission. (2010). *The Illinois public agenda for college and career success: Report to the governor, the honorable Pat Quinn and members of the Illinois general assembly*. Retrieved from http://www.ibhe.state.il.us/SJR88/Materials/FinalReport.pdf

Hossler, D., Bean, J. P., & Associates. (1990). *The strategic management of college enrollments*. San Francisco: Jossey-Bass.

Hossler, D., & Kalsbeek, D. (2008). Enrollment management and managing enrollment: Setting the context for dialogue. *College and University Journal, 83*(4), 2–9.

Huddleston, T. (2000). Enrollment management. *New Directions for Higher Education,* (111), 65–73.

Illinois Community College Board. (2010). *Data and characteristics*. Retrieved from http://iccb-dbsrv.iccb.org/databook/2009/section1.cfm

LoBasso, T. (2005). *An evaluation of enrollment management models of the 28 Florida community colleges*. Unpublished doctoral dissertation, University of Central Florida, Orlando.

McMillan, J. H. (2008). *Educational research fundamentals for the consumer*. Boston: Pearson.

Penn, G. (1999). *Enrollment management for the 21st century: Institutional goals, accountability and fiscal responsibility*. ASHE-ERIC Higher Education Report 26 (7). Washington, DC: George Washington University, Graduate School of Education and Human Development.

Pulley, J. (2009, July 14). Obama proposes $12 billion for community colleges. *Community College Times*. Retrieved from www.communitycollegetimes.com

Simon, S. (2012). *Illinois Community College: Focus on the Finish. A report to Governor Pat Quinn and the Illinois General Assembly*. Retrieved from http://www2.illinois.gov/ltgov/Documents/CC%20REPORT%20Jan%2019%20FINAL.pdf

Spellings Commission. (2006). *A test of leadership: Charting the future of U.S. higher education.* A report of the commission appointed by Secretary of Education Margaret Spellings. Retrieved from www.ed.gov/about/bdscomm/list/hiedfuture/reports/pre-pub-report.pdf

CHAPTER TWELVE

Paradigmatic Consciousness Raising

What Moves Me

KRISTA ROBINSON-LYLES

Watch your thoughts, for they become your words, watch your words for they become your actions. Watch your actions for they become your habits, and your habits your character, and your character your destiny.

—HRABOWSKI, 2007

I watch the news, and I am saddened. I listen to the radio, and I am stunned. I look at the world around me, the one constructed for me and the one constructed by me (is there a difference?) and I am at once resigned to make a difference, and concerned that I cannot. I try to envision what the world will be like for my children, Jordan—nine years old—and Sydnee—six years old—and I am afraid. The fact that many Americans (myself included) take so many human, material, and natural resources for granted, that Americans live in a throw-away society, concerns me. That our society thrives on material goods and acquisition of them to obtain, define, and tout self-worth, to proclaim achievement and to claim our "rightful" place in the socioeconomic disorder—I mean order—perplexes me. That many children have poor or no healthcare, little in the way of decent food, shelter, and clothing, and have a bleak future outlook, sickens me. The idea that poor children and children of color spend six to eight hours each day in schools, where they are likely to feel devalued, disengaged, and disregarded, alarms me. That my children have entered the world of schooling, microcosms of this larger and very economically skewed society, scares me . . . and motivates me to seek change.

It is critical, then, that I continually consider what meaning my children will make of their lifeworlds (Habermas, 1984); look at what I want for them and what I am preparing them for; and try to determine my purpose in their lives and how I impact their knowledge and learning through the paradigms that I offer them. As I watch my children explore, discover, make judgments, ask questions, make friends, observe, etcetera, I am amazed at this process of knowledge acquisition and overwhelmed, at times, by how much I and others will impact how that happens for them. As a teacher educator I feel this same awesome responsibility and, because I have even less control over what my students are exposed to outside of the classroom I share with them, the responsibility seems even greater. The challenge in my work in teacher education has been trying to encourage adults to consider more than the surface issues in teaching, as I also struggle to do the same—akin to what Regenspan (2002) calls *parallel practices*. I have struggled with how to teach in a way that will encourage and move my students beyond basic lesson planning to a consideration of the curriculum writ large; to a consideration of children's lived experiences; and to a consideration of how what we teach (implicitly or explicitly) will impact how children view and interact with the world.

Although I have come to learn that conversations and experiences designed to expose conscious or unconscious preservation of status quo, even when challenging, are actually a step forward rather than a step backward in the journey toward critical teaching, I still struggle. I struggle because as a teacher I can often see where my students are on the continuum of conscientization, but as a teacher (and a parent), I not always certain where I fall on that continuum and how that impacts my teaching, learning, and living, how it affects what I teach them, and what they teach their students. With these struggles in mind, and my own wavering between hopefulness and consternation, I wonder how other teacher educators prepare themselves to teach against the status quo and for social justice. I wonder what it is like for them to live these experiences themselves and with their students. It is an understatement to simply say that teaching for social justice is important, yet that is the basic premise of my work, and I believe that a critical democratic approach presents the necessary pedagogical and theoretical means for doing that.

Honoring Paradigmatic Name-calling: Theorizing and Problematizing Democracy

> Well they passed a law in '64 to give those who ain't got a little more
> But it only goes so far because the law don't change another's mind

When all it sees at the hiring time is the line on the color bar
That's just the way it is, some things will never change
That's just the way it is, but don't you believe them.
—BRUCE HORNSBY & THE RANGE, 1986

The American public school curriculum promotes democracy. At least, I am certain that teachers in most American public schools would say that they are concerned with producing citizens who can contribute to the existence and future of our society; therefore, the ideals promoted by schools are *democratic*. This curriculum (and by using the term *curriculum* I include paradigms, pedagogies, practices, textbooks and other literature, and policies as well as inaction) may, as Gerzon (1997) notes, work toward developing children's self-esteem and ability to clarify values, or train students to become "good corporate citizens" who respect authority. It may also promote other tenets of democracy that are hard to argue with, including the right to vote, freedom of speech, and free will. And it is perhaps hard to argue with a capitalist economy when you are one of the owners of the economic and cultural capital.

While, in that sense, schools certainly do promote and teach for a democratic society, I assert that the narrow definition of democracy from which American public schools operate does not look critically enough at what democracy really means and leaves much to be desired. Inherent in this narrow definition is an assumption or dismissal of the fact that voting, for example, benefits the privileged who have access to polls and public figures who represent and push forward the needs and desires of particular groups. It includes a privileged speech that assumes the superiority of dominant culture and ignores altogether the relativity of speech, language, and hearing. Although by virtue of living in the same universe as others, we all either pay the price for, or benefit from, this privilege and relativity, some pay more dearly and more regularly than others, and will for generations to come. That is unless we look critically at what kind of a democracy we live in, particularly when, as Brown (2004) notes, "Students of color and low socio economic status consistently experience significantly lower achievement test scores, teacher expectations and allocation of resources," which leads to "persistent, pervasive and significantly disparate" gaps in achievement (p. 340). I find a society that allows this reality troubling and so find myself questioning whether democracy is the issue or whether it is the kind of democracy we live in that is the issue.

If schools are the places charged with turning out responsible citizens, don't we, as citizens, have a responsibility to examine what *responsible* means, and what *citizens who can contribute to society* means? If knowledge is even partially socially constructed, and schools are preparing students for citizenry in society by passing on the knowledge constructed by the social order, and if that social order is oppressive to some and not truly democratic, are schools not responsible for preparing students who can challenge, envision, and contribute to the transformation of that social order? Critical pedagogy, critical race theory, and social reconstructionism demand a resounding yes to these questions, which requires both an unlearning and a relearning (Toffler, as cited in Barth, 2001) of schooling. They require that we critique and change a curriculum that uses "access, power, and privilege based on race, culture, gender, sexual orientation, language, background ability, and socioeconomic position" (Brown, 2004, p. 340) to determine who succeeds and who does not. Nieto talks about critical pedagogy as requiring a "concerted anti-oppression and emancipator approach to education" (as cited in Nagda, Gurin, & Lopez, 2003, p. 167). Extending that notion, Nagda and colleagues note the need to problematize the practice of creating and maintaining social structures that create dominate and subordinate structures as central to critical pedagogy. They go on to say that the goal, then, of critical pedagogy is "to analyze social life through a lens of diversity and social justice and to prepare students to be transformative democratic agents…employ[ing] a language of critique, and endors[ing] pedagogies of resistance, possibility, and hope" (p. 167).

Johnathon Kozol laments on the American consciousness as he talks about the selective yet "deep-seated reverence for fair play in the United States…a genuine distaste for loaded dice that applies to all aspects of living, except education, health care and wealth inheritance" (as cited in Ayers, Hunt, & Quinn, 1998, p. xxxii). If schooling is one means, and by far the most coveted means, for educating children in America—and it is—then schools should seek to educate all of its students, without preferring and privileging one group over another. That means questioning what kind of democracy we live in and how schools contribute to that democracy, for at the very heart of critical democratic education, by definition, is democratic education, begging the question, what is democracy really?

Paradigmatic Praxis: Researching the Personal and the Political

> The researcher's curiosity and excitement inspires the search, personal history brings the core of the problem into focus.
>
> —MOUSTAKAS, 1994, P. 104

I have espoused the need to work toward social justice by creating a society where people do more than tolerate each other: a need that requires a deeper understanding of what it means to be in the world together. I have asserted that schools have a role in creating the real and perceived notions of democracy in our society, and I have agreed with Brown (2004) who calls educators "moral stewards in a global, diverse, and complex society" (p. 340), saying that we must invest more in reconceptualizing, rather than reproducing, schools and the status quo on which they are based. However, I have also questioned the reality of this kind of schooling in American public schools, for as Kahne and Westheimer (as cited in Ayers et al., 1998) point out, many teachers, schools, and districts do not maintain critical democratic education and social justice as their goals because there are significant incentives not to.

As I have continued to walk the path of learning to teach for social justice, I have come to recognize that this particular research, of which my own personal journey is a part, not only asks what but also why and how. In trying to understand the work that teacher educators do and have done in the name of social justice, I realize that it is also important to try to comprehend how their complex, nuanced, and contextualized selves have come to be. Accordingly, my research seeks to illuminate for myself and for others exactly how their footsteps are rooted in working for social justice. It describes and interprets how four teacher educators have journeyed to the conscientization that Cochran-Smith (2004a) describes. It is a look at what these teacher educators' grounded knowledge (Chang, 2005) looks like, how it is informed and sustained, challenged and enhanced, by asking: How have teacher educators' lived experiences informed and transformed their conscientization and contributed to their work with preservice teachers?

In light of the theoretical and pedagogical lenses that frame the problem and the question I have articulated, the methodological framing for my research is both phenomenological and hermeneutic, informed by a lens of critical pedagogy and explored through the process of narrative inquiry. While I could have chosen multiple ways to organize the exploration of this question, a qualitative study using narrative inquiry provided the best connection among theory, research, and practice. It allows for clearest description and interpretation of the phenomenon of teaching for social justice. Having posed the question of how teachers' lived experiences inform their conscientization, my work employs social phenomenology as it "seeks to describe the schemata or themes that constitute experience" (Polkinghorne, 1983, p. 213). Specifically, this work is grounded in Freire's praxis of existential phenomenology as it "attends to the life structures through which experience is organized and made meaningful" (Polkinghorne, 1983, p. 206). In an attempt to examine and describe teacher educators' experiences of schooling, freedom, democracy, and social change, I employ the notion of education as the praxis of freedom, which requires reexamining and rejecting, and, therefore, rewriting education as domination (Kneller, 1984, p. 53). According to Kneller, this requires that the marginalized become re-creators rather than spectators and that we rewrite not only our own narratives independently but also with and as a part of each other. In focusing on these educators' autobiographies, rather than their biographies, I am seeking an understanding of the phenomenon of their experiences in working toward conscientization—asking that they write their own realities and their own futures (Kneller, p. 55).

Just as social phenomenology requires a description of the lived experiences of these teacher educators, critical hermeneutics, as embodied by the work of Habermas (1984), also grounds this work as it attempts to interpret and analyze a praxis that has an effect on others and the natural world as much as it is affected by others and the natural world (Polkinghorne, 1983, p.216). Through this work I am searching for an understanding of the human realm by using reflective experience to study it from within itself (Polkinghorne, 1983, p. 216) in an effort to challenge the past reality of democratic education, and support the transformation of its future reality as critical democratic education. I am not seeking to test a hypothesis or prove or disprove a particular theory. My goal is to deepen the conversation of what it means to teach for social justice by looking at and interpreting critically what that has meant to four specific teacher educators.

Coming to know and describe the stories of educators whose convictions, circumstances, and life histories have compelled them to this work required that I "sit for a while" (Michie, 2005) in the midst of not only what they do but also why, where, with whom, and how. I selected narrative inquiry as the tool for applying social phenomenology and critical hermeneutics to this exploration of the praxis of critical democratic education, because there are stories to be told about where each of the educators in my research has been—how they have been transformed. There are stories to be told about how their steps are imprinted as they are in their life histories; stories to be told about why they now stand where they do—what it means that their feet are imprinted in the here and now of teaching for social justice; and stories to be told about where they see their footsteps leading—what the path of their footsteps will say and where they will lead their students, and the students of their students. Branigan talks about the power and relevance of storytelling, saying, "When people tell stories, anecdotes and other kinds of narratives, they are engaged in a perceptual activity that organizes data into a special pattern which represents and explains experience" (as cited by Cortazzi in Imam, 2001, p 55). Therefore, using narrative inquiry as a phenomenon and a method (Chang, 2005, p. 63) allowed the participants to tell their stories, as they engaged in "the process of constructing and reconstructing the self…a meaning-making experience in which [they] define[d] [them]selves based on [their] families, [their] past, and [their] lives" (Chang, p. 64).

According to Clandinin (1992), this process is more than just sharing stories, it also involves "data collection, mutual narrative interpretation by practitioners and researchers, more data collection and further narrative reconstruction. The narrative inquiry process itself is a narrative one of storying, restorying, and restorying again" (p. 128). Through this notion of storying and restorying, I was able to identify themes among the unfolding stories that help describe and interpret the individual and collective existence of these educators within the larger realm of teaching for social justice (Polkinghorne, 1988 as cited in Chang, 2005).

In preparing to gather, describe, and interpret these stories, I conducted purposeful sampling of teacher educators in Midwestern universities in the United States. I wanted a sample that would bridge gender, age, depth, and breadth of experience, as well as racial-cultural boundaries. It was also critical that I specifically look for those whose teaching practices, scholarship, and professional and personal interactions and "voice" demonstrated critically conscious praxis. I recognize that the definition for teaching for social justice is broad and can and has been defined in a variety of ways. However, for the purpose of this research, I use a definition derived from a critical theoretical standpoint. It involves those who "believe that schools in a democracy can and should prepare citizens to work actively and collectively on problems facing society" (Grant, 2007, p. 258) and those who guide, support, and move students toward a questioning of status quo that will result in action to disrupt the status quo as they evolve and progress along their journey. Such parameters include those whose work considers:

> the organizational structure and policies, interpersonal dynamics, instructional practices and curriculum content and whose work help[s] move children[and adults] toward values of social bonding, caring, responsibility and justice, as well as help them embrace antisexist, antiracist and proglobal environmental attitudes. (Goodman, Kuzmic, & Wu, 1992, p. 163).

As I prepared to select participants, I found myself agonizing over whether or not my own story constituted a valid voice in the research. After all I was sure I knew my own narrative, but I was unsure about whether or not my inclusion in the inquiry would add any real insight. I struggled with everything from the validity of self-study, to how I would tell my own story without appearing self-righteous. I ultimately acknowledged that I selected this research because of what it means to me personally and professionally, making it impossible to completely remove myself. The more I wrestled with this notion, the more Polkinghorne's (1998) proclamation that "there is no way for the knower to stand outside the lifeworld to observe it" (p. 240) spoke to me. I also thought about Huberman's (2002) assertion that a good qualitative researcher should be familiar with the phenomenon under study, and familiar I am. As I considered my purpose for conducting the research, as well as the nature of the research, I found that quite fitting as I am living the questions I was to ask the other participants— have often questioned those very questions. However, what I had not yet done was frame the inquiry of myself in a new way, I had not systematically engaged in a self-study (Cochran-Smith, 2004a). In the end, I decided that a narrative inquiry that included my own voice as self-study was both appropriate and scholarly. So, my story constitutes the fourth in this collection.

Research as Paradigmatic Meaning Making: Purposeful Storytelling

> We purposefully move ahead, having discovered our work and giving our hearts to it, (Barth, 2001) knowing, struggling with, and believing that working for critical democratic education "requires an ongoing process of changing the environmental, cognitive, and pedagogical contexts in which teaching and learning occur."
>
> —GAY, 1995, P. 160

I said earlier that the focus of my research was not on proving or disproving any theory, but rather on exploring the praxis of critical democratic education by asking how teacher educators' lived experiences have informed and transformed their conscientization and contributed to their work with preservice teachers. Using narrative inquiry I gathered individual stories through engaging in interviews with, and reviewing scholarly work provided by, four female teacher educators of varying ages and ethnic identities, with affiliations with different Midwestern American universities. As part of the data-gathering process I used semi-structured interviews along with pre- and post-interview narratives, interview notes, and ongoing coding and member checks to make explicit some themes that are specific to our lived experiences. The resulting stories focused on our past experiences, current practices, and ongoing challenges as we try to make sense of where we have been, where we are, and where we are headed in our journey to teach for social justice. In analyzing the data, I looked for emergent and recurring themes within and across the individual stories, which allowed me to describe our lives and our work in the context of teaching from a critical democratic stance and, thus, tell a collective story out of which three umbrella themes, and subsequent subthemes, emerged:

- The power of reflection
  - Positive experiences
  - Painful experiences
- The need for the intersection of teacher and student journeys
  - Building trusting relationships
  - Explicit teaching about perceptions, privilege, and democracy
- The acknowledgment of challenges
  - Issues of identity
  - Dealing with perceptions, privilege, and democracy
  - Issues of silence(ing)

The research results show that moving toward a conscientization rooted in a critical democratic pedagogy requires a constant process of reflecting, questioning, perspective, and action-taking as well as challenge-facing. It is clear from the data that, for the four of us, using critical democratic education as a means for teaching for social justice is not only non-negotiable, it is also not a destination at which you can simply arrive. It is a recursive act of storying, restorying, and restorying again (Clandinin, 1992), of learning, unlearning, and relearning (Toffler, as cited in Barth, 2001).

Reflection: Going Way Back

Clearly reflection is a theme that is woven and embedded throughout this work. Perhaps then it should follow that I would have expected powerful narratives as I asked participants to reflect on key experiences that brought them to the here and now. The truth is, however, I did not. And even if I had presumed to know the power of these experiences, I still would have underestimated how critical a role they have played in shaping our conscientization. Going way back in order to share our personal and professional lived experiences revealed long-standing, deep, and sometimes painful milestones in our journeys. Each of us identified specific positive familial influences on our teaching actions, from open discussions about status quo and giving back to the community, to loving expectations of greatness. For Diane, that reflection also represented a duality in the influence of a loving family that was characterized by male-dominant modeling that has taken her years to understand and unpack.

Our stories also exposed negative experiences with schooling and society that have greatly impacted our decision to teach as we do. We all shared examples of inequities we have seen in schools and how we cannot bring ourselves to settle for that kind of schooling, nor do we see it as a problem with the children but rather as a problem with our democracy. And there were also examples of vivid, painful lessons about race and gender outside of school that made us question what a democratic America really means. These reflections on our lives before we entered the realm of teacher education are all part of the confounding array of experiences that have demanded that we work toward a transformation in our conscientization.

Journeying Together: In the Classroom

A dominant theme in all of our stories centered around trust and how critical it is that we not only trust ourselves to take and use what we have learned as we have been transformed by our lived experiences, but also the critical role of trust in the relationships that we build with our students. We realize that is not a given that all of our students will be willing to "drive from one side of the city to the other"

(Zwerdling, 2006) and see for themselves the devastation of the inequities that exist in schooling. But we also understand that even if they take that drive, what they see will be colored by where they were before they got there. If our students see us as trustworthy, we are better able and more likely to open the door to classrooms that invite real, sometimes challenging, discussions about teaching and learning. As teacher educators we have found that we have to know what it is we are asking students to do and how personal that is by building trust through sharing ourselves, our struggles, and our journeys with our students.

In other words, we found that we need to engage in parallel practice by scaffolding opportunities in the classroom for our students to look critically at their own thinking, living, and teaching by opening ourselves up to our students, talking about our transformative experiences, making sure that they understand that we too are on a journey, and that we are also doing what we ask of them. When Diane talks to her students about her fears, and Amy and I talk about our guilt, and when we all make ourselves available to our students outside of the classroom, we are working to establish the kind of trust that will build relationships that allow teaching and learning about issues of perception, perspective, privilege, and democracy to occur.

Part of that work is making it clear to students that we also expect them to embark upon their own journey. It became clear that we each, in our own ways, emphasize the notion that it is not enough to merely hear about our journeys, or for students to stop at merely reflecting on their own experiences, beliefs, and understandings. Rather they have to act on those reflections by working to understand what their lived experiences mean to them and with regard to others, by visiting and revisiting what kinds of pedagogies they operate from and by making explicit how that impacts their teaching.

Challenges: Like Pushing a Rock Uphill

Finally, in analyzing these stories it became evident that the lived experiences of the past, as well as our teaching actions with preservice students, are wrought with complexities and challenges that, for us, involve issues of identity and voice that mirror the very things we want to teach against. In teaching against these things, we come face to face with them and find ourselves struggling to live through them while we also try to teach in spite of and against them. For example, Diane is completely disconcerted by the fact that she has had to rationalize herself out of being uneasy when an African American man happens to be behind her; I am pained by the thought of the things to which my children have access that other children do not. Amy battles frustration with her neighbors who are completely complacent in her neighborhood but completely unnerved if they have to go to Chicago, and incredulous that she is "so brave." Patricia is still struggling with the great disappointment she found in being compelled by her spiritual and racial identity to support African American students in the form of a writing group, but having that support relegated by her university to the category of "other" work. Thus, it appears that trying to find and understand one's identity in this work means constantly dealing with our own, as well as larger society's, notions and living of class, race, and gender, and the contradictions therein.

Establishing one's identity, for us, also includes struggling to break the silence that status quo imposes in academia. While we each feel that the people in our universities are generally well intentioned, we seek more and we are consistently disappointed. That frustration level is especially high when, as Diane says, we feel as though we are constantly pushing that rock up the hill, and it seems that we have few others at our universities to take that journey with us. Or even worse, when, as in Patricia's example, we dare to break the silence and find ourselves silenced not only by the absence of conversation but also by blatant dismissal of it. We could each, I am sure, pick out the people in our institutions who are willing to have these conversations or are already doing so. We also know that some never will.

It is not that we are talking about our institutions or colleagues as lacking integrity, or not caring about their students, or not doing a good job of teaching. Rather, what we are asking is what constitutes integrity, what perceptions are given about which students are cared about, and what exactly it is that we are doing a good job of teaching, and how do we know? These are the same questions we ask ourselves, the same questions we ask our preservice teachers to ask themselves. In voicing our concerns, we are seeking to "normalize teaching for social justice and make transparent policies that keep that from happening" (Cochran-Smith, 2004b, p. 20). There were not only individual stories of struggles with our institutions, but the collective concern and distrust of our universities to model practices in policy, conversation, and instruction that are in the interest of social justice. We all shared concerns about the work of our universities toward the promotion of social justice when we have coded conversations, if any, about issues of equity, diversity, perception, and teaching. The surface discussions are there, there is perceived broad agreement that the world is diverse, that diverse perspectives are important, that schools are inequitable, and sometimes even a nod to the fact that institutions of higher learning contribute to those inequities. However, we have all found that there is a void in terms of deeper conversations like Cochran-Smith (1999) describes in her self-study, where we look at what we mean by diversity, social justice, and the like, and then look at what that looks like in our classrooms and in each other's classrooms. We have come to the conclusion that we cannot teach it if we have not lived it, but we do not know how we get others within our institutions to break the silence so that it is apparent that they are living it and teaching it too.

While there is greater visibility of a call for teacher educators to not only teach preservice teachers to teach for social justice, but to live it themselves, Cochran-Smith (2004b) projects that a significant number of teacher educators have yet to struggle with and learn from their own issues with "isms." With hope for that to change, she notes the growing body of research focusing on teacher educators striving for parallel practice, as she also calls for the need for continued growth in the gathering and analyzing of data that questions and explores the practices of teacher educators. In order to strengthen the research base, she talks about the power in the use of different forms of practitioner inquiry, including narrative research and self-study, which focus on

- The range and variance in the praxis of teaching for social justice
- Making explicit the role of teacher educators in maintaining status quo
- Coming to terms with struggles that perpetuate status quo, in spite of teacher educators' advocacy against it.

So while this research is useful as a means for studying and reinventing my own practice, in seeking to provide "a potentially deeper and more valuable understanding of the experience" (Clandinin, 2007, p. 21), my hope is that it also adds to the knowledge base on teaching for social justice that acknowledges the work as a journey that requires ongoing reflection, transformation, and action, by grounding these notions in a particular context for particular teacher educators at particular points in their journeys (Clandinin, 2007, p. 21). At the very least it can provide another window into the journey that Cochran-Smith (2004a, 2004b) confirms is necessary, ongoing, and challenging. It can serve as a springboard for discussion for colleagues and programs or departments who are so inclined. As in Cochran-Smith's (1999) self-study, such conversations are not expected to provoke broad agreement or even all-encompassing changes in pedagogy and practice. It can, however, open the door to conversations about what teaching for social justice means, how it is actualized in teacher education programs, and how people get to the point of even teaching for social justice in the first place, resulting in purposeful and significant changes in how more and more teacher educators view and enact their praxis.

Bibliography

Aronowitz, S., & Giroux, H. (1991). *Postmodern education: Politics, culture and social criticism*. Minneapolis: University of Minnesota Press.

Ayers, W. (2004). *Teaching toward freedom: Moral commitment and ethical action in the classroom*. Boston: Beacon.

Ayers, W. (Ed.). (2004). *Teaching the personal and the political: Essays on hope and justice*. New York: Teachers College Press.

Ayers, W., Hunt, J.A., & Quinn, T. (1998). *Teaching for social justice*. New York: Teachers College Press.

Barth, R. (2001). *Learning by heart*. San Francisco: Jossey-Bass.

Beane, J. (2005). *A reason to teach: Creating classrooms of dignity and hope*. Portsmouth, NH: Heinemann.

Brosio, R. (2000). *Philosophical scaffolding for the construction of critical democratic education*. New York: Peter Lang.

Brown, K. (2004). Assessing preservice leaders' beliefs, attitudes, and values regarding issues of diversity, social justice, and equity: A review of existing measures. *Equity & Excellence in Education, 37*, 332–342.

Chang, Y. (2005). The pedagogical content knowledge of teacher educators: A case study in a democratic teacher preparation program. PhD dissertation, Ohio University, Athens, Ohio. Retrieved February 16, 2008, from ProQuest Digital Dissertations database. (Publication No. AAT 3197294).

Clandinin, D. J. (1992). Narrative and story in teacher education. In T. Russell & H. Munby (Eds.), *Teachers and teaching: From classroom to reflection* (pp. 124–137). New York: Falmer.

Clandinin, D. (Ed.). (2007). *Handbook of narrative inquiry: Mapping a methodology*. New York: Sage.

Cochran-Smith, M. (1995). Color blindness and basket making are not the answers: Confronting the dilemmas of race, culture and language diversity in teacher education. *American Education Research Journal, 32*, 493–522.

Cochran-Smith, M. (2004a). *Walking the road: Race, diversity and social justice in teacher education*. New York: Teachers College Press.

Cochran-Smith, M. (2004b, November). Defining the outcomes of teacher education: What's social justice got to do with it? *Asia-Pacific Journal of Teacher Education, 32*(3), 193.

Cochran-Smith, M., Albert, L., Dimattia, P., Freedman, S., Jackson, R., Mooney, J., et al. (1999). Seeking social justice: A teacher education faculty's self-study. *International Journal of Leadership in Education, 2*(3), 229–253.

Cochran-Smith, M., & Zeichner, K. (Eds.). (2005). *Studying teacher education: The report of the AERA panel on research and teacher education*. Mahwah, NJ: Lawrence Erlbaum.

Dewey, J. (1916). *Democracy and education*. New York: Free Press.

Eager, J. (2007). *From multiculturalism to social justice*. Presentation at the Indivisible: Teaching for Social Justice through Literature for Children and Adolescents Conference, National Louis University, Chicago, IL.

Freire, P. (1990). *Pedagogy of the oppressed*. New York: Continuum.

Freire, P., & Macedo, D. (1987). *Literacy: Reading the word and the world*. London: Routledge.

Gay, G. (1995). Mirror images on common issues: Parallels between multicultural education and critical pedagogy. In C. E. Sleeter & P. L. McClaren (Eds.), *Multicultural education, critical pedagogy, and the politics of difference* (pp. 155–190). Albany: State University of New York Press.

Gay, G. (2000). *Culturally responsive teaching: Theory, research, and practice*. New York: Teachers College Press.

Gay, G. (Ed.). (2003). *Becoming multicultural educators: Personal journeys toward professional agency*. San Francisco: Jossey-Bass.

Gerzon, M. (1997). Teaching democracy and doing it. *Education for Democratic Life, 54*(5), 6–11.

Goodman, J. (2006). *Reforming schools: Working within a progressive tradition during conservative times*. Albany: State University of New York Press.

Goodman, J., Kuzmic, J., & Wu, X. (1992). *Elementary schooling for critical democracy*. Albany: State University of New York Press.

Grant, C., & Gillette, M. (May, 2006). A candid talk to teacher educators about effectively preparing teachers who can teach everyone's children. *Journal of Teacher Education, 57*(3), 292–299.

Grant, C. A., & Sleeter, C. (2007). *Turning on learning: Five approaches for multicultural teaching plans for race, class, gender, and disability* (4th ed.). Hoboken, NJ: J. Wiley & Sons.

Greene, M. (1988). *The dialectic of freedom*. New York: Teachers College Press.

Habermas, J. (1984). *The theory of communicative action* [Theorie des kommunikativen Handelns]. Boston: Beacon.

Hornsby, B., and the Range. (1986). *That's just the way it is*. Retrieved August 10, 2006, from http://paperclippings.com/list/bs/bhornsby-wayitis.html

Hrabowski, F. A. III. (2007, November). *Education for the 21st century: Creating a climate of success for all students*. Keynote address at the annual meeting for the National Association for Multicultural Education (NAME), Baltimore, MD.

Huberman, M., & Miles, M.B. (2002). *The qualitative researcher's companion*. Los Angeles: Sage.

Imam, S. A. (2001). Six Muslims living in the Midwest in the presence of negative images in the public curriculum. EdD Dissertation, National-Louis University, Chicago, IL. Retrieved November 15, 2007, from ProQuest Digital Dissertations database. (Publication No. AAT 3042248).

Kahne, J., & Westheimer, J. (2004, Summer). What kind of citizen: The politics of educating for democracy. *American Education Research Journal, 41*(2), 237–269.

Kneller, G. F. (1984). *Movements of thought in modern education*. New York: Macmillan.

Kozol, J. (1991). *Savage inequalities*. New York: Crown.

Ladson-Billings, G. (1995). Toward a theory of culturally relevant pedagogy. *American Reading Education Research Journal, 32*, 465–491.

Ladson-Billings, G. (2001). *Crossing over to Canaan: The journey of new teachers in diverse classrooms*. San Francisco: Jossey-Bass.

Macedo, D. (1994). *Literacies of power*. Boulder, CO: Westview.

Macedo, D. (1996). Literacy for stupidification: The pedagogy of big lies. In P. Leistyna, S. Sherblom, & A. Woodrum (Ed.), *Breaking free: The transformative power of critical pedagogy* (pp. 31–58). Cambridge, MA: Harvard University Press.

McLaren, P. (2003). *Life in schools: An introduction to critical pedagogy in the foundations of education* (4th ed.). Boston: Allyn & Bacon.

Michelli, N., & Keiser, D. L. (Ed). (2005). *Teacher education for democracy and social justice*. New York: Routledge.

Michie, G. (2005). *See you when we get there: Teaching for change in urban schools*. New York: Teachers College Press.

Moustakas, C. (1994). *Phenomenological research methods*. Thousand Oaks, CA: Sage.

Nagda, B. A., Gurin, P., & Lopez, G. (2003, July). Transformative pedagogy for democracy and social justice. *Race, Ethnicity and Education, 6*(2), 165–191.

Nieto, S. (2006). Solidarity, courage and heart. *Intercultural Education, 17*(5), 457–473.

Noddings, N. (1992). *The challenge to care in schools: An alternative approach to education*. New York: Teachers College Press.

Noddings, N. (1999, April). Renewing democracy in schools. *Phi Delta Kappan, 80*(5), 579–583.

Noddings, N. (2002). *Educating moral people: A caring alternative to character education*. New York: Teachers College Press.

Noddings, N. (Ed.). (2005). *Educating citizens for global awareness*. New York: Teachers College Press.

Polkinghorne, D. (1983). *Methodology for the human sciences: Systems of inquiry*. Albany: State University of New York Press.

Polkinghorne, D. (1988). *Narrative knowing and the human sciences*. Albany: State University of New York Press.

Reeves, P. (2006). *Lebanese PM appeals to Arab nations for help*. Retrieved August 7, 2006, from http://www.npr.org

Regenspan, B. (2002). *Parallel practices: Social justice-focused teacher education and the elementary school classroom*. New York: Peter Lang.

Zeichner, K., Melnick, S., & Gomez, M. L. (Eds.). (1996). *Currents of reform in preservice teacher education*. New York: Teachers College Press.

Zwerdling, D. (2006). *The slow pace of recovery*. Retrieved August 7, 2006, from http://www.npr.org

CHAPTER THIRTEEN

Culling Methodological Tools, Honing Research Skills

A Paradigm of Critical Discourse Analysis on Neoliberalism

BAUDELAIRE K. ULYSSE

Mining answers for research questions as well as calibrating one's findings necessitate efficient tools. Here, tools refer to methods. As such, methods putatively enable the researcher to delve in depth into a particular subject and to advance consciously and cautiously along its charted as well as uncharted paths in order to cull relevant and sound answers. Charted paths represent extant scholarly works on a particular subject, while uncharted paths represent the possibilities of latent theories, perspectives, and new interpretations of established assumptions that may lie beneath extant data, waiting to be unearthed. However, the search for an efficient method is daunting because there is a multitude of methods.

Critical Discourse Analysis as a Method or Tool for Research

Researchers from a wide array of disciplines are using critical discourse analysis (CDA) as a tool in research (McCloskey, 2008), and this trend is even more rampant in educational inquiries (Rogers, 2011). McCloskey uses discourse analysis as a tool to conduct research in the field of nursing and has found that the structure of this field inheres policies and practices that reflect the fiber of discourses. By the same token, Rogers does not simply use discourse analysis in her research but also teaches discourse analysis. In fact, her work taps into quantitative data from her own students' understandings as well as effective use of critical discourse analysis. Her data analysis provides insights into the arduous process of students wrestling to understand the tool of critical discourse analysis and effectively use it in their own research. The deep understanding as well as the effective use of critical discourse analysis apparently yields multilayered interpretations of how discourse operates within social spheres of human societies. Overall, Rogers' research adds credence to the credibility and validity of discourse analysis as an effective research tool.

Assumptions of Critical Discourse Analysis

Similar to a theoretical lens, CDA has a few assumptions. It maintains that language is a social phenomenon (Fairclough, 2001), which means that individual human beings, institutions, and social structures have values and meanings that are expressed through language in systematic ways. Thus, according to Fairclough, language is becoming more important in what people do, what multinational corporations do, what goods and services they produce and sell, and is increasingly a matter of particular ways of using language. Further, he believes that a significant part of providing goods is the way language is used in interactions between staff and customers, in printed documents and signs, in publicity for the hotels, and so forth. This use of language means that the struggle to impose or resist the new order is in large part a struggle for or against a new language. As a result, the critique of documents such as policies, academic publications, and press releases related to discourse practices becomes imperative before one can successfully delineate as well as assess the discourse of neoliberalism (Fairclough, 2001).

Perhaps more pertinent to the current study is CDA's interest in the nexus between language and power (Fairclough, 2001; Gee, 2005). According to Gee, this relationship between language and power pervasively manifests itself in that "language-in-use is everywhere and always political" (p. 1). In this relationship, language emits and solidifies power, and in turn power reinforces language, which nurtures both to coexist and self-perpetrate in a domination matrix. By the same token, Fairclough (2001) is insightful regarding the relationship between language and power. He coins the notion of "power behind discourse" and outlines three aspects of how power plays out in a discourse—*standard language*, *effect of power*, and *power and access to discourse*.

In all three aspects, discourse is engendered and maintained by the interest of power-holders. In this type of discourse, "the whole social order of discourse is put together and held together as a hidden effect of power" (Fairclough, 2001, p. 46). All three aspects, as discussed by Fairclough, have the dynamics of power and domination directly manifest in them. Here I should like to highlight the third aspect—

power and access to discourse. I am highlighting this particular aspect because it touches on the issues of inequity and inequality that are evidently part and parcel of the discourse on neoliberalism and economic globalization.

According to Fairclough (2001), power and access to discourse play right into how the value of free speech is implemented in actual social practice. He argues that the notion of free speech is in fact a myth primarily because there is "a plethora of constraints on access to various sorts of speech and writing" (p. 52). Essentially, these constraints determine what group gets access to cultural capital in a given society.

Inequity and inequality represent major concerns of my study in the same breadth they are represented in CDA. Thus, I maintain they are inextricably connected to the causality of power dynamics within the neoliberal discourse. Consequently, it is the onus and focus of my analysis in this study to delineate these issues, critique them, and present an alternate discourse that is consistent with social justice principles such as freedom, equality, and equity in all contexts of human societies.

Gee (2005) credits Fairclough, Wodak, and Meyer, among others, with the use of CDA within the discourse analysis tradition, and he suggests they all share the foundational sketch of discourse analysis, albeit they differ in tools of inquiry and linguistic tradition (pp. 116–117). However, they are all interested in language-in-use and its effects on societal structures. As such, they are linguists interested in how language is used onsite to enact activities and identities (little-d). A combination of the little d discourse (language-in-use) and non-language "stuff" to enact specific identities and activities yields big-D Discourse (p. 7).

Non-language stuff is understood by Gee (2005) as ways in the world—acting, feeling, believing, and valuing. "All life for all of us is just a patchwork of thoughts, words, objects, events, actions, and interactions in discourses" (p. 7). To Gee, language has meaning only in and through social practice. We use language when we make things significant, when we engage in certain activities, build relationships, and share or make a case for our perspectives.

Also important is that contemporary approaches of discourse analysis assume a *reflexive* of the relationship between language and context. "Reflexive here means that, at one and the same time, an utterance influences what we take the context to be and context conversely influences what we take the utterance to mean" (Gee, 2005, p. 57).

Fairclough (1995, 2001, 2008) links Gee's framework of discourse to critical theory. Hence, Fairclough (1995) vehemently emphasizes discourse analysis as that which is both analytical and critical. As such, CDA as a method serves as "a resource for people who are struggling against the domination and oppression in its linguistic forms" (p. 1). Central to Fairclough's (1995) discussion of CDA are the notions of text, discourse practice, and sociocultural practice. Hence Fairclough expands the boundaries of discourse analysis from linguistic analysis to textual analysis, which includes language, written text, and social institutions. Accordingly, texts for Fairclough could be the content of linguistic texture and structure in written documents, in which case ideologies are likely embedded in them.

Also, texts are viewed as social spaces wherein identities of individuals of a particular society are being formed. These individuals, or peoples in general, are being formed precisely in social spaces through certain processes, which Fairclough (1995) alludes to as cognition and representations of the world and social interaction. Elsewhere, he elaborates, stating, "Discourses include representations of how things are and have been, as well as imaginaries—representations of how things might or could or should be" (Fairclough, 2008, p. 207). Thus, these elements, cognition, representation, and social interaction are integral parts of discourses, and they should be factored into any CDA research design. In Gee (2005), these elements would be considered as little-d discourses that contribute to the big-D Discourse.

Based on this understanding of discourse as text, Fairclough (1995) argues that the successful analysis of any text or discourse must meticulously and critically analyze one or more of its key elements:

> Such analysis requires attention to textual form, structure and organizations at all levels; phonological, grammatical, and lexical (vocabulary) and higher levels of textual organization in terms of exchange systems (the distribution of speaking turns), structure of argumentation, and generic (activity type) structures. (p. 7)

Fairclough (1995) does not seem to relegate the primary preoccupation of CDA with language. Instead, he views language or linguistic patterns as a broader structure, encompassing written texts and spoken texts (speech or other delivery systems) along with the vital components necessary for their proper functioning. I think Fairclough's schema, which stresses text, discourse practice, and sociocultural practice as key components of discourse, expands the scope of discourse and thus provides ample targets and texts for analysis.

By the same token, Reisigl and Wodak (2009) stress an understanding of text as an embodiment of power and domination, and thus are sites of social struggle:

> Texts are often sites of struggle in that they manifest traces of differing ideological fights for domination and hegemony. Thus, we focus on the ways in which linguistic forms are used in various expressions and manipulations of power. Power is discursively exerted not only by grammatical forms, but also by a person's control of the social occasions by means of the genre of a text, by the regulation of access to certain public spheres. (p. 89)

In the preceding statement, Reisigl and Wodak espouse and aptly argue for a broader view of text, which is similar to that of Fairclough (1995). Hence, this broader view of language or text as an embodiment of domination and oppression serves as a suitably fertile framework to not only understand and interpret the phenomena associated with global neoliberalism, but also to critique and deconstruct neoliberalism's hegemonic and oppressive agenda.

Wherever we discuss methodology in a particular research, method becomes indispensable; wherever we plan to use a method, a mine of data or data sources wherein we can use our chosen method in search of evidence and insights are also requisites. In this study, I am working with the presuppositions of CDA. One of those presuppositions is that discourse uses texts (both spoken and written) to control as well as enact practices (linguistic, social, cultural, institutional, and political) in societies, which is believed to embody group domination and oppression (Fairclough, 1995, 2001, 2008; Wodak & Meyer, 2009). Another such presupposition is that discourse ironically is "resisted in text and talk in the social and political context" (Van Dijk, 1993).

Accordingly, in my critical analysis of the discourse of neoliberalism in the global economy context, I consider texts from a variety of sources and disciplines: published materials for and against the neoliberal discourse; institutions such as government, schools, or educational systems, primarily those in Haiti and the United States, with special attention given to how they support and embody the neoliberal discourse; and materials written on intergovernmental institutions such as the International Monetary Fund (IMF), World Bank (WB), World Trade Organization (WTO), and United Nations Educational, Scientific and Cultural Organization (UNESCO). As such, the analysis draws data from various strata while concentrating on key aspects such as those proposed by Van Dijk (1993): analysis of semantic macrostructure, topics for macrostructure, analysis of local meanings, analysis of subtle structure, analysis of global and local discourse forms, analysis of specific linguistic realization (hyperbolas), and analysis of content. I do not take those aspects to represent a process that should include all or none; rather, I think they should be viewed as a comprehensive list from which one may select a few elements to focus on that are consistent and necessary to one's topic, research questions, or purposes. While I am not referring specifically to Van Dijk's aspects throughout my analysis of the discourse of neoliberalism, I plan nonetheless to touch on most of them, except the aspect of analysis of specific linguistic realization.

To successfully analyze these various aspects of the discourse of neoliberalism, I draw from an array of books, journal articles, and respected newspapers that extensively address globalization's history and its current juncture—social, political, educational, and economic—through the prism of neoliberal ideologies. Also, to the degree that this is relevant to the analysis, I intend to integrate my voice as a subject whose phenomenological narrative is inevitably being shaped in the context of the discourse. Essentially, the data sources referred to above are delineated, analyzed, compared, contrasted, expounded on, and synthesized in order to unveil and critique the nature of the discourse or discourses as well as its embodied injustice.

In keeping with Gee's (2005) vernacular, particularly his differentiation between big-D Discourses and little-d discourses, I pay close attention to the subtleties and complexities of how power and politics are embedded in languages in local settings as embodied in written content. Thus, initiatives such as educational reforms, school textbooks, enactment of trade agreements, and privatization of public assets could be said to represent little-d discourses that take place in local settings while contributing and shaping, both subtly and explicitly, the big-D Discourse within the macrocosm of neoliberalism and economic globalization.

Neoliberalism as a Discourse

Neoliberalism, as an ideology, is currently exerting a tremendous influence on human societies all across the world (Davies & Bensel, 2007). The influence of neo-liberalism does not lend itself simply to one aspect of these societies but reaches and impacts many aspects that profoundly affect the material conditions of social, economic, and political structures. One of the pivotal shifts in the material conditions of societies engendered by neoliberalism is that of moving from a social welfare state to a neoliberal market-driven state serving as an apparatus for individual entrepreneurial interests (Nafstad et al., 2007). Other shifts caused by neoliberalism are manifest in social policies enacted in certain societies around the world. For instance, these various shifts engendered by neoliberalism have led many to conclude that the neoliberal agenda has been very effective on a global scale.

Jilberto and Mommen (1993) have perceptively concluded that "neo-liberalism as political and economic ideology has been one of the most successful elements of the reconstruction of capitalist hegemony over the global system" (p. 3). Similarly, Apple (1999), Hill (1998), and Miraftab (2004) have each painted neoliberalism as a powerful ideological tool that is drastically transforming the fiber of many societies around the world. Miraftab examines the role neoliberalism plays in the governance of different states around the world, and he paints a rather stunning picture of how neoliberalism relates to politics and economies in developing countries:

> Neo-liberal policies and structural adjustment programs have deeply slashed governments' budget for public expenditure and have redefined the state's responsibilities for public services. For example, in developing states in the 1950s–1970s the primary agenda for national economic growth was

to provide basic services and infra-structure. But that role has now been shifted to private firms, both local and international, in a market-led strategy for providing basic public services and infrastructure. (p. 240)

While Miraftab's depiction reflects realities as well as actualities in the developing world, neoliberalism's growing influence is by no means confined to that segment. After all, neoliberalism has long achieved a certain pinnacle regarding global dominance, making it undeniably a full-fledged ideological discourse. As Miraftab (2004) points out, neoliberalism has attained such global dominance precisely by strategically creating alliance, albeit coercively at times, with what one might call client governments around the world. If there is doubt about neoliberalism being a discourse or about neoliberalism's global reach, Apple (1999) provides a stunning portrayal of neoliberalism that is sure to dispel such doubt. His work, titled *Freire, Neoliberalism, and Education*, traces the connection between American conservative ideologies and neoliberalism. This work represents by far one of the most courageous assessments of, and thus a verdict against, neoliberalism in terms of the subtle way in which neoliberalism controls policies related to the U.S. economy and education.

Analyzing Neoliberalism: A Paradigm of Discourse Analysis

Davies and Bensel (2007) discuss the shift to or the emergence of global neoliberalism. They trace the development of neoliberalism back to the economic policies of Great Britain and the United States. Davies and Bensel also show how neoliberalism started spreading across the world through the concerted effort of neoliberal stakeholders such as France, Great Britain, and the United States. Essentially, they postulate that the spread of neoliberalism has been facilitated by the consent of nation-states' official governments in countries across the world. When these governments grant consent, neoliberalism becomes endowed with unlimited political and economic leverage to influence or undermine existing laws as well as enact new ones that favor the unfettered operation of multinational corporations and other interest groups. This relationship or arrangement between governments of nation-states and global interest groups begets as well as controls the framework within which the neoliberal discourse is promulgated, implemented, and sustained.

Operative within this discourse are various philosophies or notions. These terms, which have surfaced in earlier discussions in no respective order, are *capitalism*, *hegemony*, *neoliberalism*, *colonialism*, and *imperialism*. The assumptions of the study posit that the discourse, which embodies neoliberalism and economic globalization, subsumes most, if not all, of the terms highlighted above.

Capitalism

Capitalism is by no means a new phenomenon. It is an economic system or philosophy that has been implemented in many economies around the world, particularly in Western economies such as Great Britain and the United States (Frieden, 2006). It does not lend itself to a restricted definition, but most economists would concur that capitalism refers to and embodies values such as free market and free choice. Because of its putative element of freedom, capitalism is thought by many to be ideal and most compatible with human societies (Bernstein, 2005).

Placing this philosophy in the context of a local economy, it becomes characterized by five distinct features: private property and freedom of choice, self-interest, markets and prices, competition, and limited government intervention (Friedman, 2002, 2007). Thus, the global economy is essentially capitalism driving the economies of both developing and developed countries into an integrated whole, which entails a "closer integration of the [economies of] countries of the world through the increased flow of goods and services" (Stiglitz, 2003, p. 4).

Hegemony

Hegemony, being understood as the dominant discourse (Apple, 2004), tends to be the concurrent enforcement of a particular ideology by those in control, or an ideology resulting from the domination by others. It is a fascinating phenomenon in that it can be implemented through either coercion (Clayton, 1998) or in a subtle medium such as spoken languages, educational systems, curricular approaches, and publications. From the vantage point of colonialism and imperialism, the cultures and educational systems of previously colonized countries are steeped in the legacies of their colonizers (Ginsburg & Clayton, 2006), thereby perpetuating and enforcing hegemony.

The type of hegemony discussed and illustrated above reflects more or less a subtle domination, however strategic and intentional. Although this type of hegemony should not be equated with empire, it is more often than not the result of imperial legacies perpetuated through education, cultural, and linguistic devices. However, hegemony also inheres an aggressive dimension that is particularly manifest in economic implementation of neoliberalism and its political ramifications in the global context. Agnew (2005) thinks this kind of hegemony is U.S.-infused and argues that the United States usually enlists the help of other countries in perpetrating it. Thus, he defines it as "the enrollment of others in the exercise of your power by convincing, cajoling, and coercing them that they should do what you want" (p. 1).

For Agnew (2005), this characterizes the relationship between the United States and the rest of the world, particularly in the context of globalization. In fact, he views globalization, without qualification, as a "hegemonic project intimately connected to the geopolitical calculus of U.S. government" (p. 2), thereby dismissing neoliberalism, or "liberalization" as he labels it. I do not equate globalization with liberalization or neoliberalism because there are various factors contributing to the globalizing process. However, I posit that the current engine of economic globalization, or the global economy, is being propelled by neoliberalism as the dominant discourse. Hence, contrary to Agnew, I contend that hegemony of neoliberalism in economic globalization cannot be viewed simply through the American prism. My argument throughout this study has been that economic globalization should be viewed as a broader coalition among the most powerful and elite economies of the world, including the United States. Ultimately, this coalition is committed not only to incubate and implement neoliberalism but also to propagate it in other countries, particularly countries in the developing world.

Ideologies of the Neoliberal Discourse

Having become the preferred economic philosophy in the context of a global economy, capitalism has given rise to a capitalist expansion known as *neoliberalism*. Neoliberalism represents a hegemonic discourse in the context of globalization (Giroux, 2004; Harvey, 2007) and is manifest particularly in economies, government, and education globally (Giroux).

Privatization

Megginson (2005) defines privatization as a "deliberate sale by a government of state-owned enterprises (SOEs) or assets to private economic agents" (p. 3). As such, privatization favors private enterprise and private ownership over public or government enterprises. Similar to deregulation, privatization is another neoliberal ideology that advocates for less publically run or government-sponsored services. Further, it maintains that private ownership and enterprises ultimately foster entrepreneurship, individual responsibility, and competitions in the market and in society.

Since its introduction, privatization has rapidly become the darling of all economic reforms in developed economies and is a major component of neoliberalism as a dominant discourse. Megginson (2005) notes that Chile and Germany experimented with privatization in the 1970s, but he suggests those two countries harvested nominal results from the implementation of privatization. According to Megginson, Great Britain has been particularly singled out as an exemplar that successfully implemented privatization in the early 1980s. Further, other countries such as "France, Austria, Belgium, Canada, Chile, Denmark, Holland, Italy, Jamaica, Japan, Malaysia, Singapore, Spain, Sweden, and the United States all executed significant privatization through public share offerings during the mid-1980s" (p. 17).

As those countries embarked on the journey to implement privatization, there was an overwhelming aura of optimism that privatization would make their governments more efficient, raise financial capital for their gross domestic product (GDP), and ultimately boost their economies. To date, other countries have launched similar privatization projects. Accordingly, Megginson (2005) estimates that "the cumulative value" of all privatization undertakings "now has surpassed 1.5 trillion dollars" (p. 21). Apparently, there is very much to be had when governments privatize.

It is no wonder that privatization is being pushed in many developing countries around the world. Haiti is one among many developing countries where privatization as a neoliberal economic reform is currently being implemented. Neoliberals have been courting Haiti on such reforms for a long time. The 1994 return of Aristide, the then-exiled and now ex-president of Haiti, served as the turning point in this pursuit since Aristide supposedly agreed to a deal that guaranteed his return in exchange for the implementation of neoliberal reforms. However, Aristide had been reluctant to follow through on such reforms because they were not popular among the Haitian masses that rely heavily on public services (Girard, 2005). As it turned out, Aristide's reluctance did not earn him favor with powerful neoliberal interest groups, which arguably became the ground for a second ouster that sent Aristide into exile in Africa.

Since Aristide's second exile, which occurred in 2004, and with the advent of the reelection of Mr. René Préval for a second nonconsecutive term as president in 2006, much funding had been disbursed to Haiti through WB and IMF, purportedly from neoliberal interest groups whose precondition was the implementation of a neoliberal agenda (Girard, 2005). Privatization is one focus of this agenda and is typically sold to developing countries as a catalyst for economic development. Harvey (2007) explains how neoliberalism ties privatization to economic advancement:

> Neoliberals are particularly assiduous in seeking the privatization of assets. The absence of clear private property rights—as in many developing countries—is seen as one of the most institutional barriers to economic development and the improvement of human welfare.... Sectors formerly run or regulated by the state must be turned over to the private sphere and be deregulated (free from any state interference). (p. 65)

Economic reforms of this nature pervade many countries, both developed and developing, around the globe. I consider Haiti a country at the juncture of economic development in the context of neoliberal economic discourse. As a direct result of neoliberal economic reforms in Haiti, a few institutions or services previously run by the Haitian government have been privatized. For instance, Haiti's flourmill and cement factory, which were formerly run by the Haitian government, have been privatized. In 2010, former Haitian president René Préval announced that privatization plans for Téléco, the Haitian national telephone company, were being finalized (Sprague, 2009). Although the then-president claimed privatization to be in the best interest of the Haitian economy, many Haitians, especially those intimately affected by it, are not particularly thrilled with privatization or other reforms.

The fire of neoliberal reforms in Haiti is currently being fanned, and it will likely remain sparked and aflame for a long time because the cash-strapped Haitian government has apparently bought into neoliberal ideologies, and neoliberals have been able to exert incredible influence on the political process in Haiti. Recent evidence of such influence is seen in the exclusion of the most popular political party in Haiti in the April 2009 senatorial elections. With no constitutional or legal ground, the Haitian national electoral council banned politicians of that party from participating in the elections (Reuters, 2009; Sprague, 2009). Critics of this decision suggested that politicians from this popular party were likely to get elected but unlikely to support the neoliberal agenda. So to clear the way for unfettered and undeterred neoliberal reforms in Haiti, neoliberals purportedly colluded to orchestrate the political hacking, resulting into conundrum in Haiti (Gupta, 2010).

The point of contention regarding privatization is that it rarely delivers on what it purports to do. Giroux (2004) perceptively notes that neoliberalism "pushes for the privatization of all non-commodified public spheres and the upward distribution of wealth. It supports policies that increasingly militarize facets of public space in order to secure the privileges and benefits of the corporate elite and ultra-rich" (p. xxiv). Despite the fact that privatization serves the interests of only a select few, its proponents continue to sell it as a catalyst for widespread economic development in poor countries.

Free Market

From a policy standpoint, regulation represents rules or interventions by the government intended to contain the market's reach and protect investors from erratic turns (Reback, 2009). Presupposed in the government's regulatory interventions in the market mechanism is a clairvoyance that "the market system may not function ideally in monopolistic or oligopolistic industries" (Baumol & Blinder, 1986, p. 272). For instance, regulation restricts what prices firms and corporations can charge and, in many situations, how the products are distributed to the markets. Also, regulation enacts and enforces antitrust policies to deter monopolistic business practices (Reback, 2009). These aspects of regulation, among many others, are intended by the government to create competition and fair business habits among firms and to protect consumers and investors who do business transactions on the market (Baumol & Blinder; Reback).

In stark contrast to regulation, deregulation seeks to minimize the government's intervention since government intervention is usually perceived as interference that inhibits the market and prevents it from naturally stimulating competition in pricing and the production of better products. Further, much like liberalism, this deregulation element of neoliberal ideology holds and professes an unwavering trust in the market, touting the market as sovereign and capable of independently running itself smoothly, equitably, and fairly (Friedman, 2002; Oatley, 2008). Highlighting neoliberalism's influence on economies for the last 20 years and the emphasis on free market, Oatley notes:

> Neoliberalism is highly skeptical of the state's ability to allocate resources efficiently and places great faith in the market's ability to do so. And in contrast to structuralism's advocacy of protectionism and state intervention is neoliberalism's advocacy of the withdrawal of the state from the economy, the reduction (ideally, elimination) of trade barriers, and reliance on the market to generate industries that produce for the world market. (p. 139)

Further, neoliberalism's proponents argue that deregulation reduces prices on products, improves services, renders the market more competitive and accessible, and makes entry of new businesses feasible and profitable (Baumol & Blinder, 1986). However, it should be noted that these advantages of deregulation do not represent the norms of the markets or across industries. Further, others have suggested that regulation initiated by government toward the market fittingly represents the sole, albeit imperfect, restraining force against the excesses of the market (Reback, 2009). In fact, critics have viscerally and adamantly contested this neoliberalism's trust in the market, suggesting the market lacks the moral fiber to operate in a socially just fashion (Stiglitz, 2003).

Regarding the issue of moral fiber of the market, Giroux (2004) writes, "Within the discourse of neoliberalism, democracy becomes synonymous with free markets while issues of equality, social justice, and freedom are stripped of any substantive meaning and used to disparage those who suffer systemic deprivation and chronic punishment" (p. xviii). These points made by Giroux adeptly capture some of the issues revolving around the supremacy awarded to the market mechanism.

Milton Friedman was perhaps the most astute and prominent advocate for this supremacy of the market. In fact, Friedman (1990) co-authored *Free to Choose* with his wife. They attributed the success of American capitalist economy to the notion of free market, particularly the capitalist philosophy that advocates and demands that the market be freed from political influence. Grounded in the arguments originally advanced by Scottish philosopher Adam Smith (1723—1790) in his *The Wealth of Nations* (1776), their thesis postulates that in almost all cases where the U.S. government has intervened with the goal of protecting the public good and the interests of its citizens, it has managed to produce just the opposite. To corroborate their thesis, they extensively examined services such as education, social institutions, social security, employment, and fiscal matters where the government has frequently yet unsuccessfully intervened.

Having espoused the ideal of free market, they suggested that it is through the "voluntary exchange" among self-interested individuals that an economy develops, grows, and sustains itself. According to them, this voluntary exchange is dictated and facilitated by the pricing structure inherent in the market system and not by some outer commanding force such as governments. As far as government is concerned, Friedman and Friedman (1990) suggest that its role be confined to the protection of its citizens and the administration of justice. This will secure the parameters of a free society wherein its people are free from outside coercion and free to engage in transactions that are mutually beneficial for all parties involved. Overall, their view can be summed up as such: "Economic freedom is an essential requisite to the political freedom. By enabling people to cooperate with one another without coercion or central direction, it reduces the area over which political power is exercised" (pp. 2–3).

Hence Friedman and Friedman effectively linked the Declaration of Independence to the economic principle of free market, and they supposed that the parties operating in the market equally enjoy the same freedom. However, I surmise this is precisely where Harvey (2007) seems to sharply disagree. The implication of Harvey's disagreement is that political freedom does not necessarily translate into freedom for everyone making transactions in the market, and that neoliberal application at its core immensely undermines both personal and political freedom. By the same token, Chua (2003) suggests neoliberal ideology destabilizes democracy globally; Giroux (2004) argues, "Neoliberalism devitalizes democracy" (p. 69); and Stiglitz (2003, 2010) stipulates how neoliberalism extorts developing countries and brings the global economy to the brink of sinking.

Freedom is assumed for everyone in Milton Friedman's view, which represents a major premise in his argument for capitalism or its most current form in neoliberalism. However, I posit that Friedman has oversold the notion of freedom as understood and practiced in capitalism and neoliberalism, which I think Harvey correctly demonstrates by portraying the market not as a leveled playing field where equals play fairly. Evidently, the market is a field where unequal people, by virtue or the extent of their power to affect the outcome of transactions carried out in the market, mingle unevenhandedly. This process is sanctioned and enjoined by neoliberalism itself, which makes freedom virtually impossible to be enjoyed on an equal basis. Therefore, the ethos of freedom in neoliberalism seems more symbolic than material; hence its paradoxical nature is warranted. As such, it is used to create an illusion of democracy and choice to lure weaker players. In fact, the structure, the principles, and the practices of the neoliberal market embed this lack of evenhandedness in transactions, resulting in social inequality and economic and educational inequities within the hegemonic, oppressive, and exploitative discourse (Giroux, 2004). Further, Stiglitz (2010) suggests Friedman, along with his followers, is partly responsible for the asphyxiation of freedom and the failure of neoliberalism.

Through the preceding pages, I have attempted to depict neoliberalism as a discourse. In addition, using critical discourse analysis, I have demonstrated a variety of ways through which dominant groups insinuate, propagate, implement, as well as reinforce their ideologies in social domains. More important to my demonstration are the overwhelming evidences corroborating how the insinuation, propagation, implementation, as well as the reinforcement of such ideologies are performed, both overtly and covertly, through linguistic equivocation, the use of coercion, and consent. Ultimately, neoliberalism, as the embodiment of those discursive practices and ideologies, effectively predetermines as well as controls, both consciously and subconsciously, the thoughts and behaviors of people in their respective societies.

References

Agnew, J. (2005). *Hegemony: The new shape of global power*. Philadelphia: Temple University Press.

Apple, M. (1999). Freire, neo-liberalism and education. *Discourse: Studies in the Cultural Politics of Education, 20*(1), 5.

Apple, M. (2004). Creating difference: Neo-liberalism, neo-conservatism and the politics of educational reform. *Educational Policy, 18*(1), 12–44.

Baumol, W., & Blinder, A. (1986). *Economics: Principles and policy*. Orlando, FL: Harcourt Brace Jovanovich.

Bernstein, A. (2005). *The capitalist manifesto*. Lanham, MD: University Press of America.

Chua, A. (2003). *World on fire: How exporting free market democracy breeds ethnic hatred and global instability*. New York: Doubleday.

Clayton, T. (1998, November). Beyond mystification: Reconnecting world-system theory for comparative education. *Comparative Education Review, 42*(4), 479.

Davies, B., & Bensel, P. (2007). Neoliberalism and education. *International Journal of Qualitative Studies in Education (QSE), 20*(3), 247–259.

Fairclough, N. (1995). *Critical discourse analysis: The critical study of language*. London: Longman.

Fairclough, N. (2001). *Language and power*. Harlow, UK: Longman.

Fairclough, N. (2008). *Analyzing discourse: Textual analysis for social research*. New York: Routledge.

Frieden, J. (2006). *Global capitalism: Its fall and rise in the twentieth century*. New York: W. W. Norton.

Friedman, M. (2002). *Capitalism and freedom*. Chicago: University of Chicago Press.

Friedman, M. (2007). *Milton Friedman on economics: Selected papers*. Chicago: University of Chicago Press.

Friedman, M., & Friedman, R. (1990). *Free to choose: A personal statement*. Orlando, FL: Harcourt.

Gee, J. (2005). *An introduction to discourse analysis: Theory and method*. New York: Routledge.

Ginsburg, M., & Clayton, T. (2006). Imperialism and education. In D. Levinson, P. Cookson, & A. Sadovnik (Eds.), *Education and sociology* (pp. 387–392). New York: Rutledge Falmer.

Girard, P. (2005). *Paradise lost: Haiti's tumultuous journey from pearl of the Caribbean to third world hotspot*. New York: Palgrave Macmillan.

Giroux, H. (2004). *The terror of neoliberalism*. Boulder, CO: Paradigm.

Gupta, A. (2010, February). The U.S. in Haiti: Neoliberalism at the barrel of a gun. *Indypendent*. Retrieved from http://www.indypendent.org/2010/02/18/us-in-haiti/

Harvey, D. (2007). *A brief history of neoliberalism*. Oxford: Oxford University Press.

Hill, D. (1998). Neo-liberalism and hegemony revisited. *Educational Philosophy & Theory, 30*(1), 69.

Jilberto, A., & Mommen, A. (1993). The political economy of global neo-liberalism. *International Journal of Political Economy, 23*(1), 3–12.

McCloskey, R. (2008). A guide to discourse analysis. *Nurse Researcher, 16*(1), 24–43.

Megginson, W. (2005). *The financial economics of privatization*. New York: Oxford University Press.

Miraftab, F. (2004). Making neo-liberal governance: The disempowering work of empowerment. *International Planning Studies, 9*(4), 239–259.

Nafstad, H., et al. (2007). Ideology and power: The influence of current neo-liberalism in society. *Journal of Community & Applied Social Psychology, 17*(4), 313–327.

Oatley, T. (2008). *International political economy*. New York: Pearson/Longman.

Reback, G. (2009). *Free the market: Why only government can keep the marketplace competitive*. New York: Portfolio.

Reisigl, M., & Wodak, R. (2009). The discourse-historical approach (DHA). In R. Wodak & M. Meyer (Eds.), *Methods of critical discourse analysis* (pp. 87–121). London: Sage.

Reuters. (2009, November 26). Haiti bars ex-'president's party from elections for parliament. *New York Times*. Retrieved from http://www.nytimes.com/2009/11/26/world/americas/26haiti.html?_r=1

Rogers, R. (2011). Becoming discourse analysts: Constructing meanings and identities. *Critical Inquiry in Language Studies, 8*(1), 72–104.

Sprague, J. (2009, April). Haiti: Fanmi Lavalas banned; voter apprehension widespread. *Interpress Service News*. Retrieved from http://ipsnews.net.asp?idmews=46537

Stiglitz, J. (2003). *Globalization and its discontents*. New York: W.W. Norton.

Stiglitz, J. (2010). *Free fall: America, free markets, and the sinking of the world economy*. New York: W.W. Norton.

Van Dijk, T. (1993). Critical discourse analysis. *Discourse & Society, 4*(2), 352–371.

Wodak, R., & Meyer, M. (2009). Critical discourse analysis: History, agenda, theory, and methodology. In R. Wodak & M. Meyer (Eds.), *Methods of critical discourse analysis* (pp. 1–33). London: Sage.

CHAPTER FOURTEEN

Locked Gates and Chain-link Fences

A Generational Phenomenological Story of Disability

SHARON DUNCAN

Roots Planted: A Story

Once upon a not-so-distant time and in a not-so-distant land lived three little girls. Their lives revolved around playing Barbies, games of "ghost beware" at dusk, sewing lessons, riding the bus to Ford City, buying penny candy at the pet shop, and square-scooped sherbet cones at Prince Castle. At times their lives seemed to them idealistic and somewhat fairytale; as they were growing up in a middle-class suburban neighborhood in the 1960s, with stay-at-home moms and dads who arrived home at five for family dinner. The girls were connected by proximity, living in houses separated only by cyclone fences and a grassy alley. They lived so close you could call out, "Yo, Laura," or "Yo, Sharon," or "Yo, Debbie" till someone would answer the door. They shared the same Catholic faith, attended the same parish school, and were all about the same age. They shared dreams and made up fairytale stories while lying on blankets under Sharon's big backyard tree, sipping Kool-Aid from shiny metal tumblers, while munching on sugar wafer cookies. "So what do you want to be when you grow up?" "Where do you think we will live?" "Think we'll still be friends when we're old and married?"

Three girls, three friends for life ... and they lived happily ever after?

In order to understand the present, one has to look into the past. I (Sharon) am the collector of the group. I am compelled to collect the stories, to uncover the lived experiences that were interwoven in the fabric of our lives…the common threads that bound us together then and continue to link us in the present.

The nine-year-old me runs through the kitchen, pulls open the pantry door and grabs an eight pack of empty Pepsi bottles from the floor. I have a shiny quarter in my pocket just waiting to be spent. With the sixteen cents I would get from the bottles, I would be able to get a lot of penny candy. "Mom, I'm going," I yelled. "Where are you going young lady?" my grandmother Mere inquires. "Just up town with Laura and Debbie." "Be careful." "Don't worry Mere." I run by my Aunt Jackie washing dishes at the sink. I grab her apron string pretending to untie it and she slaps my hand. "Oh, Sharon, what a kidder." "See ya!" I run out the screen door and it slams behind me. I hear Mere yelling in the distance, but I'm off…across the porch…down the steps…crisscrossing my fenced backyard, running through the back gate, which is hanging slightly open. I give it an extra shove to open it all the way and I head across the alley to Laura's yard. "Yo, Laura." She comes to the door with a brown bag in her hand holding two empty quart bottles from beer. (She will get five cents each for those.) "Ready? Let's go get Debbie." We travel down the driveway toward Central Avenue to go next door to Debbie's. We approach the fenced-in yard. A locked double gate extending across the driveway stops us in our tracks. Laura takes her free hand and opens the latch while I take my free hand and pull up the pole. In we go. We are sure to lock the gate again or face the wrath of Mrs. E., Debbie's mom. The gate must remain locked at all times. "Yo, Debbie," we call out on her back stoop. "Hi guys! I can go, but I have groceries to buy for my mom at Freshline." She goes back in the house and comes back out with her mom's old brown wallet and a list in one hand, and her little brother Chuckie's small chubby hand tightly clenched in the other. "I gotta bring Chuck; my mom gave me money so we can get sherbet cones from Prince Castle on the way back." We walk down the drive. Laura and I open the gate and Deb pulls Chuck through. We lock it behind us. Looking both ways, we cross Central Avenue. Mere's "be careful" rings in my brain. Laura and I take the lead. "Come on Chuck, walk faster," Deb says. As we make our way from our neighborhood and the safety of the locked gates and cyclone fences into the vast world…we called: UPTOWN.

> Fenced yards, protecting Chuckie, shopping for groceries, locked gates, teasing Aunt Jackie, being corrected by Mere; the roots of our childhood; the common strings that joined our lives.

As I embarked on my research, I returned to the past: to the relationships, the values, the truths, that connected our experiences. I was compelled to provide a visual to represent the people and the relationships, which represent the roots of this inquiry. I was determined to seek a fluid representation for the connected history.

Visually, I was drawn to a root structure and all the little threads that come from and connect to the root. The cyclone fence (like the one that surrounded my back-yard and Debbie's whole yard) with its supporting bar and all the angular connec-tions, kept coming to my mind. I visualized the fences and the gates, keeping us in, locking us out, but still allowing us to see out to the other side. The fence provided safety but was imprisoning at the same time. We could lift the lock, pull up the pole, and get out from time to time, but we were compelled to go back into safety.

One can see the correlations with the structure of a chain-link fence and rhi-zome in the view point of Kurokawa (2001) in an essay covering Deleuzio-Gual-laria's architectural theory: "A rhizome is an interlocking web. It is a conjunction of dynamic relations producing bulbs here and there, interweaving with great com-plexity, reaching outward in its continuing growth" (p. 1031).

Linkages through Disability Studies

It is critical for a disability study to investigate various ontological and episte-mological assumptions underpinning the field and the lived experience of disabil-ity. My purpose was to examine the whole of the experience. As a field, disability studies challenge the stereotypes historically associated with disabilities yet does not restrict one to have a singular epistemological understanding of disability (Barnes, Oliver, & Barton, 2002). Disability studies developed as a field in response to a problem, seeking clarification about the place and meaning of disability in so-ciety (Albrecht, Seelman, & Bury, 2001).

Disability studies embrace an eclectic approach with the ultimate goal of emancipation and self-fulfillment in all areas of life for individuals with disabili-ties. Disability studies do not emphasize barriers but, instead, they focus on pos-sibilities. Relevant to a disability study is resistance theory that "maintains the social model's focus on the politics of disablement and adds to it recognition of the complexities of resistance" (Gabel, 2005, p. 8). Resistance theory proposes to look at the entire experience of disability. Looking at the totality of the experience is imperative when uncovering meaning, the body and medical support cannot be totally disregarded. Elements of disabled identity are the voice that cannot be heard in a typical way, the brain that works in a particular fashion, or ambulation with a wheelchair.

The rhizome and the fence metaphorically represent the resistance scenario, as they are juxtaposed in "a push me-pull me" connectiveness; the fence with the shut-ting out but providing protection, and the rhizome, open to all the possibilities that occur in the lived experience of disability. A theory of resistance embraces disabil-ity in all its complexity and entirety. My perspective of disability is grounded in dis-ability studies and rooted in resistance theory.

Looking Back, Going Forward—Phenomenologically

Phenomenology allows the researcher to explore the symbolism, the words, and experiences that give meaning to living. Phenomenologists are challenged to describe the lived experience in a manner that portrays person-world intimacy. The *lifeworld* (one of the key notions in phenomenology) includes all the everyday goings-on in life. My lifeworld, as well as my family's and friends' over three generations, and the interconnections to disability were the subject of our story-making. Viewing the lifeworld offers the opportunity to explore the intricacies that hold people and their world together, and view the physical, aesthetic, spatial, and emotional aspects of human life.

This research was a return to my roots, it served as an opportunity to dig into the soil and let it run through my fingers. I delved into the memories, the thoughts, and the lived experiences. Phenomenology served as the "till" for my research. Founded by Edmund Husserl (1859–1938), phenomenology is considered to be one of the most important philosophical movements of the twentieth century (Morse & Richards, 2007). Phenomenology is the study of human experience (Moustakas, 1994; Van Manen, 1990; Seamon, 2000); it serves as a means to give "a rigorous description of human life as it is lived, and reflected upon, in all of its first person concreteness, urgency, and ambiguity" (Pollio, Henley, & Thompson, 1997, p. 5).

Phenomenological inquiry allowed me to explore endless possibilities of the rhizome and to uncover its multiple meanings. Phenomenological "root strands" of an event are more clearly understood when we bring ourselves "wholly to the transparency of the imaginary, to think about it without the support of any ground, in short, withdraw to the bottom of nothingness. Only then could we know what moments positively make up the being of experience" (Pollio, Henley, & Thompson, 1997, p. 111).

I sought to "bring into the nearness that which tends to be obscure, that which tends to evade the intelligibility of our natural attitude of everyday life" (Van Manen, 1990, p. 57). It is with a fresh sense of wonder that I immersed myself in research to reveal a story (Merleau-Ponty, 1962). Phenomenology is about revealing, uncovering, exposing, and connecting. The rhizome as an image of thought serves as a model of an open-ended interactive system. There are roots in place, grounded in friendship, family, proximity, history, and disability. The rhizome is fluid and has the ability to grow and change, tiny threads will emerge from the root, linking to other threads, which will grow and flourish over time. Rhizomes are about possibilities, whereas the fence served as a protective boundary, protecting us from the dangers that lurked just outside.

"Go home Sharon…bye,…we already started" ("but I have all my Barbie Stuff"), "take your Barbies and just go"…(My lip starts to quiver and tears come to my eyes), "You're a big crybaby! You act retarded, just like your mongoloid Aunt Jackie and we don't want to play with you!"

Girls from the neighborhood were sitting at the picnic table playing Barbies. I had rushed and gathered my stuff when I saw them out there. The twin girls that lived just on the other side of the fence, right behind my house, yelled at me in unison, adding to the insults in a tag team fashion. I was upset, and I really wanted to play Barbies that day. At first I was mad that they told me to leave, but then my eight-year-old self realized that they called my Aunt Jackie retarded. "No, Jackie's not retarded, Debbie's brother Chuck is retarded, and I heard him called mongoloid, too." Those words described Chuckie, not my Aunt Jackie. Jackie could talk. Jackie took care of me. I ran away, dragging my Barbie cases, and finally I threw them on the ground (I heard the girls laughing at me in the background). I ran faster through the yard and into the house. By now, I was crying loudly in my typical dramatic fashion.

Throwing open the back screen door, I yelled into the house, "M-o-o-o-om, the twins said Jackie is retarded." My grandmother gave me a dirty look (my voice was bellowing through the house). My mom ushered me into the bedroom and told me to "ssh" (now I'm thinking Jackie must have been in hearing distance as the first floor of our house was not large). Between my sobs, my mom tried to speak. She closed the door and said, "I should have told you, but I couldn't." She explained Jackie was "slow." She did not say retarded, she did not say mongoloid. I was told to stop crying and to not say anything to Jackie or in front of my grandmother (Jackie's mother).

Over time, I came to realize both Jackie and Chuck were born with Down syndrome. In the late 1960s, Down syndrome was often called "mongoloid." So Chuck and Aunt Jackie actually were the same, as far as a disability category anyway. They were my roots.

I go back to the past and return home. I was situated in a particular circumstance of disability. I lived in a home where disability and "retard-ness" (as it was referred to then), was somewhere else, not in our house. Although my Aunt Jackie had a disability due to an intellectual disability, my grandmother refused to call or label her disabled. The norm when my aunt was born in the late 1930s was for children who were declared retarded or mongoloid to be put away. Children like those were sent to institutions. My maternal grandparents, but most especially my grandmother (Mere), defied the norm and made Jackie fit. She taught Jackie to walk, talk, count, read, close her mouth (drooling was not an option) and was determined that she reached those milestones in typical developmental stages.

Although as a child, I never thought of Jackie as different, I always knew Chuckie, my friend Debbie's brother, was "different." He could not read; he needed help with everyday tasks and went to a "special" school. I thought the experience of disability was beyond my fenced yard. It was over there; in Debbie's fenced-in house on the next block. However, as I grew older and more aware of the stares and heard the names, the reality began to hit home. My mom explained to me at ten years old, after my grandmother passed away (at fifty-three years old), that Jackie and Chuckie both had Down syndrome (much nicer sounding than mongoloid). Laura, Debbie, and I continued to be friends, from high school into young adulthood until today. Our lives were still connected like the links in the fence. Our friendship was a stronghold, and we could always return back to our girlhood memories and the stories of our shared experiences.

> *Friendship, history, labels, families and the impact of disability from the past to the present, and into the future; the links that continue to connect our lives.*

There is a profound story here; a story that crosses generations and stereotypes. This story is "our social construction of what happened" (Ferguson, Ferguson, & Taylor, 1992, p. 5). A broad theme of phenomenology is intentionality a "basic structure of human existence that captures the fact that human beings are fundamentally related to the contexts in which they live" (Pollio, Henley, & Thompson, 1997, p. 7). Home and in-home experiences have been addressed by many phenomenologists. Day (1996) studied "at-homeness," signifying a timeless quality, positive attunement to the present moment, the relatedness to a lived interplay between safety and familiarity. Home offers an attunement into oneself in relationship to others; home relates to healing and personal well-being. Home for us was more than houses on Central or Parkside Avenue. Home was an emotional place where we felt protected and loved. Home is the sense of no matter what occurs around me, I have a place where I am safe emotionally, physically and psychologically. Home is where a person can truly be free, just to be.

Phenomenological incentive to go "back to the things themselves" (Husserl, 1970) prompted me to return again and again, through reflection, to the interviews with family members and with the individuals with disabilities.

Reflections on Perceptions

The eight-year-old me had no thoughtful concept of disability. Rarely were people with disabilities in the public eye in the early 1960s. I never thought of my Aunt Jackie as disabled. The word people used to describe people with intellectual disabilities at the time was "retarded," but even that term was rarely said out loud in my personal experience. Sometimes I noticed Jackie did and said silly or inappropriate things. Yet, for some reason Jackie did not do those "not so adult-like things" around my grandparents or other adults. She seemed to have two distinct personas, the one who acted like an adult and the other who was my own personal silly friend.

I had this internal nagging tension about when to listen to Jackie or not, or why Jackie did things at times that most adults did not do in public. There was also an unspoken rule in my household not to ask about Jackie, especially around my grandmother. Chuckie, my girlfriend's brother with Down syndrome, was never discussed either. Chuck was the only person I knew as a young child with a disability. Jackie, who often said out loud what she was thinking, did talk about Chuck and very sympathetically called him "poor 'tarded Chuck." I share these vignettes about life as I knew it then, because as an adult, I have come to realize that my childhood experiences with Jackie served as a catalyst in forming my own theory about disability. The nagging questions of the little girl, who was to be seen and not heard, are ever present in this adult, as I engage in thoughtful introspection. My view of disability is rooted in my past experiences as a little girl hanging out with Jackie and Chuck. My past cannot be disregarded or set aside but serves as a connective root strand now watered by a disability studies perspective.

Jackie, Chuck, Jonathon, and Jamee made and are making their own histories. Society, cultural factors, family situations, and their particular place in time had much to do with the formation of their personal histories.

Rhizomes and Stories

By virtue of her year of birth in 1991 and her place in this connective rhizome, Jamee has reaped the benefits of the rich soil that has been watered by the experiences of those who have come before her in time. Once upon a time there were three young girls living in the 1960s who were linked by proximity, friendship and disability. These three girls—Laura, Debbie, and Sharon (me)—are connected intricately with Jamee through the offshoots of the rhizomic experiences that have connected our lives through the generations. Jamee is the great-granddaughter of Dorothy, the courageous mother of Jackie who was determined to defy the social constructs of disability imposed on her in the late 1930s.

Stubborn will power and steadfast determination flow through the blood of Dorothy's granddaughter Colleen, the mother of Jamee, as she advocates for choices for her daughter. Colleen (my sister) never knew our grandmother Dorothy (Mere), she was only two years old when she passed away, but when I look at Colleen, I see my grandmother's sense of control, strong will, and dominance. It is almost as if Colleen had some predisposition to be Dorothy in another time to raise a child with a disability.

Colleen walked up town with Laura, Debbie, Chuck, and I as a young child. Colleen played in Chuck's yard and shared swing time with him. Growing up as

Jackie's niece, and sharing personal space with Jackie for more than twenty years, gave Colleen an understanding of living with and loving a person with an intellectual disability. Laura gave birth to a child with a disability (Jonathon) four years previous to Jamee. Laura has been very helpful to Colleen, providing her with the names of orthopedic specialists and programs to support Jamee. Three girls, three families connected through the generations and still growing, continuing the rhizomic connections established between the fences of our youth.

Connections and Revelations

A connective strand that united the families was a fear of the unknown. Typically, when a new baby comes into the world, the family is filled with anticipation and dreams for the future. The birth of a child is a joyful experience. These families had little time to bask in the happiness of a new life. Instead they embarked on emotional quests searching for answers. Initially, the parents sought answers so they could understand their role as parents. They wanted to find the means to assist their children. All of the families in this research went through emotional struggles with the professionals. The parents in this story were all subjected to "category bound activities" (Sacks, 1972).

Parents of children with disabilities are looked at in a particular manner. The parents were told by medical professionals they could not handle their child, or nothing was wrong in Jamee's case. The professionals put the parents in categories. Colleen, Dorothy, and Mrs. E. (Chuck's mom) were dismissed as young mothers. Laura was thought of as being too assertive. Social constructs of which the families had no control caused additional anxiety to these families who were already under much pressure. Upon realizing that the professionals did not have all the answers, after time, the parents discovered that they had the answers all along. All of the parents found the strength from within themselves to do whatever was necessary for their children.

Externally the families went about their lives, yet within the spatiality of their homes their experiences were complex. Without any training, my grandmother took on the roles of therapist and teacher. She discovered that neckties and belts were useful in supporting Jackie as she learned to walk, and match sticks could be used as manipulatives as Jackie learned to count. Chuck's parents discovered that elastic bands could be used to stretch Chuck's limbs. Jonathon, born with agenesis of the corpus callosum, was sent home from the hospital to die. Laura and her husband Steve decided their son was going to live and found programs to support his growth. Colleen and Bob kept bringing Jamee to doctors to treat her medical difficulties and sought help from anyone and everyone. All the parents took action, but fear remained under the surface.

Fears

Fear connected the families, but it was manifested differently in their lived experiences. Historically, parents or siblings of children with disabilities often wondered what they did to deserve this fate, or if they did something wrong for this to occur in their family. My grandmother is representative of this as she was trying to place the blame on someone for Jackie's "condition." Much of this blame had to do with the time in history. People did not understand the medical reasons for Down syndrome. I cannot fathom the deep anxiety a mother would feel upon realizing their beloved child was viewed by society as subhuman, a burden, or a product of sinfulness (Castles, 2004). Parents who gave birth to children with obvious disabilities in this era were often fearful of people trying to come and put their child in an institution. Due to this particular time in history, as a member of the silent generation (Strauss & Howe, 1992), my grandmother did not discuss her feelings regarding Jackie's disability. She repressed her fears and had emotional breakdowns.

With the progress of medical science over the decades and having a clearer understanding of the etiology of their children's disabilities, the other parents did not have the same type of fears as my grandmother. Yet fear was a connective element experienced by all the families in this research. Chuck's parents are not preparing financially or psychologically for Chuck's future. Laura still checks on Jonathon when he sleeps too long. Colleen worries if caregivers in Jamee's future will care for her medical needs and provide her with choices. Jenna, Jamee's sister, cried as she discussed her worries about Jamee's physical fragility. Jonathon fears being alone and is purposely working on overcoming his shyness. The fear was ever present, but it was accompanied by resilience and resistance.

Resistance

The rhizomic strand of resistance was evident as the stories were told. This was demonstrated by my grandparents refusing to call Jackie anything but Jackie and demanding that she attend the local Catholic school with her sister. Chuck's parents (Mr. and Mrs. E.) moved to the suburbs to find a school for Chuck, and continued to fight the school district for funding because their son was happy at his private school. Chuck resisted societal expectations when he is the "man in charge" on his work crew. Laura confronted the doctor when he did not think baby Jonathon should have prostheses because of his fragile state. She continued to resist the expectations of doctors and other professionals throughout his childhood. Demonstrating resistance, Jonathon enrolled in anatomy and physiology classes against the advice of his counselors and received *A*s in the classes. Colleen demonstrates resistance by living in the moment; she does not dwell on the past, but moves forward, providing Jamee with choices in her daily life. Jamee, through making choices and navigating her environment with the support of her communication device and power wheelchair, is resisting the social constructs assigned to individuals with significant intellectual and physical disabilities. The families in this story had unique perspectives and situations, yet self-fulfillment for their own child was a personal goal in each circumstance.

Mother to Mother

A common strand, linking story to story, generation to generation, is the inner strength of the mothers. The mothers are resilient and strong, taking on doctors, teachers, and anyone who denied their children opportunities. These women played the dominant role while the husbands played supportive roles (Herbert & Carpenter, 1994). The women were grounded in actualization and hope; negativity was not an option. Each of the women was fenced in by the constraints of the times in which they lived. Historicality served as a fence for which they had no control.

Historicality

Jackie was born in the era of when disability was regarded as sinful, deviant, or a societal burden (Kevles, 1995). In the 1930s, institutionalization was recommended for most people with disabilities. My grandparents did not give in to the societal expectations of the time. As Jackie's parents, they negotiated their lived experience through rebelling. By putting their daughter "out there" in the local Catholic school, the community, family gatherings and social situations, they were quietly, but forcefully, rebelling. Particularly revealing was the fact that my grandmother put Jackie out into the world full of pride, but internally she was fighting her own emotional difficulties. The literature (Blancher & Baker, 2007) does indicate that many parents with children with disabilities have internal and emotional struggles. Unfortunately, my grandparents' personal and emotional struggles support the studies that indicate that parents could exhibit depression or emotional shock.

The 1930s and 1940s was a difficult era to live openly with a child of disabilities and my grandparents were victims of the societal fences of their times. The fact that Jackie lived in this time, yet portrayed a level of self-confidence and did not see herself as disabled, had much to do with the fences they collectively built to protect their daughter.

Chuck was born in the time of parent involvement (Schwartzenberg, 2005). Down syndrome now had a biological explanation, so once he was diagnosed his parents at least had a name and a reason for his particular disability. While the Mr. and Mrs. E. did not define Chuck by a label, they needed to have a diagnosis to understand why Chuck was not developing like his sister Debbie. While medical science had come far, there were still many misconceptions about Down syndrome. At the time of Chuck's birth, Down syndrome was still being referred to as "mongoloid" (Trent, 1994). The Es were told Chuck would not live long and were also told to think about placing their son in an institution. The Es resisted the advice offered to them and began to make plans for their son. They sought a new life in the suburbs because they had heard there were schools nearby "for children like Chuck." Chuck had a special school to attend, and during his school years, laws were written to mandate education for children with disabilities. They, like many parents in the 1960s, joined with other parents to support their child with a disability.

White, middle-class parent advocacy groups were able to help society make the shift from disability being thought of as undesirable, sinful, or lower class (Trent, 1994). The Es were representative of their particular time in history, their son was not hidden away and they were creating programs for his support. As a grassroot organization, Chuck's school was representative of the time (Kliewer, 1998; Winzer, 1993). My grandparents could be considered cutting edge in their accessing an inclusive education for Jackie in the 1940s, the Es' situation is representative of the historicality of disability in the mid-1960s.

Jonathon and Jamee went to school in the era of inclusion (Friend, 2008). They were the products of school systems in the infancy stages of such practices. The school districts in both Jonathon's and Jamee's early educational experiences were working through the kinks in their own school settings. Their education was full of fences and rhizomic possibilities, isolation and inclusion involved in an intricate dance with everyone trying to learn the new steps. Initially, both families desired an inclusive school experience for their children. Jamee's parents, while philosophically embracing inclusion for all people with disabilities, had to act in the best interests of their daughter and transfer Jamee to a more secluded school setting. For two years Jamee's parents worked with the school district to bring about changes in the inclusion program. During this time Jamee was actually regressing. The community school was experiencing constant personnel and philosophical changes and lacked the training and understanding to support students with significant disabilities. Colleen and Bob could no longer risk their daughter's personal growth in order to bring about change in the school. There are circumstances when parents have to make difficult decisions to support their child that may not necessarily reflect their philosophical stance.

Another example of a philosophical conundrum was when Jonathon entered high school and Laura and Steve felt it was in his best interests to be in a more secluded freshman program. Laura had fought for the least restrictive learning environment for Jonathon throughout his elementary years and yet supported his placement in the freshman learning center program. Jonathon himself faces a struggle with his own personal philosophy as he accesses support in college. Jonathon told me he does not embrace the label of "disabled," yet he must have a disability label to navigate in the university setting. He also recalled that his high school counselor seemed angry when he insisted on enrolling in a higher level physiology and anatomy class. Mercer (1973) describes this construct and states, "People with disabilities are rewarded for behavior that conforms to the social expectations associated with the disability role and are punished for behavior that departs from the expectations" (p. 73). Jonathon had his own personal expectations, which did not coincide with the counselors desire to keep Jonathon within a particular construction.

Jonathon and Jamee did benefit, however, from a society that had grown in awareness both philosophically and technologically. They both had the benefit of technology to assist them in accessing their education, which was not available for Jackie and Chuck. Their parents also reaped the benefits derived from a historical era that was beginning to be more open about disability. Laws had been implemented to not only educate but also to include children with disabilities in school. Parents of children with disabilities in contemporary times have the ability to engage in mediation and voice their concerns. Laura and Colleen were not products of the silent generation, and as such they were able to voice their concerns in a more open forum than my grandmother and Mrs. E.

Exposure

A theme that represents the stories of the families and the corporality and temporality of their situations is: "They were there." They put themselves and their children out in the community to face whatever life had to offer. Simultaneously, the parents were there to protect their children from whatever society put in their way. They exposed them to opportunity, but put up fences whenever necessary. To these families, life was and is something to partake and opportunities are not only for the strong, but for everyone. Laura and Colleen stressed over and over, "It is what it is." In fact, all of the parents used those words to describe their lives of raising their children. The rhizomic strand that served as a connection in the shared stories is acceptance. The parents sought answers for the purpose of helping their children, and they focused on the possibilities, not the disabilities. Laura said she "wasn't going to have a pity party." Colleen said she never said, "Why me?" Mr. and Mrs. E. told people, "Don't feel sorry for us, Chuck is a gift, not a burden."

Roots

The neighborhood of our youth served as the soil for our rooted experience. Representing the existentials of spatiality and relationality, it served as the place where the families became connected. Disability was not thought of as something abnormal, it was life. It was our life. The neighborhood was surrounded by busy streets; danger right outside Laura's and Debbie's front doors, but there was the grassy alley that protected us, separated us, and connected us. We could cross the alley and be together. As children, we had an idealistic view of life. We knew if we yelled loud enough, someone's mother would come and save us, we knew our Dads would come home at the same time for dinner every night, and most important we knew we had each other. In our lived space, Jackie would entertain us, we would take our siblings uptown or to the park; life was simple. The "fence" was difficult to break through. In many ways the fence kept us naïve and unaware of the big world outside. Children were seen and not heard. We did not question why Jackie could not drive, or why Chuck and Debbie always had to play in their yard. We were so blinded by simplicity that we did not even realize that Chuck and Jackie looked alike, until someone pointed that out to us in a cruel way. We held Chuck's hand both figuratively and literally and walked him home.

It's Just Life

Perhaps because as children we were steeped in this particular lived experience, Laura and Colleen, upon giving birth to children with disabilities, understood the experience as life. They went about the business of mothering their children. It was not different for them, it was life. Colleen tagged along with Laura, Debbie, and I when she was a toddler. The strands of the rhizome connected Colleen back to Laura as an adult. Jamee continues to receive physical therapy from the therapists recommended by Laura more than fifteen years ago. The rhizomic threads still continue to connect the families generationally, mother to mother.

Gardening

I am the gardener, keeping the roots fed, watering the soil, making sure the root strands stay strong. I could never surmise that I truly understand their lived experiences, but I know my life is intricately linked to theirs; passing on information, being there to listen, or just being present. We are linked because we were there. We share our beginnings; we know where we came from, surrounded by strong women, caring men, and air filled with the aroma of protection.

Jackie, Chuck, Jonathon, and Jamee have taken all of us linked to their lives, places we never thought we would go. They have forced us to look outside ourselves, to be empathetic involved people. While others may see disability as wrong, it is normal for us.

Jackie's Life

Compared to the majority of the individuals born with disabilities in the late 1930s, Jackie led an accomplished life. Most important, Jackie did not think she was disabled, just "short." Disability to Jackie was "poor 'tarded" Chuck across the alley, or the people in wheelchairs at her club—it definitely was not her. Disability was not her identity. Shakespeare and Watson (2002) remind me that "to assume that disability will always be the key to [their] identity is to recapitulate the error made by those from the medical model perspective who define people by their impairment" (p. 22). Disability did not define Jackie.

Jonathon's Perceptions

Jonathon refuses to call himself disabled. Yet he is well aware of his blindness, his brain agenesis, along with a myriad of medical issues. He is supposed to have an intellectual disability, but he has a different type of intelligence and he has determined how to negotiate school and life using his intelligence. Rapley (2004) suggests that it is not necessary to theorize or retheorize intellectual disability: "Maybe we should just refuse to do so" (p. 206). Jonathon is an example of just such refusal. He has constructed a fence blocking out disability. The fence has served him well, leading to possibility as he now exemplifies a college graduate with a medical research degree.

Chuck's World

Chuck is not able to voice his feeling about disability. Based on immersing myself in the world of Chuck, he appears content with his life. He has activities he enjoys, work which has given him a level of self-assurance, his girlfriend Lee, and parents who are very dedicated to his well-being. Chuck does not appear to mind living in a protective environment. His needs are simple and watching his TV programs and being a part of a day program brings him a certain level of comfort and joy.

Happy Jamee

Jamee is a happy young woman. Her difficulties with mobility and communication do not appear to affect her spirit. She has never known life as anything different. Jamee has definite interests and is able to express them in her individual manner. Utilizing an augmented communication device for her school work, she can access her education on her level. Routine is clearly important to Jamee and her family recognizes and honors this need. Within her structured world there are choices. Her quick smile and pleasant personality denotes a young woman who is content. Her contagious laughter resonates with pure joy.

Connected Individuals

Through watering the rhizome with independence and fertilizing it with love, these individuals identified themselves as Jackie, Chuck, Jonathon, and Jamee, not as intellectually disabled, retarded, or a person with Down syndrome. To be called "retarded is to have one's moral worth and human value called into question" (Bogdan & Taylor, 1982, p. 14). Jackie was referred to as Jackie, Chuck is just Chuck, Jonathon is "what he is," and Jamee is Jamee. They are one of us.

Uncovering Meaning

The purpose of this research was to uncover the meaning of the lived experiences of four individuals with intellectual disabilities and their families over three generations. While this journey took me to places I never imagined, I believe I uncovered the meaning of their lived experiences by sharing their stories. Van Manen (1990) asks, "Can phenomenology, if we concern ourselves deeply with it, do something with us?" (p. 47). This process was revealing for me and yes it did something to me. I am not the same person I was when this root was planted. I have evolved and find myself in a new place.

In this new place I am further convinced that a theory of disability must be malleable. There must be a meeting at the fence. Individuals with disabilities must bring the dominant culture into their "yards" and the gates to the world must be universally designed so everyone can have access. The gate keepers must be the individuals with disabilities themselves, not members of the dominating social institutions. For change to evolve there must be negotiation. Resistance theory allows Jonathon, for instance, to push against the stereotype, yet to negotiate a system of support. I especially found Jonathon's idea about disability refreshing—and truthful. He has his own theory about disability. He said, "When you call someone 'blah, blah, blah' then you expect them to act 'blah, blah, blah' and you think they need 'blah, blah, blah.'" He refuses to be defined. Jonathon has never read a book about disability theory or models of disability, yet in those words, he is describing the medical model of disability that ascribes certain attributes to people with disabilities. He is also rejecting such notions. Jonathon has come to this philosophical viewpoint through his lived experience. His voice is a voice of resistance. A theory of disability based on resistance can bring society into to Jonathon's way of knowing and understanding.

The stories must be written, lives must intersect; able and disabled can meet at the fence and open the gates. Rich stories written within a phenomenological perspective can allow people who have not been heard to have a voice. Stories can bring about social reform and understanding.

Three childhood friends, four families, four individuals with disabilities connected by proximity, understanding, and love. Together, we wrote a story.

Once upon a time lived three little girls, their lives were connected by friends, family, and disability.

References

Albrecht, G., Seelman, K., & Bury, M. (2001). Introduction. *Handbook for disability studies* (pp. 1–10). Thousand Oaks, CA: Sage.

Barnes, C., Oliver, M., & Barton, L. (2002). *Disability studies today*. London: Polity.

Blancher, J., & Baker, B. (2007). Positive impact on intellectual disability on families. *American Journal of Mental Retardation, 106,* 173–188.

Bogdan, R., & Taylor, S. (1982). *Inside out: The social meaning of mental retardation.* Toronto: University of Toronto Press.

Castles, K. (2004). Nice average Americans. In S. Noll & J. Trent (Eds.), *Mental retardation in America* (pp. 351–370). New York: New York University Press.

Day, M. (1996). *Home in the postmodern world: An existential phenomenological study.* Paper presented at the International Human Science Research Conference, Halifax, VA.

Ferguson, P., Ferguson, D., & Taylor, S. (1992). *Interpreting disability: A qualitative reader.* New York: Teachers College Press.

Friend, M. (2008). *Special education, contemporary perspectives for school professionals.* Boston: Pearson.

Gabel, S. (2005). *Disability studies in education: Readings in theory and method.* New York: Peter Lang.

Herbert, E., & Carpenter, B. (1994). The secondary partners: Professional perspectives and a father's reflections. *Children and Society, 8*(1), 31–41.

Husserl, E. (1970). *The crisis of European sciences and transcendental phenomenology.* Evanston, IL: Northwestern University Press.

Kevles, D. (1995). *In the name of eugenics: Genetics and the uses of human heredity.* Cambridge, MA: Harvard University Press.

Kliewer, C. (1998). *Schooling children with Down syndrome.* New York: Teachers College Press.

Kurokowa, K. (2001). Towards a rhizome world or chaosmas. In G. Gensoko, G. Deleuze, & F. Guattari (Eds.), *Critical assessments of leading philosophers* (pp. 1027–1034). London: Routledge.

Mercer, J. (1973*). Labeling the mentally retarded.* Berkeley: University of California Press.

Merleau-Ponty, M. (1962). *Phenomenology of perception.* London: Routledge & Kegan Paul.

Morse, J., & Richards, L. (2007). *Users guide to qualitative methods* (2nd ed.). Thousand Oaks, CA: Sage.

Moustakas, C. (1994). *Phenomenological research methods.* Thousand Oaks, CA: Sage.

Pollio, H., Henley, T., & Thompson, C. (1997). *The phenomenology of everyday life.* New York: Cambridge University Press.

Rapley, M. (2004). *The social construction of intellectual disability.* Cambridge, UK: Cambridge University Press.

Sacks, H. (1972). On analyzing the stories of children. In J. Gumper & D. Hynes (Eds.), *Directions in sociolinguistics: The ethnography of communication* (pp. 329–345). New York: Holt, Rinehart & Winston.

Schwartzenberg, S. (2005). *Becoming citizens: Family life and the politics of disability.* Seattle: University of Washington Press.

Seamon, D. (2000). A way of seeing people and place: Phenomenology in environment behavior research. In S. Wapner, J. Kemick, T. Yamamoto, & H. Minami (Eds.), *Theoretical perspectives in environment-behavior research* (pp. 157–178). New York: Plenum.

Shakespeare, T., & Watson, N. (2002). The social model of disability: An outdated ideology? *Research in Social Science and Disability, 2,* 9–28.

Strauss, W., & Howe, N. (1992). *Generations: The story of America's future 1584–2069.* New York: Morrow.

Trent, J. (1994). *Inventing the feeble mind: A history of mental retardation in the United States.* Berkeley: University of California Press.

Van Manen, M. (1990). *Researching lived experience.* New York: State University Press.

Winzer, M. (1993). *The history of special education from isolation to integration.* Washington, DC: Gallaudet University Press.

Once upon a Time, the Message of Love Was Born

ANTONINA LUKENCHUK

What is truth is real.
What is not truth is not real.
It's an illusion, but it looks real.
Love is real.
It's the supreme expression of life.

—TOLTEC WISDOM BOOK

Before the curtain falls on the work of this book, I would like to reflect on aspects of it that I deem are particularly meaningful in terms of its conception and advancement. Rather selfishly, I must admit, I have received absolute satisfaction from being able to engage in this work. Coincidentally, throughout the process of composing this manuscript, my ego had a chance to be transformed into a sense of self with a new level of understanding. The process has enabled me to dialogue with myself, to come to terms with my intellectual discontents and emotional frailties, and to evoke my redemptive self (McAdams, 2012). I have traveled a full re-search circle only to realize all over again that at the end of this journey, my inquisitive self has emerged with a renewed sense of wonder.

Wonder is natural to human beings and it sparks a desire within to pursue unimaginable projects. We may never know many details of how our ancestors went about their lives, but the vestiges of their existence reflect different stories of heroes, warriors, craftsmen, magicians, and builders. The coded messages of our ancestral tales tell us that ancient people also contemplated existential questions: Where do we come from? What are we? Where are we going? They were, in brief, philosophers and their pursuit of knowledge has been essentially through the exchange of ideas (Kenny, 1997).

The beginnings of philosophy, which are as ancient as humankind, can be rightfully considered the beginnings of research. Like philosophy, research begins in wonder and attempts to answer multitudes of questions and to solve myriads of problems pertaining to the human realm and its near and far surroundings. Like philosophers, researchers have at their disposal many and varied intellectual and methodological tools to employ in their quest to know. Extraordinary opportunities are open, especially for twenty-first-century researchers who can choose from among many and alternative paradigms of knowledge to pursue projects focusing on specific issues and amplifying our understanding of them contingent upon conceptual and methodological boundaries. Competing paradigms of knowledge do not necessarily imply privileging some of them over others. Instead, existing paradigms compete for the best available explanation or understanding, taking into account new vistas in the future that can challenge them.

Epistemological pluralism is the fact of the day even though some may not agree with or accept it. Contemporary researchers and scholars seek new ways of understanding themselves and their realities within and beyond the boundaries of their geographical locations. Modern marvels of communication and travel afford them the possibility of crossing the borders of the world's continents and countries much faster and to go farther than their predecessors could in the remote past. It is no surprise that the exchange of ideas and learning experiences among different people transpires at an unprecedented rate in this day and age. The accounts of most Westerners' journeys to other parts of the world are no longer accounts of conquest, colonization, enslavement, or prejudice. In the twenty-first century, most Westerners undertake pilgrimages to learn from the global world and, as a consequence, have an opportunity to rethink their personal identities, stories, and histories.

Imagine a white American woman, a professional psychologist, venturing on a spiritual quest around Mount Kailash, one of the three sacred mountains in Tibet. Mount Kailash is a spiritual center to the religions of Hinduism, Buddhism, Bön (a syncretic religion in Tibet), and Jainism. The sacred ritual of prostrations around Mount Kailash is said to have been attempted by only a few representatives of these religions, and certainly not by many foreigners. What drew Tracy Allyson to this sacred pilgrimage was the spiritual passion she considers integral to her practice as a professional psychologist. Without any special training or preparation, except for her prior travel to and knowledge of Tibet's cultural and spiritual traditions, Allyson performed prostrations around Mount Kailash at an elevation of 14,500 feet, with the highest point of the path located at an altitude of 18,500 feet. "I did not know," writes Allyson (2008), "if my body would hold up. There was nothing to encourage myself, nothing to gauge progress, and really, this is as it should have been. There is no progress, no goal. There is the experience and there is surrender to the invitation to attempt this" (p. 91).

Circumambulating Mount Kailash is called *khora*. It took Allyson 28 days to finish the prostrations:

> Doing khora was an invitation that came to me in prayer. I felt that my role was to show up and do the best I could each moment. Khora is surrender in the not-knowing. The Void filled me. It wrapped itself around me. It was inside and outside of me. It was infinite, it was everything. I let the Void hold me because I just did not know; I could not assess or control my experience; I could only show up or not show up. There is an enormous freedom when we let go of the illusion of knowing. After all, life is enacting itself along some pattern, some dance, but that dance is not for me or you. It is for itself, it is dancing itself. (Allyson, 2008, p. 91)

To Allyson, doing khora turned into the most difficult and most meaningful experience of her life. She returned home "more mature, more open, less knowing, more conscious, more loving, more humble, and more confident" (p. 91).

The twenty-first-century paradigms of knowledge offer educational researchers endless possibilities to advance rigorous inquiry that can illuminate economic, social, political, psychological, or spiritual dimensions of the human realm and their power to transform the lives of individuals and communities. For many people who hold spiritual beliefs dear to their hearts and minds and who practice various forms of spirituality, an engagement in social and political arenas constitutes an integral part of their day-to-day existence. Many of them consider the various aspects of their lives as manifestations of the whole, or wholeness of the experience. Spirituality can be conceived as life force, wholeness, or interconnectedness (Tisdell, 2000). Spirituality and social justice efforts can be integrated into empowering ways of life and doing research. Researchers may find themselves inspired by "new insights from different paradigms and … spiritual traditions" (Tisdell, p. 84).

Russell (2009) shares his experience of participating, with a group of Hispanic Roman Catholics, in an annual, hundred-mile pilgrimage to a shrine of healing dirt in New Mexico. To him, this journey becomes a discourse on social compassion. Driven by the desire to know, this "middle-aged, Anglo professor from Brooklyn" with a "recalcitrant agnostic spirit" trod the path that challenged his "niche in academe" and offered him a "model of compassion to sustain social concern" (p. 583). Prior to taking this journey, Russell researched, spoke, and wrote about pilgrimage. Yet he admits that it was *walking* the pilgrimage that had shifted the conception of it from description to performance, from telling to showing: "Walking is integral, a connecting thread of movement as coherent as a thread of thought. In pilgrimage, walking becomes a medium for understanding spiritual participation in the world" (p. 584).

The *performance* of pilgrimage is a way of knowing, a way of learning to walk— learning through singing, healing, sacrifice, mistakes, humility, vulnerability, and learning step by step. It is also learning to return.

> My lessons in pilgrimage began with unlearning. I had been ignorant of my cultural resistance to the rich symbolism and embodied practice of Roman Catholicism. My old, familiar *habitus* was shaped by a Protestant, middle-class aesthetic more comfortable with a priest in a white lab coat than a black cassock. Religious sacrifice seemed superstitious to me.... My Anglo culture's ignorance and my middle class discretion about the messiness of [these] issues seemed Victorian in its avoidance of physical and emotional contact. The pilgrim community of compassion was a startling alternative to the stoic despair of my secular world. (Russell, 2009, p. 591)

Russell's return home illuminates the most significant lesson that he has learned throughout the journey and along the path: that the practices of pilgrimage "teach compassion for others"; that the routes themselves represent "the moral and ethical strength of [the] experience"; and that "the paradigm of walking to a holy place is a paradigm of access to power, [which is] compassion, the only healing power we truly possess" (Russell, 2009, pp. 600–601).

The possibilities of choosing among many alternative paradigms entail responsibilities of educational researchers to master their craft beyond the technical knowledge of *how* and to develop creative approaches to research and the innovative ways of its representation. Our capacity to wonder enables us to choose the paradigms that resonate with our artistic sensibilities and the new ways to see (Leavy, 2009; Stanczak, 2007). Visual research methods, such as photography, film, digital images, and website designs, represent shifting relationships between the production of a written text and new digital possibilities (Stanczak). Arts are known for being "emotionally and politically evocative, captivating, aesthetically powerful, and moving" (Leavy, p. 12). The practice of arts-based research is "one about fusion, affinity, resonance, and above all *holistic approaches to research*" (Leavy, p. 253). Image conveys meaning. Visual and arts-based research practices are about "composing, weaving, and orchestrating—creating tapestries of meanings" (Leavy, 254):

> Finally, my heart understands it: I hear a song,
> I see a flower,
> Behold, they will not wither! (Unknown Aztec philosopher-poet)

Truly, we live in a remarkable time when the sky becomes the only limit to pursuing inquiries of our own liking. Scientific, spiritual, socioeconomic, political, pragmatic, or arts-based paradigms of research as multiple and alternative ways of knowing call forth our imaginative powers to know, to understand, to test, to emancipate, to deconstruct, or to reveal the truth.

Reflecting on this journey granted me the opportunity to reenact the story of my personal quest for knowledge. I was accompanied on this journey by a few dedicated pilgrims with whom I had the privilege to share the path. Many roads lead to the truth and each of us chooses our own road. What can bind us together in the long run is the paradigm of walking—an act of communion that evokes the redemptive and healing power of compassion. We learn to love as we walk together.

> Love cannot be contained within our speaking
> or listening; Love is an ocean whose depth cannot
> be plumbed.
> Would you try to count the drops of the sea?
> Before that Ocean, the seven seas are nothing.
> Love cannot be found in erudition and science,
> books and pages. Whatever is discussed by people—that is not
> the way of lovers.
> Whatever you have said or heard is the shell:
> The kernel of Love is a mystery that cannot be divulged.
>
> —RUMI

References

Allyson, T. (2008). One woman's journey around Mount Kalish. *Quest, 96*(3), 87–91.

Kenny, A. (Ed.). (1997). *The Oxford illustrated history of Western philosophy.* New York: Oxford University Press.

Leavy, P. (2009). *Method meets art: Arts-based research practice.* New York: Guilford.

McAdams, D. P. (2012). Exploring psychological themes through life-narrative accounts. In J. A. Holstein & J. F. Gubrium (Eds.), *Varieties of narrative analysis* (pp. 15–32). Los Angeles: Sage.

Russell, L. (2009). Learning to walk. *International Review of Qualitative Research, 1*(4), 583–602.

Stanczak, G. C. (Ed.). (2007). *Visual research methods: Image, society, and representation*. Los Angeles: Sage.

Tisdell, E. J. (2000). Spirituality and emancipatory adult education in women adult educators for social change. *Adult Education Quarterly, 50*(4), 308–335.

About the Contributors

The Editor

ANTONINA LUKENCHUK is Associate Professor at National Louis University, Chicago, Illinois, where she teaches graduate courses in educational foundations and research. She received her BA and PhD degrees in English and general linguistics from Chernivtsi University, Ukraine. Her MSEd is in educational foundations from Northern Illinois University, and her EdD is in adult education from Northern Illinois University.

Antonina's research and scholarly interests are in philosophy of education, epistemology, critical discourse analysis, semiotics, cross-cultural studies, service-learning, and imaginative education. She has conducted workshops and seminars on the pedagogy of service-learning, paradigms of research, and qualitative research in several Midwestern universities and internationally.

Some of Antonina's recent publications include "Itinerary of the Knower: Mapping the Ways of Gnosis, Sophia, and Imaginative Education" (in I. Semetsky, *Jung and Educational Theory*, 2012), "Exploring Cultural Dynamics of Self-Other Relations: University Faculty and Students Engage in Service-Learning with Refugees (with E. Barber, in T. Stewart and N. Webster, *Exploring Cultural Dynamics and Tensions within Service-Learning*, 2011), "Imagining a Better World: Service-learning as Benefit to Teacher Education" (with V. Jagla and T. Price, in *Journal of Research on Service-Learning and Teacher Education*, 2010), and *Reflections on the*

Nature of Self in the World and in Adult Education: A Search for Inclusive Ways of Knowing (Germany: VDM Verlag, 2009).

The Contributors

EIRINI ADAMOPOULOU is a professor in the Psychology Department at the Business College of Athens, Greece. She completed her doctoral degree in Educational Psychology and Human Learning and Development at National Louis University, Illinois. She has worked as a school psychologist at Chicago Public Schools for five years. Her research interests include social-emotional learning, cognitive development and assessment, early intervention, diversity in learning and development, school-family partnerships, youth risk behavior, and cyber bullying.

NANCY W. BENTLEY holds a PhD in higher education leadership and policy studies from Loyola University-Chicago. She is currently an adjunct professor in the College of Education and Health Sciences at Benedictine University in Lisle, Illinois. She recently retired with more than thirty years' experience in higher education administration at both two-year and four-year institutions, including serving as chief student affairs officer at three institutions. Her research interests include student affairs research and assessment of student support and counseling programs, college student success and persistence, underrepresented student populations, and community colleges.

SHARON DUNCAN completed her doctoral degree in Disability and Equity Studies at National Louis University. Sharon's research interests include literacy for students with significant intellectual disabilities, models of disability, transition practices, and family stories. She has worked in Puerto Plata in the Dominican Republic, providing training for special educators and caregivers. Sharon is passionate about advocating and supporting individuals with disabilities and is the director of the Abide in Me charitable organization, which provides assistance to individuals with disabilities for leading engaged lives. Sharon is currently a Clinical Assistant Professor of Special Education in the Graduate School of Education at Purdue Calumet University in Hammond, Indiana. Sharon's dissertation, *Locked Gates and Chain-link Fences: A Phenomenological Generational Story of Disability*, is published in the Disability Studies in Education Series by Peter Lang (2012).

MARIA E. HERNANDEZ-RODRIGUEZ holds her doctoral degree in Educational Psychology and Human Learning and Development from National Louis University. She is currently working as a school psychologist at Woodland District 50, Gages

Lake, Illinois. Maria is a native of Spain and a former professional ballerina. Her interests are in educational philosophy, child's psychology, cultural diversity, poetry, visual and performing arts, and arts-based education. Growing up an islander, at the heart of the Canary archipelago, Maria has always been curious as to what lies beyond the horizon. She is intrigued by the unique and exclusive shapes that the ocean waves deposit on the shore with every movement, as much as she is enchanted by a rainy day.

EILEEN KOLICH holds a PhD in curriculum and instruction from the Pennsylvania State University. She is currently Professor of Education in the College of Education and Health Sciences at Benedictine University in Lisle, Illinois. Eileen cofounded the doctoral program in Higher Education and Organizational Change (HEOC). She teachers a number of HEOC courses, including qualitative research methods, and supervises doctoral dissertations. Her research interests are in scholarship of teaching and learning as it relates to instructor collaboration in the development of curriculum for qualitative research courses. The research addresses the potential of practitioner collaboration for enhancing curriculum, teaching and learning venues, and student engagement as the expertise and talents of both educators become inextricably connected.

CHRISTINE L. KRAMP PFAFF has a doctorate in Educational Leadership from National Louis University. She is currently an elementary school principal in Kildeer Countryside District 96 near Chicago with more than twenty years of experience in teaching and leadership. For fourteen years, she was a middle school teacher instructing mathematics and language arts, and for the past nine years she has been a school administrator at both the elementary and middle school levels. Dr. Pfaff's work focuses on developing learning communities for students, teachers, and parents as well as fostering positive school environments.

ANDREA LEHMACHER is the Director of Marketing at Joliet Junior College. Prior to her current position, Andrea was the Director of Marketing at University of St. Francis, Illinois, and the Director of Admissions at Robert Morris University, Illinois. Andrea has more than fourteen years of higher education experience in branding, marketing, new media, market research, and enrollment management. Andrea earned her bachelor's degree in Media Communications at Governors State University, Illinois. Andrea holds an EdD in Higher Education and Organizational Change from Benedictine University, Illinois.

ANNE PERRY has a doctoral degree in Higher Education and Organizational Change from Benedictine University, Lisle, Illinois. She is currently Associate

Dean of the College of Liberal Arts and Sciences and interim Associate Dean of Health Sciences at DeVry University, Illinois. Her research and scholarly interests are in assessment of student learning and improving their career decision making. Anne is a member of the Academy for Leadership and Development, the National Career Development Association, and Sigma Beta Delta honor society.

KRISTA ROBINSON-LYLES is Associate Professor in Elementary Education at National Louis University, Chicago. She received her EdD in Curriculum and Social Inquiry at National Louis University. She has served as teacher and administrator in both public and private schools in the Chicago area, as well as provided mentoring and coaching in literacy and general classroom instruction in various schools in Illinois, Indiana, and Oregon. Some of her scholarly interests include critical literacy, equity pedagogy, gender studies, and curriculum and instructional practices in urban public schools.

REGINA SCHURMAN holds a doctoral degree in Higher Education and Organizational Change from Benedictine University, Lisle, Illinois. She is currently the Administrative Program Director of the Master of Science in Clinical Exercise Physiology program at Benedictine University. Regina's passion lies in the area of preparing her master's students to be successful in a challenging job market. Her research and scholarship interests are in developing models and strategies for making practitioners successful in the field of clinical exercise physiology. Regina values a scholar-practitioner tandem in enhancing capabilities of students to transition from classroom to the workplace via clinical internships.

VLADIMIR TROSTIN completed his doctoral degree in Educational Leadership at National Louis University. He is currently teaching high school language arts in the Chicago northern suburbs. Vladimir is an ethnic Russian born in Harbin, China. His immigration journey took him from China, through Kazakhstan, Siberia, and Latvia, to the United States. He resides in Lyons Woods, Illinois, with his wife Cyndi (born in Chicago area), their two birds: Pod (Amazon from Mexico) and Rocky (Cockatoo from Indonesia). Vladimir is the proud father of Natasha (born in Latvia), Peter (of Czech ancestry), and Kate (of her own ancestry), and proud grandfather of Oliver (of Chinese-Russian roots) and Rollie (of Czech-Norwegian ancestry). In his free time he enjoys symphony, country, and bluegrass music, and his daughter's and son-in-law Tim's (of Chinese ancestry) concerts (both are concert pianists), working out, and feeding the nightly wildlife visitors to his home backyard.

BAUDELAIRE K. ULYSSE holds a doctoral degree in Curriculum and Social Inquiry from National Louis University. He is currently teaching at National Louis University and the community colleges in the Chicago area. His research interests span across various topics such as globalization, educational economics, faculty development, neoliberalism, Haitian history and politics, philosophy, theology, and religions.

MATTHEW WOOLSEY'S expertise spans communication, leadership, team development (including cross-cultural teams), and strategic visioning for human capital in domestic and international markets. The recipient of the Edward R. Murrow Award for Excellence in Broadcasting from Washington State University, Dr. Woolsey holds a bachelor's in Communication (Broadcasting), a master's in Education Administration, and a doctorate in Higher Education and Organizational Change. His expertise and learning programs have received recognition by the Association of Professional Communication Consultants, Consulting.Com Magazine, and Experience.com. His current research interests include Asian Indian leaders in America's higher education institutions with future projects targeting leadership competencies specific to this community of practice. Currently, Dr. Woolsey is an adjunct professor teaching courses in Public Speaking, Critical Thinking, and a senior capstone class on Society, Ethics, and Technology.

.

Index

A

Abulafia, A., 51
access, 221
Achieving the Dream, 196
advocacy, xxvi
Against Method, 42
Agnew, J., 226, 227
Albrecht, G., 236
Allyson, T., 252, 253
American Association of Community Colleges, 190
American Physical Therapy Association, 148
Analytics, 8
Anfara, V.A., xxv, 65
Anfossi, J., 157
Angold, A., 176
Appiah, A.K., 54
Apple, M., 224, 225, 226
Aquinas, 5
Arendt, H., 35
Aristotle, 8, 13, 34
Aristotle of Stageira, 9
art, 22

arts-based research, 254
Asian Indians
  diaspora of, 104
  risk aversion and, 114–15
  self-identity, 113
Association of Supervision and Curriculum
    Development, 139
at-homeness, 239
Audi, R., 37, 49
autobiography, 96–99
autoethnography, 92–93, 94, 99–101, 143, 146
  interpretive paradigms and, 93–94
  storytelling and, 94
  writing, 143
Avenarius, R., 14
Awareness of Dying, 150
axiology, 8
Ayers, W., 207, 208

B

Bachelard, G., xxiii, 39, 40, 84
Bacon, J., 115

Bailey, K., 144
Baker, B., 243
Ballard, H., 48
Banaszynski, J., 94
Barnes, C., 236
Barnhardt, R., 53, 54
Barrett, K.C., 171
Barth, R., 140, 207, 211
Barton, L., 236
Basics of Qualitative Research, 151
Bass, B.M., 105, 139
Baudrillard, J., 45, 46
Baumol, W., 229, 230
behavioral sciences, 62
Behringer, L.B., 105
Being and Time, 25
Belenky, M., 46
Bell, C.H. Jr., 192
Bell, D.A., 48
Belli, G., 180
Benedictine University, 149, 153
Bennett, J., 13
Bennis, W., 112
Bensel, P., 224
Bensimon, E.M., 106
Benzing, C., 157, 158
Berger, P., 93
Bernstein, A., 226
Berry, R., 160
Bertrand, R., 132
Besevegis, G., 181
Bhadha, B.R., 113
Bhagavad Gita, 11
Bhattacharya, G., 113
Bickman, L., 138
Biklen, S.K., 73, 82, 153
biometrics, 16
bios politicos, 35
Birnbaum, R., 106
Bishop, S., 13
Blackburn, S., 13, 14
Blancher, J., 243
Blinder, A., 229, 230
Bochner, A.P., 95, 143
Bogdan, R.C., 73, 82, 153, 248
Bohm, D., 55
Bohman, J., 27, 28

Bolman, L.G., 114
Bonner, A., 151
Bontrager, B., 191, 192, 193
Bordbeck, B.C., 106, 116
Borthwick, A.M., 161
Bouhoutsos, J.C., 177, 178
Boyd, T., 55
Brady, I., 94
Brandt, R., 141
Brilliant, C.D.G., 129, 130
Bronfenbrenner, U., 179
Brown, D.J., 53, 54
Brown, K., 207
Brown, S.P., 158
Bryant, A., 151, 152, 153, 154, 155, 156
Buber, M., 24
Buddhism, 9, 11–13, 50, 51
Budhwar, P.S., 106
Burns, B.J., 176
Burns, J.M., 105, 139
Bury, M., 236
Butt, J., 113

C

Callahan, G., 157, 158
capitalism, 225, 226
Career Decision Profile, The, 172
Career Decision Scale, The, 172
Career Thoughts Inventory, xxix, 79, 166, 170–71
Carlisle, E., 132
Carney, C., 172
Carpenter, B., 243
Carrette, J., 26
case study, 143
Castellano, M.B., 54
Castles, K., 242
CASVE, 167–68
category bound activities, 241
Chambers, E., 143
Chang, H., 143
Chang, M.J., 105
Chang, Y., 209
Charmez, K., 152, 154
Chethimattam, 10, 11
Chhokar, J.S., 106, 114

choreography, 95
Christian existentialism, 21
Chua, A., 231
Churchill, S., 132
Cintron, R., 48
Clandinin, D., 209, 212, 215
Clark, V.L.P., 109, 110, 151, 193, 194
Clayton, T., 226
Cleaver, J., 93
Clement of Alexandria, 9
Clemetsen, B., 194
clinical exercise physiology, 148, 149
    academic preparation, 156–57
    boundaries of expertise, 161
    career satisfaction, 158
    compensation, 159
    credentials for, 159
    employment in field, 156–58
    expertise of, 161–62
    job market, 157
    licensure and, 149, 160
    professional development, 157
    professional identity, 158–59, 160, 161
    professional recognition of, 158–63
    scope of practice, 160–61
    study of, 150–52
Coach, M., 24
Cochran-Smith, M., 210, 214, 215
codes, 154
cognitive information processing, xxix, 166–68
    conclusion of study of, 174
    negative thinking and, 168
cognitive therapy, 167
Cohen, E., 104
Cohen, L., xxv, 66, 69, 109, 144, 145
Coleman, M., 132
Coles, R., 94
Collingwood, R.G., 84
colonialism, 225
commitment anxiety, 169, 170
Community College Survey of Student En-
    gagement, 194
Comte, A., 14, 62
conceptual repertoire, 65
Confusianism, 50
constructivism, xxvi, 151
Coons, A.E., 105

Cooper, J., 159
Corbin, 151
Costa, P.J., 172
Costello, E.J., 176
Cottage Hill Junior High School, 137
counter-spaces, 48
counter-stories, 48
Cranmer, S., 158
Crants, J.T., 56
Craver, S.M., 4, 15, 20, 23, 24, 77, 150
Crease, R.P., 56, 57
Creswell, J.W., xxv, xxvi, 66, 68, 69, 70, 74, 80, 107,
    109, 110, 111, 123, 144, 145, 151, 181, 193, 194
critical
    democratic education, 208, 211, 212
    ethnicity studies, 48
    hermeneutics, 43, 209
    pedagogy, 207
    race theory, 48, 207
    theory, 27, 28, 221
critical discourse analysis, 83, 219–20
    assumptions of, 220–24
    neoliberalism and, 225
    texts and, 223
crystallization, 95
Cummings, T.G., 192

D

Daiger, D., 172
Dalton, M., 106
Dantley, M., 72, 101
Daode Jing, 50
Daresh, J.C., 138
Darwin, C., 16, 19
Dasein, 25
Davies, B., 224
Davis, K., 138
Davis, S., 159
Day, M., 239
de Beauvoir, S., 23, 46
decision-making confusion, 169, 170
decision-making skills domain, 167
DeCsipkes, C., 129, 133
Dei, G.J.S., 55
Delgado, R., 48

Delgado-Gaitán, C., 128, 129
Dellassoudas, L.G., 178
Deleuzio-Guallaria's architectural theory, 236
deMarais, K., 73, 74, 81
Denzin, N.K., 93, 95, 123, 143, 145
Derrida, J., 45
Descartes, R., 8, 13, 17, 37, 38
Deslandes, R., 132
devotion, 9
Dewey, J., 18, 19, 100, 152, 153
Dharma, 12
dialectic materialism, 27
Díaz, D., 129
Dilthey, W., 25, 123, 124
Dionysian principle, 22
Diotima, 52
disabilities/disability studies, 49, 83, 84, 236
    exposure and, 245
    fears and, 242
    historicality, 243–55
    reflections on, 239
    resistance and, 242–43
    uncovering meaning of, 248–49
discourse, 222
Discourse, 222
double consciousness, 48
Down syndrome, 238, 239, 243, 244, 248
Drath, W., 107
Drummond, K., 129
Du Bois, W.E.B., 48
Dunn, E.W., 115

E

ecological systems theory, 79
education, xxii, 3
educational inquiry, 3–5
educational research, 3
    paradigms in, xxv
    philosophical inquiry and, 5–7
    pragmatic diversity and, 61
    purpose of, xxiii–xxvi
    transformational leadership and, 139–40
Einstein, A., 55, 63
Eisai, 51Ellis, C., 93, 94, 143
Emergence vs. Forcing, 151

Emerson, R.W., 71
empirical-analytic paradigm, 66, 79
empiricism, 13, 14
empiriocriticism, 14
enlightenment, 12
enrollment management, 189–90
    demographic shifts and, 192–93
    research regarding community colleges, 191
epistemological pluralism, 41, 49–55, 252
epistemology, 7, 39, 40
    philosophy of science and, 31–38
Erikson, E., 91
erklären, 62
Essed, P., 48
ethnographic impressionism, 109
ethnography, 81, 107–8, 143, 146
    ethical considerations of, 110–11
    interviews, 144
ethnomethodology, 69
Eurostat, 181
Evans, R., 157
Everatt, J., 178
evolutionary philosophy, 19
executive processing domain, 167
existentialism, 21, 22, 23, 137
experimentalism, 19
external conflict, 169, 171, 172

F

Fairclough, N., 220, 222, 223
faith, 5
Fakiolas, N., 177
Falk, C.F., 115
Farahmandpur, R., 28
Farmer, E.M.Z., 176
Farver, J.M., 113
feedforward, 100
Feldman, D., 158
feminist poststructuralist theory, xxv
Ferguson, D., 239
Ferguson, P., 239
Feyerabend, P., 42, 58, 63
Feyman, R., 56
Fisher, R.A., 16
Flick, U., 107, 108, 111

Foley, M., 4
Foster, C., 160, 163
Foucault, M., 45
foundationalism, 8, 37, 43
Four Noble Truths, 12
Francis, K., 151
Frankfurt School, 26, 27
Franklin, J., 94
free markets, 229–32
Free to Choose, 230
Freire, P., 28, 208
Freire, Neoliberalism, and Education, 225
French, W.L., 192
Frieden, J., 226
Friedman, M., 230, 231, 232
Friedman, R., 231
Friend, M., 244
Fullan, M., 114
functionalism, 18

G

Gabel, S., 49, 236
Gadamer, H.-G., 25, 26, 122, 124, 125, 127, 133
Gallos, J.V., 114
Gandhi, M., 117
Gans, C., 92
Garber, D., 13
Gari, A., 176, 178
Garman, A.N., 157
Gaspar de Alba, A., 48
Gauguin, P., xxii
Gautama, S., 11, 12
Gee, J., 221, 224
Geistenwissenschaft, 62
genetics, 16
Georgas, J., 176, 177, 181
Georgouleas, G., 178
German Romantic movement, 20, 21
Gerzon, M., 206
Geuss, R., 27, 28
Gilligan, C., 46
Ginsberg, M., 226
Giotsa, A., 177
Girard, P., 228
Giroux, H., 227, 229, 230, 231, 232

Glaser, B.G., 150, 151, 152, 153, 154, 155
Glennon, L., 50
Gliner, J.A., 171
Global Leadership and Organizational Effectiveness, 106
Gnosticism, 51, 52
Goldberg, D.T., 48
Gonzales, K.P., 145
Goodall, H.L., xxviii, 143
Goodman, J., 210
Goossens, L., 92
Gracia, J.J.E., 130
Grant, C.A., 210
Gratling, A.C., 8
Greek parents
    education of children, 176–78
    childrens' mental health and, 176
    childrens' special education services, 177
    study of children, 178–82, 182–85
Grey, E.A., 105
Grof, S., xxii, 55, 57
grounded knowledge, 208
grounded theory, 81, 150, 151, 152–53, 154, 158
Groves, J., 15
Guba, E.G., 107, 109, 110, 111, 144
Gubrium, J.F., xxiv, xxviii
Gupta, A., 229
Gurin, P., 207
Gutek, G.L., 19, 22

H

Habermas, J., 26, 43, 44, 45, 66, 69, 70, 124, 205, 209
Haiti, 228–29
Hall, B.L., 55
Hall, S., 92
Hallinger, P., 138
Haraway, D., 46, 47
Harris, T., 192
Harvey, D., 227, 228, 231
Hatzichristou, C., 178, 181
heart-full science, 94
hegemony, 225, 226
Heidegger, M., 25, 26, 122, 124
Held, D., 27
Henley, T., 237, 239

Hennemann, S., 157
Herbert, E., 243
hermeneutic circle, 124–25, 132–33
hermeneutic interviews, 125
hermeneutics, 24, 42, 43, 123–24
Hermeticism, 52
Hernández, E., 130
Hesse-Biber, S.N., xxv, 66, 82, 83, 107, 109, 110, 143
heterotopia, 45
Hickey, M.G., 113
higher education
    Asian Americans and, 104, 105–6
    Indian natives and, 110
    leadership and, 104–5
Higgs, J., 124, 125
Higher Education Finance Study Commission, 190
Hill, D., 224
Hinduism, 9–11, 50
Hiriyanna, M., 11
Hispanic parenthood, 121
    educating the children of, 127–28, 128–29, 130–31
    finances and, 129
    hermeneutic circle and, 125
    qualitative inquiry and, 123
    roles and responsibilities, 130
    school culture and, 122
Hofstede, G., 106, 112
Hofstede, G.J., 112
Holland, J., 172
Holstein, J.A., xxiv, xxviii
Holton, J.A., 153, 154, 155
home, 239
Hoover-Demsey, K.V., 129
Hossler, D., 192
House, R.J., 106, 114
Howe, K.R., xxiii, 72
Howe, N., 242
Huberman, M., 210
Huddleston, T., 192
Human Condition, The, 35
human perception, 17
human science research, 65
Hume, D., 8, 14, 62
Hunt, J.A., 207

Husserl, E., 23, 24, 237, 239
Hyperion, 21
hyperreality, 70
Hyson, M., 129, 133

I

Idealism, 9, 13
identity, 92
Illinois community colleges, 189–90
    cost burden of, 190
    opensystems and collaboration, 192
    statistics on, 190
    study findings, 195
    study of, 191–92, 193–95
Illuminists, 51
imagination, 39
Imam, S.A., 209
imperialism, 225
Improving Your Career Thoughts, 166, 171
inquiry, 4
    critical, 26–28
    postmodern, 26–28
    writing and, 95–96
instructional leadership, 138
instrumentalism, 19
interpretation, 25
interpretive research, 74
intervention strategy, 166
Islamic mysticism, 51
I-Thou dialogue, 24
Ives, J.C., 159

J

Jackson, A.Y., xxv
James, W., 18
Janesick, V., 95
Jankovitz, K., 159
Jantzi, D., 140, 144, 145
Jastrow, J., 17
Jilberto, A., 224
Johnson, R.B., 20, 68, 80, 123, 180
Johnson, S., 36
Johnson, T.W., 10, 19

K

Kahne, J., 208
Kakar, S., 104
Kalsbeek, D., 192
Kant, E., xxvii, 8, 71
karma, 9
Kassotakis, M., 177
Kawagley, A.O., 53, 54
Kegan, R., 138
Kemple, K., 132
Kenny, A., 9, 22, 31, 33, 34, 35, 252
Keown, D., 12
Keteyian, S.J., 161
Kevles, D., 243
Kezar, A., 107
khora, 253
Kierkegaard, S., 21
Kipfer, B.A., xxv, 65
Kliewer, C., 244
Kneller, G.F., 15, 24, 123, 208
knowledge, 3–4, 9, 10, 13, 31, 37
    of ecosystems, 54
    insight and, 52
    logocentric principle of, 34
    theory of, 32
    scientific, 38
    types of, 32–33
Knowledge and Human Interests, 44
Knudson, D., 159
Kohlberg, L., 46
Koliadis, M., 177
Komives, S.R., 106
Koschier, M., 172
Kozol, J., 207
Krauss, M., 157
Kuehn, M., 37
Kuhn, T., xxiii, xxv, 39, 40, 64, 65
Kurokawa, K., 236
Kuzmic, J., 210

L

Langdon, J., 54
language
    context and, 221

language, *cont.*
    critical discourse analysis, 222
    power and, 220
    use of, 220
Laozi, 50
Lapan, S.D., 73, 74, 81
Lareau, A., 125, 129, 130, 132
Lather, P., xxvi, 47, 66, 69, 70, 71
Lattuca, L.R., 108
Laverty, S.M., 123
leadership, 138
Leadership, 105
leadership studies, 105, 106
Leavy, P., xxv, 66, 82, 83, 107, 109, 110, 143, 254, 255
Leech, N.L., 171
Leedy, P.D., 108, 144
Lehrer, K., 37
Leithwood, K.A., 140, 144, 145
Lemert, C., 62
Lemos, N.L., 8
Lenz, J., 166
Lewis, C., 108
Li, W., 104
Lieber, E., 113
Liefner, I., 157
lifeworld, 237
Lincoln, Y.S., 93, 107, 109, 110, 111, 123, 144
Lindberg, C.A., xxvi, 61, 65, 71
LoBasso, T., 192
Locke, J., 8, 13, 37, 38
Lockridge, E., 95
logical analysis
logical atomism, 14
logical empiricism, 14
logical positivism, 14, 15, 41–43, 75, 76
logos, 33, 36
Longino, H.E., 46, 47
Lopate, P., 95
Lopez, G., 207
Low, D., 24
Lowe, E.J., 7
Luckmann, T., 93
Lugg, C.A., 48
Luther, M., 24
Lyman, S.M., 93

M

Mach, E., 14
Manion, L., xxv, 66, 109, 144, 145
Maxim, P.S., 180
Mayan civilization, 53
Mayer, J.D., 116
Mazi, M.S., 178
Mazzei, L., xxv
McAdams, D.P., 251
McAtee, K.A., 143
McClosky, R., 219
McCrae, R., 172
McLaren, P., 28
McMillan, J.H., xxv, 66, 107, 109, 111, 193, 194
Megginson, W., 227, 228
member checking, 110
memo writing, 154
Mercer, J., 245
Merleau-Ponty, M., 24, 237
Merriam, S.B., xxv, 65. 110, 143, 152, 153
Mertz, N.T., xxv, 65
Metaphysical Club, 18
metaphysics, 7
methodological pluralism, 72
methodology, 73
methods, 73
methods of analysis, xxiv
Meyer, M., 221, 223
Michie, G., 209
microaggressions, 48
Milesian philosophers, 62
Mill, J.S., 14
Miller, A.S., 115
Mills, J., 151
Minkov, M., 112
Miraftab, F., 224, 225
Mitchell, E.D., 55
mixed-methods research, 80
modern Western philosophy, 13–17
Mohan, W.J., 4
Moje, E.B., 108
Mommen, A., 224
Monadology, 55
Morgan, G.A., 171
Morrison, K., xxv, 66, 109, 144, 145

Morse, J., 237
Moser, P.K., 3, 4, 7, 8, 13, 31, 32
Moules, N.J., 124, 133
Moustakas, C., 237
Mulder, D.H., 7, 32
Mullen, P.D., 152, 154
Murphy, J., 138
Murti, T.R.V., 12
Museus, S.D., 105
Mylonas, K., 176, 181
My Vocational Situation, 172

N

Nafstad, H., 224
Nagata, A.L., 100
Nagda, B.A., 207
Nancarrow, S., 161
Narang, S., 113
narrative, 83
narrative inquiry, 210
Nat, A.V., 13
National Louis University, xxiv
natural growth theory, 125
natural sciences, 9
Nelson, G., xxv
Nenopoulou, S., 178
neoliberalism, 219, 223
   as a discourse, 224–25
   discourse analysis and, 225
   free markets, 229–32
   privatization and, 227–29
NEO PI-R, The, 172
Neumann, A., 106
Ng, T., 158
Nichomachean Ethics, 34
Nieto, S., 207
Nietzsche, F.W., 21, 22, 44
Nikodemos, S., 177
non-foundationalism, 8, 37
Norenzayan, A., 115
Noriega, C., 48
Northouse, P.G., 105
Novalis, 21

O

Oatley, T., 230
occupational knowledge domain, 167
Ogbonna, W., 106
Oliver, M., 21, 236
Olsen, W., xxv
Onwuegbuzie, A.J., 20, 68, 80, 123, 180
Origin of Species, The, 19
Ormrod, J.E., 108, 144
Orozco, G., 129
Osipow, S., 172
Other, 23, 46
Ozmon, H.A., 4, 15, 20, 23, 24, 77, 150

P

Palmer, D., 17
Papapetrou, S., 177
Papineau, D., 39
paradigm
    critical, 70
    definition of, xiv, 64, 65
    etymology of, xxv
    interpretive, 68–69
    of mixed-methods research, xxix
    poststructuralist, 66
    pragmatic, 68
    pyramid, xxvi
    shifts, 40
    six, 72
    transcendental, 71
    typology of, 64, 67–68
    wars, 20
parallel practices, 205
Parent Survey, xxix
Parker, T.L., 105
Parry, K.W., 107
Pascale, C.M., xxiv, xxv, 66, 74
passion, 64
Paterson, M., 124, 125
Patton, M.Q., 123, 142, 143, 145
Paxton, T.D., 37
Pearson, K., 16
Peirce, C.S., xxix, 17, 18, 19, 41, 68, 152, 153
Penn, G., 192

Pentland, W., 124, 125
personal narrative, 94–95
Peters, S., 49
Peterson, G., 166
Peterson, K., 138
phenomenology, 23, 237
philosophical inquiries, 5–7
    Buddhism and, 11–13
Philosophical Investigations, 16
philosophy, xxii, 4
    ancient and classical traditions of, 8–9
    branches of, 7–8
    education and, xxii
phronesis, 34, 35
pilgrimage, 253–4
Pillow, W.S., xxv, 47, 48, 71
Plano Clark, V.L., 181
Plato, 5, 7, 8, 9, 13
poesis, 35
Poincaré, H., 58
Pojman, L.P., 31, 32
Polanyi, M., 16
Polichroni, F., 178, 181
Polkinghorne, D.E., xxiii, xxvii, 15, 16, 17, 20, 24,
    25, 34, 35, 42, 43, 49, 62, 63, 65, 66, 68, 69, 70,
    73, 77, 124, 143, 208, 209, 210
Pollio, H., 237, 239
Popkin, R.H., 19, 20
Popper, K., 42
Porcari, J.P., 160, 16
positivism, xxv, 14–17, 19, 66, 75
positivistic scientific methodology, 42
postmodernism, 26, 43, 44
postpositivism, xxvi
poststructuralism, 26, 70
poststructuralist feminist research, 71
Potteiger, J.A., 148, 149
power, 221
Power, G., 172
pragmatic truths, 68
pragmatism, xxvi, 80, 150, 152
    American, 18–20
    prophetic, 20
prajna, 12
Pratt, M.L., 92
praxis, 35
praxis of existential phenomenology, 208

Prebish, C.S., 12
Préval, R., 228, 229
Price, M.W., 53
principalship, 140–42
privatization, 227
psychoanalysis, 39
Pulley, J., 190
Pythagoras, 52

Q

Qabbalah, 51
qualitative
    inquiry, 106–7, 123
    methodology, 150, 151
    research, xxv, 76, 93, 95, 142
quantitative research, 75
quantum mechanics, 56
queer legal theory, 48
Quesada, R., 129
Quine, W., 16, 17
Quinn, T., 207

R

radical hermeneutics, 45
Rapley, M., 247
Rasmussen, J., 124, 125
rationalism, 13, 14
Ravid, R., 180
Realism, 9, 13
reality, 71
Reardon, R., 166
reason, 5
Reback, G., 229, 230
redemptive self, 251
Reed, R.F., 19
reflexivity, 111
Regenspan, B., 205
Reisigl, M., 222, 223
Relational Leadership Theory, 107
resistance theory, 236, 248
Reuters, 229
Rhoads, R.A., 107
Richards, L., 237

Richardson, L., 95
Riessman, C.K., xxviii
Roberts, C.M., 180
Robertson, R., 55
Robinson, D., 15
Roe, K.V., 177, 178
Rogers, R., 219, 220
Romantics, 20, 21
Rorty, R. 17, 20
Rose, M.A., 43
Rosenberg, D.G., 55
Rota, G.C., 56
Rothstein-Fish, C., 130
Royer, E., 132
Rubin, H.J., 110
Rubin, I.S., 110
Ruiz, M., 53
Rumi, 51
Runes, D.D., xxv, 14, 40
Rush, F., 27
Russell, B., 84
Russell, L., 253, 254

S

Saldana, J., 111
Saldívar, R., 48
Salinas, A., 129
Salovey, P., 116
Sampson, J., 166, 167, 168, 171, 172
Samsara, 11
Sánchez, M., 129
Sartre, J.-P., 23
saturation, 154
Saunders, D., 166
Schleiermacher, F., 25, 123, 124
Schlick, M., 15
Schoppelrey, S.L., 113
Schutz, A., 24
Schwandt, T.A., 94
Schwartzenberg, S., 243
science, 61
science of social action, 45
science, philosophy of, 38–41
scientific inquiry, 19
scientific knowledge, 38

Scott, G., 114
Scruton, R., 8, 44, 71
Scullion, H., 104
Seamon, D., 237
Second Sex, The, 23
Seelman, K., 236
Seidman, I., 123
Self, 145
self-knowledge domain, 167
self-study, 210, 214, 215
Sellars, R.W., 18
Shakespeare, W., 91, 247
Shamanism, 53
Shank, G.D., 107, 142
Sheldon, S.B., 132
Simpson, E.L., xxv, 110, 143, 152, 153
simulacra, 70
Situated Knowledges, 47
Smart, N., 27, 53
Smith, A., 231
Smith, D., 46
social construction, 106, 207
social justice, 207, 208, 209
social sciences, 62
Socrates, 9, 33
Sophia, 52
Sophianidou, E., 178
Sophists, 36, 37
Spellings, M., 189
Spellings Report, 189
Sprague, J., 229
Stanczak, G.C., 254
standards of truth, 81
Stanley, L., 132
Stark, J.S., 108
Stefanic, J., 48
Stevenson, A., xxvi, 61, 65, 71
Stiglitz, J., 225, 230, 231, 232
Stipeck, D., 129
Stogdill, R.M., 105
storytelling, xxviii
St. Pierre, E.A., xxv, 47, 48, 71
Strategic Enrollment Management Health Assessment, xxix, 80, 194–95
  academic program innovation, 200
  marketing and, 197–98, 200–1
  recruitment and, 198, 201

Strategic Enrollment Management Health Assessment, *cont.*
  retention and, 198–99, 201
  service delivery and, 199, 201
  as a system, 196–97, 199–200
Strauss, A.L., 150, 151, 152, 153
Strauss, W., 242
Stroll, A., 19, 20
Structure of Scientific Revolutions, The, 40
subjectivity, 145
substantive theory, 151
Sufism, 51
Suppe, F., 16
Suri, R.P., 103
Sutton, S.B., 177
symbolic interactionism, 69
Symposium, 52

T

Taoism, 50
Taylor, S., 239, 248
teacher educators
  grounded knowledge and, 208
  stories of, 209–10
  storytelling, 211–15
Téléco, 229
Teranishi, R.T., 105, 106
Test of Leadership, A., 189
Test of Psychosocial Adaptation, xxix, 79, 181
Theaetetus, 8, 33, 36
theoretical coding, 154
theoretical sensitivity, 154
theory, xxvi
Thompson, C., 237, 239
Thoreau, H.D., 71
Tierney, W.G., 107
Tisdell, E.J., 72, 253
Toltec culture, 53
Toulmin, S., 16
Tradition, 51
transactional leadership, 139
transformation, 136
transformational leadership strategies, 136
transcendentalism, 71
Trenchard, W.C., 7

Trent, J., 244
triangulation, 95
Trout, J.D., 7, 32
Trueba, H., 128, 129
Trumbull, E., 130
trust, 2112
truth, 41, 71
Truth and Method, 25
Tsiantis, J., 177
Turcotte, D., 132

U

Übermensch, 44
Uhl-Bien, M., 107
Ultimate Reality, 11
understanding, 43, 69
University of Chicago Laboratory School, 19
Upanishads, 11

V

Valdés, G., 129, 132
Van Dijk, T., 223
Van Maanen, J., 109
Van Manen, M., 125, 237, 248
Van Voorst, R.E., 10, 12
Vardis, P., 177
Varma, R., 116
Vedism, 10
verificationism, 15
Verrill, D., 160, 161
verstehen, 62
Vico, G., 20
Vidich, A.J., 93
Vienna Circle, 14, 15
visual research methods, 254
Vlachos, A., 181
von Leibniz, G.W., 55

W

Wagner, T., 138, 141

Wallace, D.B., 7
warranted assertions, 19
Watson, N., 247
Wealth of Nations, The, 231
Weltanschuungen, 16
Wertsche, J.V., 108
West, C., 20
Western rationalism, 54
Westheimer, J., 208
Westphal, M., 20, 43
Whitehead, A.N., 9
Wilson, M., 106
Winer, J., 172
Winkler, K.P., 36
Winzer, M., 244
Wittgenstein, L., 14, 15, 17
Wodak, R., 221, 222, 223
Woldu, H., 106
Woodard, D. Jr., 106
Worley, C.G., 192
Wu, X., 210

X

Xu, Y., 113

Y

Yamagata-Noji, A., 104
Yanico, B., 172
Yin, R., 144
Yon, D.A., 91
Yu, C.H., 15, 16, 64, 66, 72, 73, 75, 76, 77
Yukl, G., 105, 107

Z

Zarate, M., 129
Zoniou-Sideri, A., 177
Zweck, C., 124, 125
Zwerdling, D., 213

Studies in the Postmodern Theory of Education

General Editor
Shirley R. Steinberg

Counterpoints publishes the most compelling and imaginative books being written in education today. Grounded on the theoretical advances in criticalism, feminism, and postmodernism in the last two decades of the twentieth century, Counterpoints engages the meaning of these innovations in various forms of educational expression. Committed to the proposition that theoretical literature should be accessible to a variety of audiences, the series insists that its authors avoid esoteric and jargonistic languages that transform educational scholarship into an elite discourse for the initiated. Scholarly work matters only to the degree it affects consciousness and practice at multiple sites. Counterpoints' editorial policy is based on these principles and the ability of scholars to break new ground, to open new conversations, to go where educators have never gone before.

For additional information about this series or for the submission of manuscripts, please contact:

> Shirley R. Steinberg
> c/o Peter Lang Publishing, Inc.
> 29 Broadway, 18th floor
> New York, New York 10006

To order other books in this series, please contact our Customer Service Department:

> (800) 770-LANG (within the U.S.)
> (212) 647-7706 (outside the U.S.)
> (212) 647-7707 FAX

Or browse online by series:
> www.peterlang.com